THE CULTURE OF ENGLISH
ANTISLAVERY, 1780–1860

35.00

THE CULTURE
OF ENGLISH
ANTISLAVERY,
1780–1860

David Turley

London and New York

First published 1991
by Routledge
11 New Fetter Lane, London EC4P 4EE

Simultaneously published in the USA and Canada
by Routledge
a division of Routledge, Chapman and Hall, Inc.
29 West 35th Street, New York, NY 10001

Printed in Great Britain by T.J. Press (Padstow) Ltd, Padstow, Cornwall

British Library Cataloguing in Publication Data
Turley, David
The culture of English antislavery
1. Slavery, British abolitionist movements, history
I. Title
322.440941

Library of Congress Cataloging in Publication Data
Turley, David
The culture of English antislavery/David Turley.
p. cm.
Includes index.
1. Slavery–Great Britain–Anti-slavery movements.
2. Abolitionists–Great Britain–History. 3 Social reformers–
–Great Britain–History. 4. Slavery and the church–Great Britain–
–History. I. Title.
HT1162.T84 1991 90-24525
326'.0942–dc20

ISBN 0-415-02008-5

To my Mother and
the memory of my Father

CONTENTS

PREFACE

The shape and focus of this book have evolved through a number of stages; it is to be hoped that it is now fit enough to encounter the scrutiny of others. Some bits of the research which underlies it were done long ago but there have been a number of constants over the years. One is the aid and interest of archivists and librarians in the United States and Britain from California to Canterbury and Michigan to Manchester. My gratitude is at least as constant as their assistance; the particular institutions and the materials they allowed me to consult are listed with thanks at the end of the book.

Although the last chairman of the University Grants Committee reputedly remarked that while (scientific) research was expensive scholarship was free, it is not so. I therefore gratefully acknowledge financial assistance over the years for travel and maintenance costs and the expenses of copying materials from the Faculty of Humanities Research and Travel Grants Fund of the University of Kent, the Colyer–Ferguson Fund and the Twenty-Seven Foundation.

At a time when the virtue of competition in various forms is being pressed upon the battered British educational system it is with relief as well as gratitude that I set down the names of those individuals whose co-operation, to my benefit, has distinguished them most in my eyes. My most immediate colleagues as teachers, Christine Bolt and Julian Hurstfield, have cheerfully accepted my absences on study leaves and leaves of absence and equally cheerfully done extra work where necessary. For enlightenment of my ignorance on particular points, bibliographical aid, conscious and unconscious refinement of my ideas through discussion, I happily acknowledge David Birmingham, Hugh Cunningham, Grayson Ditchfield, Donald Read and Doreen Rosman. They are in no way responsible for any errors or misconceptions which occur in the following pages; they have simply demonstrated that they are good colleagues. Sue MacDonald and the other members of the Darwin Secretarial Office offered their interest as well as their expertise in producing clean copy from successive drafts.

Finally, my pleasure in Anna, Hilary and Celia Turley has been increased by the infrequency of their concern with the culture of antislavery. Kate McLuskie has been much more frequently concerned; where my prose and argument are clear it is because I have responded to her comments; where they are not, the reason is my stubbornness.

David Turley
Darwin College
University of Kent

1

APPROACH AND CON

Antislavery in Britain had a long and fluctuating history as a reform cause; it ultimately commanded the support of leading political and religious figures and the assent of a mass of ordinary citizens as petitioners. In many places it channelled the energies of leading figures in local communities whose passage through antislavery constituted a prominent aspect of their more complex engagement in moral and social improvement. It also contributed to the continuous working out of changing relations of power in particular localities in favour of some and to the detriment of other elements in a growing but heterogeneous middle class. As a subject of study, in other words, antislavery can be appropriately placed in the larger evolution of Britain in the later eighteenth and the first half of the nineteenth century. Only recently, however, has historical writing begun to point in this direction.

When W.H. Lecky argued that the English crusade against slavery 'may probably be regarded as among the three or four perfectly virtuous pages comprised in this history of nations' he proposed a view of abolition, emancipation and efforts to suppress the international slave trade which bridged the judgement abolitionists made of their own efforts and a humanitarian historiographical tradition running well into the twentieth century; a tradition which celebrated moral progress in history, achieved by the efforts of virtuous men and women and the influence of religion in public affairs.[1]

This tendency to moral and historical complacency met its sharpest challenge in Eric Williams' *Capitalism and Slavery* (1944). In Williams' view abolition and emancipation were nothing to do with moral progress achieved by moral and religious means but the result of changing class relationships in Britain, together with shifts within the political economy of empire. It was an argument based on economic change and its effects which left little room for antislavery

1

῾mers in the process of abolition and emancipation, apart from ῾eir talents as propagandists. What really mattered for Williams was the conjunction of significant decline in the economies of the British Caribbean after the American Revolution with the shift in Britain towards industrial capitalism, generating a powerful new class attached to *laissez-faire* and free-labour ideals.

Recent, often brilliant, scholarship has thrown doubt on Williams' contention about the importance of industrial interests in the process of abolition and emancipation. Nevertheless the tensions between 'moral' and 'material' factors have remained major concerns of historians studying the end of the British slave trade and slavery. Recent work, however, has suggested that they are not necessarily alternative kinds of explanation. From very different perspectives, the writings of David Brion Davis and Seymour Drescher have focused on what importance *class* and *culture* have in locating antislavery in a complex picture of the changing economic, social and political order in Britain.[2]

The present book tries to build on these issues opened up by recent scholarship. Questions of both culture and class are addressed through the study of the active minority – the antislavery reformers, including the parliamentary and national reform leaders but, equally importantly, the zealous provincial reformers whose networks connected one locality with another and linked parliamentary and national reform leaderships to the population at large. For the features of culture and class embodied in the practices and outlook of the reformers themselves present a different sense of antislavery from either the one offered by attention to the national and parliamentary level of reform or the one produced by stressing the quantitative 'popular' aspect of antislavery.

This book, then, does not directly tackle the question of why abolition and emancipation occurred. Rather it attempts to understand antislavery as a cultural response to change in both English society and in Britain's relations with the external world. Culture, in turn, is interpreted as the range of ways of responding to and judging the world within contained limits common to a group. Understanding culture in this way implies two separate but linked questions: firstly, in what terms did antislavery activists understand and engage with a society they wished to win over; and secondly, what structures and forms of behaviour internal to the antislavery movement contributed to the group sense of reformers? The two questions are clearly linked since the reformers' successful engagement with English society would in part depend upon a clear sense of identity within antislavery groups.

In their efforts to engage with English society, the reformers dealt with a culture which offered a limited number of forms and channels through which to effect change. In order to confer legitimacy on their struggles, reformers had to come to terms with these given forms and channels. Yet to leave the question of the forms available in a culture to initiate change here is both to bypass one property of reform as re/form and court the danger of implying stasis in the formal resources of the culture. At the very least this is implausible in a study of the particularly dynamic decades from the 1780s to the 1860s. Antislavery practice expressed more general innovations in permissible ways of trying to bring about change and sometimes tested the limits of what was considered legitimate (not least by some abolitionists) as in the controversy over popular participation in the early stages of the anti-slave trade campaign. Eventually antislavery did open up wider forms of engagement with public opinion, a force which became central to its strategy for success. Nevertheless there was no simple linear development towards more democratic practices and structures. Although by the mid-nineteenth century the political and civic culture within which reformers operated was more broadly based than it had been in the 1780s the boundaries of permissible kinds and methods of change had fluctuated and sometimes contracted in the intervening decades. Antislavery shared this history with other reform agitations. In part it was an experience shaped by forces external to Britain. The increasing radicalism of the French Revolution in the early 1790s contributed to a movement in the balance of social and political confidence and initiative in Britain which briefly opened up the possibility of more popular methods of bringing about reform. Rapidly reaction to French radicalism and the consequent outbreak of war closed off again the momentarily greater space for reform activity.[3]

Within Britain popular Protestantism, its organisational and behavioural developments, was central to the forces which contributed to the space antislavery made for itself in the first half of the nineteenth century. Despite the immersion of antislavery in religious currents which impelled so much reform activity, however, abolitionists had to compete for space and attention with other agitations using a more secular tone or having a more clearly defined social constituency. In their different ways the relations of antislavery to Chartism and to the Anti-Corn Law League, explored in later pages (pp.181–95), make this point. In sum, antislavery developed within a context whose changes over three generations it could do only a modest amount to shape but, up to the 1840s at least, it was both a subject of attraction and an object of competition in its institutional forms, characteristic practices, ideas and support.

It was the substance of the antislavery *appeal*, a compound of characteristic ideas and feelings projected towards potential converts which animated these forms and practices. The purpose of the appeal was for reformers to gain sufficient *influence* to secure abolition and later emancipation. Such influence was sought directly in parliament and indirectly through agitation in the country. The position of parliament, with its capacity to regulate commerce and, as the imperial legislature, the sovereign power to end slavery in the colonies if local assemblies were recalcitrant, made the parliamentary political class a crucial target. At the same time abolitionists wanted to arouse public opinion throughout the country. These two targets were connected but separate. The parliamentary and political class constituted a relatively restricted and specialised audience and one very conscious of its position and powers. Abolitionists could expect no straightforward link from convincing the public in the country to the impact of opinion on legislators to consequent antislavery influence by politicians on legislation. Nor could the public in the country be regarded as a homogeneous body. This was likely to mean that there was some variety of emphasis and tone in the antislavery appeal as between parliament and the country. To test how far this was so, chapter 2 on ideology offers a comparative analysis at particularly significant moments in the history of antislavery of the appeal to parliament and the country. Moreover, within the appeal to the country, changes over time have to be registered as do the effects of the reformers' desire to maximise their appeal. Abolitionists tried to inculcate *common* ideas and feelings while subgroups within antislavery offered some distinctive dialectical emphases and styles of thought as more likely to appeal to particular constituencies within the population.

As this preliminary sketch of the structure of the antislavery appeal suggests, it has to be seen as the expression in thought and feeling of an alliance, or rather a series of alliances over three generations which formed the antislavery movement. The perspective on antislavery as a series of alliances entails exploring the cohesive factors beyond common intellectual and emotional ground which held reformers together, that is, taking up the question of the internal culture of the movement as distinct from its interaction with the world around it. What kinds of interactions occurred between reformers and what meanings they had; what images abolitionists had of themselves; how they tried to adjust to changes in their circumstances and outlook to maintain their sense of solidarity and how and why they sometimes failed at the cost of internal divisions and conflict are all problems which demand attention. Answers require in part an examination of the more intimate side of the culture of reform, the more informal patterns of behaviour and personal and organisational rituals of antislavery. Relevant here are the family networks and religious affiliations which existed before or developed with antislavery mobilisation and which became the vertebrae of public activity and co-operation. Collaborative activity could become so close as to form intimacies akin to friendship and friendship itself often constituted a basis for reformist action. The element of time also entered the process of group cohesion and definition; antislavery people developed their own version of their own history, created their own historical pantheon and placed themselves in an historical succession. Such a placing, especially in the later years of antislavery, was part of the function of anniversary celebrations and memorial gatherings which were public occasions whose meaning was in part private to the reformers.

The organising concept of an alliance or series of alliances is appropriate too in that antislavery depended heavily upon networks of reformers within particular localities and on their collaboration with similar networks in other communities. Evidence drawn from local reform communities not only underlines the significance of family connection, friendship and religion but exposes how often implicit and sometimes explicit *negotiation* of antislavery coherence was undertaken or attempted within and between local reform communities in order to further national mobilisation. This dimension is analysed both in relation to particular issues and through locating it in the combinations and divergences of the three religious–intellectual traditions which comprehended virtually all abolitionists from the 1780s to the 1860s – evangelicalism, Rational Dissent (which emerged in the nineteenth century as Unitarianism) and Quakerism. These traditions, it becomes apparent, underpinned and were sustained by only partially congruent social worlds.

The relevance of class in its relation to the culture of antislavery is implied by this last point, but is perhaps best approached by referring back to the earlier sketch of the fields of force, of attraction and

5

repulsion, within which antislavery operated. Even cursory acquaintance with the range of activities of abolitionists reveals how many of
them were involved in other religio-philanthropic and social reform
efforts. Antislavery was part of a religious, philanthropic and reform
complex which embraced missionary activity, temperance, peace, free
trade and limited political reform. Juxtaposing and analysing this
range of commitments offers entry to the distinctive forms of
consciousness, religiosity and behaviour of those middle-class elements comprising a major component of the liberal segment of the
bourgeoisie by the mid-nineteenth century. In describing the underlying assumptions of the often influential provincial citizens in this
complex – the continuities and breaks in their loyalties across a
spectrum of philanthropy and reform – particular attention is focused
on how they saw the appropriate balance of liberty and control and
the contest of civilisation and barbarism within England and in the
wider world. This placing of antislavery allows some judgement about
how ideologically paradigmatic it was in defining the outlook of the
liberal bourgeoisie in the first half of the nineteenth century.

Equally significant so far as the ideological and social identity of
antislavery activists is concerned was the ambivalence or opposition
of most of them to agitations which not only drew heavily on popular
support but challenged middle-class notions of appropriate relations
of power in society and implicitly questioned the adequacy of
reformist procedures. To counterpoint the sketch of antislavery
embedded within a complex of middle-class philanthropy and reform,
chapter 6 examines the relation of abolitionists to the democratic
movement of the 1790s and Chartism. It is important, however, to
maintain a distinction between the social *identity* of antislavery
activists and the potentially and often actual cross-class character of
the antislavery *appeal*. Frequently present in the articulation of
antislavery attitudes and relevant to the appeal both to middle- and
working-class audiences was the claim to the legitimacy of antislavery
as a *patriotic* crusade, pursued in the interest of the nation as a whole,
when that interest was properly understood. Even at times of political
and social crisis in the 1790s and 1840s a minority of abolitionists
tried to bridge social and ideological gulfs and to accommodate
pressures from largely opposed groups. In less fraught years middle-
class reformers secured lower-class support by various means for the
antislavery project which they refused to see as limited by class. The
process of defining the boundaries of antislavery through tracing the
patterns of engagement with and ambivalence and opposition to

other contemporary movements for change and of dealing with explicit ideology, underlying assumptions and practice – *in toto* culture – also therefore necessarily reveals something of the complex class character of the movement's appeal.

Tensions in antislavery were sometimes acute but would have been less so amongst English abolitionists if many of them had not developed strong links with American reformers. The Anglo-American aspect of antislavery arose both from the transatlantic relations of religious dissent and the increasing attractions of the liberal and democratic features of American society for English reformers. The intensity of this relation was perhaps greater in the case of antislavery than in other strands of philanthropy and reform. It expressed both the reformers' fear of failure to undertake a universal religious duty in striking at slavery wherever it existed and anxiety at the subversion of American claims to be the very model of the liberal society which the existence of slavery threatened. When the struggle for liberal advance in England commanded widespread loyalty the maintenance of slavery in America appeared an obstacle.

The idiom of antislavery was predominantly religious and religious organisations became an important factor in the power of antislavery. Before exploring the nuances and implications of this, an indication of the changing structural and social characteristics of Protestant religion in England in the later eighteenth and the first half of the nineteenth centuries offers preliminary guidance to the organisational and social texture of antislavery.

There were two striking features about organised religion in England in the century between the mid-1700s and the mid-1800s. The first was the great evangelical wave which swept through most denominations gathering support as a proportion of both the religious and the total population; the second the change in the relative strengths of different religious groups which, on one calculation, left the Church of England 50 per cent weaker in 1830 than it had been when Methodism originated in the 1740s. Recovery of the Established Church in terms of more buildings and more clergy in the 1830s and 1840s by no means regained all the ground lost earlier.

Denominational competition was a fact of religious life of which leaders and many followers in church, chapel and even meeting-house were conscious, especially as the evangelising impulse gained strength. Methodism formed the leading edge of the great evangelical wave and reached its greatest relative strength by the beginning of the

1840s, though it continued to grow in absolute numbers while remaining distinctly smaller than membership of the Anglican Church. Almost as important as evidence of the power of evangelicalism was the surge in support for Congregationalists and Baptists, becoming especially noticeable in the late eighteenth century and continuing swiftly through to the 1830s in the case of Congregationalists and the following decade in the case of the Baptists.

Even the stirrings of recovery within Anglicanism evident by the 1830s must be attributed in part to the strengthening of the evangelicals. Gilbert calculates that in 1800 perhaps only 10 per cent of Anglican clergymen were in the evangelical camp and they, and even prominent lay evangelicals, were often regarded with some suspicion by hierarchy and laity alike as troublesome and 'Methodistical'. The evangelical impulse however gained strength remarkably after the withdrawal of Wesley's followers. Evangelical abolitionists within the church were thus part of a rising tendency.[4]

✓   Evangelicalism was none the less paradoxical in its effects. While fuelling the competitive drive between denominations to recruit souls it also potentially provided enough common ground theologically and in perspective on the world to allow co-operative activity with evangelical dissenters, as well as parallel activity in some spheres. Such a blurring of denominational lines in some aspects of righteous activity, including antislavery, also entailed collaboration across lines of social difference at times when the sense of social tension was not too acute. It is an important point that in a society of such material inequalities and consciousness of hierarchy a common commitment to biblicism, the *experience* of a vital religion and an expansive desire to gather in souls could open up such possibilities. In its early stages, Anglican evangelicalism no doubt 'derived its leadership and style from the upper classes and strove to avoid all that Methodism emphasized'. Practical initiatives as well as sentiment on particular issues at times and in particular localities crossed these implied social and behavioural barriers. In doing so these activities linked elements of the gentry and the urban middle classes with efforts by humbler social groups whose commitments were to evangelical dissent. Artisans were the largest element in all the evangelical nonconformist denominations and probably included people who were small employers, employees and independent craftsmen. Wesleyans and later Primitive Methodists had an element of miners and labourers amongst them, more so than Congregationalists and Baptists who in turn had more members amongst retailers, small traders and some merchants and manufacturers. This picture of cross-denominational and cross-class collaboration is, however, somewhat modified over time and in the case of reform activity like antislavery by the recognition that leaders and ministers who were especially prominent were always likely within dissent to have come from more 'respectable' strata than the rank-and-file. Even Wesleyanism showed a clear move towards respectability amongst ministers. To Cobbett's jaundiced eye, 'They quitted the tree, the hovel and the barn; and saw themselves elevated in elegant pulpits and stately temples.'[5]

Religious groups less caught up in, or even actively resistant to, the evangelical revival underwent a chequered history. Quantitatively the non-Catholic, largely non-evangelical groups declined towards marginality. The prominence and influence of some leading Quakers and Unitarians however tells another story. The Society of Friends, from a membership on one sober estimate of 60,000 in 1680 had perhaps 20,000 by 1800 while their own unofficial census of 1840 computed 16,227 members. It is, however, too simple to interpret these figures as evidence of loss of influence in society as a result of entry into a quietist phase after the proselytising years of Fox and Penn. However by the early decades of the nineteenth century some evangelical influences had begun to permeate part of the Society as had an often related willingness to take part publicly on some questions in a form of moral or philanthropic politics. In a number of respects Quakers were well placed to undertake such activities. Whether as individuals they were touched by evangelical influences or not, Quaker reformers were part of a denomination which on average was significantly wealthier than the ranks of evangelical dissent. Their leading figures often had a recognised status in society outside their own ranks; they were conscious of their predominantly middle-class character and high level of education. By the period of slave emancipation in the 1830s the largest element in membership was in London, Birmingham, Bristol and the industrial towns of Lancashire and the West Riding, with historic clusters in smaller centres like Norwich, Kendal and Banbury. Friends were composed of 'gentlemen', bankers, merchants, professional men and manufacturers in those major urban centres but sustained in the smaller towns and in significant numbers in the cities by substantial retailers, independent craftsmen, foremen and skilled workers and farmers. The family names of the elite engaged in antislavery and other public, including political, activity were widely known – Pease, Gurney, Allen, Clark, Crosfield, Fry – in part for their prominence in the country's economic life. Some of these names identified dynasties over several generations based in the case of Samuel Gurney of the bankers Overend and Gurney, of G.W. Alexander of Alexander's Discount Company and of Edward Pease and Joseph Pease MP of the Stockton and Darlington Railway and other north-eastern interests on earlier substantial economic success by family members.[6]

A similar paradoxical relationship between numbers and public prominence and influence existed in the case of Rational Dissent transmuted into Unitarianism, though in this case without any substantial evidence of a proselytising evangelical coloration. In the late eighteenth century Rational Dissent was the result of a convergence between heterodox Presbyterian congregations, the followers of Theophilus Lindsey after his withdrawal from the Church of England in 1773 over the test of the Thirty-Nine Articles and some unorthodox elements from the General Baptists (Old Connexion). It was an intellectually powerful, rationalist tendency which emerged, largely Unitarian in theology, with high standards for the training and intellectual performance of the ministry and resistant to 'enthusiasm' in religion. A rationalist tradition in religion had developed in such centres as the Mill Hill Chapel in Leeds and dissenting academies in Northampton, Warrington and Taunton during the course of the eighteenth century, and in the last decades the intellectual influence of Joseph Priestley encouraged an active faith directed 'to remove the distresses of our fellow creatures'.

But neither in Priestley's time nor later were Rational Dissenters or Unitarians numerous. In 1830 there were about 200 congregations in England and the 1851 Religious Census indicated about 50,000 attenders. This does not suggest any significant expansion let alone one comparable with the evangelicals. Modest numbers however disguise the presence of chapels in the major towns throughout the years of this study where they were centres of substantial wealth and influence. Essex Street in London, Cross Street in Manchester, Bowl Alley Lane in Hull, Hanover Street in Newcastle-on-Tyne, Westgate in Wakefield, Renshaw Street in Liverpool, Upper Chapel in Sheffield, High Pavement in Nottingham, as well as chapels in Birmingham, Norwich, Derby, Leicester, Bristol and smaller centres like Bridport, Bridgewater and Stockton were the locations of circles which united landed and mercantile wealth, leading local members of the professions and in some places manufacturers. Both within the cities as ordinary members of elite-led congregations and more prominently in the smaller towns congregations also contained

10

shopkeepers, small-scale manufacturers, and dealers and school-masters. Dissent expressing this kind of socially confident rationalism had links in the late eighteenth century with some liberal Whig grandees. In several towns, well before municipal reform in 1835, members of chapel elites held local office and became members of corporations. In a few places they were dominant – Bridgewater, Portsmouth and Nottingham – elsewhere they constituted an opposition to Tory–church dominance. After the institution of reform of the corporations they accumulated greater influence in urban politics. By the 1820s and 1830s a younger generation of Unitarians had also registered a substantial advance in the world of London in influential professional positions, as writers and journalists and soon as administrators and politicians. In the mid-1830s of fourteen MPs who were dissenters thirteen were said to be Unitarians. Members of this metropolitan and provincial minority, although not all were reformers and relatively few were radical, like the Quakers were especially visible in the different phases of antislavery.[7]

One final context is necessary; what was Britain's changing relationship to the international economy and the international political order, particularly in those features which impinged upon the perspectives of abolitionists and their possibilities of action? Aspects of the pattern of trade in the late eighteenth and earlier nineteenth centuries appeared to give the slave-based Caribbean territories a secure place in British economic fortunes and thus to reduce the likelihood of abolition and emancipation if they were to be considered purely as a matter of economic calculation. This is not to suggest that the direction, extent and value of commerce is a sufficient yardstick for measuring the importance of a particular area and concentration upon this variable in this section does not imply this. But it has the virtue both of adopting a criterion common in the historical literature and, more important, of highlighting the widespread antislavery conviction that exploitation of the cosmopolitan character of British commerce could further emancipationist objectives. After 1815 projects for the suppression of the transatlantic slave trade and the extension of freedom in Africa and the Americas were framed in antislavery minds by evident British predominance as a naval power and influence as a diplomatic negotiator alongside an enhanced capacity to expand trade and tap even more cosmopolitan markets.

Recent scholarship on the Industrial Revolution in Britain has stressed the relatively long drawn out and uneven movement towards a large-scale, mechanised manufacturing sector. While the pace of development in general quickened from the 1780s the growth in overall industrial output up to 1800 occurred at only about half the rate achieved by the 1820s. It was only in that decade also, it is argued, that the rise in productivity in manufacturing began to be rapid enough to outstrip the pressure of a growing population on resources. Whatever the implications of these arguments for the influence of manufacturers in society and for felt evidence amongst the population at large of the material benefits of industrialisation, they should not disguise the rapid impact on the content and pattern of British trade of cotton textiles.[8]

The remarkable rise of cotton textiles to a central place in British exports occurred between 1780 and 1806 and initially seemed to make slave societies of the Caribbean even more secure within Britain's commercial system. For much of the eighteenth century British exports had largely consisted of a variety of woollen goods and traditional manufactures traded to both Europe and British colonies. This commerce paid for rising imports of sugar and tobacco from the West Indian and North American colonies. The maintenance of territorial empire, especially in the Americas, as a resource for raw materials and staples and as a market for traditional British products was an important part of a consensual mercantilism up to the American Revolution. Cotton textiles in the post-revolution years became important as traditional European markets for woollens were lost to continental competitors and Britain emerged with an early competitive advantage in an attractive new line of goods. Initially the Caribbean was an important market along with North America and from the late 1790s Europe also, despite war conditions. Such a burst of production required secure supplies of raw cotton and these were drawn in large measure from the West Indies through to the early years of the nineteenth century. The trade in sugar of course continued. As Drescher and other scholars have suggested the West Indian territories remained of major importance to Britain as partners in trade at least to the time of abolition of the British slave trade.[9]

The quite rapid transfer of raw cotton supply from the colonial West Indies primarily to an independent United States from the early 1800s might be thought to have presented considerable potential difficulties in guaranteeing supply. The changed situation presented no serious problems, however, in Britain's new circumstances after 1815. Whatever the qualifications as to the pace and extent of industrialisation the British had a considerable industrial lead in the post-war years. Moreover, they had unchallenged naval and maritime predominance and together these factors put them in a position to secure markets and develop reciprocal commerce, including the supply of raw materials.[10]

Growing industrial production and an expanding and increasingly cosmopolitan commerce underpinned London's position as the dominant financial centre in the international economy. A number of writers in recent years have seen the resumption of gold payments in 1819 as laying the foundations for a gold–sterling standard as the universal referent around which international trade and financial transactions came to turn. This was the context within which the British could not only expand trade but move towards free trade, a process likely to be of benefit to a country with its existing advantages but potentially threatening to slave-based colonial economies.

The volume of British exports expanded enormously between 1815 and 1850. In the same period there was also both liberalisation of trade and some shifts in the relative importance of the various directions trade followed. Some recent writers – notably Hilton, Cain and Hopkins and Ingham – have argued persuasively that liberalisation began in the 1820s not through pressure of manufacturing interests seeking new and expanded markets for their products but as a result of the attention policy-makers paid to developing and maintaining London's financial role and to the problems of food supply. Rising population suggested that British self-sufficiency in basic foodstuffs was coming to an end. Loosening restrictions on trade was expected to provide resources for the importation of increased quantities of foodstuffs.[11]

Much of the substance of liberalised trade, although there was no unified manufacturing interest in support of liberalisation in the 1820s, came from cotton textiles and other products of the industrialising sector. In this way in the 1820s and 1830s, the currency of free trade and free-labour ideas was much greater and provincial manufacturers were more closely interested in policy-making than they had been. At the time of the social crisis of which Chartism was an expression, according to Cain and Hopkins, many industrialists were strongly in favour of expanding export markets through the drive towards free trade, in part because they hoped the prosperity which would result could contribute to social calm.[12]

Whether or not this was a large consideration, in the 1840s cotton textiles remained important in commerce but their markets indicate significant shifts of emphasis in the patterns of trade. After 1815 a relative loss of markets for textiles occurred in Europe and the United States and the value of trade – in textiles and overall – increased in commerce to Africa, Asia and Latin America. Some colonial markets, including the West Indies, shared this relative loss of importance in the era of emancipation. The increase in the average value of trade with Europe, the United States and traditional markets including the Caribbean between 1816–20 and 1838–42 was £1.9m; in the same period to Africa, Asia and Latin America it rose by £8.4m. From the mid-1840s foreign trade became even more cosmopolitan in character and grew in volume at the remarkable annual average rate of 4.7 per cent through to the early 1870s.

The nature of the West Indian loss of significance within British commerce in the post-war years is highlighted by the crucial item of sugar. Although the total value of sugar imports to Britain rose more than fourfold between 1784–6 and 1814–16, and continued to come overwhelmingly from the West Indies, a sharp post-war depression in the sugar trade almost halved the value of sugar imports by 1824–6. True, thereafter, they rose consistently to near the value of 1814–16 by 1854–6 but the West Indian share declined progressively. By emancipation West Indian sugar constituted 80 per cent of the total value imported and by the mid-1840s, at the time of the equalisation of the sugar duties, little more than 50 per cent. The difference was made up by increasing contributions from East Indian, Indian, Mauritian and African sources. Thus the West Indies became less important as a market for cotton textiles and other manufactures roughly in phase with the reduced position of the islands as sugar suppliers.[13]

The increasing cosmopolitanism of British trade as it impinged upon antislavery was apparent in three other ways. With only a brief interruption, occasioned largely by the war of 1812, the United States continued to be the main supplier of raw cotton to Britain after it had replaced the West Indies in the early years of the nineteenth century. By the early 1850s, however, India had become a noticeable source and there were also modest amounts imported from Egypt and Brazil. It was in these later years that India also became an important market for British cotton textiles. Both commercial tendencies coincided with the campaign of some abolitionists to erode American slavery by proposing the further development of Indian cotton production based on free labour as a replacement for American slave-grown cotton. In this they worked parallel to, and sometimes in contact with, parliamentarians like John Bright whose parliamentary committee of

1847–8 reported favourably on cotton expansion in India, looked to railway development to encourage it and showed support from cotton trading and manufacturing interests in Bombay, Liverpool and the Lancashire mill districts.

The aspiration of British antislavery reformers to have Britain deal less in southern cotton was complemented by their hopes that good commercial links with the United States could be sustained through bringing in corn from the free states of the Middle West. In the 1840s and 1850s at the time of and following the repeal of the Corn Laws, the need to increase imports of temperate foodstuffs was apparent and traders did buy in sharply increased quantities of American corn so that by the mid-1850s the United States was the largest external supplier of corn to the British market.

As far back as the 1780s humanitarians in Britain also demonstrated a concern to persuade African suppliers of slaves to European traders in the transatlantic slave trade that they could both prosper and develop their societies by switching from slaving to 'legitimate' trade and find alternative commodities to human beings. There was periodic encouragement from Britain to West Africans, both those under and those outside British political control, to develop such a commerce with Britain. Whether as a result of such efforts or not, as part of the tendency to greater trade with Africa a sharp increase in legitimate commerce, particularly in palm oil, occurred in the 1840s and 1850s.[14]

In the years after 1815 then, when Britain was the predominant naval power, London the major international financial centre, British industrial development a vital source of the rise of an increasingly cosmopolitan commerce, British horizons were wider than ever before. Politicians and theorists and, in their more limited way, antislavery reformers worked for the construction of a liberal international order in politics and economics at a time when Britain had the power and could expect to be the main beneficiary. The British, policy-makers and abolitionists, were confidently free in pressing other powers into diplomatic agreements to end the transatlantic slave trade and on occasion were prepared to use naval squadrons to ensure enforcement. It was a context in which the British did not have to choose between 'informal' or 'formal' empire but could respond with a good deal of latitude to particular situations and one in which governments sometimes acceded to humanitarian pressures. Such a case was Buxton's Niger expedition, which resulted in quasi-imperial policies in pursuit of liberal objectives.

Antislavery became a reflexive feature of the British official and to some extent popular outlook on the world. As the following chapters demonstrate, however, that conclusion masks a variety of changes and complexities.

2

ARGUMENT AND ID.

Quakers, evangelicals inside and outside the Church of England and Rational Dissenters and Unitarians all articulated a powerful abolitionist and emancipationist appeal over more than half a century. The fundamental dynamic driving towards reform in these three religious–intellectual traditions differed subtly but the appeal demonstrated considerable coherence and continuity from earlier to later phases of antislavery. From the late 1780s onwards, often fierce dialectical conflict with pro-slave trade and pro-slavery spokesmen was central to the intellectual experience of the antislavery movement. In controversy abolitionists found arguments in common whatever their religious affiliations. The deployment of particular arguments both in response to their opponents and when they went beyond those limits, revealed a family resemblance in fundamental ideas. Antislavery success, it was assumed, would be a large step towards creating a proper moral order in the world and from that could be expected to flow greater social and political harmony. Such a moral order was legitimate since it was consonant with the dictates of Providence or, in different intellectual terms, expressive of the natural order progressively opening to the minds of Enlightenment intellectuals through scientific investigation and freedom of thought.

The very capaciousness of the idea of proper order as well as the changing dialectical requirements of controversy meant that *absolute* agreement on fundamentals was unnecessary. Indeed part of the attraction of the picture of the world abolitionists presented, that is, a contribution to the success of their *appeal*, was that their world-view or ideology was capable of accommodating differences of emphasis and expression while recognisably having the same basic shape. Quakers, evangelicals and Rational Dissenters could reach a similar commitment by their own intellectual and theological routes and

17

derstand it as having somewhat different implications for desirable social and political arrangements. The same considerations of ideological convergence in broad terms and participation in public controversy encouraged the development of antislavery argument after the Napoleonic Wars in directions only lightly indicated in the early stages of the anti-slave trade argument. Especially important were the growing certainties of liberal political economy and the theme of antislavery as expressing the national interest and, as an important moral component, the sense of national duty the British people owed the world and themselves.

What were the dynamics within the religious–intellectual traditions which committed some adherents to public action for reform and provided theological rationales which sustained antislavery over many years? To begin with Quakerism, Friends taking the initiative against the slave trade in the 1780s drew on the colonial American Quakers Benezet and Woolman. The groundwork of a powerful testimony and action against the trade in slaves was laid by their writings. This result might seem puzzling given the conventional characterisation of most Friends in the eighteenth century as quietist 'following their habit of attending religiously to their internal impressions'. But the truth is more complex; it is difficult to find a hard and fast line absolutely distinguishing quietists from other Quakers. If quietism entailed abnegation of the self the better to experience the Light Within, it could also imply a moral optimism about the future. The future Quaker abolitionist, James Cropper of Liverpool, accepted the necessity 'for a humble, dependent state of mind naturally arising from the knowledge of the superior wisdom and goodness of the will and ways of God to our own' and found gloom about the future banished. Cropper's implication that in this way God's concerns became a man's own and, potentially, were the basis for activism in the world, indicates the difficulty of reading the language of quietism in a purely passive way. Elizabeth Fry was more explicit about spiritual direction. The power she experienced descending upon her had its value in 'the sensible and constant direction of the Spirit of God in men'. Nothing short of this 'can really help forward the cause of righteousness on earth'. God's presence understood in this way led to moral teaching or particular action on behalf of righteousness. In Mrs Fry's case this meant prison reform, but also, at least formally, antislavery. The self-abnegation of Friends, emptying themselves the better to be filled by the Light Within, did not

18

then necessarily exclude the pursuit of righteousness in the world; equally, in the outlook of growing numbers of Quakers in the early nineteenth century, this stance could merge with a stress on the *experience* of grace which aligned them with evangelicals.[1]

It was Mrs Fry's brother, the antislavery Quaker minister Joseph John Gurney, who was a prime source for the absorption of evangelical elements into Quakerism, reiterating the typical evangelical emphases on Christ's atonement and the centrality of the biblical message. Full absorption of the meaning of the atonement allowed the Spirit to work the conversion of the sinner. When the converted attained the faith they were no longer merely formal Christians and were predisposed to work for a righteous world. This tendency was not unchallenged amongst Quakers but its impact was substantial, perhaps predominant, in the Yearly Meeting by the later 1820s.[2]

It was the clear differentiation of 'real' from 'nominal' Christianity which was the most obvious point of convergence between Gurney-influenced Quakerism and evangelicalism inside and outside the Anglican Church. 'Real' Christianity, in Clarkson's words, depended upon 'a *total change of heart or of mind* so as to produce a *corresponding change of Life*'. This transformation could only occur in the heart of the individual if, anguished at his sinfulness, he recognised his complete reliance upon Christ for assured salvation and then attained utter conviction that Christ's redeeming grace had infused him. The 'real' Christian was then able scrupulously to follow the scriptures as a divine standard and guide through the contending opinions of men.[3]

In this way evangelicals understood the individual to achieve a right relation with God and to do so within a providential order in the world. Despite disagreement over the extent of providential intervention in the flow of human events evangelicals had no doubt that 'there is a God who governs the world and intimately directs all the concerns of his rational and immortal creatures'. It was a conviction which promised moral and spiritual progress. One other element however was essential to provide the dynamic for righteous action by evangelicals; certainty of God's government was combined with conviction of free human will and agency. Not only could the possibility of salvation be rejected, both James Stephen and Clarkson affirmed, but men and women had sufficiently free will, 'to render us justly responsible . . . for all the sins we commit in this our state of trial'. Equally, for the regenerate, free agency effectively imposed the duty of good works in the world; they had the capacity to overcome 'the

;s of passion or inclination' or interest and act in accord with ishes.[4]

.. ..t in this way furthered the Kingdom of God through the expression of man's benevolence. Neglect of opportunities to act on such feelings, Granville Sharp believed, was 'as great an offence before God as if we had denied assistance to *Christ himself* '. Benevolence contributed to harmony within God's order. Slaveholders fostered misery amongst their slaves; they clearly did not act upon the precept of loving their neighbours. Yet, as Sharp expressed it, Christ taught 'that all *mankind*, even our *professed enemies* . . . must necessarily be esteemed our neighbours . . . so that the same benevolence . . . is indisputably due, *under the Gospel*, to *our brethren of the universe* '. The related evangelical image of humanity as one 'great family' similarly incorporated the imperative of proper order within local and national communities, though it was far from meaning that the existing pattern of society was left untouched. It also indicated the slave trade as a peculiarly appropriate object upon which many evangelicals could exercise their benevolence since it constituted a burden of individual and national guilt and in its international character provided a way of extending and giving reality to the notion of mankind as a family.[5]

The third religious tradition in antislavery, Rational Dissent, increasingly expressed in Unitarian ideas, came into open conflict with the other two traditions at the end of the eighteenth century. Unitarian tendencies were found amongst some Quakers in both England and Ireland in these years and the Liverpool abolitionist William Rathbone's sympathetic treatment of them led to his disownment by the Friends and the passage of his family to Unitarianism. Wilberforce attacked Unitarians as lacking fixed religious dogmas and was attacked in turn, along with other evangelicals, for promoting irrationality in religion precisely through dogmatism about the divinity of Christ and the Trinity while also stressing the reality of the Devil and Hell. Rational Dissenters themselves exemplified a variety of doctrinal positions derived from their commitment to individual enquiry in matters of belief. Some followed Priestley in his necessarianism which envisaged all mental and moral life, since it was derived ultimately from matter, operating according to natural laws. Within that structure men's own actions and decisions were necessary to link cause and effect and any properly considered action must have an effect on the system of moral life. Necessarianism was thus not fatalistic but optimistic in its concern for properly effective motive, encouraging constant effort. Other Rational Dissenters held back from Priestley's particular arguments but shared with the Priestleyans an urgent commitment to influencing moral life through advocacy of 'great and universally allowed principles of religion and morality ... in all their boundless and beneficent application to the concerns of public and private life, of national and individual conduct, of politics, literature, art, philosophy and the condition of society' (W. J. Fox). The common imperative to activism amongst Rational Dissenters drew upon the conviction of an ordered universe revealed progressively through rational investigation and scientific enquiry. This is less distant from the other religious traditions discussed than might be supposed. The cumulative revelation of an ordered universe convinced most Rational Dissenters, following Newton, that greater understanding brought them closer to God through familiarity with His design. Like Quakers and evangelicals, Rational Dissenters relied upon the characteristic of human benevolence to underpin their advocacy of 'great and universally allowed principles of religion and morality' and to act them out. Combined with their conviction of man's capacity for utilitarian calculation of the effects of his actions, or, in Priestleyan terms, properly judged motive, this was an outlook able to be squared with the Quaker and evangelical pursuit of righteousness. As Cookson has noted, in this sense Christianity fitted man's propensities and the revelation afforded by the Bible complemented man's reason and his progressive moral inclinations. In respect of a common activist orientation towards achieving a providentially sanctioned order in the world, based upon faith in man's capacity for moral progress, the tensions between Rational Dissent/Unitarianism and the other religious traditions in antislavery reform were of secondary importance.[6]

What themes emerged in public argument against the slave trade and how do they relate to the basic concern with good order and the imperative of action to achieve it?

The arguments contained in *The Case for the Oppressed Africans* (1783) issued by the Friends in advocacy of abolition set useful signposts to the general lines of persuasion adopted for the following twenty years. The Quakers anticipated results from the claim that abolition was required by 'justice and humanity, but is also consistent with sound policy'. It was the duty of the government to bring 'terror to evil doers'. The penalty for failure to do so was likely to be dire because not only individuals but nations were chastised for their sins 'and can it be expected that He will suffer this great iniquity to go unpunished?'

These arguments suggest the importance of the direct appeal to feelings of humanity but also their link to religious-based ideas of justice. Equally the portrayal of the trade in slaves as opposed to sound policy suggests a complementary appeal to traders themselves, associated interests and politicians, to those whose sense of personal, community or national interest screened out the appeal of justice and humanity. It was a point which opened up a line of argument opposing the 'true' national interest of abolition to the false claims of the traders of national necessity for what they were doing. Yet it was also to emerge that for some antislavery controversialists 'impolicy' itself arose from abrogating the natural order in the form of the laws of liberal political economy; consistency and principle together would bring greater prosperity. Finally, the question of national guilt and its expiation was to have a long history in relation to abolition and emancipation involving a definition of national interest as meeting national duty by observing the religious conception of proper order in the world.[7]

From the late 1780s onwards evangelicals contributed substantially to the pamphlet literature against the slave trade. As Wesley had done, and as Rational Dissenters very frequently did, they alluded to the natural rights of all men. But a more characteristic evangelical understanding of how the slave trade abrogated God's good order stressed the interposition by trader and slaveholder of a harsh human power between God and some of His creatures. This intervention ignored the fact of creation as a 'comprehensive system of goodness' in which all men and women, Africans included, influenced by 'communicative goodness' were to be 'instrumental in promoting each other's happiness'. All were in this sense brethren and capable through redemption of striving to abolish sin. Not only did trader and master subvert that sense and render the victims of the Middle Passage 'incapable of deriving any benefit from Christianity' but slave trading and slavery were a context conducive to sinfulness by loosening constraints on passion. Put in slightly different language slave trading blocked the operation of Christian benevolence arising from man's innate ability to distinguish good from evil and strengthened 'by various communications of his revealed Will'. The imperative to act upon the promptings of benevolence was crucial to some notable opponents of the slave trade; its frustration by the traders amounted to disruption of providential means to harmony. Slave traders fomented a kind of disorder which was characteristic of relations *outside* God's rule. Justice entailed bringing all relations within the ambit of divine order.[8]

This point provides the key to the full meaning of the many arguments in pamphlet form – and on occasion in parliamentary debate – which underlined the brutalities and cruelty of the slave trade. They were aimed at arousing horror and warm sympathy, leading to action on behalf of their victims. But they could be expected especially to move a religious audience committed to a divine order comprehending all men. Cruelty against fellow creatures with God-given souls constituted an unjust and blasphemous misuse of power which could, Clarkson argued, drive a fellow human being to madness, suicide or desperate revolt; to bring on moral disorder ran the risk of provoking psychological and social disorder.[9]

Within all of the religious currents sustaining antislavery, the Bible was taken as a vital revelation of God's will and a guide to right action. Any attempt to use the scriptures to vindicate the slave trade was thus bound to provoke energetic efforts by abolitionists to controvert the arguments; failure to do so would have yielded an authority to the pro-slave trade position by sacrificing one of the main ways religious reformers had of grasping the essential spirit of the Christian moral order. The biblical argument over the slave trade and slavery was thus of immense significance but took on particularly sharp controversial form in Liverpool over the Rev. Raymond Harris' (Don Raymondo Hormaza) *Scriptural Researches* (1788) which tried to ground the legitimacy of the slave trade in scripture. The local slave trading and mercantile community was loud in its support for Harris' intervention and happy to see, at this early stage of antislavery mobilisation, its interests defended quite as much in general scriptural terms as it was on the broad basis of national interest and community prosperity. This bespoke greater *intellectual* confidence than was to be evident at later stages of controversy. Equally significant, the community strength and religious confidence of the pro-trade argument prompted vindications of the antislavery impulse of scripture across religious traditions. Abolitionists were alert not only to the particular issue of the slave trade but to the larger need to safeguard their deployment of scripture as a powerful instrument of insight into right and wrong.

Harris tried to argue the consonance of the slave trade with 'the Mosaic Dispensation and the Christian Law'. William Hughes and the Unitarian William Roscoe, following Granville Sharp's argument in

23

the 1770s, asserted the scriptural sanction of slave trading to have only particular application; they tried to bolster scripture as a reliable instrument of antislavery revelation by insisting that Harris' reliance on the Old Testament had to be modified or abrogated by the New Testament. It required, in familiar language, '*all mankind* are to be esteemed *our brethren* '. The Anglican Henry Dannett provided a further fall-back epistemological basis for vindicating antislavery perceptions of the moral order by arguing that even 'if scriptural decisions should appear to contradict our ideas of right and wrong we are still bound to follow those ideas because we cannot be so certain that we rightly understand and justly limit those scriptural decisions as we are of our own ideas of right and wrong'. Individual conscience repaired the weaknesses of individual scriptural interpretation. It was an appropriately Protestant justification for refutations of Harris (of foreign, Catholic origin, 'a Spanish Jesuit') whose reading of the Bible was 'well worthy of one of the disciples of Loyola'.[10]

Arguments advanced by Rational Dissenters against the slave trade revealed a sense of providential order quite as strong as that of Quakers and evangelicals. But they drew more explicitly upon Enlightenment ideas and liberal political tradition and so expressed their anxieties about infractions of the right order in language which often sounded more secular. A reading of anti-slave trade and antislavery tracts by Rational Dissenters in the late eighteenth century thus reveals concern about abrogations of a man's 'natural right' to liberty. A properly harmonious order in the world, the argument ran, depended upon a just recognition of man's God-given constitution, his rights and capacities. Stress on man's nature and the rights expressive of that nature pointed in some cases to a more radical politics than was embraced by other antislavery advocates. It was an outlook formed in a number of Rational Dissenters active against the slave trade, by adherence to the 'Real Whig' tradition of liberalism, so copiously analysed in recent years. Central was a commitment to the universality of natural rights and the need to protect them by maintaining balanced systems of government in which concentrations of power were avoided. Checks and balances required an alert and informed populace. Analogies with the slave trade and slavery and the movement against them were apparent to such reformers. The natural right to liberty also began to be combined, though much less regularly than in the 1820s, with the conviction from liberal political economy of the greater efficiency and wealth-creating properties of free labour.[11]

The anti-slave trade committee in Manchester was an apt source of these arguments in 1789. Though chaired by the latitudinarian Anglican, and radical, manufacturer Thomas Walker, it contained a number of Rational Dissenters in the professions – lawyers and doctors – several of whom had an intellectual bent and were active in the discussions of the Manchester Literary and Philosophical Society, a significant regional conduit for Enlightenment thinking. The committee gave the Scots scholar, James Anderson of Monkshill, the brief which led to his *Observations on Slavery*. The pamphlet began its argument for the dependence of harmony and order on the recognition of man's true nature by distinguishing man from other animals. Chiefly he was different by virtue of his sense of 'self-love'. When brought into operation it stimulated hope, emulation and friendship, the maturing of the social affections. At best man 'idolized by all . . . feels an irresistible impulse to confer upon them fresh benefits . . . and he runs on in his magnanimous career with alacrity and joy'. Slavery and the slave trade, however, denied self-love to the slave, provoking permanent discontent and possible rebellion.

Similarly Joseph Priestley concluded that men were treated as 'mere brutes' in the slave trade 'so that they are deprived of every advantage of their rational nature'. The enlightened Baptist minister Robert Robinson in Cambridge denounced the trade as an encroachment on natural rights and envisaged its end as the result of a general offensive, congenial to Rational Dissenters, making 'the natural connection between civil and religious liberty'. Further, his evident linkage of slavery and the slave trade with the political concerns of the Real Whig tradition was plain in his wish that children should be taught about 'the histories of consciences oppressed, property plundered, families divided and flourishing states ruined by exercises of arbitrary power'. The radical Unitarian, Thomas Cooper, proclaimed opposition to the slave trade as a particular duty of Englishmen 'who claim Freedom as our birth-right . . . we are in honour bound to assist in exterminating the most diabolical exertion of political tyranny which the annals of oppression can exhibit'.[12]

It was Anderson in his Manchester pamphlet who most conspicuously at this early stage of the antislavery campaign raised the free-labour argument and implicitly defined its appropriateness to man's nature. In an argument no doubt intended to be attractive to Manchester's merchants and employers – local abolitionists had specifically asked him to write on the *impolicy* of slavery and the slave trade – he declared that freedom produced cheaper labour than slavery. His reasoning was that the productivity of free workers was greater than slave labour if the labourers were offered sufficient inducement through piece-work and high rates for day labour; the cost of getting the same amount of work done by slaves was greater than the cost of the higher rates offered as an inducement. A free, contractual basis for labour thus pointed to progress and prosperity. Priestley concurred and offered explicit references to 'Dr Smith'. The dictates of true order properly understood were not only just but superior in terms of interest.[13]

The argument tying increased prosperity to increased freedom was intended to demonstrate to individuals, groups and communities whose interests were involved with the slave trade and slavery that they were impolitic in their understanding of their own interests. But abolitionists also had to face powerful arguments formulated by slave trading interests in terms of the *national* interest of the commerce by the mercantilist criteria which underpinned much existing commercial legislation. The assertions of the Liverpool trader, Robert Norris, can be taken as a representative example. Sugar production, he argued, was extremely important in the imperial economy and for the foreseeable future plantations would rely upon fresh labour from Africa to maintain production. As well as commercial prosperity the slave trade contributed to Britain's security by enhancing her naval superiority through the provision of sailors and ships. And, in an argument utterly characteristic of the mercantilist view of a conflict-ridden world, Norris raised the bogey of the old rival France; he claimed that France's naval power had been so strengthened by her own involvement in the slave trade that if Britain discontinued it not only would her commercial prosperity decline but she would lose naval predominance.[14]

A more insidious appeal to the national interest on behalf of the trade came from those controversialists who appeared to concede much of the abolitionists' case with one hand only to withdraw it with the other. Granting evils in the slave trade and colonial slavery it was none the less argued that government could more easily influence planters and traders through better regulation than they could control the situation on the West African coast. Once those involved in slaving recognised that self-interest dictated decent treatment of the Africans natural population increase would occur amongst the bondsmen, making the continuation of the slave trade irrelevant. Alternatively, in attempts to deprive antislavery of the dynamic of evangelism, it was sometimes argued that the task of evangelising and civilising Africans, whether in Africa or the Americas, necessitated the disciplines of slavery and the slave trade rather than being a reason for abolition or emancipation. Progress within bondage had to take precedence over liberation to secure the safety of any eventual freedom. Decisive action would exacerbate existing evils and undermine Britain's strength.[15]

As the climate of controversy became sharper at the end of the 1780s reformers countered these varieties of the national interest argument both by emphasising the potential for the country in alternative patterns of commerce and production and, more defensively, by trying to reconcile abolition with the nation's interest in security and order. At this time they operated largely within the mercantilist premises of their opponents. They believed the existing system worked to the enrichment of only a small number; national benefit could be derived from legitimate commerce with a fertile Africa only if the slave trade did not create misleadingly attractive alternatives. Numerous products from Africa could give British merchants the opportunity to push Dutch carriers out of supplying European markets and provide in Africa resources for the purchase of British manufactures. As to British naval power, the slave trade militated against rather than enhanced it through the high mortality of sailors engaged in it. Further, slave traders helped rather than hindered the power of France by supplying slaves to the booming colony of St Domingue and thus indirectly encouraged the growth of the French merchant marine engaged in carrying colonial produce.[16]

The issue of stability or order at the political and social level, and its relation to the interest of national strength and security was also a significant factor in shaping the *particular* arguments abolitionists advanced to influence the economic interest groups and policy-makers. The fundamental stress on proper moral order as the basis of a healthy society could be dangerously two-edged; it could plausibly be turned against the reformers by the assertion that abolition and emancipation would cut off the civilising influence of Europeans on Africans and result in social and political upheaval in the colonies. Reformers were even more acutely aware of the need for effective dialectical counters on this point as the French Revolution developed an increasingly radical edge and slave revolt overtook St Domingue. By the early 1790s the argument was conducted in an atmosphere in which projects for reform were presented by their enemies as tantamount to a threat to stability and the preservation of civilised life in Britain.

Abolitionists handled this delicate problem for the efficacy of their 'persuasion' or appeal in two ways. Both before and during the events of 1789–92 in France and St Domingue they distinguished their aim of abolition of the trade from the larger question of emancipation of the slaves. They acknowledged that if emancipation were eventually to come it would require the moral progress and demographic increase consequent upon a conscious policy of a more equal sex ratio amongst slaves; education and religious instruction; the reorganisation of the work of the slaves to provide a progressive increase in the time devoted to autonomous labour from which earnings could be directed to self-purchase; possibly too recognition of obligations to the former master even after the date of legal emancipation. All of this was admitted to be long term. The virtue of immediate or shortly forthcoming abolition of the trade abolitionists proclaimed as an act of justice and humanity which at the same time offered the greatest stimulus to reform of slavery on the plantations. At the very least it would make it a more rationally and humanely organised system likely to be more productive; at best it would provide the conditions for eventual emancipation should that decision finally be made.[17]

With the experience of revolution in France and her colonies a few of the more enthusiastically radical abolitionists – notably Clarkson and Thomas Cooper – adopted the higher risk tactic of accepting both the virtual inevitability of slave revolt and its justification. Salvation for the slaveholders lay only in their own willingness to accept abolition and undertake amelioration of slavery on their estates. Paradoxically, these abolitionists were arguing that fear was supposed to induce reason and humanity and provoke policies which squared reform with stability and both with the interest of the nation.[18]

In one other sense fear was promoted by abolitionists as a motive for demanding abolition in the national interest – fear of divine judgement falling upon the guilty nation as a whole. It was a fear expressed across the religious spectrum of antislavery and a major source of the conviction, particularly of Unitarians, that the slave trade was a subject not for sectarian difference but for the united opposition 'of the various denominations of *Christians* '. Divine judgement on a sinning nation was foreshadowed in the growing conviction that the corruptions of unrestrained power in the plantation colonies were beginning to stain the social and political fabric in Britain. Luxury, too, based upon exploitation of the bondsmen spelled destruction.

The spreading leprosy taints ev'ry part,
Infects each limb, and sickens at the heart.
Simplicity! most dear of rural maids,
Weeping resigns her violated shades:
Stern Independence from his glebe retires,
And anxious Freedom eyes her drooping fires;
By foreign wealth are British morals chang'd,
And Afric's sons, and India's smile avenged.

The struggle to avoid the wrath of divine judgement on the nation and conviction that the crisis of the French Revolutionary and Napoleonic Wars both revealed God's displeasure and offered an opportunity to vindicate the nation's purity, contributed powerfully to substantial ideological coherence over the slave trade, embracing politically a range from the Toryism of James Stephen to the liberal wing of dissent. The necessary correlative, particularly amongst liberals, before and during the wars was caution about threatening the social order; it would also mark a form of corruption in the Christian dynamic of antislavery. Robinson expressed it most explicitly:

> The execution . . . of the Saviour's plan required the prudent application of wise and well-judged measures so as not to injure private property, not to disturb civil order, not to expose Christianity to the scandal of sedition, not to obscure the glory of a Kingdom *not* of this world.[19]

The abolitionist appeal in parliament revealed subtle differences. In the 1792 debate, abolition is portrayed as in the national interest economically through the liberation of legitimate trade to and from Africa. In mercantilist terms, the nation would benefit by the protection of mariners from the horrors of the Middle Passage. Equally parliamentarians spoke of cruelty, inhumanity and tyranny as features of the slave trade and slavery, often providing vivid examples. It is clear though that familiarity with such an approach was thought to make it less effective in 1806 than in 1792. But familiarity was not the only factor. The rhetoric of cruelty and inhumanity in 1792, and more clearly in 1806, aroused ambivalence as to its persuasive effect in parliament, even amongst some abolitionists, because they feared the impact of 'enthusiasm' upon their colleagues. Fox in 1792 and Romilly in 1806 were prepared to take the risk. They used the language of murder about the slave trade and Fox proclaimed himself an enthusiast for 'that zeal and warmth which arose from a sense of justice and was that kind which made men act with energy in a noble cause'. Other opponents of the trade, however, deliberately distanced themselves from 'fanaticism'. In 1792 Whitbread stressed his commitment to 'a cool and moderate proceeding in the course of justice and humanity'. In 1806 proponents of the trade, Gascoigne and Rose, tried to marginalise Romilly's attack by portraying it as a form of extremism. Leading opponents of the trade, however, also adopted a different tone. Wilberforce doubted that humanitarian zeal had sufficient staying power despite his own and others' expression of it in 1792. By contrast the interest behind the slave trade created a passion which 'is cool, collected, steady and permanent'. The 'compunctions of conscience are in general of a far more fleeting nature'. The implications of this change in tone emerged explicitly in Grenville's setting aside of 'the effusions of a blind and generous passion' in favour of 'cool judgement' since the issue involved 'a large portion of the interests of the British empire of which it is your Lordships' duty, as an House of Parliament, to take care'.

At one level, then, leading abolitionists in parliament came to the conclusion that the language of practicality, of plausible calculations about population increase in the future in the West Indies if importations from Africa were stopped, were more likely to be effective on their colleagues. This arose in part from a strong sense of parliament's unique place and function in the political system. In sharp contrast to his 'enthusiasm' of 1792, in 1806 Fox introduced the abolition resolution by reminding the Commons what was owed to its own reputation after its 1792 decision for gradual abolition was not carried through; he appealed to the memory of Pitt and the arguments of Burke; he looked to parliament to speak for the nation on 'a question in which party feelings, arising out of political connections, can have no share'. Abolition was to be a vindication of the capacity of parliament to bring about nationally agreed change in difficult times.

Full realisation of the meaning of the partial divergence in styles of appeal between parliament and country requires recognition of at least the limited equation of 'enthusiasm' with popular opinion. It thus posed a threat to the calm, deliberative function of the legislature. Rose was critical of Romilly for being carried away by 'heat and popular prejudice'; Romilly himself linked his denunciation of the barbarities of the slave trade with speaking on behalf of the wishes of 'the people of England'. Differences in style and content of appeal to a considerable extent mirrored divergent estimates of the virtues of parliament and people, as well as differing assessments of how to win over a self-conscious political class.[20]

By the time of the abolition measures of 1806 and 1807 abolitionists had failed to convince their opponents that they were not also looking forward to emancipation. West Indians and their supporters were substantially correct in their suspicions. Much of the attack on the slave trade from as early as the end of the 1780s to the debates of 1806 could equally have been, and was, an attack on slavery. It was not only to meet the argument of demographic decline if the trade stopped but to avoid the embarrassingly radical charge that they wanted rapid emancipation that antislavery reformers argued the consequence of abolition would be virtually automatic improvement in the conditions of slaves. And in many abolitionist minds this would ultimately lead to emancipation; slaves would not only gradually become more able to live in freedom but better conditions would so enhance the population of labourers in the West Indies that it would be cheaper to employ workers on a waged basis than as slaves. There was one significant qualification; emancipation was the *ultimate* objective. In 1806 Fox described it as 'not now and not soon'. In 1818, even in private correspondence, Wilberforce still envisaged 'the almost insensible result of the various Improvements' to be 'Slaves *gradually transmitted* into a free Peasantry'.[21]

Initially in the years following abolition most antislavery reformers, though James Stephen was a notable exception, assumed that little if any government intervention was required in West Indian affairs to bring about improvements in slavery; the self-interest of the planters would be sufficient. Concern with labour productivity, they believed, would lead slave-owners both to behave more humanely and find ways of giving slaves greater autonomy in their labour. From the antislavery perspective this would also make them readier to assume the responsibilities of freedom. These calculations account for the enthusiasm with which some reformers embraced and recommended models for the development of *self-regulation* amongst slaves. Reformers showed some knowledge of Spanish American provisions of work for wages to allow self-purchase by slaves at a formally agreed price. But most attention was given, and especially by Clarkson, to the ideas and experiments of Joshua Steele of Barbados. His activities had been known to some antislavery figures long before, but in 1814 his *Mitigation of Slavery* was published along with an extensive and favourable account by the Scots abolitionist William Dickson in the form of *Letters to Thomas Clarkson*. Clarkson publicised it to colleagues, to American abolitionists and to reform-minded West Indian proprietors like 'Monk'

Lewis. Steele's starting point was that slaves as much as all other men were subject to the law of human behaviour which said that conduct could be modified through the deployment of rewards and punishments; the point of his experiment was to offer rewards to his slaves for defined tasks when in the past they had primarily experienced punishment. He and his later antislavery advocates argued that the results demonstrated the greater efficiency of the work done – a genuine experiment because the whip had previously been removed from overseers and offences amongst the slaves dealt with by a jury of elders amongst the slaves themselves. Ultimately Steele divided land amongst his slaves for which they paid rent; they received wages for other work. They had time for their economic activities and were free to choose the form of payment for their other work. Although Barbadian law forbade emancipation Clarkson concluded

> he advanced above three hundred debased field negroes who had never before moved without the whip to a state resembling that of contented, honest and industrious servants and after paying them for their labour, tripled the annual neat [*sic*] clearance of his Estate.

Self-interest had been successfully combined with civilising and training slaves 'to the threshold of liberty'. The worst effects of slavery – dependence, lack of motive – could be removed even before the end of the institution was agreed upon.[22]

The whole orderly structure of argument and assumption of course depended on slave-owners seeing the force of and benefit to them of these laws of development. James Stephen did not believe they would ever reconcile their pursuit of profits with policies of amelioration. It was Stephen who was particularly intent on government and parliamentary intervention via a Registry Bill for West Indian slaves and wanted to create an attractive alternative model of agricultural labour by settling free blacks on Trinidad land under metropolitan government control. Within a few years other reformers, including Wilberforce and Clarkson, recognised that their belief in virtually automatic improvement in the population and condition of slaves was naïve. At the very least, if the best conditions for improvement were to obtain, they saw the need to ensure that illegal importations did not occur and that it was valuable to have information which would allow a judgement as to whether the slave population was increasing. By the early 1820s conviction grew amongst reformers that it was not.

They were now in a position which needed large efforts on their part, as much in renewing and adapting the antislavery argument as in practical action. James Losh, the north country reformer, later remarked that after abolition 'the country at large seemed to settle into a state of indifference on the subject of negro slavery' or at any rate to accept reformers' own assurances that amelioration would follow from the cut-off of new labour supplies from Africa. Reformers had to overcome the effect of their own earlier confidence. The way forward could only be through a measure of government intervention and inevitably it provoked at the time and in its later consequences, or lack of them, sharp controversy which did much to form the particular arguments reformers used to articulate their basic ideological assumptions.[23]

Even so, initially, with the formation of a new Anti-Slavery Society in 1823 (the African Institution had for years primarily acted on the international slave trade), there was no major break in abolitionist ideological assumptions. James Cropper who was at the centre of the efforts to establish a national antislavery body to work directly for emancipation declared roundly, 'We have no wild schemes of emancipation . . . we rather wish the thing may work its own way by the force of faith and the operation of circumstances.' Activists had the job of implicating West Indian proprietors in the public mind with the lack of progress since 1807 but to do it 'wisely and prudently' by seeking 'to second or to remove the impediments out of the way of the free operation of the Laws which the Creator has fixed in the nature of things'. Evidently the attainment of an ordered world consonant with divine laws remained the ideological framework of antislavery. A relative shift of emphasis however became apparent in the 1820s.

Many, particularly evangelical and women abolitionists, remained primarily concerned with antislavery as the path to true moral order; evidence from local provincial associations will be cited on p.34. But God's laws 'fixed in the nature of things' were as, if not more, frequently understood as the economic laws and the laws of human nature embodied in the doctrines of classical political economy. The freeing of economic forces to operate, it was believed, would produce developments which spelled the death of slavery and should lead to a prosperous, morally appropriate and stable order. Finally, in continuity with some elements of the earlier anti-slave trade argument, Buxton, Stephen and Clarkson all saw British pride in the achievement of abolition and the moral stature this accorded the nation, at least in its own eyes, as requiring the step of liberating those who had been stolen from Africa before 1807 and their descendants since the principle of hostility to man stealing remained the same. Indeed, not only the earlier act but God's especial blessings to the British nation in the form of a tradition of civil liberties imposed a particular duty on it to act as exemplar to other nations and work for emancipation. It would be a vindication of the country 'blessed as we are above other nations with the pure light of Christian truth'.[24]

The force of religious antagonism to slavery was maintained as part of the basis of the antislavery appeal at the level of the national Anti-Slavery Society, at the international conventions of the early 1840s and through local associations as they multiplied after 1823. Slavery's denial of the full 'creatureliness' of human beings, in the words of Leicester abolitionists its annihilation of 'the dignity which belongs to a reasonable and accountable nature', constituted one aspect in this religious perspective on its inhumanity. Its injustice was expressed in its provocation of human pain and disorder as 'ties of kindred may be torn violently asunder' and because law in the plantation colonies was no guardian of order for the slave victims. Moreover, ' "Let this people go" ' the Birmingham female reformers asserted, were the words of 'the voice of reason, of conscience, of revelation'. Slavery, to Sheffield female abolitionists, was essentially unlawful; human laws could only take away what they could create.

> Could they legitimately take from man those primary rights by virtue of which they have their existence, they would destroy their own foundation, break the moral chain, give a chaotic impulse in the universe and introduce confusion, in the works of Him who *is not* the God of confusion but of order.

The institution, summarised the 1840 General Anti-Slavery Convention, was a violation of 'the immutable principles of equity and justice' and sinful by the light of revealed religion. Moreover, it constituted a barrier to carrying God's order to other parts of the human family. The evangelical missionary impulse was brought to bear in the verse of Josiah Conder's antislavery hymn:

> What though of different hue and race,
> Brethren by blood, coheirs of grace,
> Our prayers, our sympathy they claim,
> Their wrongs our sin, their bonds our shame.[25]

More striking by the 1820s than the continuity of the theme of the incompatibility of slavery with a true moral and religious order was the much fuller expression than at the end of the eighteenth century of the precepts of economic liberalism as part of the antislavery appeal; abolitionists now clearly departed from mercantilist policy assumptions. One source was the *Edinburgh Review* tradition, exemplified in antislavery circles by Brougham. But these ideas were equally powerfully present in reformers of more obvious religious sensibility. The Quaker Cropper translated those 'laws which the Creator has fixed in the nature of things' into a campaign for the superiority of free labour, freer trade and particularly in favour of equalisation of East Indian sugar duties with West Indian in the British market. The Unitarian William Roscoe was equally in support of economic liberalisation as a way to bring on emancipation. In terms of an element in their appeal antislavery reformers saw this line of argument as an effort to exploit the material interests of public and policy-makers and even slave-owners and therefore a second order argument only, despite their ability to relate liberal economics to a conception of the natural order of things. But it was in Cropper's and Roscoe's home town amongst liberal men of religion that agitation of the economic arguments had first substantially begun.

At the time of the new commitment to a national campaign for gradual emancipation, initially understood as compatible with support for Canning's amelioration policy announced in parliament on 15 May 1823, both Cropper and Roscoe in private correspondence adopted the equation between free labour, higher productivity and colonial prosperity. It was the intellectual or doctrinal basis for antislavery's main economic appeal thereafter. It soon appeared in public in Cropper's own pamphlet addressed to Wilberforce and in the writing of his and Roscoe's colleague in the Liverpool Anti-Slavery Society, Adam Hodgson. The interest of Hodgson's argument lay in two things: the pedigree he sketched for his contention about the greater economy and productivity of free labour and the comparative dimension historically and geographically of his argument. Hodgson wanted to emphasise both the long understood wisdom of his argument – he referred to Pliny as concurring – and the support of some of the best modern minds in Hume, Beattie, Franklin and Brougham. Comparative land values indicated the superiority of free labour; Steele's Barbados experiment was taken as a success economically as well as morally; evidence comparing hired out slave labour in Virginia with the maintenance of free labour in Pennsylvania indicated the relative cheapness of free labour. Such inducements to good sense on the part of slaveholders and their political supporters were underlined by assertions about population increase and rising revenues from the enfranchisement of former serf villages in Poland. Hodgson believed that the case had been made for an entirely open, competitive labour market in the West Indies. Resistance by planters was evidence of economic irrationality. From the point of view of consumers of produce grown by slave labour the advantage was going to be equally clear; supplies of cotton from free-labour sources had begun to enter the British market and were substantially effective in reducing prices. The point was to get slaveholders to recognise that they would have to adopt 'the most economical mode of cultivation'. Leicester abolitionists regarded all of this as 'classed with the most established maxims of political economy' while Josiah Conder in a pamphlet bluntly titled *Wages or the Whip* pointed to what he saw as the disastrous economic effects peculiar to the slave system – exhaustion of the soil, no change in crops cultivated, little rotation, lack of use of livestock and a low level of technology.[26]

These convictions had become sufficiently general amongst antislavery reformers by the mid-1820s that local associations in, for example, Norwich, Beverley, Hull and Whitby all dismissed comprehensively the argument in *Cobbett's Register* and *Blackwood's* that labourers in Britain suffered worse material conditions than West Indian slaves. It was considered self-evident that it was in the general national, indeed imperial, interest to move towards free labour. Abolitionists did not expect immediate conversion by slaveholders; it was not necessary in so far as they were sure planters could not for long resist the economic imperatives. It was possible to settle for Canning's amelioration policy which, if it worked properly (and about this there was some scepticism), should itself bring enlightenment to slave-owners as to their own best interests. This was a position which also continued to express the preference of most abolitionists that government intervention be limited to policy guidelines to be rendered into detailed legislation and implemented by local assemblies and officials except in the Crown Colonies. But the amelioration policy, filtered through the structures of local government in the West Indies, could only work properly if the case for planters recognising the virtues of a movement towards free labour was urgent. It was in this context that the Liverpool abolitionists in particular began their campaign for equalising duties in the British market on slave-grown West Indian sugar and free-labour East Indian sugar. Cropper looked for support from the African Institution for the removal of the West Indians' financial advantage in the sugar trade, privately assuring Zachary Macaulay that the introduction of free-labour sugar was opposed by the planters because they knew it 'will destroy their *System* of cultivation, tho' it can be proved to be the only means of establishing West Indian property on a lasting foundation'.[27]

Liverpool abolitionists drew upon Hodgson's investigations in the United States, information from Americans and their own reading in the writings of the political economists to document pamphlet arguments for the equalisation of duties on sugar from free and slave-labour areas. They claimed substantial effects would follow from the removal of the higher duties on East Indian and Indian sugar and the termination of the 6 shillings per hundredweight bounty paid by Britain to West Indian producers for the export of their surplus to European markets. The results were predicted to be of two kinds. Firstly, since free labour was cheaper and more productive than slave labour, East Indian sugar could be sold, if allowed to compete on equal terms, at a lower price than West Indian in both the British and European markets. This would compel West Indians to produce more economically, and this they could only do by moving towards free labour and engaging the labourers' personal material interests in their work. Dickson's recommendation of Steele's experiments was seen as an appropriate guide in making the transformation smoothly and fairly rapidly. If in the process of transition West Indian proprietors experienced temporary losses Cropper was confident that 'our country will cheerfully grant indemnity'. Secondly, the opening up of the sugar market was perfectly compatible with an amelioration policy designed to improve slaves' conditions and prepare them to take responsibility for their future freedom. Lower prices for West Indian sugar, according to American evidence which had been gathered, would encourage the use of more land and slaves in food production; the result would be much better feeding of slaves than under a regime where owners took advantage of artificially high prices for cash crops to maximise profits and imported insufficient food for their labour force. An increase in the slave population also seemed a likely result of better conditions arising from a redistribution of resources within West Indian economies promoted by market competition.[28]

Davis has indicated the reluctance of the London committee to adopt officially the equalisation policy as a path to emancipation. It was a policy he presents largely as Cropper's. The reality was that provincial reformers generally took the ideological initiative away from London on this important point. What Liverpool abolitionists initially expressed other local associations – in Hull, Norwich and

Leicestershire for example – rapidly adopted. The London committee's acquiescence in 1825 was in part a mark of the force of provincial abolitionist attitudes. They were attitudes which permitted no doubt about free-labour sugar driving out the produce of slaves or the consequent steady march towards emancipation through the rigours of the market combined with amelioration. The gradualist emphasis was explicit and virtually universal up to the mid-1820s. Mission work to civilise the slaves and the extension of responsibilities to the labourers for their own work were only thought likely to be successful if they were cumulative experiences for the slaves. Beverley, Chester, Newcastle and Norwich abolitionists all distanced themselves from calls for immediate emancipation. Beverley and Liverpool reformers in 1824 went to the point of envisaging no substantial changes in the structure of West Indian agriculture with the arrival of emancipation. Planters could anticipate services from the black population 'in a better and safe form' through the conversion of 'a set of dangerous slaves into useful, industrious labourers'.[29]

Initially after 1823 progress to the proper moral and natural economic order was seen as a gradual, almost automatic business which avoided irreconcilable conflicts. The insistence that emancipation was in the national interest expressed this. It was, moreover, a national interest understood as the interest of all. Slaves were to obtain freedom, missionaries black souls, British consumers cheaper sugar, manufacturers and traders new markets in other sugar producing areas benefiting from the ending of the West Indian monopoly and, did they but realise it, slave-owners themselves were to benefit not only in terms of possible compensation but through being forced to become more efficient and to modernise their operations. The abolitionist prospectus was one in which everybody gained and nobody lost; conflict was both unnecessary and irrational. In its combination of sentimental piety and intimations of economic progress the description of the frontispiece to the Sheffield abolitionist volume *Negro's Friend* (1826) held up the perfect image of success.

> Christianity is clearly shown to be both the foundation and the superstructure of the important change. The sun is arisen and is breaking forth in splendour over the Christian Church (which is founded on a rock) dispersing the clouds of night and illuminating, with his new-born light the benighted land. A beacon crowns the summit of the highest mountain. A happy family of

freed negroes occupy the foreground. The husband and father on his knee is fervently pressing the sacred volume to his lips. The devout and thankfully expressive countenance of the wife and mother is too admirably depicted to be overlooked or mistaken by anyone as she is occupied with those two most delightful of maternal duties, suckling her infant and teaching her child to pray to God. The shackles, the whip and the hoe, these emblems of slavery, lie broken and scattered on the ground; while the plough, the sickle and the flail, emblematical of improved and free labour are conspicuously displayed. The group are shaded and protected by the branches of an aged English oak which, at the same time, embraces and supports a declining West India palm. A noble vessel leaving the port shews that extended commerce has been the result of the change from slavery to freedom.[30]

The circumstances of the 1820s and early 1830s, however, in two particular respects reminded the abolitionists that not all the elements of the situation could be shaped by them. The slaves themselves intervened dramatically by rising in revolt in Demerara in 1823 and in Jamaica at the end of 1831 and the beginning of 1832. Their masters too refused to play their assigned parts; despite some legislation in the islands in accord with Canning's programme, evidence accumulated of slave-owner resistance to the progress of ₤ amelioration. |Emancipation was not to arrive without conflict| and growing recognition of that truth stimulated a more radical strain in antislavery which took the form of the demand for immediate emancipation. In the face of slave rebelliousness abolitionists denied that their support of gradual emancipation had anything to do with the Demerara revolt or that 'rash philanthropy' had produced slave disorder on earlier occasions in Guadeloupe, St Domingue or Barbados. Governments which recognised the freedom of former slaves, they argued, had found that they did not abuse it. Careless talk or dark allegations about the true intent of such moderate measures as the Registry Act by slave-owners themselves in Barbados had brought on the trouble there in 1816. In the case of Demerara, removal of the slaveholders' symbol of authority, the whip, by government, without adequate attention to the moral education of the slaves, it was implied, vindicated the evolutionary approach of the reformers rather than challenged it. Speakers at a Beverley antislavery meeting in 1824 did not believe that slaves needed 'foreign stimulus' to make them rebel;

their own sufferings were sufficient. Norwich reformers agreed, claiming that amelioration properly carried through made them more long-suffering. Both local associations pointed unambiguously to slavery itself as the disruptive factor; only with emancipation would 'a Population of turbulent Slaves [be] converted into one of peaceable Colonists'. By early 1832 the insurrection in Jamaica had so underlined in many abolitionists' minds the presumption that slavery was the source of social disorder they unambiguously demanded 'nothing short of the total and immediate Abolition of British Colonial Slavery'.[31]

In fact the growing demand for immediate emancipation had captured organised antislavery at the national level by the spring of 1831. The rising intensity of immediatism began with Mrs Heyrick's pamphlet of 1824 and developed in step with the conviction that amelioration was being blocked by slave-owners. Gradualism had failed to secure the collaboration of masters or their agents in educating or providing religious instruction for the slaves. How long could their own obstruction permit the slave-owners to claim the slaves were unfit for freedom? By 1830 the speaker at a meeting of Durham abolitionists was part of a formidable chorus when he argued

> It was futile to invest him [the slave] with moral dignity while under the weight of slavery . . . . There was a gulph [*sic*] between slavery and freedom which could neither be filled up nor closed over and across which the slave must leap ere he alighted on the other side and found himself a free man.

This amounted to a reversal of the earlier gradualist assumption that a virtually full preparation of slaves for freedom was possible within the structure of slavery. Only the experience of freedom could now make slaves fit for it.[32]

The announcement of the success of this conviction within the national antislavery movement came with the establishment of the Agency subcommittee of the Anti-Slavery Society in the spring of 1831. Its travelling lecturers were required to accept and transmit the proposition that slavery was 'a crime in the sight of God and ought to be immediately and forever abolished'. This position appeared to cut through earlier concerns for a smooth transition achieved by education and the inculcation in the slaves of self-reliance. Liberation, however, did not contradict order. It was to inaugurate the movement of the freedmen from the private and irresponsible authority of master or steward to proper restraint under judicial power. The

Agency lecturers, in other words, stressed that the freedmen were to become citizens with responsibilities as well as rights. The radicals of the Agency committee were as concerned as Buxton in his plea to the slaves on the eve of their emancipation that they 'by every motive of duty, gratitude and self interest . . . do their part towards the peaceful termination of their bondage'.[33]

Abolitionists were also therefore demanding direct intervention by the imperial government to end a species of property and override the role of local assemblies with which they had earlier been prepared to collaborate. This change of outlook was the result of a fusing of perceptions over some years about the character and behaviour of the West Indians as partners in the project of amelioration and gradual emancipation. The slave-owners had acted in bad faith over amelior-ation; there were so few exceptions to the 'state of debauchery and debasement' of the colonists that reformers were fully justified, they believed, in their condemnation of 'the present state of corrupted morality and religion in the West Indies'. Slave-owners of this character, in frustrating gradual reform, had shown 'language and conduct . . . such as fall very little short of actual rebellion'. They had stood out against 'the general voice of the whole British population' for emancipation 'was not a party question; all denominations, whether Whig or Tory, Saint or Radical were united upon this one great point'. The need for metropolitan government intervention of a swift and direct kind and its ideological justification were contained in this moral and political marginalisation of the West Indians.[34]

Examination of the debate on Buxton's resolutions for gradual emancipation of 15 May 1823, of his resolution for parliament to take up general emancipation of 15 April 1831 (the resolution was interpreted in the debate by other speakers as being immediatist) and, more briefly, of the debate on Stanley's government resolutions for emancipation followed by a period of apprenticeship of 14 May 1833 indicates a clear shift to acceptance of abolitionist assumptions. The debates also constitute evidence of reformers' realisation of the need politically to isolate the West Indians and an ambivalent attitude to the usefulness of moral condemnation as a way of winning over MPs.

The starting point for the case for gradual emancipation made in 1823, largely by the freeing of children of slaves born after a certain date, was the agreed failure of the expected automatic amelioration of slavery after abolition of the slave trade. Initially both Baring for the West Indians and Canning for the government tried to limit the effectiveness of the emancipationist case by defining its impulse as inappropriate for parliament to act upon. Any measure of change 'should be dictated by prudence and reason and not by the new lights of enthusiasm and madness'. Canning equally looked to 'justice and judgment' not 'impulse and feeling' since 'that is not a ground upon which parliament can be called upon to act'. The reformers were charged with placing an abstract moralism above the discipline of the historical and present reality of slavery.

Abolitionists underlined their familiar moral attack and claimed the unacceptability of ownership of another human being as the basis for Buxton's wish to free slave children. William Smith, the veteran Unitarian associate of Wilberforce, in particular introduced a tone of some urgency over the nineteenth century's need to make 'quicker progress in the annihilation of slavery'. Buxton proclaimed himself an 'enthusiast' and in theory wanted existing slaves freed too. That was the logic of his moralism, as Canning had pointed out; he met the charge of dealing in moral abstractions by recognising that slavery had damaged its victims and 'brutalized their minds'. Existing slaves would have to be carefully prepared for liberation.

Two other features of the 1823 appeal in parliament are to be noted. Pro-emancipationists indicated their reliance on popular opinion expressed in petitions from the country and went along only reluctantly, and sceptically, with the government's hope for co-operative measures of amelioration by colonial assemblies. Doubt that the West Indians would do much was widespread amongst parliamentary abolitionists before the experiment even began.

By 1831 the attempt to portray antislavery in parliament as an exercise in abstract moralism was absent. Buxton, for example, relied on statistical evidence indicating slavery's destructive and freedom's beneficial demographic effects. He asserted explicitly that he appealed 'not . . . to the feelings or the passions of the House but to the stubborn facts, incapable of contradiction'. He now believed that reference to individual cruelty cases hindered the argument of the cause. Perhaps he had concluded that the moral argument had been won by antislavery 'out of doors' in the country. By a statesmanlike not an enthusiastic appeal Buxton may have calculated on maximising pressure for policy revision and politically isolating the West Indian interest, believing that they were already on the defensive morally and ideologically. Certainly by 1831 it was generally supposed on both sides of the Commons that the 1823 approach had failed and that even on its own terms the government was committed to revising its policy.

However to judge by the veteran abolitionist Lushington's intervention in the 1831 debate the powerful demand for immediatism from abolitionists in the country was still somewhat muffled in parliament; he approved of it if understood as 'measures immediately brought in now and adopted which might lead to the gradual extinction of slavery'; Buxton had avoided completely talking of immediate emancipation. What was striking about the instant response to Stanley's emancipation proposals in 1833 was that it came from Howick, until recently in charge, at the Colonial Office, of the emancipation question, and that his strongest dissent arose from the failure of the plan to chart a move as soon as possible directly from slavery to free labour without bothering with an apprenticeship stage. It was a significant measure of the progress of abolitionist ideology even within the walls of parliament.[35]

The campaign against apprenticeship in 1837–8 required no great dialectical ingenuity or intellectual departures by the abolitionists. News from missionaries, investigative visits and subsequent writing on the West Indies by Charles Stuart, Joseph Sturge and others provided the kind of detail which permitted attacks on the operation of the system as too little different from slavery to be supported as substantial progress. In broader ideological terms the Sheffield female abolitionists neatly illustrated the intellectual continuity of the opposition to apprenticeship with the fundamentals of the emancipationist outlook. They declared their hostility to apprenticeship since they regarded it as a delay in ridding the colonies of slavery. Only immediate action was appropriate in abolishing a system which infringed divine law. But if apprenticeship was to work as its devisers hoped it relied upon the *interest* of freedmen in working for themselves in the time they were allotted and their *generosity* if their work for their former masters was to be energetic. Such a situation was inconsistent with the 'two springs of action which keep the universe in motion – *force* and *incitement*'. The half-way house of apprenticeship thus accorded neither with God's law nor man's nature.

With the premature end of apprenticeship came abolitionist anticipation of a new era of orderly progress in liberty. As Birmingham abolitionists expressed it at their celebratory public breakfast in the Town Hall on 2 August 1838, with slaves 'relying on their own peaceful and persevering efforts for the removal of every vestige of oppression' and with 'the continued vigilant aid of the British people, under the blessing of Divine Providence' they foresaw

43

'the progressive development of the glorious results of free institutions and the reconstruction on purer and better principles of the now disorganised elements of colonial society'. Joseph Sturge, who had assumed a leading part in the fight against apprenticeship, anticipated triumphs on a broader imperial and international scale which would confirm Britain's moral leadership in the world. He quoted approvingly,

> Slaves cannot breathe in England. If their lungs
> Inhale our air, that moment they are free.
> They touch our country and their shackles fall!
> That's noble and bespeaks a nation proud
> And jealous of the blessing. Spread it, then,
> And let it circulate through every vein
> Of all your empire, that when Britain's power
> Is felt, mankind may feel her mercy too.[36]

The theme of this chapter has been that a great deal of antislavery argument grew out of a fundamental concern for proper order in the world. Distinct but, from the abolitionist perspective, compatible conceptions of order permeated the reformers' rhetoric; they spoke out of convictions about a moral order sanctioned by Providence and a 'natural' order in which Providence was understood through the laws and qualities of God's creation, human, animate and inanimate. More secular, Enlightenment notions of order harmonised with the idea of natural order, particularly relevantly in the 1820s, in the form of the laws of liberal political economy. Abolitionists thus aspired to make their actual metropolitan and colonial societies conform more closely to these underlying ideas of order. Leaving aside antislavery as a convenience for particular interests, an obvious question occurs. Why did this kind of ideology have sufficient attractions as an appeal or persuasion to inform the language of the many antislavery associations and contribute to widespread popular petitioning against the slave trade and slavery?

The history of antislavery as an ideology coincided in Britain with an era of complex and quite rapid economic, social, cultural and political change. Such changes generated tensions and ambivalences in society and raised questions about economic and social organisation and its justification; about the quality and character of the relationships between people; about the exercise of power and what kinds of authority were appropriate. In the broadest sense antislavery took its place with Smithite liberalism and Owenism, democratic radicalism and anti-Jacobinism as an aspect of a peculiarly intense self-scrutiny by a society conscious of the significant change it was undergoing.

The slave trade and slavery subsumed many of these tensions and ambivalences, giving a focus to the categories of question troubling many English men and women and did so by directing powerful anxieties on to phenomena at some geographical and social distance from most people. The religious developments sketched in chapter 1 also in part expressed these tensions while providing a framework – without offering simply and divisively *political* answers – within which anxieties expressed through the issues of the slave trade and slavery could be handled. The idea of an underlying providential moral or natural order which the earthly order of things should attempt to express, it may be supposed, demonstrated the need for change while offering security and assurance about its legitimacy. At a time of flux, antislavery struck an ideological balance between mere stasis and the sensed need to overcome a loss of control.

It offered itself also as an ideology of movement against aspects – abolitionists feared and hoped symptomatic aspects – of the established system of the later eighteenth and earlier nineteenth centuries without requiring confrontation with the central features of the metropolitan order. This may well have provided relief and reassurance to those many antislavery people who were at the respectable fringes rather than the centre of religious, social and political power as well as for different and obvious reasons those who were closer to the centre. As an ideology of movement antislavery proposed a purification of social morality and socially ordained authority on the assumption that the result would be more stable. The dangers of both divine wrath and colonial disruption would be diminished.

Antislavery ideology in its economic features may have been an attractive persuasion for paradoxical reasons. It offered opportunities for the reception and use of the precepts of economic liberalism and thus a break from intellectually old-fashioned mercantilist conceptions of public policy. It absorbed and demonstrated the relevance of a particularly *modern*, even insurgent, current of thought; it combined the seductiveness of the intellectually advanced with the supposed certainty of prosperous results. At the same time, however, liberal political economy in its antislavery guise sought to maintain the link between private motives and public consequences, to check the anxiety arising from perceptions of the divorce between morality and economic development in the era of industralisation.

Finally, antislavery promised change which was compatible with, indeed directed towards, the protection and enhancement of the homogeneity, security and strength of the Empire when Britain had to undergo the potentially difficult adjustment to the loss of most of the Old Empire and the crises of the Revolutionary and Napoleonic Wars with their domestic impact. Thereafter, as the British recognised their predominant position in the world, antislavery laid claim to putting moral fibre into the exercise of international power and in doing so promised to help sustain that predominance by prescribing as fundamental features of other societies forms of commerce and labour in accord with British values.

3

MAKING ABOLITIONISTS
Engaging with the world

Like other movements to bring about change in the same period antislavery had to find ways of attracting the attention and gaining the support of those who could advance the cause. Beginning with efforts to rid Britain herself of slaves, traversing the abolition and emancipation campaigns and the less dramatic struggle to suppress the international trade in slaves and assist liberation in foreign countries, British abolitionists had an exceptionally long history as reformers. They were compelled to consider the most appropriate forms of action in changing circumstances and practise a great variety of methods to engage the commitment of potential supporters and of both makers and executors of policy. There are several main questions which have shaped the analysis of antislavery activity in this chapter. To what extent were the forms of antislavery activity developed in struggle with the organisation and institutional structures of the West Indian interest; did the forms change according to changing objectives? What was the relationship between different reformers' conceptions of how to bring about change and the methods adopted by the antislavery movement? How willing were abolitionists to challenge both the accepted ways of acting publicly and by whom the action should be undertaken? How best is the recurrent tension in the antislavery movement between what will be termed 'agitation' and 'influence' to be understood? Does the history of antislavery reflect the progressive adoption of more popular forms of social and political activity in accord with a changing balance of forces within the larger culture of nineteenth-century England? This last problem particularly requires discussion of the recent contention that antislavery petitioning demonstrated a recurrent popular mobilisation, a mass antislavery latent even in seemingly quiescent years which spearheaded dramatic changes in the political culture and had a direct impact on legislature and executive.

It is appropriate to begin with the forms of propaganda adopted to convey the particular arguments and the broader ideological perspectives analysed in the last chapter. According to Walvin the Anti-Slavery Society alone published nearly 3 million copies of tracts in the campaigning years 1823–31. Other tracts, printed speeches and sermons and local publications by antislavery bodies in those years and earlier added to the vast quantity of printed material. Earlier, in the 1780s, antislavery arguments appeared in newspapers and sometimes, as in the case of Thomas Cooper's *Letters on the Slave Trade* (1787), were republished as a pamphlet, in the Cooper example at the urging and expense of 'some Gentlemen', to allow wider, because free, distribution. In turn Zachary Macaulay's *Negro-Slavery* (1823) was extracted by Clarkson for East Anglian papers and both papers and pamphlet were made locally available. 'We have three well-frequented news and reading rooms at Ipswich, and every one of these has a "Negro Slavery" also.' In the 1820s, as well as having pamphlets and papers produced under its aegis, the Anti-Slavery Society adopted the writings of other abolitionists if the committee on publications approved the content. Thus the Liverpool pamphlets of Hodgson and Cropper discussed in chapter 2 received the sanction of the national antislavery body. Particularly when petitions were being raised in the country large quantities of pamphlets and other printed material were sent out to local activists to help mobilise opinion. In 1823, in the weeks before Buxton's parliamentary motion of 15 May, material went to '38 counties in England, Edinburgh & Glasgow, Dublin & Belfast, Neath for S. Wales'.[1]

The reciprocal relationship between pamphlet and newspaper insertion was only one way in which reformers used both the London and provincial press. On his early anti-slave trade tours Clarkson secured the support, for example, of William Cowdray, editor of the *Chester Chronicle* whose readership spread into east and north-east Wales as well as Cheshire. To take a London example, in 1832 the *Tourist* became the mouthpiece of the Agency committee. By the late summer of 1831 so crucial did regular sympathetic treatment in the metropolitan press seem to Thomas Pringle, secretary of the Anti-Slavery Society, that he discussed a plan with provincial abolitionists for the purchase of a part share in the *Morning Herald* which would also be distributed to country subscribers.[2]

At the point when abolitionists turned to making the emancipation issue a mass campaign they published their own news-sheet, the *Anti-Slavery Monthly Reporter* (1825–30), followed by the *Anti-Slavery*

Reporter (1830–3) and thereafter the mark of an antislavery organisation with claims to national standing was a paper of this kind.
Such papers as the *Reporter*, and the *British Emancipator* were in
part intended to win abolitionists for the emancipation and anti-
apprenticeship campaigns. Ipswich abolitionists in 1828 circulated
bound copies of the *Reporter*. Allying with the denominational press
at the end of 1829 the Anti-Slavery Society allowed copies of the
Reporter to be stitched under the cover of the *Baptist Magazine*. But
the specialist papers were also 'house' journals, increasingly so as
active antislavery subsided in the 1840s and 1850s. The *British and
Foreign Anti-Slavery Reporter* in those decades must have been dull
or impenetrable to all but the dwindling band of initiates. There were
modest alternatives available to an antislavery readership but they
either propounded the outlook of a minority tendency as did the *Anti-
Slavery Advocate*, edited by the Irish Garrisonian Richard Webb in
the 1850s, or had a predominantly local circulation as was likely with
the short-lived *Anti-Slavery Watchman* of Manchester produced by
the Garrisonian group around George Thompson and his son-in-law
F. W. Chesson, or propounded a particular remedy for slavery in the
case of the Quaker Richardson family in Newcastle through the
Slave's stress on the free produce movement. At a more sophisticated
level of writing, antislavery was able to infiltrate the pages of the
Edinburgh Review through Henry Brougham's own contributions
and his influence with Francis Jeffrey. Similarly, the *Westminster
Review* under the sympathetic direction of T. Perronet Thompson
provided space.[3]

These prestigious locations for antislavery discussion were also one
way of internationalising the argument. The circulation of the great
reviews in the United States included the South and their antislavery
content was welcomed as a boost to their cause by American
abolitionists. As to the involvement of various European states in the
international slave trade the old Quaker campaigner, George
Harrison, proclaimed the possibilities of inserting material in the
foreign press since 'The Freedom of the Press, now in good Degree
established, affords the Opportunity.' It was subscriptions from
Friends through the Committee for Sufferings which contributed
substantially to funding propaganda efforts in Europe in the 1820s
and 1830s including the translation of existing materials into various
languages and the production of new items for European readers.[4]

There was also a belief in the antislavery movement that images
were a particularly striking form of propaganda. Drescher has noted

the pervasiveness of Wedgwood's image of the kneeling slave, first designed for a medallion at the time of the 1788 petition campaign but afterwards widely translated to other formats. The plan of a slave ship issued by Clarkson was also extensively taken up and became an antislavery print. Its effect was remembered well into the nineteenth century in Birmingham; at that later time the campaigners against apprenticeship in the West Indies reproduced and distributed a magazine plate of a Jamaican treadmill on which apprentices were employed, in the conviction that 'pictorial representations have a far more powerful influence on the mind than letter press descriptions'.[5]

Large-scale deployment of the printed word and the image was such a powerful feature of the culture of antislavery because reformers could exploit technical developments and geographical expansion in printing, tendencies to specialisation in publishing and the establishment of a coherent national distribution network for books and pamphlets. All of these took place on the eve of or during the decades of greatest activity in antislavery. In the early nineteenth century a number of different iron hand presses reached a sufficient stage of development for widespread application in the printing of books and required no great skill or preparation in their use. Mechanised steam-powered presses, beginning with *The Times* in 1814, contributed to the expansion of newspaper printing in the 1820s and 1830s and had spread to book printing by the 1850s. These changes roughly coincided with the progressive mechanisation of paper-making. Equally important for the print culture of antislavery was the considerable expansion, judged on conservative criteria, in provincial printing presses in the second half of the eighteenth century. Mitchell has calculated that on average in the 1760s two new towns per year appeared as the source of printed material and that this had grown to an average of seven per year in the 1790s. Conditions were thus ripe by the height of the emancipation campaign in the late 1820s and early 1830s for the cheap and rapid production of vast quantities of antislavery material and for the expansion and relative cheapness – and consequent probable expansion in readership – of newspapers. Historians of publishing have also detected some tendency towards specialisation amongst publishers by the 1780s and 1790s and this may have helped the appearance of antislavery writing. Certainly Johnson of St Paul's Yard, who published antislavery items at the end of the eighteenth century, specialised in liberal and dissenting publications and probably saw antislavery writing in this context.[6]

Calculations based on antislavery titles published year by year in

Britain from 1781, with information on places of publication, offer support to the view that the conditions discussed above are relevant to antislavery's print culture. The rhythm of publication of antislavery titles is one which matches quite closely parliamentary initiatives, petitioning and some other activities on slavery. There was a clustering of publication in 1788 and 1789, 1791 and 1792, a lower peak in 1807, a high level of titles between 1823 and 1833 (though with relative dips in 1827 and 1829 and 1831 and 1832), quite high peaks in 1838, 1840 and 1848. The years picked out up to 1833 reflect fluctuations in the 'popular' aspect of abolitionist and emancipationist activity. 1838 coincided with the culmination of the anti-apprenticeship campaign, 1840 with the first World Anti-Slavery Convention in London and 1848 with the high point of the controversy over whether to maintain the West African naval squadron as the main instrument of slave trade suppression. These correspondences indicate the rapidity with which writers and compilers but also printers and publishers were able to respond to developing events. During most, but not all, of the years of high levels of antislavery publication a significant proportion of titles (50 per cent in some years) were published in provincial towns or in the provinces and London at the same time.[7]

The later eighteenth century also marks the appearance of national advertising of books and pamphlets through the press and the fixing of a pattern of nationwide distribution through provincial booksellers. This was a system abolitionists used in the early 1800s. It seems however to have been supplemented by more informal methods. We know that Olaudah Equiano spread successive printings of his autobiography after its first publication in 1789 by selling them with antislavery as well as personal benefit in mind to his audiences after meetings. Clarkson sold some of his writings, including his history of abolition, through a system of subscriptions raised by acquaintances in religious networks, particularly Quakers. Finally, the national network of antislavery societies auxiliary to the London body which covered the country during the emancipation and apprenticeship campaigns provided channels for pamphlets, prints and papers.[8]

Whatever the methods of distribution and sale were, the evidence on who were the intended recipients of printed antislavery arguments suggests that further distinctions as to types of material and their immediate purposes are necessary. Printed materials published or distributed to accompany petitioning campaigns, in 1792 and 1823–4 for example, were clearly in the first instance intended to produce as many petition signatures as possible; the mass of petitions was to be the weight behind the parliamentary initiatives of Wilberforce and Buxton. General statements of the antislavery case particularly suited this purpose. Zachary Macaulay's 1823 pamphlet, *Negro Slavery*, was a good example. However, from the issue of the 1783 Quaker protest onwards abolitionists sent some of their material directly to persons of influence; in the Quaker case members of the royal family, the principal officers of state and members of both Houses of Parliament. In 1784 the Friends extended the distribution to people of influence throughout the nation, defined particularly as JPs, clergymen, members of corporations and 'merchants concerned in the West India and Guinea trades'. Just as there was no absolute separation of the rhetoric of appeal directed to the country as compared with parliament but some differences of emphasis, so printed material circulated to decision-makers, without ignoring humanity and justice, probably relied more on evidence drawn from Privy Council and parliamentary investigations and focused on questions of national interest and economic benefit. In post-emancipation international appeals on the slave trade and foreign slavery, issues over which the British government had little, and British abolitionists no direct leverage, circulations were either in the form of general pieties to political leaders signed by such venerable reformers as Clarkson or Christian appeals from antislavery corporate religious bodies to similar organisations, particularly in the 1830s and 1840s to the United States. Print propaganda aimed then to stimulate 'agitation' in the hope of shaping or sustaining antislavery public policies 'by a loud, strong and solemn expression of the public opinion' and establish direct 'influence' with individuals who exercised power and authority. In the phases of large-scale antislavery mobilisation within Britain these two purposes were pursued simultaneously, though sometimes using different printed materials. Beset by relative impotence in the international arena only rarely could abolitionists provide sustenance from 'agitation' for antislavery diplomacy or politics as when the 1814 petitions were seen as support for Castlereagh's negotiations on suppressing the transatlantic slave trade at the peace congress. And on that occasion print propaganda appears to have played only a minor part.[9]

The previous chapter argued that the ideological terms of antislavery were developed in part through contesting a pro-West Indian intellectual barrage, often presented in the rhetoric of national and imperial interest. Similarly, an analysis of the organisational and institutional forms adopted by the West Indians and the abolitionists reveals how strikingly they mirrored each other. Most of the forms of publicity through print discussed in the first section of this chapter were taken up by the West Indians. Much of their machinery of print propaganda was organised centrally through the West India Committee. This body originated in an organisational fusion of West India merchant and planter groups in 1775 to face the difficulties posed for traders and producers by the American War of Independence. The threats of abolition and then emancipation maintained a united West Indian front. Particularly in 1792–3 and from 1823 onwards, the West India Committee organised and co-ordinated defence and counter-attack against the abolition and emancipation campaigns. They conducted propaganda war through a slave trade subcommittee which spent £2,000 on propaganda in 1792–3, and in 1823 a literary subcommittee, with £1,000 initially to fund favourable articles and pamphlets. The London-based committee was in contact with ministers, tried hard to persuade the island legislatures to initiate measures of amelioration to make the West Indian position more tenable in British eyes and managed to raise some petitions on slavery's behalf, though few compared with the abolitionist flood. This pattern of organisation and activity was connected to West India groups in some of the outports. The Liverpool West Indian and African traders were especially well organised through a committee which instructed Liverpool delegates giving evidence before parliamentary and Privy Council committees, dominated the common council and mayor's office in Liverpool and, by means of local government, funded propaganda and maintained a stream of pro-slave trade petitions.

With the exception of William Roscoe's brief election to the Commons for 1806–7, West Indians also controlled Liverpool's parliamentary representation. The local MPs formed part of a visible West India group in the Commons throughout the abolition and emancipation periods. On fairly conservative criteria this parliamentary force numbered perhaps thirty-five in the first half of the 1790s, twenty in 1806 and between thirty-five and sixty in the parliaments from 1812 to 1831, dropping to about thirty in the reformed parliament of 1832. In addition the upper house seems to have contained a little over thirty peers with West Indian connections in the crucial dozen years after 1821. The West Indians were alert to any erosion of their parliamentary position even at a time when the principle of maintaining slavery was virtually lost. In late August

1832 the West India Merchants' Committee still attacked as thoroughly improper the abolitionist practice of pledging parliamentary candidates to immediate emancipation and publishing pledge lists in the first post-reform election.[10]

This system of national, local and parliamentary organisation wielded by the West Indians both provoked and was a response to a structure with many similarities developed by the abolitionists. The reformers established a succession of central bodies claiming national leadership and co-ordination of the cause and adjacent to political power in London; the Abolition Committee (1787), the African Institution (1807), the Society for the Mitigation and Gradual Abolition of Slavery throughout the British Dominions (the Anti-Slavery Society, 1823), the British and Foreign Society for the Universal Abolition of Negro Slavery and the Slave Trade (the successor to the Agency committee from 1834), the Central Negro Emancipation Committee (1837) and the British and Foreign Anti-Slavery Society (1839). However, while the condition of struggle with the West Indians remained a constant, at least until 1838, in providing a rationale for national organisations, how they were conceived as operating at various times, and even at the same time by different reformers, varied significantly. All could agree on the need to secure appropriate action from parliament and government, but how far this required agitation of mass support at different times and how much deference should be paid to the judgement and tactics of parliamentary abolitionists were points of tension both early and late within antislavery.

In June 1788 Clarkson proposed that the London committee promote widespread agitation through forming local committees. He may have been influenced by the views of the parliamentary reformer Major Cartwright who at this time was on an organisational subcommittee. In the same spirit the main committee intended a general meeting in London against the trade. On both of these Wilberforce intervened to modify the idea of local committees and to have the public meeting abandoned. 'He desired to appeal to the moral feelings of the nation and approved therefore of promoting petitions to parliament; but he distrusted and disowned the questionable strength which might be gained by systematic agitation.' As an insider, sensitive to MPs' sense of their own constitutional centrality, Wilberforce wanted to avoid causing offence to them. He approved of Clarkson's travels to secure witnesses for the Privy Council hearings but not as a focus for popular agitation. By the autumn of 1788 a number of local committees were established but the process seems not to have seriously breached Wilberforce's guidelines. In the next few years, however, as later discussion on petitioning will demonstrate (pp.63–7), there emerged in practice a dialectical relationship between 'agitation' and 'influence', 'pressure from without' and 'manoeuvre within'.[11]

With the achievement of abolition in 1806 and 1807 the new objective of the national antislavery organisation, the African Institution, was essentially consolidation of the victory achieved, best advanced by a different balance of methods. In trying to expand legitimate commerce with Africa so as to provide an attractive alternative for both Africans and European traders to slaving, the African Institution proposed spreading information about African products and making communication easier by establishing written versions of African languages. Securing the suppression of the foreign slave trade might be achieved in part in wartime by naval power but otherwise was mainly seen as requiring lobbying of and consultation with ministers, communicating with British diplomats and naval commanders for information and to provide stimulus to intervention in particular cases and pressing arguments upon foreign leaders, particularly during the Congress phase of European diplomacy in the years following the defeat of Napoleon. Striving for influence almost submerged the dialectic of influence and agitation except for the one brief but massive burst of petitioning in 1814 on suppression of the international slave trade. It was an episode which showed that the conviction of the virtuous power of public opinion had become firmly fixed in the antislavery movement and it provided the source of growing unease about the African Institution by the early 1820s. Both Buxton and Wilberforce deplored its relative ineffectiveness and inactivity. Buxton believed that it had lost the confidence and interest of the country because of its practice of negotiating secretly with ministers instead of acting in the open. The result was that people cared little about slavery.[12]

From this perspective the establishment of a new national Anti-Slavery Society in 1823 proposed a renewed dialectic of agitation and influence, pressure from without and manoeuvre within, extra-parliamentary movement and parliamentary tactics. It was thus necessary to reanimate local antislavery societies, renew the propaganda war, and once more undertake large-scale petitioning. Yet even within this dialectic in the decade after 1823 the balance of methods was a source of tension. How publicly should emissaries from the national body be encouraged to set up local associations? Were the London committee and its parliamentary spokesmen showing enough urgency by the early 1830s? What role should travelling lecturers play in mobilising popular support? Were they a challenge or complement to parliamentary leaders? This was the source of the divergence between some of the old committee of the Anti-Slavery Society and the Agency committee.

Emancipation brought the apprenticeship system in the majority of the West Indian territories but, until its operation began to cause ripples of concern in 1835, a mood of satisfaction prevailed amongst many reformers. As in the aftermath of abolition there were signs of a 'consolidationist' outlook at least amongst some of the older generation of reformers and those parliamentarians like Buxton who felt bound to support the legislative compromise solution of 1833. Clarkson saw the model of the African Institution in these circumstances remaining relevant. A new national organisation he believed should be on a smaller and more economical scale than required by the struggle up to 1833; functioning as a watchdog over legislation and supplying information to ministers and public its style had to be 'very prudent and discreet'. It was clear that Clarkson wanted a fresh start in a style distant from the Agency campaign discussed below (p.62).[13]

By contrast members of that younger and more 'populist' group of abolitionists envisaged addressing the universal abolition of slavery through the British and Foreign Society for the Universal Abolition of Slavery and the Slave Trade – reorganised from the Agency in March 1834 – and more permanently with the British and Foreign Anti-Slavery Society (BFASS). Their methods were to be essentially agitational – employing lectures, insertions in the daily press, travelling agitators in foreign parts and a campaign of publishing. And in practice, when the issue of ending apprenticeship became more urgent, it was a revival of antislavery mobilisation in the country which was most striking – with publications, local organisation and intervention in parliamentary elections. The shift in balance in the style of operation embodied in the anti-apprenticeship campaign was revealed in the gathering of a conference of antislavery delegates from around the country in London in November 1837 and their appointment of a Central Negro Emancipation Committee drawn from activists able to be permanently or frequently in London. This reversal of earlier antislavery history in which London-based committees had sought to mobilise the provinces from their self-anointed positions of leadership was a sign that an aroused antislavery public expected its demands to override tendencies to parliamentary compromise and to render manoeuvre within virtually irrelevant.[14]

From 1838 onwards the discipline imposed by struggle with the West Indian enemy inside the British political system largely disappeared. As abolitionist ambitions widened in geographical scope the ability of reformers to effect them declined in respect both to an informed public opinion able to be mobilised and on finding policies which could bring results through the use of practical methods. These turned out to be the basic difficulties facing the BFASS in the 1840s and 1850s. Such a different environment for antislavery work gave different meanings to bodies which claimed national antislavery status. Within Britain, with the unifying factor of a common West Indian opponent gone, one function of antislavery organisation was to make a competitive claim against other tendencies within antislavery to be the true legatees of a triumphant cause. Sturgeites in the BFASS, Buxton's supporters in the Society for the Extinction of the Slave Trade and for the Civilization of Africa (the 'Civilization Society', 1839–43) and British Garrisonians in the British India Society and the Anti-Slavery League all made gestures towards identifying their different preoccupations as legitimate developments in new circumstances of antislavery in its most successful period. Struggle for the sanction of the aged Clarkson was one indication of this. Claims to leadership of national antislavery opinion also involved hopes of influencing British government policy where it might make a difference – for example, in negotiations over the continuing problem of slave trade suppression and on particular issues such as American fugitive slaves in British territories or terms for British recognition of the independence of Texas. Even though active support for antislavery organisations declined after 1840, leaders of abolitionist organisations wanted to be recognised as speaking for a reflexive, if latent, antislavery sentiment.[15]

An interim conclusion is now possible from the discussion of national antislavery organisations. In the half-century between 1787 and 1838 the overall organisational and institutional forms of antislavery were powerfully shaped by the need for meeting the propaganda and political challenge of the West India interest. At the height of abolitionist and emancipationist campaigns this involved a mutually reinforcing relationship between 'agitation' and 'influence', popular mobilisation and political manoeuvre, an extra-parliamentary movement and parliamentary initiative and tactics. But the organisational and institutional history of antislavery at this level does not demonstrate any simple linear development culminating in an open, 'democratic' style of operation. The movement recurrently exemplified conflict typical of the wider political culture between more and less 'open' styles. This was a matter both of the outlook of individuals and groups and the product of periodic reassessments by abolitionists of both circumstances and objectives and therefore of the most appropriate forms of activity. Here is an explanation of the differences between 1792 and the methods of resumption of abolitionism in 1804; the 'consolidationist' priorities and methods after 1807; even in part the divergences of 1831–2. Ultimately however there did emerge an asymmetry in activity between West Indians and abolitionists glimpsed by the West India Committee at the beginning of the emancipationist campaign. '[They] act upon a more extensive system and with greater means of influence upon the public mind.' But abolitionists did not reach that position along a single straight path.[16]

Refinement of interim conclusions based on national antislavery organisation will concentrate first on the elements of 'agitation' in winning over support to antislavery by paying attention to local antislavery committees or societies, types of antislavery meeting and petitioning. Whether the conception and practice of antislavery organisation and methods expanded resources for change in English political culture should then become clearer. The following section will then analyse the practice of 'influence' in relation to the electoral process, parliament and executive.

Local committees or associations fluctuated drastically in numbers in different periods of antislavery history despite the proclamation of the Liverpool society in 1823 that 'the present age', in making the organisational discovery of the local philanthropic or reform association, had made the era noteworthy 'for the rapid and surprising improvement which has taken place in the moral character and disposition of mankind'. Local abolition committees spread in 1788 prompted by Clarkson's visits and perhaps by the Manchester committee's circular letter to other towns. They worked up petitions to parliament while engaging in some correspondence with each other. These procedures were even more extensive by the time of the petition campaign of 1792. The culmination of abolition in 1806 and 1807 was much less marked by local committee activity and the African Institution did not expend great efforts on recreating or maintaining a national network of local groups. A few *were* deliberately encouraged, but only where they could further the Institution's 'watchdog' function. In 1809 Clarkson went to Liverpool to promote a local committee under William Roscoe's leadership to monitor the observance of the slave trade law in the largest former slaving port. Similar committees in Bristol and London appear to have been established. But only with the opening of the emancipationist campaign in the 1820s did local societies again become a major organisational feature of antislavery. During the course of his national lecture tour to promote petitions in 1823–4 Clarkson assisted in the foundation of about 200 local groups. That number had risen, according to George Stephen, as a result of the efficiency of the Agency committee system of itinerant lecturers, to 1,300 by the summer of 1832.[17]

The achievement of emancipation from 1 August 1834 clearly indicated final victory to many abolitionists and many local auxiliaries of the Anti-Slavery Society stood down, even as George Thompson who had been an Agency lecturer helped the establishment of new auxiliaries in the mid-1830s in pursuit of universal abolition. There were signs of reluctance to take seriously the need for revival of activity at the local level to overthrow apprenticeship before its due term under the act of 1833. Some of this was the product of the growing identification nationally of antislavery with political liberalism and thus fear, as in the case of Canterbury, of seeming to be 'acting from party feeling only'. But by 1837 local groups were active again in working against apprenticeship. The most zealous founders of the BFASS in 1839 were amongst those who had worked hardest to revitalise the local society network in the mid-1830s and so Joseph Sturge, John Scoble and the Quaker banker George Alexander toured areas of the country in 1839–40 to give the new national body the support of auxiliaries consciously orientated to universal abolition. The truth is, however, that it was much more difficult to maintain interest and organisation in the country for this purpose than for British abolition and emancipation. In total no more than a few dozen local groups existed at different times in the 1840s and 1850s. Within this much smaller number of local societies several – notably Glasgow, the Hibernian in Dublin and later the Bristol and Clifton Ladies – repudiated any auxiliary status to the BFASS. This outbreak of local and regional autonomy appears to have had its origin in hostility to compensated emancipation and the temporary vacuum in effective national leadership in the mid-1830s. It was strengthened by the impact of American abolitionist divisions in Britain in the 1840s.[18]

Even in the periods of local committee or society expansion, although the groups were intended to draw in supporters to the cause, their operation did not provide unambiguous evidence of the politics of popular mobilisation. It is clear from Clarkson's *History* that in the early years of the anti-slave trade agitation local organisations were established through existing religious networks (an example would be the Quaker Lloyds in Birmingham) or contact by Clarkson or others with a small group of prominent individuals who already had an interest in the issue. On occasion these contacts were accompanied by quasi-public events like Clarkson's antislavery sermon in Manchester at the end of 1787, but by no means invariably. In the expansive period post–1823 some local groups paid due heed to rank and influence in society; Beverley, for example, had different levels of subscription and those prepared and able to provide a sizeable financial stake were guaranteed additional influence: 'Subscribers of 10s.6d. and upwards shall be of the Acting Committee of the said Association'. The Swansea and Neath association announced its social respectability in its president, the Marquess of Bute, and a roster of vice-presidents entirely aristocratic, gentry, and wealthy businessman in character. Abolitionists assumed that social deference could be a valuable impulse to support for reform. More striking is evidence of reluctance by local groups to launch out into direct engagement with the public in open meetings. The Swansea and Neath Society was founded in December 1822 but made no appeal through a public meeting until January 1826; the Manchester Society, although becoming active at the beginning of 1824, issued no report to the public until March 1827 and had only had its first public meeting on 22 March 1826. It was this sort of situation the Agency committee had in mind in justifying its activities because 'provincial associations have become inert and inefficient' with the result that local groups concluded 'their own individual exertions were too little sustained by those of similar bodies elsewhere to be of real utility'. It was to break through this impression that Agency lecturers began to address large meetings and out of a groundswell of popular conviction produce affiliated societies of which George Stephen claimed 'all were well disciplined and eager for work'.[19]

The attitude to public meetings by local antislavery organisations was one test of how seriously reformers tried to mobilise popular opinion. However, since not all antislavery public meetings were under the aegis of local societies or linked to their establishment, the fact that some abolitionist groups were chary of a 'populist' style of

activity before the early 1830s does not exclude democratic implications from all antislavery usages of meetings. Moreover, the
significance of public meetings in the late eighteenth and earlier
nineteenth centuries differed according to both their type and the
changing general political context. Some early petitions in 1788 to the
Commons on the slave trade came from county meetings held in
customary county meeting places. At these gatherings only
freeholders (including gentry and clergy) were allowed to speak and
vote; they were usually summoned by the sheriff on the application of
a number of freeholders and the county members might often attend.
These meetings had a constitutional if non-statutory status and their
use by abolitionists, far from opening the democratic floodgates, put
the authority of precedent and the county elites behind them. Some
other meetings in 1788 in corporate towns extended beyond local
officials but were not open and general; yet other gatherings were
restricted to membership of particular denominations. Drescher,
however, has demonstrated that there were at least twenty-seven
public meetings for anti-slave trade petitioning in 1788. By 1792 the
general, public character of antislavery meetings for petitioning was
evident even though, according to Clarkson, efforts were made to
prevent public meetings in some places.[20]

However, 1792 did not establish for all time antislavery as a
movement of popular mobilisation demonstrated in the use of general
public meetings. Even at that point such meetings were touched by
the rumbling fear of the authorities of political disorder; after all, as
recently as 1779–80 such a hallowed institution as the county meeting
had provided the basis for a powerful, though short-lived, movement
for political reform under Wyvill's leadership. By 1794–5 democratic
radicals were using public meetings against the war and domestic
social crisis in such a way as to constitute in the eyes of the authorities
'tumultuous petitioning' and potentially seditious attempts to coerce
parliament. Abolitionists had to face the fact that for many of their
fellow countrymen during the next thirty years open public meetings
continued to have this resonance. In the abolition efforts of 1805–7,
rousing support deliberately excluded the use of public meetings in
both London and the provinces. The African Institution dealt in
business 'which Parliamentary men alone could manage' and this did
little 'in the way of creating or organizing public feeling' by meetings
or other means. Davis has noted the unease as late as the mid-1820s of
some members of the committee of the Anti-Slavery Society over
Cropper's desire to see public meetings addressed by travelling agents

because of the association of such methods with other, divisive reform causes. In deference to these views Cropper seems to have met groups of 'influential citizens' and spoken to clearly defined religious gatherings. Only in the later 1820s is there clear evidence not only of the pursuit of mass public meetings, as at Liverpool in April 1828, but collaboration in setting up similar meetings in other major centres. Liverpool and Birmingham, Cropper and Sturge, worked together through these meetings (2,000 at Liverpool) to 'have a powerful effect on Parliament and they must do their duty'. Logically, these two provincial Quaker activists were foremost in support of the Agency committee in 1831.[21]

The enthusiastic embrace of large-scale public meetings came from the 'Young England' abolitionists engaged in the Agency campaign. In the previous chapter (p.41) it was argued that this was the period when a major ideological stress of antislavery was its embodiment of the national interest across class and denomination, and such meetings offered dramatic demonstration of aristocratic support (the Duke of Bedford at Woburn), 'the elite of the town, churchmen and dissenters' (at Dunstable) and caught up audiences, already stirred by 'an intensity of feeling on the fate of the Reform Bill', into an almost equally excited interest in emancipation. The lecturers' meetings became a form of theatre as they encouraged opposition the better to silence it before the expectant crowd. In the post-Reform Act atmosphere of an impending election the large antislavery meeting could become a collective expression of anticipated triumph. In Sheffield in July 1832 George Thompson wrote of speaking before 'Montgomery the Poet – also before Buckingham who is perhaps the most accomplished lecturer of the day – also all the four candidates for the representation of the Town and a fearful array of parsons of all denominations and critics of every grade. Yet was my success triumphant.' The unqualified use of the public meeting in the later stages of the emancipation campaign was the product both of an urgency amongst primarily a younger generation of abolitionists and a changed political context. The campaign for parliamentary reform had drawn the population in, in part through great reform meetings. Abolitionists were no longer exposed in their use of public meetings; indeed, compared with the disorder which sometimes accompanied agitation for parliamentary reform, large antislavery meetings were able to project the eminent respectability which could be attained by popular reform enterprise.[22]

These developments also reveal a basic change in the conception of the travelling agent whose existence went back in some form to the beginning of organised antislavery in the 1780s. Both members of the London Anti-Slavery committee and some of the Liverpool abolitionists who encountered him were doubtful about Clarkson's attitudes and methods in gathering information from participants in the African slave trade. Currie in particular stressed the need for respectable sources rather than 'the lowest class of seamen'; impartial enquiry, the need to find the truth, required informants of integrity. Encouragement of such careful discrimination was perhaps also reflected in agent Clarkson's other main function in the late 1780s – the establishment of local committees through consultation with influential individuals in communities. When Clarkson and Cropper in the 1820s once again set about gathering evidence they were more strongly aware that they were fighting a war. Abolitionists saw themselves less as seekers after impartial truth than partisans whose gathering of facts was defined in military metaphor as 'a Corps de Reserve against the hottest of the Battle'. The agents or lecturers became not only dramatic figures in the theatre of the public meeting but combatants, for example on the occasions when Thompson and some colleagues debated the West Indian Peter Borthwick and associates at Glasgow in 1833 and in 1836 the American defender of slavery, Breckinridge.[23]

Both the activities of local antislavery associations and public meetings engendered petitions and the recurrent presentation of large numbers of them to parliament was a striking feature of antislavery history. There is no doubt that they played a major part in maintaining interest in abolition and emancipation through different phases of antislavery. They were also an important link between agitation out of doors and influence within the walls of parliament. Until the restrictions of the 1830s presentation of petitions guaranteed MPs opportunities to raise the grievances on the floor of the House before the business of the day. The phenomenal rise in antislavery petitions is now widely appreciated: from 102 in 1788 to 519 in 1792, over 800 in 1814 and repeated waves of hundreds virtually every parliamentary session from 1823 onwards, culminating in over 5,000 at the climax of the emancipation campaign in 1833. Petitioning remained a weapon of agitation against the apprenticeship system up to 1838. Seymour Drescher's work has recently sought to underline the significance of petitioning by comparison with its role in French antislavery and as a high proportion of all petitions to the British parliament in particular years.

It is clear that in 1788–92, then in 1823–33 and, with some uncertainty in various localities, up to 1838 petitioning expanded concern with the slave trade, slavery and apprenticeship. Petitioning grew with local antislavery organisations, circulation of massive amounts of literature and the ideological acceptance of emancipation as a matter of national interest and a component of national identity. Yet there is a danger of reading too much into petitioning unless it is given a firm context. Though antislavery petitioning was a very prominent element of parliamentary petitioning in the years mentioned above, they were years in which petitioning as a habit grew remarkably. Petitions did not begin simply to be pressed on parliament in large numbers on a few issues; the *range* of grievances expanded in petitioning. The annual average of petitions in 1785–9 was 176 and rose in 1811–15 to 899, in 1828–32 to 4,656, in 1833–7 to 7,436 and in 1838–42 to 14,014. Nor should the novelty be exaggerated of abolitionists advancing petitions from a relatively popular base and on grounds of the general interest in 1788 – *relatively* popular because calculation from Drescher's estimate of 60,000 signatures in 1788 suggests an average of 600 signatures per petition and, with Manchester producing 10,639, some were clearly much smaller than the average. Petitioning on public interest, if not humanitarian, grounds and from a quasi-popular base had recent precedents in the later eighteenth century. In 1769 Middlesex and London petitioners, concerned with seating Wilkes as member for Middlesex, mounted a general assault, couched in terms of the public interest, against the policies of the king's government. In 1779 Middlesex petitioners demanded an investigation 'into the true cause of those misfortunes which have reduced this once powerful and flourishing empire to a state which words cannot describe'. They initiated a campaign embracing twenty-four counties and eleven of the largest towns and cities in which petitioning was combined with parliamentary initiatives. Some of the county meetings which originated the petitions contained 'popular' elements. Broad justifications for petitioning were as familiar to both politicians and abolitionists as the sectional interest justifications of the petitions on economic and commercial issues in the 1780s which Drescher stresses because of their contrast with the humanitarian and general interest grounds of the anti-slave trade petitions of 1788. Moreover, since the 1788 petitions were not part of a movement pursuing significant change in the political system or attacking the *range* of government policy, the application of humanitarian and general interest criteria to a question of trade probably appeared relatively innocuous to those who were not directly involved.[24]

Recurrent bursts of petitioning on an ever larger scale played a central part in developing and maintaining the dynamic of anti-slave trade agitation up to 1792 and of the emancipation campaign from 1823. They do not however provide conclusive evidence through their cumulative impact of a *continuously developing* popular social movement over fifty years, using the same methods for winning over support. There was a very long gap of years between the mass petitioning of 1792 and that of 1823–4 with the single exception of the 1814 campaign against the reopening of the French slave trade after the war. Whether that campaign should be interpreted as a link maintaining popular continuity across years when there was little other popular involvement in antislavery becomes crucial. The term 'antislavery' is itself deceptive; the 1814 campaign was against allowing a defeated enemy to reopen a cruel trade which the British were proud of having ended amongst their own fellow-countrymen. It occurred at a time when abolitionist leaders hoped for improved treatment of slaves in the West Indies but had not focused on emancipation as an objective and had not specifically propagandised for it. Whatever it says about an achieved consensus on the slave trade, the 1814 campaign provides no support for a developing popular antislavery which incorporated emancipation. Even on the slave trade a comparison of the places petitioning in 1792 with those of 1814, despite an increase in the total number, indicates quite sizeable geographical discontinuities in support. In 1792 519 petitions were raised but forty-eight of them were institutional. Of the remaining 471 area petitions a number contained signatures from several places; 542 places in all petitioned in 1792. It is clear that the North of England and especially Scotland contributed to the large advance of 1792 over 1788. But of the 542 places petitioning in 1792 only 283 also petitioned in 1814 – a 'persistence rate' of only 52.21 per cent. Of the places which did not petition in 1814, although they had done so in 1792, some 40 per cent were in Scotland. But what of the 'new' places, within the larger total of petitions in 1814? 483 of these have been located.

This indicates that, excluding Wales, 76 per cent of 'new' petitions in 1814 were from places in the Midlands and East Anglia southwards. If this is combined with the previous result of 40 per cent

Regional distribution of 1814 petitions from places not petitioning in 1792

Region	Number of 'new' petitions nationally	Number of 'new' petitions	% of Total
London and S.E.	483	80	16.57
Elsewhere in s.	483	63	13.04
South-west	483	68	14.07
Midlands (n. to Derby)	483	83	17.18
East Anglia (inc. Essex)	483	75	15.52
North of England	483	58	12.00
Wales	483	19	3.93
Scotland	483	29	6.00
Ireland	483	8	1.65

[1792 & 1814 lists from 8th Report of the African Institution (1814), pp. 40–7 (1814) and pp. 51–67 (1792)]

of places 'lost' in 1814 as against 1792 being Scottish the conclusion is that the 1814 petitioning was not only much more English than 1792 but even much more English south of the North Country. Since the gap between the two campaigns was twenty-two years this cannot be described as 'volatility' in antislavery support but it does indicate a complicated picture of simultaneous large expansion and significant (though quantitatively less) erosion, using the yardstick of petitioning. This picture of antislavery support is at an early stage of a shift towards the objective of emancipation; the completion of the transition took several more years even for abolitionist leaders. It would not be surprising if, to gain popular support for emancipationist petitions, reformers had to work very hard. After several months of touring and organising in 1824 Clarkson claimed 200 local associations and 225 petitions, just over one-quarter of the number gained in one month in 1814. The implication of the argument is that 1823–4, so far as petitioning to gain mass support was concerned, should be seen primarily as a new start in many places.[25]

One other feature of emancipationist petitioning is now well established. Reformers often worked through sympathetic religious networks in the localities, the names of members of which were known from earlier years; more important, petitions came increasingly from congregations and denominational organisations of an aroused dissent. The evangelical antislavery imperative in the 1820s formed a conjunction with a reaction against West Indian treatment of nonconformist missionaries and powerful leadership in antislavery activism by major figures of dissent: Jabez Bunting and Richard Watson of the Wesleyans, Joseph Ivimey of the Baptists, the Congregationalists Henry Waymouth and John Angell James. The abolitionists worked hard to maintain this denominational momentum as a source of petitioning and Joseph Sturge noted that they would simply be paralleling the tactics of the campaign against the Test and Corporation Acts. In a routine way by September 1830 the committee of the Anti-Slavery Society sent for insertion a short notice requesting petitions 'to the Editors of the Provincial Newspapers and of Religious Periodicals'. In 1833, of 5,020 antislavery petitions the Wesleyans provided 1,953 and other nonconformist bodies 873, though Drescher points out that a higher proportion of signatures came on community petitions.[26]

The presentation of a petition could have a dramatic, if momentary, effect on parliament. Priscilla Buxton recounted how four MPs brought in the huge rolls of the ladies' petition of 1833 and 'heaved it on to the table among loud laughing and cheers. It was soon and very unceremoniously dragged away again by the officers'. Miss Buxton's last sentence, however, is significant. By the early 1830s the very 'glut' of petitions so held up the normal business of the day that, although an exceptional petition like that of the ladies could make an impression, the House of Commons acted to refer petitions to a committee and deny immediate speech on them on the floor of the House. Although the campaign against apprenticeship brought a renewal of petitioning, by 1838 the Scots abolitionist William Smeal was expressing his disappointment at how 'cavalierly' petitions which had taken so much effort were received by the Commons.[27]

Whether working in an expansive phase in which the techniques of 'agitation' were widely used or in a 'consolidationist' period in which 'pressure from without' assumed less importance, antislavery needed to maximise its influence in parliament and the administration in order to translate aspiration into policy and ensure that policy was effectively executed. Alongside whatever direct impact petitions had on MPs, some printed material and very particular kinds of evidence were channelled straight to parliamentarians – especially the results of quantifying aspects of the slave trade and slavery and the direct testimony of witnesses whose authenticity was expected to impress. In addition, reformers tried to obtain antislavery pledges from parliamentary candidates or MPs and at critical moments called national conferences to 'shadow' parliamentary deliberations. In the 1830s this provoked significant tension between antislavery parliamentarians and activists in the country. By the 1840s abolitionists in England had long experience in less public ways of reaching into the government and its administrative arms. Consultations with ministers, the provision of information to administrators, direct communication with diplomats and naval officers, all fell within the ambit of less public means of attempted influence and can be most clearly illustrated from the record of the African Institution which has been somewhat overlooked by earlier writers. The two General or World Anti-Slavery Conventions of 1840 and 1843, held under the aegis of the BFASS in London, tried to influence the British government on some questions of policy. They helped maintain concern, but ultimately also divisive debate, over suppression of the transatlantic slave trade and whether or not the encouragement of free-labour staples, combined with consumer boycotts of slave-grown produce, could convert slaveholders into emancipators by forcing them to revise their calculations of economic interest. 'Hard' evidence of a quantitative kind was never neglected by abolitionists since they appreciated that it was more likely to impress parliamentarians who were conscious of their role as 'cool' arbiters of the national interest and who consequently distanced themselves from 'enthusiasm'. Thomas Cooper provided some basic calculations on the extent of demand for slaves in European colonies in the 1780s, what likely mortality was in Africa to supply the demand and estimates of total imports of slaves since the trade's commencement. In Liverpool William Rathbone extracted figures from the muster roles which Clarkson used as the basis for the statistics on mortality, disease and desertion amongst seamen engaged in the slave trade and which apparently impressed the Privy Council committee. Other ways of guaranteeing the reliability of antislavery evidence to MPs and government included appeal to acknowledged experts such as the Scots scholar and historian Principal Robertson on the likely ramifications of ending the trade and the personal appearance or signed testimony of first-hand witnesses – naval captains, inhabitants of or travellers to the West Indies and the occasional victim of the slave trade. Much of this was then recycled to MPs through careful abridgement of the evidence given to parliamentary committees. In the early 1820s the comparative material gathered from the United States by Liverpool abolitionists was used for parliamentary purposes.[28]

Face-to-face lobbying of MPs was initially adopted by Quakers hostile to the slave trade in the 1780s. Its appeal for Friends perhaps lay in its resolution of the tension within the Quaker outlook between a perfectionist separation from worldly activities and the moral relativism involved in the direct exercise of power. At any rate in the spring of 1784 it was Friends who resolved to accompany their delivery of their anti-slave trade pamphlet prepared by the slave trade committee of the Meeting for Sufferings with lobbying of MPs. In May 1788, immediately after Pitt had persuaded the Commons to agree the slave trade would be debated in the next session, the mainly Quaker members of the London committee, accompanied by Thomas Walker and Thomas Cooper from Manchester who had come to the capital to inspire urgency, formed a deputation to prepare MPs for the forthcoming discussion. As a result of their conversations they were able to draw up a list of MPs favourable to abolition. In December 1790 the Quaker committee, which maintained its existence alongside the London body, prompted Friends in the country to lobby their local MPs, particularly those elected for the first time in 1790. Other, non-Quaker, abolitionists had experience of lobbying as a technique in the 1780s – in the cases of Josiah Wedgwood and Thomas Walker over protection of commercial and industrial interests. It was a habit which remained a stand-by of abolitionists in the campaigns for emancipation and against apprenticeship; Wilberforce was convinced however that, contrary to the practice of 1790, pressure near the end of a parliament was likely to be more effective as MPs' minds were concentrated by the approach of an election. MPs were the targets of their local antislavery societies, though in addition reformers concentrated on members in strategic places or prominent enough to command support from some other members of the House. Thus in 1831 Cropper instructed Edward Prothero, one of the Bristol MPs: 'he is a nice young man; very willing and open to hear; but a good deal uninformed'. And in 1836 a deputation of Birmingham reformers saw O'Connell on apprenticeship; they could already assume help from Birmingham and Black Country MPs.[29]

To extract a pledge from candidates for parliament and, at least by implication, make votes conditional upon it, was to go a stage beyond lobbying. It was also a form of behaviour initially associated with political and constitutional radicalism. In a political system in the later eighteenth century in which political position and parliamentary place were still largely a function of kinship with, or being in client status to, political notables parliamentary seats were frequently uncontested to reduce the role of opinion in the political process and to save money. To attempt to commit candidates to a position at elections was therefore to challenge the main working assumptions of the system. In the early 1770s it was Supporters of the Society of the Bill of Rights who attempted pledging with only limited success. In 1779 it was the more radical of the parliamentary reformers and in 1790 it probably told against supporters of the third effort to do away with religious tests that they tried such unconventional methods. Significantly then, apart from isolated evidence of attempted antislavery pledging in 1792 in the middle of a parliament, it did not become a systematic technique of abolitionists until the culmination of the emancipation campaign in the early 1830s when parliamentary reform politics also triumphed. In Gloucester in 1831 all three candidates adopted an antislavery stance as a result of being questioned, one going so far as to have 'cards in his constituent hats with "No Slavery" printed up on them'. In the post-Reform Act election of December 1832 abolitionists published pledges from over 160 candidates; 132 pledged MPs were elected. This was the most successful moment of the pledge technique, though it was employed in the 1837 election to end apprenticeship and suggested in 1841 by the BFASS to create a parliamentary bloc ready to abolish slavery in British India. But in 1837 there is evidence of broader intervention in the election. In Wellingborough abolitionists used the electoral machinery of the Whig candidate to circulate anti-apprenticeship material and in Gloucester reached the electors with a separate electoral address. In Leicester a prominent Baptist abolitionist and town councillor, J. F. Winks, targeted the Tory candidate W. E. Gladstone and organised a public lecture on slavery and apprenticeship to highlight the Gladstone family's West India interests. Despite his action as an individual, Winks recognised the problem of alienating Tory abolitionists. They existed in significant numbers in the town at a time when there was restiveness amongst some antislavery people at the growing identification of antislavery with political liberalism and the demands of religious dissent.[30]

The 1830s was not only the most successful decade abolitionists in England experienced in their history but also the period in which the fluctuating interaction of agitation in the country with manoeuvre by and within the political class was most nearly resolved into parliamentary and administrative activity as a direct expression of mobilised grass-roots attitudes. This was the aspiration of increasing numbers of provincial antislavery militants; how closely they approximated their aim and what tensions it provoked with parliamentary abolitionists, especially Buxton, can be observed in part through examining the use of the delegate conference or convention. Like the practice of pledging, summoning conventions of delegates to deliberate on public policy, especially if they questioned the legitimacy of political institutions, had a radical pedigree. The history of the convention in England since the 1770s, however, more frequently indicated its possibilities for focusing 'pressure from without' on the political class than it pointed to a fully fledged anti-parliament. Both in 1780 when a divergence between metropolitan radicals and Wyvill's gentry in the county associations was evident and in 1793–4 with the calling of a British and then an English Convention, the contradictory potentialities of the convention were part of the substance of debate amongst participants. If the convention as anti-parliament is understood as assuming that the people's wishes must prevail, that the convention better expressed those wishes than parliament and therefore in any contest between the two popular loyalty should be to the convention, as abolitionists employed it in the 1830s, it was closer to a focus for intensifying 'pressure from without' than an alternative to parliament. At moments, none the less, abolitionist conventions challenged the moral, though not the constitutional, legitimacy of parliament. They escaped the reaction of state authority, unlike the radicals of 1793–4, because they did not pose a direct constitutional challenge, were composed of representatives primarily of the provincial, nonconformist middle and business classes and met in a political context judged less threatening by the authorities.[31]

In what context did abolitionists resort to the convention? It was adopted by those abolitionists who in a growing mood of frustration had also developed the agency system. Their frustration arose not only from the belief that amelioration was failing in the West Indies, but from lack of action by the Whig government and the little urgency displayed, in the eyes of many activists, by the London committee of the Anti-Slavery Society and their parliamentary allies. Thus the conventions expressed a provincial assertiveness and dissatisfaction at both parliamentary manoeuvre and the sense of apartness manifested by Buxton in his parliamentary role. At the end of 1830 Birmingham abolitionists were so disappointed at the failure of progress towards immediate emancipation in parliament that they floated the idea of a national delegate conference with the London committee to bring stronger action. Disappointment and frustration began to accumulate in criticism of Buxton as parliamentary leader of the cause. He had the difficult task in 1832-3 of reconciling his sympathy for the Whig government with pressing for the sort of positive action on emancipation which was acceptable both to a majority in the political and parliamentary class and antislavery militants in the country. Buxton revealed his awareness of conflicting pressures and the source of his determination to pursue his own course in a letter to Althorp on the eve of the 1832 motion on emancipation.

> However insignificant in myself I am the Representative on this question of no mean body in this country who would be . . . disappointed and chagrined at the suspension of the question – But further – and this is a consideration far more really influential on my Conduct – I cannot but feel myself the Representative of a Body who cannot speak for themselves and for whom I must act without other guide than my own Conscience.

Buxton's strength was his sense of conscience on behalf of distant slaves but it was also a weakness from the perspective of militants in the country because it resisted dictation from collective antislavery opinion. He had to rebut charges of acting for the convenience of his political friends. Worried that the government might retreat from an emancipation measure a convention of 339 antislavery delegates assembled in London in early spring 1833. Many of them were chosen by public meeting and Cropper and Sturge were prominent in encouraging organisation for the convention in the north and the West Country. Stanley's government proposals on emancipation in mid-May provoked hostility amongst delegates on the grounds of compensation and the apprenticeship scheme. Convention delegates marched through the streets of London committing themselves by 'all legitimate means' to bring about complete and immediate emancipation. Buxton was initially in despair at Stanley's proposals but, judging that total rejection ran the risk of abandonment of emancipation, refused to divide the House on the principles of the bill on second reading and hoped for amendment at the committee stage. Divisions amongst delegates appeared over Buxton's stance; the anger and the grounds for it amongst many provincial militants were clear in the report back to a meeting of the Birmingham Anti-Slavery Society. Divisions were such that

> the old Anti-Slavery Society committee [was not prompted] to

make a vigorous opposition to the grant of Twenty Millions and one parliamentary leader T. F. Buxton felt so much doubt upon the propriety of turning the attention of the country prominently to it that there was on this subject a want of cordial cooperation with those who wished to make use of it to its full extent.

A second convention met in July 1833 and in an effort to improve the bill had a delegation denounce apprenticeship to Stanley's face and managed to unite behind a Buxton amendment that apprenticeship should be for no longer than was required for the welfare of the slave. The amendment was lost by only seven votes; Stanley reduced the length of the intended apprenticeship terms. On everything else delegates felt a sense of 'dissatisfaction and complaint'. In response to continued encouragement from the localities they protested until the final passage of the legislation in August.[32]

The next antislavery use of the convention was in 1837–8 as a weapon to push parliament to end apprenticeship. It constituted an even clearer expression of provincial mobilisation and disregard for parliamentary initiative and manoeuvre than 1833. Growing conviction that apprenticeship was essentially slavery by another name came to a head with Joseph Sturge's return from an investigative visit to the West Indies in May 1837. After urging measures upon the virtually comatose London committee of the Anti-Slavery Society he concluded urgent action would not follow 'unless the friends of the Cause in the Country exerted themselves without waiting for information and instructions from London and that many of our friends in London would be strengthened by a spontaneous movement in the Country'. Spontaneity was given organised form on 11 October when antislavery delegates from Bath, Bristol, Exeter, Gloucester, Taunton, Devizes and Westbury met at Bath and resolved to work for the end of apprenticeship by August 1838. Encouraged by the resolutions of the Bath meeting Sturge summoned a conference in Birmingham on 25 October of delegates to the 1833 convention and opponents of slavery from all the Midland counties. They proposed a convention of delegates to meet at Exeter Hall on 14 November 1837. Significantly no places within 10 miles of London were contacted about the convention and a delegation from the old Anti-Slavery Society was only suggested at the last moment. In practice it soon withdrew. Given that, in 1837, Buxton initially opposed an immediate move against apprenticeship it is doubtful how much deference would have been shown his leadership by the convention, but he had anyway lost his seat at the recent election. The delegates, again often chosen by public meetings, saw themselves as the aroused mass of principled antislavery, cutting across the political and religious differences of their communities. After their initial meeting they reconvened in March 1838 and lobbied parliament heavily. So intensive was this that Lord Holland concluded MPs from 'populous' constituencies were intimidated. A quasi-national meeting in Birmingham on 19 April maintained morale and a third meeting of delegates convened in Exeter Hall on 19 May. Delegates were divided into sixty lobbying groups which tackled a majority of members of both Lords and Commons. When Sir George Strickland's motion (having no force of law) for complete emancipation was passed on 22 May but the government reversed the decision, delegates posed 'the Philanthropic and Christian Public' whom they represented against such parliamentary manoeuvring. They published voting lists of the relevant divisions and denounced unsympathetic MPs as 'unworthy of the support of a free and Christian people'. The attempt to convey the moral illegitimacy of the government's and parliament's continuation of apprenticeship was fierce. In fact, unknown to the convention, the pressure they exerted had much to do with the Colonial Secretary Glenelg writing to the colonial governments, even before the Strickland motion, to encourage local decisions to dispense with apprenticeship; the system came to an end in the summer of 1838. Abolitionists successfully used the convention drastically to reduce the freedom of parliamentary action and to claim that it was more representative of national opinion than the legislature. Much of the substance of Wilberforce's supposition as to the effects of aroused opinion in the country on the legislature had finally come to pass a half-century later.[33]

One reason why some of the most energetic of antislavery activists in the 1830s resorted to the mass public meeting, the public lecture, the organisation of vast petitions and the delegate convention was that they lacked the easy personal access to ministers and administrators which an earlier generation of antislavery leaders possessed. Buxton retained that access into a period when almost no other prominent active antislavery leader had it, though in accord with changing times, he saw the usefulness also of popular mobilisation. In contrast Sturge reflected in 1841 that he and fellow activists were 'not now in favour in High Quarters here'. Their more popular style of public activity was a measure of their marginality in relation to the

political class. In antislavery's earlier years Wilberforce's close connection with Pitt has been well documented and his and Stephen's
collaboration with Grenville to bring about the abolition legislation of
1806 and 1807 is established. Within the framework of the activities
of the African Institution Stephen and Zachary Macaulay had a
considerable impact on the formulation of legislation and policy for
the suppression of the slave trade and its execution. Stephen in
particular had a strong sense of British power through the country's
naval forces to end the international slave trade, 'to compel other
powers to renounce it too'. Personal and institutional links between
reformers and government were supported by the 'Saints' and their
associates in parliament. George Stephen remembered how as a youth
he heard 'many a semi-domestic debate as to the extent to which
parliamentary manoeuvring could be successfully carried out with the
ministerial benches'. Deficiencies, so far as British subjects were
concerned, in the anti-slave trade laws were able to be documented
through a network of correspondents in Liverpool (particularly
William Roscoe), Bristol and London and abroad. Such information
formed the basis of interventions by the African Institution to draft
new legislation and push it through parliament (the Slave Trade
Felony Act of 1811). The network centring on Macaulay as secretary
of the African Institution also provided evidence and argument which
persuaded the Admiralty to order naval vessels to act against foreign
slave traders, even to the point of illegality. But the African
Institution went further; it directly contacted the naval officers
concerned with enforcing the anti-slave trade laws

> respecting the provisions of the Legislature on this point and
> the manner in which these provisions have been eluded, as well
> as to point out the pecuniary advantages [the system of bounties
> which the abolitionists had themselves promoted] which would
> accrue to them from a vigorous enforcement of the Abolition
> Laws.

As early as 1812 the African Institution was also in regular communication with civil officers on the West African coast. It was
monitoring by abolitionists which prompted the seizure by customs
officers of a Spanish vessel fitting out at Gravesend for entry into the
Cuban slave trade. The antislavery body also claimed effective access
to government on the aspect of anti-slave trade policy which
complemented suppression; after pressure over some years for the

British government to reduce discriminatory duties on commercial products from West Africa originating with information by Roscoe, duties on cotton wool, ginger, coffee and palm oil were lessened. Not surprisingly, the active members of the African Institution saw themselves not simply as a successful pressure group but as something like an unofficial arm of government.[34]

Despite these links, however, reformers in the African Institution could not always get what they wanted. One such area was the treatment of slaves and administration of justice in the West Indies. Scandals in Nevis and Tortola were publicised by the African Institution but Whitehall was reluctant to challenge the constitutional convention which consigned such questions to the colonial authorities. A more oblique approach, a project of the elder James Stephen, was to create a central registry of slaves intended not only to provide evidence of the extent to which the anti-slave trade legislation was being evaded, but to illuminate the demographic trends within the slave population and indirectly the conditions and treatment of the bondsmen. About 1815, Clarkson made the assumption explicit that Great Britain had a right to see her colonies managed on principles, and a morality not contrary to her own. But once more an effective mechanism for translating the conviction into practice was thwarted by the British government's tenderness for West Indian constitutional susceptibilities. Stephen was close enough to his fellow evangelical, the Prime Minister Spencer Perceval, to be allowed to draft an order in council for a registry in the Crown Colony of Trinidad in 1812. But the succeeding Liverpool administration was more cautious. Stephen felt compelled to try to force the government's hand in extending the registry. Persuaded by him, Wilberforce introduced a bill for a registry in 1815 to cover both crown and legislative colonies. It met such opposition in Jamaica that Wilberforce was persuaded to withdraw it and settle for registries by colonial legislation. Stephen left parliament disillusioned; virtually all the colonies passed legislation by 1820, and although it was unsatisfactory in some respects to the reformers they were constrained by the existence of the legislation. The final example of failure by reformers in the African Institution period, despite their access to ministers, ambassadors and political leaders of foreign governments, was in getting agreed international action to suppress the slave trade through the international congresses of powers from Vienna to Verona, 1814–22. Personal approaches to Talleyrand and Tsar Alexander I were combined with priming the Foreign Secretary, Castlereagh, so that the Foreign Office circulated British representatives in foreign capitals to obtain allies for suppression. The Duke of Wellington, both when ambassador in Paris and later as representative at the Congresses of Aix-la-Chapelle in 1818 and Verona in 1822, was enlisted in the campaign and in 1814–15 Clarkson and Macaulay, in 1818 Clarkson and in 1822 William Allen all spent time at the congresses meeting political leaders and arguing for defining the slave trade as piracy under international law. The difficulty lay in the inability, not the unwillingness, of British political leaders to persuade the French or the tsar to act decisively. The African Institution had to accept defeat on collective action and hope for efficient bilateral arrangements between Britain and other powers.[35]

Finding the institutional means to strike at the slave trade and slavery internationally posed even greater difficulties for those abolitionists of Joseph Sturge's generation who were more distant from the centres of political power in Britain. The habit of this dominant Quaker in the BFASS of arranging deputations to ministers and approaching kings and emperors brought even less of a result than it had in earlier generations. There was widespread scepticism about such methods of making reformers out of rulers. It was a context in which British antislavery, peace and temperance reformers (there was a considerable overlap) all devised another institutional instrument – the general or international conference or convention. The Anti-Slavery Conventions in London in 1840 and 1843 were mainly Anglo-American in membership but also drew delegates from western Europe and some free blacks from colonial territories. The meetings encouraged exchange of information and perhaps boosted morale. The British found a role as recent emancipators in advising others, though they had to acknowledge the continued participation of British capital and goods in the slave trade and the possession of slaves by British functionaries abroad. They and their closest American collaborators asserted the superiority economically as well as morally of free labour systems as central to the international emancipation campaign and sought to purify slaveholding societies by purifying Protestant denominations and missionary enterprise of slaveholders. All these policies were enthusiastically adopted in the fellowship atmosphere of the conventions; the problem remained of persuasion and enforcement outside. The conventions issued addresses to both peoples and rulers of western European empires and to southerners and Christian denominations in the United States. No doubt they hoped that their pleas and arguments would receive attention. They were also hoping by these means to avoid causing resentment at infringement of separate national sovereignties which would be a possible result if they enlisted the aid of the British government. But since response from ministers by the 1840s was extremely circumspect the reformers were probably making a virtue of necessity. They rarely succeeded in making an antislavery question into a diplomatic issue, though they occasionally tried to exploit an existing issue for antislavery purposes.[36]

After 1838, therefore, neither 'agitation' nor 'influence' either separately or together provided very powerful instruments for achieving antislavery ends. Shortage of funds and opportunities for popular mobilisation as well as 'outsider' status in relation to leading public men were the disabling features of antislavery in the 1840s and 1850s. There remained one other tactic in these years, which had an earlier antislavery history too, designed to provide a role for individual abolitionists in England and convince them that they were contributing to advancing freedom internationally; it was the tactic of economic boycott of slave-grown raw materials or goods produced from them. By the 1840s it was mainly American-grown cotton which was at issue and a tactic largely adopted by Quakers. Some supporters of what became known as the free produce movement none the less had earlier experience of boycotting West Indian rum and sugar. Though not entirely restricted to Friends, it was an approach particularly appealing to people in whom quietist instincts remained strong both before and after the direct political involvement exemplified by the election of Joseph Pease to parliament in 1832. One interpretation of the intermittent energy which Joseph Sturge put into the free produce movement in the 1840s is that it constituted an attempt by a Friend who had launched out into public and even political life to maintain links with more traditionally quietist brethren who none the less looked for greater perfection in the world.

As a mechanism for weakening the slave trade, British colonial slavery and American slavery, the abstention from slave-grown produce was marginal in giving reality to abolitionist arguments about the 'impolicy' of the trade and in no way qualified, despite the evidence it provided, the later reflexive ideological commitment of abolitionists to the superior efficiency of free labour. Throughout its fluctuating history in antislavery it remained a badge of 'purity' and a mark of earnestness. It did however reflect a sense of Britain's central role in a world-wide economy and permitted individuals to believe they could contribute to a good cause without relying upon government or becoming enmeshed in politics. As such, and as dealing with questions of household consumption, it was a form of activity doubly appropriate for women. By the 1820s they were especially prominent in the campaign for abstention. Even then the older amongst them could look back to the early 1790s when debate about, and the practice of, abstention from slave-grown colonial sugar was claimed by Clarkson to have drawn in about 300,000 families. It was Clarkson's response to the stubbornness of West Indian legislatures over amelioration in the mid-1820s to encourage ladies' antislavery associations to promote abstention as a superior alternative to the use of force by the government. James Cropper went further in hoping for, but failing to do anything about, improving the quality of free-labour East Indian sugar as an alternative for British consumers if it was allowed to compete on fairer terms with West India produce. The Sheffield Ladies' committee canvassed the East Indian alternative in the town and reported 'grocers have stated the demand for it has been doubled since the commencement of the canvass'. But, in the case of cotton, balancing the evil of consumption against the possibility of widespread loss of employment in Lancashire caused some perplexity. These doubts were still widely encountered at the time of the 1840 Convention but a debate there and at the 1843 meeting stimulated the search for a reliable supply of free-labour cotton to reduce dependence on the slaveholders of the American South. Provincial tours and propaganda by Sturge, Alexander and Scoble identified the BFASS with the free-produce tactic and prompted a flurry of interest in 1845–6. Encouragement and promises to aid in supplying free-labour cotton came from American Friends and Elihu Burritt took up free produce as one of his reform themes during his recurrent visits from the United States. But, as disappointed abolitionists in the country reported, adequate supply remained crucial. So too did the quality of goods manufactured and their relative dearness – given supply difficulties and lack of bulk orders to manufacturers. These problems were never entirely overcome and fluctuations of enthusiasm in the use of the economic boycott/free-produce tactic depended on temporary external factors rather than permanent solutions to the difficulties. Free produce, like antislavery generally, received some publicity from the visit of Mrs Stowe and her husband in 1853 but ebbed in popularity when the Richardsons of Newcastle who had been prime propagandists for the movement had to withdraw in 1854. Voluntary personal abstention continued in a modest way through to the end of American slavery but plans positively to develop free-labour cultivation in the American South, India or West Africa came to little in the 1850s and the the British government never gave any serious consideration after equalisation of the sugar duties beginning in 1846 to a policy of discriminating in favour of free-grown produce. Overall, within the culture of antislavery economic boycott and free-produce activities worked much less significantly as a way of drawing in support than as a mark which some abolitionists chose to display of their antislavery identity.[37]

It can now be concluded that while initially forms of antislavery activity were in considerable part shaped by the struggle against the West Indians, they moved beyond these limits and assumed some of the characteristics of a popular movement. Yet even when 'agitation' played a large role, until the 1830s – and even then the traditional view was maintained by an older generation of abolitionists – it was seen as giving strength and support to parliamentary initiatives, backing to 'influence' over political leaders and entailing deference to the consensus of the leaders of parliamentary antislavery. That relationship was eroded in the 1830s and the main parliamentary associations of antislavery organisations in the 1840s and later were clearly with radical and strong reformer politicians. Militants in the country became increasingly impatient of parliamentary manoeuvre and calculation because they became more critical, particularly as to the position of the Anglican Church, of both Tory and Whig politics. Riding a numerical surge of dissent, provincial abolitionism came to distrust even an antislavery politics practised with any ease within the confines of Westminster and Whitehall. This is not to say that the emergence of more popularly-orientated styles of activity expressed a displacement of sectarian religious feeling but antislavery none the less did become an important channel for religious feeling which looked to a broader moral enhancement of English society and in turn that had to involve the full-hearted commitment of a myriad of individuals and groups. The evidence reviewed in this chapter does not however demonstrate even in the earlier agitational aspects of the anti-slave trade campaign that antislavery took up radical methods and challenged the normal modes of bringing about change. Certainly abolitionists used techniques which had a radical pedigree – this was a source of Wilberforce's concern – but most of them did not tie them to programmes of large-scale reconstruction of the political order and sought to portray the economic change involved in abolition and emancipation as a smooth transition to a more profitable state of affairs. Nor did they continue to deploy the full panoply of radical techniques in moments of perceived social and political crisis. In this way radical techniques became reformist techniques.

4

BEING ABOLITIONISTS
Harmony and tension in the internal culture of antislavery

Looking back from 1808 Clarkson had no doubt of the enormity of the task which had faced him and his collaborators a little over twenty years earlier.

> The slave trade may be considered, like the fabulous hydra, to have had a hundred heads, every one of which it was necessary to cut off before it could be subdued. And as none but Hercules was fitted to conquer the one, so nothing less than extraordinary prudence, courage, labour and patience could overcome the other.

The heroism portrayed as necessary to triumph over the slave trade drew upon a sense of working in harmony with fellow reformers, fired in part by an ideologically convergent commitment and of acting upon that commitment in similar ways. The first part of this chapter begins with the structural factors – especially the religious, family and community links – which drew and held abolitionists together in that sense of fellowship. These structures were informed by common elements of personal and group experience and knowledge. When the antislavery movement as a movement began to have a history, the writing of it by participants or writers dependent upon the perspective of participants contributed to a unifying consciousness central to which was a veneration of the heroic first generation who in their functional and religious diversity confirmed the possibility of unity in common endeavour. A purpose of Clarkson's *History* was thus not only to delineate a common pattern of consciousness but to promote it as a contribution to energising the internal networks of antislavery for future struggles. The first section also suggests that a cohesive consciousness could be registered in the construction and development of antislavery rituals and occasions and iconographic expressions or visual representations of a common antislavery identity.[1]

None the less, the necessity to reach out to others – to make abolitionists – even from a strong sense of a mutually supportive movement could contribute to tensions and conflicts between individuals and groups of reformers, as the previous chapter indicated. Lines distinguishing different groups and generations could not be completely erased by the building of a sense of common commitment and endeavour. What was a contribution to harmony in one context could become a support for disharmony in another set of circumstances. Religious networks could make for a unified effort or become the vertebrae of different segments of reformers whose conflicts were expressed in organisational diversity and competition. In the form of the consciousness registered in the antislavery celebrations of the 1830s, manifestations of a triumphant unity could betray evidence of very different senses of who had primarily achieved the triumph and how. Similarly, post-emancipation abolitionist accounts of antislavery history, in their strategies and silences, indicate colder considerations of priority in the cause, status and the relative significance of different contributions which both reflected a changed context and added to tensions of sect and party within antislavery. These themes form the substance of the second part of the chapter. There it is also argued that it is from the legislation of emancipation onwards that the tensions and forces making for conflict grow significantly stronger than the cohesive factors sustaining antislavery culture. A subordinate theme from the late 1830s remains a striving to restore a commonality in antislavery, involving a conscious mediation between a weakened common antislavery identity and loyalty to separate circles and reform interests. But the need openly to handle such divergent pressures when their earlier expression had been largely submerged by common and complementary work to be done and the high excitement of periodic achievement, was itself a mark of the decline of a cohesive internal culture of antislavery.

At the level of national antislavery leadership the Clapham Sect illustrated the dense personal texture underlying co-operative activity in combining close friendships, ties of kin, connections by marriage and, with the exception of William Smith, attachment to the evangelical wing of the Church of England. The Thorntons were kin of the Wilberforces; Gisborne was a close friend of Wilberforce and married Babington's sister while Babington himself married a sister of Zachary Macaulay. James Stephen the elder took Wilberforce's sister as his second wife and in the next generation James Stephen the younger – the under secretary at the Colonial Office in the crucial emancipation period – married a daughter of John Venn, the rector of Clapham. In the early decades of the nineteenth century the creation of Anglican evangelical networks in the country in the form of clergymen active in parishes, energising lay commitment through a plethora of activities, including antislavery, became noteworthy. Thornton patronage in Colchester placed the Rev. William Marsh there in 1814 and in the following years an evangelical connection was established across southern East Anglia. From 1829 Marsh was translated to Birmingham to a diocese under the direction of the first evangelical bishop in the Anglican hierarchy. Marsh's appointment was but one aspect of an evangelical 'saturation' of pulpits in the city in the 1820s and 1830s. A member of the Spooner family, connected to Wilberforce by his marriage to Barbara Spooner, became Archdeacon of Coventry with responsibility for Birmingham and had close links to the evangelical Calthorpes, landowners and philanthropists in the city. Antislavery, temperance and other favourite evangelical reform endeavours became an everyday part of evangelical activity.[2]

Readers of Annan's classic essay are equally certain to know of the elaborate interconnections in the Quaker world of philanthropy and reform. Kin and marriage ties in the eighteenth and earlier nineteenth centuries bound together such antislavery families as the Gurneys, the Frys, the Hoares, the Hodgkins, the Foxes and the Barclays. Marriage also connected the Gurneys to the Darlington Quaker dynasty of bankers and philanthropists, the Backhouses, who in turn were cousins of the Peases. Their senior branch of railway promoters and philanthropists produced the first Quaker MP Joseph Pease as well as marrying back into the Gurneys. A junior branch through Joseph Pease, the India reformer (uncle of the MP) provided one of the main strands of support for American Garrisonian abolitionism in Britain, in the form of Elizabeth Pease Nichol and her connections. At this level Friends linked antislavery in the north-east, East Anglia and the West Country together; local Meetings of Friends provided the organising framework and fellowship for Agency lecturers in many places in the 1831–2 campaign of mobilisation.[3]

Marriage perhaps played a less important part in the network of Rational Dissent in the late eighteenth century, though Josiah Wedgwood did become a relation by marriage to Sir James Mackintosh and thus in touch with the world of Brougham and the

Edinburgh Review. More evident were the personal and intellectual connections of prominent ministers and scholars and the friendship of educated liberal families clustered round a particular chapel or linking one congregation with another. Although the chapel communities of Rational Dissent, largely identified with Unitarianism by the early nineteenth century, were fiercely proud of their constitutional autonomy, there was a framework of cultural institutions which drew them together in book societies, college trusts and publishing networks. The circle of Norwich families centred on the Octagon Chapel added friendship to common intellectual and literary interests. These embraced the daughter of the famous Octagon minister Dr John Taylor, Susannah, the Opies, the Barbaulds; the antislavery poetess Mrs Barbauld was an Aikin daughter and made a link between antislavery and the liberal political journalism of her father and brother in the *Annual Review*. The Martineaus were also part of this cultivated group for whom antislavery was an aspect of their general liberalism. Such a circle as the Octagon, despite its special qualities, was connected with a broader network. In visiting Susannah Taylor whenever he was on circuit in East Anglia the barrister and antislavery literary journalist, Henry Crabb Robinson, was in part resuming the connections of his youth. His friend William Pattisson had been a pupil at Rochemont Barbauld's school near Diss and, although an Independent, was familiar with the Octagon circle. Pattisson and Robinson after their 'Jacobin' youth in Norwich maintained their friendship into more conservative middle age and bound together the remnants of the Norwich network with reform-minded nonconformity in the chapels of Suffolk, Essex and parts of Cambridgeshire. The Roscoe–Rathbone circle in Liverpool constituted a somewhat similar predominantly Unitarian intellectual–literary–reformist complex.[4]

Circles centring on prominent individuals could maintain and encourage common antislavery feeling. Like the Robinson–Pattisson connection they could also easily cross lines of religious affiliation. One such emanated from the friendship of Thomas Clarkson and the popular, and antislavery, poet Bernard Barton. A network extended to draw in sympathetic local Anglican clergymen in their part of Suffolk, Arthur and Jane Biddell (Clarkson's agent, a wealthy farmer and his wife) and, via Mrs Biddell's membership of the Ransome family, to the Quaker iron manufacturing and philanthropic family in Ipswich.

Cross-denominational association of this sort in particular localities was not uncommon and could be reinforced through collaborative reformist and philanthropic action as in the common efforts for moral and civic improvement of such Quaker and Unitarian families in Birmingham as the Cadburys, Lloyds, Kenricks and others. At the level of national leadership in antislavery the separate networks sketched above were structurally linked by the mediating roles of individuals or by marriage. Clarkson remained an Anglican and an evangelical but was extremely close to a host of Quaker reformers. William Smith's friendship with Clapham was strong enough to license their toleration of his Unitarian views and he kept them in touch with more liberal and heterodox elements. The Liverpool Quaker, James Cropper, married a daughter of Zachary Macaulay and after her death the widow of her brother, H.M. Macaulay, while another Cropper married a son of Lord Brougham.[5]

Perhaps even more than in the case of energising Anglican evangelical clergymen like William Marsh, in the ranks of evangelical nonconformity the powerful leadership of some ministers shaped the attitudes of chapel communities and led them into collaboration across denominational and church/chapel lines. Within the lively political and religious life of Leicester in the 1820s and 1830s the Baptist Mursells, father and son, shaped a commitment to missionary work and its support, antislavery and political liberalism and launched the young Congregationalist Edward Miall on his notable career in journalism and reformist religious politics. Davidoff and Hall have recently underlined not only the strong conception of ministerial leadership possessed by John Angell James at Carr's Lane in Birmingham – 'We occupy a very public station; like the angel standing in the sun we must be seen' – but demonstrated his ability to lead his chapel in alignment with Anglican reformers to work for antislavery, temperance and projects of moral benevolence within the community. These examples suggest that while antislavery could not become an explicit test of membership of chapel communities it did in many cases become a norm of memberships and of a minister's identity. The heavy congregational and denominational petitioning in the last years of slavery suggests this; so does the image of ranks of black-coated nonconformist ministers at the antislavery conventions of the 1830s. Antislavery thus had a further institutional base but it was thereby also vulnerable as regards united action to the outbreak of warfare amongst religious parties.[6]

Chapter 2 offered a short discussion of how a number of antislavery reformers derived an intellectual orientation towards reform from the different religious traditions sustaining antislavery. Yet even when this is added to the evidence of bonding and enabling structures of family, kin, friendships, religion and community sketched above, something is missing. That element is the *emotional* quality in the commitment of many individuals to the cause, a quality which contributed noticeably to the tone and texture of the internal life of the antislavery movement. The first generation especially in the history of organised abolitionism could not derive the quality of their commitment from pre-existing norms or groups. Individuals in that generation of whom we know most seem to have grappled uncertainly with how to deal with their growing understanding of and revulsion from the slave trade; sometimes it was almost to their own surprise that they arrived at a commitment sufficiently deep to devote a major portion of their time and energies to the cause.

It was not that evangelicals or Quakers or even more rational Christians doubted their ultimate dependence on Providence. A number of the earliest abolitionists, however, experienced a difficult and anxious passage before they recognised the particular *role* providentially required of them. In the case of the elder James Stephen's commitment to antislavery, it came after the experience of working in the West Indies as a lawyer, but more precisely, that experience helped direct into antislavery the expression of his gratitude 'for the infinite mercy of God' in extricating him from the depths of sin brought on by sexual passion and setting him on the path of prosperity and happiness. His language, in the remarkable autobiography about his young manhood written for his grandchildren, plays on the language of enslavement and emancipation.

> At length these bitter fruits of sin, and a sense of dependency on his Providence for the averting those dreadful consequences with which others were imminently threatened, brought me to the repentance and gave me a victory over those guilty passions by which I had been so long enslaved. He then heard my earnest indefatigable prayers and by a train of events the most impossible and unexpected released me from the cruel bondage in which the enemy of my soul had bound me.

The result was 'peace and happiness' and a commitment to antislavery work.[7]

Clarkson's account of his entry into his antislavery role stressed the long period of crisis in which he indecisively debated with himself and James Ramsay what to do. 'At length I yielded . . . in obedience I believe to a higher Power. And thus I can say that both on the moment of this resolution and for some time afterwards I had more sublime and happy feelings than at any former period of my life.' These pioneers had the happy assurance of providential selection for their tasks. Later abolitionists exemplified in Buxton and Cropper, though it might have seemed easier for them to adopt antislavery as a routine, not only maintained vital feeling in their commitment but possessed sufficient accompanying serenity – 'we have more than human help' – to accommodate setbacks and 'to triumph over the storms which surround them'. Appropriately the imminent passage of the emancipation legislation at the end of Wilberforce's life provoked in him feelings so strong that he wrote 'I have not time to open the Stopper of ye jar that hardly prevents the bursting forth of my [joyful?] feelings abt. Emancipation'.[8]

In the language of religious contemporaries abolitionists were people who experienced and expressed 'christian joyousness', secure in 'the divine authority of our principles.' It was the basis of a security which never allowed even the more worldly of them, like Brougham, to take seriously the possibility of ultimate defeat. Even when the obstacles seemed great there was 'no room for despair' and 'we may indulge the gratifying and cheering reflection . . . we may . . . in reality be on the very verge of its attainment'. The 1 August 1834 Wardlaw proclaimed a Jubilee day: 'Thousands that had slept in servitude awoke independent freemen . . . it was the sound of the *Jubilee* trumpet that awakened all the ecstasy of emotion'. The joy Wardlaw celebrated with his fellow reformers extended beyond the former slave as its object; the colonies which had been blighted by an 'offended God . . . frowning in vengeance' were to be transformed into prosperous lands. Britain itself had escaped retribution; Africa would assume its full role in the spread of Christian truth and the British example, awakening American emulation, would result in the two countries jointly shaming the rest of the world into ending bondage. In this version, abolitionist joy anticipated a qualitative transformation of history.[9]

Amongst Unitarian abolitionists an emotional quality in antislavery commitment was also present but it may often have had different origins from the antislavery of Evangelicals and Quakers. Unitarians were very conscious that they too had suffered discrimination; they were a group who, because of their heterodoxy, were 'everywhere spoken against'. This gave them sympathy for the victims of the slave trade and slavery and, as the abolitionist John Bowring stressed, formed a strong bond of union between them. In the revealing words of one antislavery minister, he and his fellow Unitarians were 'theological negroes'. In consequence they hoped for fellowship with others in the cause with particular ardour.

The Unitarian minister and editor Edwin Chapman underlined that desire to overcome separation when in his thanksgiving sermon on Emancipation Day in 1834 he proclaimed that it was the Christian principle evinced by *all* the sects and parties which had brought on the victory. In commemoration of the end of apprenticeship in 1838 John Relly Beard looked on behalf of religious liberals as much as had the evangelical Wardlaw to the 'genius of Christianity' producing future success in the US and the wider world.

The dangers of routine and passivity to the often joyful and serene spirit which infused abolitionists grew greater as direct British targets for the cause largely disappeared from the late 1830s onwards. When 'scarce anything [was] more likely to mar a . . . man's reputation than to be thought opposed or indifferent to the cause of abolition' but when slavery was a distant and foreign institution, the urge to respectability could predominate over the vital flame in antislavery. While the drama of the mass mobilisation phase remained, however, with its engendering of collective determination and the warmth of fellowship, rank-and-file abolitionists could shake off 'coldness and opposition' and 'Be steadfast. Be active'.[10]

A feeling commitment was also the continuing outcome of the rigorous self-scrutiny religious men and women undertook as a matter of course and especially in retrospect at the end of the year. The change of the calendar was a time to repair faults and omissions and vow rededication. Abolitionists provided themselves with a collective equivalent to the practice of personal scrutiny in their annual meetings. Leaders not only brought supporters up to date with the position of the cause but resolutions took the form of reiteration of basic commitments as well as referring to current developments. But the meetings could have greater resonance than this suggests and provide powerful reinforcement of a sense of fellowship. The 1824 annual meeting of the Anti-Slavery Society offers an appropriate example. The report was able to recount what had been done in the first year of effort of the newly-organised national campaign for emancipation but to stress continuity through reliance on the circulation of pamphlets by Wilberforce and Clarkson; reformers were 'thus enabled to proceed under the conduct of the same veteran Champions who had first led the battle against the African Slave Trade and who had pursued it to its final extinction'. James Stephen provided encouragement at signs of progress in the operation of amelioration measures in the Crown Colonies but required recommitment from the representatives of the cause in the work still to be done, particularly in pressing change upon the legislative colonies. The range of speakers called upon seemed consciously designed to stress Christian collaboration within the movement and equally its vitality across generations. In addition to Stephen, Wilberforce represented Clapham and the Anglican evangelical veterans; William Smith registered Unitarian liberalism and William Allen the Friends as components of the movement. The young T.B. Macaulay, like Baptist Noel earlier in the meeting, consciously took upon himself the mantle of a new generation 'who, although they have not contributed to your past success, are ambitious to participate in your future labours . . . the good cause shall not therefore want fresh champions, nor, if it must be so, fresh martyrs'. It was almost superfluous after the 'loud cheering which lasted several minutes' for Calthorpe to assure his fellow abolitionists that victory was certain if other members of the new generation descended from old advocates of the cause showed similar energy.[11]

Such occasions were constructed to confirm the high value of the cause, to energise the ranks and maintain and strengthen the internal links in the movement. They did as much if not more for the internal cohesion of antislavery as in impressing the outside world. The gatherings were devices to construct a sense of a vital present for the movement linked by the 1820s to a successful past and with the potential for a triumphant future. Abolitionists thus presented themselves to the world and to each other as part of a continuous progress despite the significant disjunctures in the movement's history discussed in the last chapter (pp.65–6).

Important additional sustenance for this cohesive 'myth' of antislavery came in the deployment by abolitionists of their own history prior to the main drive for emancipation. To substantiate this point it is proposed to offer brief readings of aspects of both Thomas Clarkson's *History* and Prince Hoare's *Memoirs of Granville Sharp Esq.* which drew heavily not only on Sharp's papers but accounts and memories of him by fellow abolitionists. Clarkson believed that a narrative of abolition produced not only 'the most pleasing and grateful sensations' but that lessons relevant to future success emerged. Encouragement to reformers to maintain their commitment would bring its reward since 'no virtuous effort is ever ultimately lost' but such effort depended upon 'a union of wise and virtuous individuals' who recognised the providentially sanctioned nature of their cause. Virtually the whole of the first half of his first volume was devoted by Clarkson to discussing individuals and intellectual and religious traditions whose contributions to antislavery converged in unity in the organisation of the committee of 1787. It was a body defined in terms of its unity and perseverance, bringing together all the

> classes of which I have been giving a history . . . a committee which labouring afterwards with Mr. Wilberforce as a parliamentary head did, under Providence, in the space of twenty years, contribute to put an end to a trade which . . . was the greatest practical evil that ever afflicted the human race.

Collectively its dedication, despite all difficulties, constituted an unimpeachable example. Each individual abolitionist demonstrated the victory of the better over the worse side of his or her nature, of 'pure power' over interest, but some particular individuals elicited especial admiration and reverence. Abolitionists began to create their own pantheon of heroes, veneration of whom contributed both to longitudinal solidarity over time and horizontal solidarity between groups. Of Sharp, taking his lead from Wilberforce, Prince Hoare wrote 'there are few who will not find him to have been one [a hero] and who would not exult in possessing among the members of their family such a relative'. Clarkson stressed Sharp's priority in the cause and his unwearying employment of talents and substance. He was also presented as exemplifying the qualities for unifying supporters of philanthropic activity, 'a churchman in faith, in charity a universalist'. Clarkson's narrative revealed his own perseverance and commitment until exhaustion and financial difficulty overtook him in 1794 and Hoare fastened upon Clarkson's continuing 'zeal'. If chronological and organisational priority were attributed to Sharp and Clarkson, Wilberforce emerged unambiguously as the third member of an heroic triumvirate whose efforts crowned with success the struggle for abolition. The moment when he was drawn in as parliamentary leader was 'an event . . . which gave preponderance to the scale of African freedom'. His talents and character perfectly qualified him for his role and his motives expressed 'an awful sense of his duty as a Christian'. Divisions between them abolitionists saw, unlike later, as being purely functional; the *cause* was harmonious. Such heroic examples, concluded Brougham, looking both backwards and forwards in 1822, permitted reformers to have confidence for the future.[12]

This early writing by abolitionists on their own history also gave them assurance that they were vindicating their country. Clarkson and Hoare interpreted Sharp's success in the Somerset case as 'restoring the beauty of our constitution' and preventing 'the continuance of our national disgrace'. Collectively antislavery showed 'no country has shone with more true lustre than our own'. At a time of 'awful crisis, when constitutions of kingdoms are on the point of dissolution the stain of the blood of Africa is no longer upon us' thus removing 'a mill-stone about our necks, ready to sink us to perdition'.[13]

Abolitionists marked their respect for their heroes in both more and less personal forms. Clarkson and Wilberforce, partly because they lived for so long, frequently sent off autographs with motto attached and Clarkson received and met requests for locks of his thinning hair. Antislavery medals, work bags, albums and china also circulated, sometimes no doubt bearing images of the heroes.[14]

At the time of the 1834 emancipation, as also at the cessation of apprenticeship in 1838, abolitionists enacted rituals of triumph and unity, though it was significant for the future that they now acknowledged differences and, ironically, different abolitionists performed different rituals indicative of unity. On 1 August 1834, after attending the wedding of his daughter Priscilla who had been such a tireless assistant to her father, Thomas Fowell Buxton and his gentlemen associates attended a 'grand public dinner' to celebrate the end of slavery with toasts and speeches. But the Buxton clan also saw emancipation as a family triumph. On Emancipation Day Buxton was presented by his family with a seal, salver and vase – the two latter inscribed with the motto 'Safe and Satisfactory'. In a flurry of further presentations Louisa Hoare handed to Buxton's wife, Hannah, a small silver cup commemorating her partnership with her husband in the abolition of slavery, while the uncles and aunts handed to Priscilla an inscribed small waiter to commemorate her role. At a celebratory meeting at West Bromwich abolitionists passed a resolution of gratitude to Buxton while the city of Plymouth conferred its freedom upon him. For many abolitionists emancipation was celebrated by raising Buxton to the pantheon of heroes.[15]

Birmingham on 1 and 2 August 1838 saw a celebration to mark the end of apprenticeship. It did not lack its central figure, for Joseph Sturge was prominent, but he was located in the events in relation to enlightened nonconformity and the power of provincial community rather than gentry family and parliamentary class. Gifts were part of the occasion too: 3,500 children gathered in the Town Hall on the morning of 1 August, 3,000 of them from the Baptist Sunday schools and the rest from the Lancasterian and Infant Sunday schools, and were each given a booklet commemorating the end of apprenticeship. On the front of the booklet was the picture of a white man giving instruction to blacks and inside prominence was given to missionary work, particularly that of the Baptist mission to the West Indies. Sturge's role in ending apprenticeship through his visit to the West Indies was picked out. After a service of thanksgiving the children were given a 'substantial meal of bread and beef'; to observers 'the whole scene was one highly creditable to the philanthropy and liberality of the people of Birmingham'. After the meal the children marched in procession to a patch of ground where a foundation stone for new school rooms in commemoration of emancipation was laid by 'the friend of the negro, the friend of the children and the friend of man, JOSEPH STURGE Esq.'. That evening and the next day there were speeches in which Sturge and Birmingham received particular notice. The celebration in the following year on 1 August was even more explicitly designed to allow the younger generation to experience being abolitionists. Tickets were distributed by William Morgan, Sturge's colleague, through Sunday school teachers.

> It is considered of the first importance that young persons should receive correct and permanent impressions on this subject and to assist in securing that object it is intended to exhibit a model of a SLAVE SHIP which was recently captured upon the coast of Africa.[16]

The deliberate juxtaposition of these rituals of celebration has been done to suggest that the 1830s were years of transition in antislavery culture in which occasions of unity indicated growing divergences within the 'movement culture'. Thus when Clarkson spoke movingly to the gathered World Convention of 1840 he was intended to symbolise continuity and provide in what he stood for a unifying focus. Benjamin Haydon's painting of the scene was planned to reinforce this:

> In the centre is Clarkson, in his own natural attitude concluding his speech. Behind, beneath and about him are the oldest and dearest friends of the cause – whilst a liberated slave, now a delegate, is looking up to Clarkson with deep interest, and the hand of friendship is resting with affection on his arm, in fellowship and protection.

At the 1843 Convention Haydon's picture was hung at one end of the room; above the chairman was a portrait of Clarkson and opposite it 'A Scene on the African Coast'. Yet in 1840 it was Joseph Sturge, having emerged as the leading figure of one faction of abolitionists, who guided Clarkson to and from the platform; Haydon's picture represented an exclusion from full recognition in the movement of some elements, especially women, on ideological grounds, and in 1843 some abolitionists refused to attend the Convention, implicitly denying Sturge's BFASS the right to claim the antislavery heritage.[17]

It is now time to deal more directly with the tensions evident in the internal culture of the movement; they were never entirely absent but the strains they imposed became increasingly hard to manage in the 1830s. By that decade different religious and social elements had become prominent in antislavery from those who had taken the initiative in earlier years. Traditional leadership of the kind provided by the landed classes had never been significant in antislavery. Mercantile, commercial and professional elements of the middle stratum with a sprinkling of manufacturers and, at a more local level, tradesmen, artisans and dissenting ministers were the sort of people who were active. Initially, if they belonged to the Church of England, they were likely to be of the evangelical tendency so disturbing to comfortable Anglican parsons and laymen. Many of them were not even that but nonconformists of both evangelical and rational and liberal kinds. The years 1806-7, however, marked the triumph of social as well as political respectability as more socially prominent names became associated with the African Institution and antislavery more generally. *Political* leadership of the cause remained, into the 1830s, in the hands primarily of the upper echelons of the Anglican middle class but mass support depended upon the activism of evangelical dissent down to and including the artisan class. By the 1830s, however, much of the old leadership was dead or retiring; Stephen died in 1832, Wilberforce in 1833, William Smith in 1835, Zachary Macaulay in 1838, Cropper in 1840 and Clarkson was in his seventies. There became room for younger, different, mainly nonconformist leaders to assert themselves, not necessarily by parliamentary means.

As these opportunities appeared, so at the same time the lines of religious party and sect hardened. Even within Anglican evangelicalism fissures appeared. Older, Clapham Sect–*Christian Observer* evangelicals who had always believed in the necessity of good deeds in the world for forming the true Christian heart, increasingly in the 1820s and 1830s regretted amongst younger 'ranters' and 'noisy professors', followers of the histrionic Edward Irving, a relative complacency about public activity beyond the conversion of individual souls. James Stephen regretted the paucity of active evangelicals combining true religious piety with cultivation 'in heart and understanding'. It was a lament which registered the weakening of a moderate, socially philanthropic evangelicalism in the face of the more strident and ultimately more bigoted brand associated with Irving and Drummond outside the church and the Recordites within it. This awareness contributed to the sense evangelicals in the Clapham tradition had of disorder within the church whose position itself appeared threatened by economic, social and political change. The obvious questions for churchmen were how best to improve order within the church and how to impress the church upon society. Whether their inclination was to enhance the symbiotic relationship of church and state or, for those of them tending towards support of Tractarianism, to reunify the church by distancing it from the state while reinforcing respect for its ordinance, hierarchy and 'Catholic' traditions, nonconformists were likely to perceive either process as antithetical to their status, rights and interests. Their numerical expansion, elaboration of denominational and educational institutions and practice of evangelical united front philanthropy gave many of them the confidence to undertake an increasingly militant struggle for equality of religious status under the law, culminating in the case of a growing number of advocacy of disestablishment as the logical end of the voluntaryist principle. An aroused evangelical nonconformity, however, in turn alarmed and alienated many of the religious liberals amongst the Unitarians and those Friends resistant to enhanced religious authority through creed, and in the office of ministers as a result of evangelical tendencies in their own Society. In these years the Unitarians were forced out of the Dissenting Deputies and had to fight for control of their chapel property against other dissenters; tensions and fractures recurrently emerged within the Society of Friends. In such a climate the emergence of provincial nonconformity within antislavery imposed severe strains on the cohesion and common assumptions of the movement.[18]

Even in 1831, at a moment of mass mobilisation, George Thompson on tour encountered conflict between dissenters in Dartford and then in Faversham confronted such distance between church and chapel abolitionists that he doubted the possibility of a lecture which could draw in cross-denominational support. Sectarian tensions within antislavery also provided the terms within which hostility to, or criticism of, individuals or groups of abolitionists were expressed. As John Scoble, with his intolerantly rigid evangelical attitudes, rose to become a prominent administrator and organiser of antislavery bodies, he became a target as a sectarian who had apparently denounced one liberal-minded Quaker reformer as 'degenerate' for suggesting that the heathen might be treated with mercy. He left the impression on Richard Webb of 'a selfwilled, tyrannically minded, narrow-souled, clever bigot'. Indeed in Webb's opinion, by the beginning of the 1840s sect, party and worldliness all undermined the antislavery movement as a whole.

> Touch *church* or touch *party* in your antislavery efforts and all
> their zeal for the slave would be scattered in the twinkling of an
> eye . . . The London Committee [of the BFASS] could not help
> being what they were . . . They loved titles and titled people –
> they are no non-resistants and their vision is clouded by wealth
> and worldly importance – though there are many kindhearted
> and munificent men among them.[19]

From less radical perspectives than Webb's also the religious and political zeal of party seemed at the root of controversy within antislavery. The venerable Clarkson, for many reformers the remaining patriarch of the movement, was not exempt by 1838–40. There is no doubt that in earlier years Clarkson's relations with some of the Claphamites had occasionally been strained. In terms of Henry Thornton's antithesis between reputation and religion and the need to sacrifice the former to the latter if it aided the antislavery cause, Clarkson had sometimes seemed too attached to reputation. He was also for much of the middle part of his life financially sufficiently insecure to look to the personal aid and patronage of others, including Claphamites, from whose psychologically stabilising intimacies he was excluded. His importunities at times embarrassed or irritated Wilberforce, Stephen and Macaulay who all also doubted his judgement on some issues. They may have believed too that he appeared too prominently in his own *History* – the desire for reputation again. However, these occasional tensions had been kept private until Robert and Samuel Wilberforce chose to make some of them public in the life of their father they published in 1838. In the view of private and public critics of the Wilberforce sons there was more than filiopietism at issue in their charge that Clarkson claimed leadership in the cause when their father was entitled to it; they suggested Clarkson had been to all intents and purposes a paid agent of the Abolition Committee. Sara Coleridge saw the Wilberforce sons claiming antislavery for their brand of Clapham evangelicalism against Clarkson's historical interpretation which had literally offered a diagram of numerous branches contributing to the cause.

> The Evangelical party will perhaps continue to exalt their hero as *partially* as *parties* always do – but the members of it will act thus only so far as they are possessed by party spirit, rather than by the pure spirit of the doctrines which they hold in common with their so-called Catholic opponents, whom adversaries style popish.

Henry Crabb Robinson equally perceived a party spirit at work but, noting the younger Wilberforces' drift away from their father's associates, defined it differently. 'Highly Conservative in politics, they are also High Churchmen'; their sectarian spirit focused on Clarkson because, although a churchman, he had been an apologist for Quakerism and in earlier days as an enthusiast for civil as well as religious liberty 'he belonged to a very liberal class' and showed support for the French Revolution.[20]

Clarkson himself, his wife and old associates such as William Smith and Henry Brougham did not rest on the charge of sectarian and party spirit but reverted to the earlier image of the antislavery movement as effectively integrating the diverse roles of individuals and groups into a successful unity. Specifically Wilberforce and Clarkson were presented as reliant upon each other's efforts respectively in parliamentary tactics and debate and in the provision of information and witnesses. Clarkson had pre-dated Wilberforce in organised work against the slave trade and had taken the initiative, it was generally agreed, in raising the issue with him. But Clarkson himself stressed Wilberforce's suitability 'for the *conduct* and *management* of the antislave trade affair' as head of the parliamentary effort. The clinching argument for Clarkson himself, however, and probably for many of the older generation of abolitionists, was the providentialist one. 'This powerful combination and union of men and measures' could not have prevailed 'if God had not bestowed His blessing on the work'. It followed that no individual should boast of his role 'but be thankful that he has been permitted to be useful'. This was the fundamental ground of the strong emotional dislike of older abolitionists for internal polemics in the movement and distaste for any derogation from a transcendent commitment to the cause.[21]

The younger James Stephen in essays in the *Edinburgh Review* in 1838 and 1843, later republished and expanded in *Essays in Ecclesiastical Biography* (1849), took up the tradition of abolitionist historical writing on antislavery and was joined in it by his younger brother, Sir George Stephen, with *Anti-Slavery Recollections* (1854). Both were evidently embarrassed by the attack on Clarkson and yet both betray a shift away from the interpretation of the antislavery movement as integrative and inclusive. James Stephen would not allow an exaggeration of Clarkson's contribution but saw the historical memory of antislavery preserved in the names of Wilberforce and Clarkson 'not by any human caprice or fortuitous accident but by the selection and appointment of the Master they served'. Similarly circumspect, George Stephen granted Clarkson priority in time but underlined how Wilberforce's prominence enabled him to make a public issue of the slave trade in a way Clarkson could never have done. Clarkson for many years, though, acted as Wilberforce's 'abolition walking stick'.[22]

This evenhandedness in relation to individuals was, in the case of both writers, however, set within an emphasis on the predominant contribution of Clapham to antislavery. James Stephen saw abolition in 1807 as having world-wide consequences as well as setting in train 'by slow but inevitable steps' the extinction of British colonial slavery. 'The mainsprings' of these developments 'as far as human agency is concerned' were found in the Clapham sect. Antislavery history thus entailed building a monument to the sect. George Stephen, moreover, agreed with his brother that, at least in the earlier stages of antislavery, exceptional individuals rather than reform associations shaped the movement for change. While James devoted considerable space to William Wilberforce and less to the elder Stephen, Macaulay and others, George especially underlined the work of his father and Macaulay who were, he claimed, the only long-standing abolitionists who had had direct experience of the effects of the slave trade and slavery and who were portrayed as replacing Clarkson as the 'crutches' of the parliamentary antislavery leadership by the 1820s. That leadership itself fell to Buxton, he argued, as a protégé of Clapham.[23]

George Stephen was not so poor an historian as to refuse credit to other parliamentarians such as Lushington, Brougham and Denman who could not be accounted Claphamites, nor to nonconformity in the country, nor to Emmanuel Cooper the Quaker for his work in the Agency nor Cropper and Sturge for their financial support of the Agency. Two further features of his narrative, none the less, register that it was composed in the changed atmosphere of 'late' antislavery. Developments in antislavery – both the spread of local associations and the splitting off of the Agency campaign – were portrayed as only occurring when they were functionally necessary and productive of minimal conflict. At the same time they were consistent with a Clapham-style leadership. The African Institution, when the time came for public agitation, was unfitted for the task because of its direction by 'men of rank and high position'. It was Macaulay, in the George Stephen account, who, through the Anti-Slavery Society, substituted the power of association. The effective creation of an urgent mass antislavery opinion, however, was dependent upon the efforts of the Agency committee and its lecturers. But after 'the first somewhat angry alienation', apart from Macaulay who remained doubtful, the honesty of the old antislavery leadership and of the Young England Agency men enabled them 'to play successfully into each other's hands. They worked separately but they worked harmoniously together'. The Agency committee was not hostile to Buxton, except for some occasional attenders, and Cooper and the working core 'maintained their faithful allegiance to the leaders to the last'. This was a rather partial view of the critical phase of the antislavery movement but it presented a satisfactorily smooth expansion beyond the 'aristocracy' of antislavery to the successful incorporation of provincial respectability in an essentially religious endeavour and led by Claphamites and their heirs.[24]

The second feature of George Stephen's narrative which gave it a markedly ideological cast was its distancing of the movement from the kind of radicalism and militant nonconformity of the 1830s and 1840s many of his readers associated with antislavery. One of the major objectives of the account was to reapportion credit within the movement since much of it had been misappropriated by those who had done little or only appeared after emancipation in 1834. Whether as a direct result of this or not, the treatment of the antislavery agent and later rhetorician of radicalism, George Thompson, was noticeably cool; he was eloquent but lacked education and was thus in 'entire ignorance of the tone of that high society from which the great bulk of our parliamentary men are taken'. He had been a 'lamentable failure' as Radical MP for Tower Hamlets between 1847 and 1852. By contrast Stephen thought the Rev. Baldwin had been much more effective as an agent being 'connected by birth with the higher orders' and because, as a religious man (which by implication Thompson was not), he lectured from the heart. More remarkably, George Stephen was virtually silent on the later antislavery commonly associated with aspects of radical politics and militant nonconformity. The cause was defined as essentially terminating in 1834; the BFASS was thus marginal to the tradition of antislavery; it was conducted, with few exceptions, by 'men utterly unknown in the great Antislavery battle'. Even Sturge, whom Stephen cast in a minor role in the heroic days, had been 'so headstrong in his peculiar notions of right and wrong' that he had embarrassed the Young England abolitionists in the 1830s and such 'eccentric principles' as his pacifism had, in Stephen's judgement, led the BFASS into error by opposing the continuation of the squadron policy in West African waters in the 1840s. The BFASS, let alone its more radical critics, was in effect portrayed as a late and illegitimate claimant to membership in the line of antislavery bodies. This was history whose tendency was neither cohesive nor energising. Rather it attempted to lay the movement to rest.[25]

With such evidence of divergent religious feeling, and at a time when antislavery was no longer disciplined by the immediate and agreed task of overthrowing colonial slavery, it is not surprising that organisational pluralism became a feature of the reform culture of abolitionists. This was a tendency reinforced by the impact of American abolitionist divisions in Britain from 1840 onwards. The different bodies mentioned in chapter 3 followed different routes to the objective of a free-labour world. They were not only evidence of disagreement amongst abolitionists but perceived by contemporaries to have different religious and political characteristics. Buxton initiated his Civilization Society in part because he feared that to wait for antislavery principles to permeate foreign societies of slaveholders, which he believed to be BFASS policy, 'would cost us half a century, and that implies the sacrifice of twenty five millions of the human race'. Equally, however, Sturge found the Civilization Society's policy 'inadequate to meet the case but as it involves a violation of my peace principles I can take no part in it'. Abolitionists who had earlier given their commitment to an integrated movement still hoped to avoid open conflict despite these tensions. Clarkson wanted to co-operate with Buxton and J.J. Gurney to 'endeavour to preserve harmony between the two Societies' and indicated his ecumenical support for other organisations advocating black improvement and different lines of attack on slavery: he mentioned Oberlin

College, the Society for Free Negroes in Canada and the British India Society (BIS). Gurney, engaged in starting auxiliaries of both the Civilization Society and the BFASS in Norfolk, urged influential figures in the county to support both. Buxton and Sturge both wished each other's efforts well and hoped they would be complementary.[26]

Such hopes, however, were likely to be fragile. Buxton's group was associated with 'great names' and, in some eyes, predominantly Tory. The Civilization Society more deliberately went out for bipartisan support and one result was that the six Conservative MPs who belonged to only one antislavery body chose to give their support to it. In attempting to maintain a broad political base and in holding together the traditions of moderate evangelical Anglicanism and moderate dissent the Buxton group sought 'a Wilberforce station' but in changed circumstances. Those circumstances included the increasingly expressed distaste of more extreme evangelical Anglicans for collaboration with nonconformists and a tendency of such people towards Toryism. Buxton, perhaps despite himself, grew anxious not to alienate Tory support, even if that meant silencing more liberal voices. In effect the Clapham tradition was no longer a viable model in the Civilization Society by 1840.

Some evidence has already been offered in this and the previous chapter of the rise of provincial radical dissent within antislavery; much of it was channelled into the BFASS from its beginnings in 1839. To one old abolitionist in 1840 the annual meeting of the BFASS was 'only composed of whig radicals' and marked a break from the political and religious ecumenicism of the antislavery tradition. Despite Gurney's effort in Norfolk, in a number of other localities local abolitionists could not find enough support for two organisations and BFASS supporters argued against auxiliaries for Buxton's society.[27]

The British India Society had no longer a life than Buxton's group (both were defunct by 1843) but its brief existence indicated further fragmentation in the internal culture of the movement. Its adherents were often politically radical and had religious outlooks tending to the liberal or antinomian. At its core were Joseph Pease of Darlington, head of the junior branch of the philanthropic and entrepreneurial family, and his daughter, Elizabeth. With her father she matched sympathy for disaffected working men with devotion to the cause of West Indian freedmen, American slaves and the indigenous population of India. George Thompson gave his rhetorical gifts to the cause for a time. But the BIS can also be seen as the project of a dissident

101

Quakerism which led Elizabeth Pease Nichol to leave the Friends on her marriage; the Peases found collaborators in the Dubliner Richard Webb whose contempt for the 'form and conventionalisms' of British reformers has already been indicated and his Unitarian associates such as James Haughton. That the BIS was a mixture of unconventional religion and radical politics was further underlined by the support of Garrison and his emissaries from the United States; British India development as a way of undermining British dependence on American cotton was equally for them part of a package, which included association with 'moral force' Chartists and hostility to evangelical 'sectarianism' in antislavery in the form of the BFASS, a view they held despite Sturge's middle-class political radicalism.

American abolitionist divisions translated to Britain had a lingering power in the 1840s and 1850s to maintain organisational friction between the London committee of the BFASS and provincial groups faithful to Garrison and hostile to the British national organisation's links with the evangelical circles of Lewis Tappan and his associates in America. Yet, loyalty to distant American factions apart, religious enmities in Britain helped split abolitionists and also had much to do with the conviction of anti-BFASS radicals that the *Antislavery Reporter* gave a distorted and very partial view of the antislavery scene in both Britain and America. It contributed to the decision of the Unitarian Dr John Estlin to fund the alternative *Anti-Slavery Advocate*, edited by Webb and beginning publication in 1852.[28]

It would, however, be too simple to portray antislavery after the late 1830s as purely a scene of contending sects more concerned with maintaining their own kinds of purity than achieving anything practical. All abolitionists in the 1840s and 1850s recognised their organisational weakness and the barrier to influence created by the widespread assumption that the main task of British abolitionism was completed. The different antislavery bodies provided much weaker foci for antislavery identity, whether they were local or national in aspiration, than the overarching organisation of the heroic days of the movement. Thus paradoxically organisational loyalties as such were less likely to be the source of permanent, unchanging estrangement of abolitionists from each other. There was some room for individuals and groups to experiment with limited co-operation across factional lines if they could temporarily forget their religious and sometimes political differences. This in turn was possible when abolitionists were provided with the occasional opportunity, by factors exterior to the small British antislavery world, to break through the torpor and indifference of opinion and mobilise popular enthusiasm of a kind not seen since the 1830s.

The rousing campaign for free trade in the 1840s impinged upon many abolitionists especially when proposals to equalise and reduce duties on sugar entering Britain, whether it originated in free-labour or slave-labour economies, were put forward. The result was not merely a blurring but a confusion, of normal factional loyalties. The BFASS divided between a Sturgeite majority advocating a continued discrimination in favour of free-labour sugar and a minority, mainly of West Countrymen, for complete free trade in sugar. Some anti-BFASS radicals, especially the Dublin circle of Webb and Haughton, supported the majority position but some of their usual British allies in support of the Garrisonians assumed their normal stance hostile to the Broad Street committee of the BFASS.[29]

More positively, both the BFASS and most of its critics in England and Scotland, though not some of the more circumspect Scots abolitionists, sounded off powerfully against the Free Church's financial reliance on southern slaveholders after its break from the Church of Scotland in 1843. The great occasion, however, of commitment to the cause transcending factional divisions came with the opportunity provided by Mrs Stowe's visit to Britain in 1853 after the enormous impact of *Uncle Tom's Cabin*. 'From the Peer to the Peasant the whole country seem boiling with indignation' recorded the Edinburgh Quaker, Henry Wigham. Although initially the visit revived divisions over attitudes to Garrison and his ideas, so great was antislavery enthusiasm that abolitionists of all kinds took the occasion to publicise the nature of American slavery and raise funds throughout the country for Mrs Stowe to employ against the southern system in the way she thought best. Mrs Stowe's impact through her book also produced the Stafford House Address from the aristocratic coterie around the Duchess of Sutherland and Lord Shaftesbury. Its inadequacies as an antislavery statement produced remarkable agreement across the range of abolitionist sentiment. The new young secretary of the BFASS, Louis Chamerovzow, described the aristocratic group as one whose antislavery feelings 'had not simply been re-awakened but in many instances actually created by Mrs. Stowe's work', distancing such newcomers from those who had laboured long in the cause. The Broad Street group, the radicals in Bristol normally critical of the BFASS, and Harriet Martineau, attacked the Stafford House preference for an amelioration policy in America as a retreat from the fundamental principle of immediatism.

Whatever their other differences, good middle-class reformers would not countenance such ideological backsliding or remain passive before fashionable aristocratic interventions.[30]

The reawakening of interest in slavery prompted by Mrs Stowe's writing and her visit to Britain thus encouraged some co-operation, or at least recognition that parallel action based on elements of agreement was taking place amongst different groups of abolitionists. One other factor converted this blurring of factional lines into a quite serious attempt at mutual reassessment of their relations by these groups; a younger generation of reformers, particularly personified in the secretary of the BFASS from 1852, L.A. Chamerovzow, and George Thompson's son-in-law, the journalist Frederick Chesson, were willing to try to overcome the hostilities inherited from the previous generation. They lacked any direct involvement in the origins of those hostilities and were clear-eyed about the depleted resources with which they had to work to arouse a usually indifferent public. Chamerovzow's succession to the long-serving John Scoble, particularly detested by critics of the BFASS, was itself conducive to aspirations for better relations, hopes which Chamerovzow built on by undertaking as editor of the *Anti-Slavery Reporter* to report abolitionist efforts in Britain and America whoever undertook them. Signs of the times appeared in a number of different places. J.B. Estlin, the Unitarian friendly to the Garrisonians, responded from Bristol to Chamerovzow's openness and in April 1853 gave his support to the BFASS, though Richard Webb remained sceptical of the possibilities of real co-operation. Mary Estlin's Bristol and Clifton Ladies' Anti-Slavery Society also warmed to the changed tone of Broad Street although they had broken from them barely a year earlier. Another inveterate opponent, William Smeal, still secretary of the Glasgow Emancipation Society, told Chamerovzow that he was willing to organise a meeting in Edinburgh during a peace convention to discuss a movement towards unity in antislavery ranks. At that meeting it was concluded that while a future conference on unity had to be based on a recognition that some differences of emphasis would always exist, they need not disrupt harmony. Thompson, making a tour of the Lancashire cotton belt, continued to regard himself as independent in late 1853 but promised Chamerovzow, 'My exhortations shall be to unite upon broad principles for a common object.' In the same year in both Leeds and Manchester stumbling efforts were made to overcome distrust and form new antislavery organisations uniting all adherents. The case of Manchester is particularly significant because, although the project started well, failure foreshadowed unsuccessful efforts to establish a single organisation nationally. A preliminary meeting in Manchester in October 1853 got the support of the BFASS committee; when an inaugural gathering was held Sturge and Thompson spoke from the same platform and it was resolved that the Manchester Anti-Slavery Union should become an auxiliary of the BFASS. The common ground Chamerovzow sketched out was a commitment to working for the importation of free-labour cotton for the Lancashire mills and a shared desire to isolate American churchmen who were not firmly antislavery. Thompson in turn deliberately recalled the days of an integrated and successful movement by praising Sturge's work a generation earlier with Wilberforce and Clarkson. All seemed set for an experiment in unity. Within a few months these hopes were dashed when a majority of the Manchester committee insisted on recognising an American evangelical, the Rev. Fred Hemming, as an official agent to raise money for the anti-Garrisonian abolitionists in America although he only had the general support of Lewis Tappan and apparently regarded the Garrisonians and their British sympathisers as 'infidel abolitionists'. The result was a schism by the Thompson–Chesson group and the formation by them of the short-lived North of England Anti-Slavery and India Reform League.

The American factor and the continued strength of a spirit of religious intolerance had proved decisive in Manchester and in 1854 they were equally to be central in the failure to find a single national organisational focus for antislavery commitment. An anniversary meeting in Manchester on 1 August 1854 showed willingness to attend a unity conference in London in November although it was under the aegis of the BFASS. The Estlins hoped that at best a merger of the BFASS and others could be achieved. Their fellow liberal Unitarian, S.A. Steinthal, however, thought the old Broad Street leadership, 'these orthodox gentlemen', were as intolerant as ever to reformers of his persuasion 'but to others they are all light'. The Glasgow Emancipation Society greeted the conference with hope but also the requirement that the antislavery platform should be of the 'broadest and most Catholic principle' avoiding 'sectarian feeling and jealousy'. In other words, different elements in antislavery approached the London conference with various doubts and some hopes but with fundamental positions unaltered.

The conference was broadly enough based to include both Samuel Gurney and the intemperate American Garrisonian, Parker Pillsbury, but although the BFASS committee supported a resolution encouraging American abolitionists of all persuasions, it refused to eat enough of its past words to single out for particular mention the American Anti-Slavery Society, associated with the Garrison's 'heretical' notions. Thompson encouraged acceptance of this compromise since in private talks with Sturge he became convinced that in return its critics would get most of what they wanted from the BFASS. Manoeuvring by the Unitarian from Liverpool, Francis Bishop, got a statement from Chamerovzow that no resolution repudiating the American Anti-Slavery Society was on the books of the BFASS. Thompson stressed that the *sine qua non* of future co-operation was that 'no man's or woman's cooperation is to be accepted or rejected by a reference to his or her peculiar religious or non-religious, political or non-political views'. He appears to have believed that this had been conceded in substance 'by the admission of all sects and all sexes, unquestioned to the Conference'. He implied, in other words, that the BFASS had been brought a long way since its restrictive outlook had so divided the 1840 World Convention. Others, notably Webb and the Unitarian minister William James from Clifton, were more concerned with the failure to get open sanction of the American Anti-Slavery Society; to obtain, that is, a repudiation by the BFASS of its own past conduct. This reflects the almost total concern with American abolitionism of some reformers as well as a liberalism about religious matters which regretted even the refusal to allow the unbeliever Joseph Barker to speak at the earlier Manchester conference. Such radicalism demanded too much, because there was little popular momentum to be gained from harmony through compromise, once the first flush of enthusiasm engendered by Mrs Stowe passed. Estlin now withdrew from the BFASS, demonstrating for one last time his use as a barometer of sentiment in intra-reform relations. Thompson, Chesson and Chamerovzow remained personally friendly but a later effort at co-operation in 1859 between the BFASS and Thompson's London Emancipation Committee produced more recriminations. The result was that at the end of the decade British critics of the BFASS, few as they were, tried to draw together once again. They reasserted their support of the American Anti-Slavery Society, sought links between their local groups and accepted the logic of being a minor adjunct of a movement whose dynamic lay in another country.[31] Even as other abolitionists refused that logic they were unable to find any means of reasserting the vitality of the emancipation cause and of recovering an integrated antislavery culture such that loyalty to their identity as abolitionists took precedence over religious and political differences. Only with the impact of the American Civil War did many abolitionists again transcend their local conflicts.

5

ABOLITIONISTS AND THE MIDDLE-CLASS REFORM COMPLEX

This chapter proposes to extend and refine discussion of the cultural identity of antislavery reformers by analysing their relation to various kinds of reform. The opportunities afforded by abolitionists' positive identification with philanthropic, moral and other reform activities, which mainly drew support at the level of subscription and organisational activity from the middle classes, are several. It becomes possible to understand on a broader social canvas both the characteristic preoccupations of reformers in the separate religious–intellectual traditions and their overlap and close collaboration on a number of questions. Because it is apparent that joint endeavour was often especially effective on issues within individual communities, the product of multiple layers of interlocking activity, a sketch of a broad front of reformers in action on specific terrain is feasible. Focus on antislavery within the middle-class reform complex also prompts recognition that parallel to its own international pretensions were other movements with ambitions for moral and material reformation abroad. Similarly, building on Britain's enhanced international political and economic position at the end of the Napoleonic Wars, English reformers sought extension of their influence through links with like reformers in other countries and through the moral and ideological penetration of territories under British rule. As abolitionists and proponents of other projects of betterment, reform circles were equally progressively permeated by liberal economic ideas, whether derived from the political economists or evangelical pundits like Thomas Chalmers; they were thus encouraged to develop connections between the new international economic order and their ambitions for improvement far beyond Britain. Some reformers at least essayed a moral reach no secular British political leader would have attempted.

Sketching such a range of concerns and activity demands an

explanation of why, to the abolitionists involved, they seemed to fit so naturally together. From the longer-term perspective of the historian, what credence can be given to different, and in some senses alternative, hypotheses advanced in recent years; that the broad and common front of reformers either had an agenda for or produced the result of social control of the English lower classes at home and legitimation of imperialism abroad; that the complex of reforms was a major way in which the relatively benevolent ideology and practice of liberalism came to exercise a powerful influence in Britain and the wider world?

The multiplicity of reform interests pursued by abolitionists is traceable from the earliest years of the period covered by this study. Amongst Anglican evangelicals of the Clapham Sect and their associates the theological and intellectual framework discussed in chapter 2 (pp.19–20) which facilitated their antislavery activism equally directed them to the moral and social regeneration on a broader front of individuals, communities, their nation and ultimately the world. In the late eighteenth and early nineteenth centuries this group within antislavery also paid particular attention to the reformation of manners and morals, though these were concerns which were also often connected to material problems. Wilberforce originated the Proclamation Society in 1787 after inducing the king to declare publicly against the dangers of vice and immorality and the prospectus was signed by a list of antislavery evangelicals including Muncaster and Sir Charles Middleton. Other early antislavery supporters behind the Proclamation Society included the MPs Sir Thomas Bernard, Henry Thornton and Charles Grant. It operated on the principle that 'The most effectual way to prevent the greater crimes is by punishing the smaller' which led to especial attention to Sunday observance, attempts to curb sexual explicitness in literature, the press and prints, attacks on blasphemous language and the like. Wilberforce and his colleagues hoped to advance their aims by encouraging their socially prominent members to become magistrates. They had some limited success in this; William Hey, Wilberforce's antislavery correspondent in Leeds, was sufficiently active on the bench that he was apparently hanged in effigy by a crowd. The similar, though more populist, Society for the Suppression of Vice was more visibly active through local associations in various parts of the country. Despite some Claphamite doubts about it, their organ, the *Christian Observer*, approved of the Hull Vice Society's action against servants and apprentices 'infesting the streets in the evening of the Sabbath', a practice 'highly injurious to their morals' which ought to be prevented by masters and mistresses throughout the kingdom. After about 1812 the Vice Society had lost some of its more rabidly populist and controversial leaders in the loyalists John Reeves and John Bowles and popular membership declined; it therefore became a more appropriate instrument for church evangelicals in the suppression of blasphemy and obscenity.

Yet suppression by social and legal authority of such manifestations of cultural and religious deviance was less important than efforts to spread the Christian word and inculcate vital religion, directed at the upper ranks of society as well as the lower. Like Granville Sharp, the Claphamites could be critical of the life-style of the upper classes; they hoped to make them better exemplars to their social inferiors through the work of the Bible Societies as well as the production and general distribution of religious tracts.[1]

The moral renovation of society particularly required influence over future generations. Hannah More established Sunday schools for the poor children of the Mendips and at the national level of Sunday school organisation the evangelicals Barham and Teignmouth were active in the Sunday School Society. Its directorate had not only antislavery links but Vice Society and missionary connections as well. Provincial evangelicals and evangelical dissenters who were active in antislavery – Hey once again in Leeds, Robert Hall in Manchester, Riland and Curtis in Birmingham – all promoted Sunday schools, sometimes through inter-denominational committees, and drew on donations from antislavery philanthropists of all the main religious strains in the movement as well as more conservative non-abolitionist sources.

Wilberforce's colleague, Thomas Bernard, took the lead through the Society for Bettering the Conditions of the Poor in working for the regulation of the hours of factory children so that they had the time for moral improvement through Sunday schools, preferably linked to 'our civil and ecclesiastical establishment'. He hoped to lay the foundation for the life of the poor man and his family 'around his cottage and garden'. Its directing committee included Wilberforce, Teignmouth and Calthorpe and Wilberforce also appeared with other Claphamites as well as non-evangelicals and non-Anglicans on the committee of the Philanthropic Society for reforming poor criminal children.[2]

In the early decades of the nineteenth century the evangelicals extended their control of benevolent organisations. According to Owen's study of philanthropy many of the antislavery core subscribed to at least fifteen societies. Wilberforce at one stage gave away a quarter of his annual income and subscribed to about seventy societies. Members of the Grant and Thornton families were equally committed. It was 'the real taste of the times'. Their talents as public men, as much as their wealth, were important for the evangelical reform front. Buxton, who in the following generation became almost as important a figure at the centre of the evangelical network as Wilberforce, in the autumn of 1816 spoke at a meeting to raise funds to improve the circumstances of the poor of Spitalfields; his speech was sufficiently effective to be printed and circulated with the result that the Prince Regent was prepared to subscribe £5,000.[3]

Quaker ambivalence about public action, fear of the 'delusion' that reform activity constituted 'the sum of Christianity', did not detract from the activism of many Friends in a range of reforms. The group around William Allen's *Philanthropist* justified philanthropy and reform as securing the happiness of others without which the reformers' own contentment was impossible. Beneficence 'acts harmoniously with the Divine intention' and promoted a nearer approach to 'the standard of perfection' whereby reformers 'become anxious to promote the welfare of all'. The first number of the journal in 1811 appropriately had items on civilising barbarous states, the slave trade and the African Institution, capital punishment, penitentiaries, the education of the poor, schools of industry for girls, refuges for the urban destitute, improving the condition of cottagers, New Zealand, West Indian slaves and American benevolent institutions.

Many of these interests placed Quakers alongside evangelicals but they especially identified themselves with certain forms of improvement. The Friend Joseph Lancaster's monitorial system of education became the basis for the efforts of Quaker reformers to provide education for a mass of children who had had none. Thomas Sturge and Anthony Sterry who both became antislavery stalwarts took the initiative in raising subscriptions amongst Friends when Lancaster got into early financial difficulties, and in later years Allen's circle stoutly defended a system which avoided the reduction of education to the religious indoctrination with which they charged their Anglican critics. Their organisational initiative as educational reformers was through the British and Foreign School Society, soon in competition with the Anglican body, the National School Society. On the finance committee Quakers took a leading role as trustees of Lancaster's Borough Road teacher training establishment where Allen pressed for longer, better quality and more expensive training. Above all, Friends vindicated freedom of religious conscience in education against successive legislative proposals on education which dissenters believed favoured the Church of England. Their efforts to provide education amongst classes of children previously beyond the reach of instruction were only partially successful however in terms of quality and social class.

Friends also adopted one particular solution to the need for popular adult education in the first half of the nineteenth century: the adult Sunday schools known as the Friends' First Day Schools. Quakers promoted adult education in Sunday schools from the early years of the century but it was Joseph Sturge in the 1840s who initiated a network of such schools. Using young Friends as teachers the school in Birmingham provided reading and writing instruction and scripture study for over-14s; a women's class and a separate adult male class were added in the years from 1848 and a national Friends First Day School Association established under Sturge's chairmanship in December 1847. The Birmingham school added a library and a savings bank.[4]

How to deal with the poor was a preoccupation near the centre of these educational efforts; experiments in and projects for improving the rural poor are also associated with the antislavery philanthropist–reformers James Cropper and William Allen. On succeeding to his father's farm in 1810 Cropper projected plans for occupying the neighbouring poor as agricultural labourers and at times of distress 'he gave employment to all who came'. He saw this as philanthropy but also as good sense in terms of political economy. He came to argue by 1817 that distress was the product of under-consumption and wanted a solution through increased production and maintenance of demand. Agricultural labour as an alternative to either emigration or parish relief made a contribution to countering the economic downturn. By the 1830s, on land at Fearnhead near Liverpool, Cropper not only employed labourers but he began to educate boys amongst them in an agricultural school, opened deliberately on the day emancipation of the slaves occurred. Religious readings and education became part of the regular diet of both the boys and adults in the community. 'Occasional and economical feasts' and meetings on temperance and other uplifting topics occurred in a large meeting room at the settlement. By late 1836 Cropper concluded 'There does seem a great desire for improvement.'

A similar interest in encouraging thrift, independence and a reduction in lawlessness, as well as diminishing the amounts spent on parish relief to counter rural poverty and underemployment, seems also to have motivated William Allen's Lindfield settlement in Sussex. Beginning in 1825, it combined schools, workshops, manual and agricultural training, domestic economy training for girls and eventually a system of 5-acre allotments to encourage both individual and community self-sufficiency.[5]

The other kind of benevolent reform outsiders particularly associated with Quakers was lunacy reform. Other antislavery reformers – evangelicals, Unitarians and Benthamites – also became involved, but the antislavery Quaker Tuke family in York became the focus of attention through their construction of the Retreat and the regime of 'moral treatment' they inaugurated. Their patients were Friends and the resources they raised were from Friends; one of the earlier channels for propagating the conception of 'moral treatment' was through the columns of Allen's *Philanthropist*. Samuel Tuke, grandson of the founder of the Retreat, extended discussion of the treatment of the insane to the need for a public policy to deal with the needs of the insane poor for appropriate accommodation and the appalling treatment of many inmates of existing asylums. The influence of such argument, the impression the Retreat made on many visitors and Tuke's distillation of his family's experience all contributed to the substance of parliamentary committee hearings called between 1815 and 1817. In the longer run legislation which encouraged and then required the construction of public asylums, the inception of regular inspection and reports and institutional regimes which in theory reduced the role of physical restraint, owed a good deal to the campaign begun by the Tukes and their associates.[6]

Just as the importance of the tradition of Rational Dissent–Unitarianism in antislavery has been too little emphasised, so the range of reform activities engaged in by abolitionists of this type has been insufficiently stressed until recently. The deep commitment of Price and Priestley, of William Smith MP and later Lant Carpenter in the struggle for repeal of the Test and Corporation Acts, 1787–90 and in the 1820s, is undeniable, yet these reformers did not restrict themselves to sectional religious projects. Removal of religious restrictions was seen as necessary in creating the conditions in which the progress bound to emerge from freedom of thought and investigation could occur. Universal tolerance and enlightenment were indissolubly linked. The priority of religious and intellectual freedom in the Rational Dissenters' perspective and their determination to pursue them were expressions of attachment to fundamental natural rights including freedom from enslavement. Recent research has confirmed the significant overlap at the parliamentary level of abolitionism and opposition to religious tests at the end of the 1780s.

Wilberforce's long-term collaborator, William Smith, the Unitarian MP for Norwich, was as active in the 1820s as in the late 1780s on behalf of the abolition of religious tests and spoke with the authority of his chairmanship of the Dissenting Deputies. His long parliamentary career and firm connections to sympathetic Whigs like Lord Holland contributed to the successful passage of repeal in 1828. Yet Smith and Lant Carpenter were clear examples of reformers who looked beyond Protestant dissent to the liberation of Jews and who worked for Catholic Emancipation too. Despite fears that 'many of our weaker brethren are anxious to steer clear of the Catholic vessel' Unitarian reformers could judge the claims of Catholics 'vastly more urgent' than their own and worked in provincial towns like Exeter and Bristol for the Catholic cause despite the orthodox dissenters and Methodists, their recent allies against the Test Act, being 'almost universally unfavourable (though with diminished violence in some cases) to the Catholic claims'. This generously liberal spirit, while it had its limitations, none the less infused the activities of this branch of dissent throughout the early decades of the nineteenth century. It contributed to Unitarian prominence in the anti-war petitioning of the Napoleonic years when liberals frequently held the waging of war responsible for economic difficulties and the further growth of a corrupt and authoritarian governmental system. Educational development, a potential source of enlightenment in the people at large, attracted the antislavery Carpenters to schooling and William Roscoe and other Unitarians to the Society for the Diffusion of Useful Knowledge or Mechanics' Institutes. The antislavery Strutt family in Derby supported local Lancasterian schools and civic improvements embracing street lighting and widening, public buildings and bridges, the establishment of an Infirmary in 1810, a Sunday school and, in 1840, an extensive arboretum. In the later decades covered by this study antislavery Unitarians S.A. Steinthal and Francis Bishop continued their denomination's educational interest as well as work in Domestic Missions for the urban poor. William Shaen's membership of the London Emancipation Committee in the late 1850s was a minor part of public activity which embraced education for women in the establishment of Bedford College and work for women's suffrage. So far as antislavery Unitarians were concerned by mid-century 'The very reason that causes them to work for oppressed humanity when they hear its cry for help coming across the Atlantic fires them to hear that same voice when lifted up in England.' Unitarians worked with other groups on many of these issues; their approach through a consistent intellectual liberalism and optimism about human reason, however, did distinguish the basis of their activism.[7]

The power of evangelical dissent was demonstrated in the years immediately before slave emancipation by its ability to inundate parliament with petitions on behalf of the repeal of religious tests and the liberation of the colonial slaves. But reform activity in a subordinate role by dissenters stretched back before the 1820s. There was support, behind Unitarian leadership, for civic improvements in, for example, Manchester in the 1790s and mobilisations to petition for peace at various times in the war years. It was in the 1830s and 1840s, however, that evangelical dissenters became especially militant on a number of issues essentially linked to a sense of religious grievance. They did not always agree about tactics and particularly about the desirability of political action. Yet most would have accepted the Rev. Andrew Reed's formulation: 'We ask, in short, that we shall be free: in labour, free; in trade, free; in action, free; in thought, free; in speech, free; in religion, free – perfectly free.' Miall and Mursell were prominent in the early efforts of the Church Rates Abolition Society established in 1836 and helped mobilise out-of-doors support for the elder Edward Baines' parliamentary attack against this mark of Anglican privilege. The antislavery journalist, Josiah Conder (of the *Eclectic Review* and the *Patriot*) initiated the Religious Freedom Society in 1839 when the sharp parliamentary attack failed to make headway and many antislavery dissenters moved into Anti-State Church Societies and then the Liberation Society. This route was pioneered by leading antislavery dissenters who were present at the large Anti-State Church convention in the spring of 1844. Voluntaryism in religion was here combined with a sharper-edged voluntaryism in education. The militancy in education grew with the confidence of success after dissenters fought Graham's education proposals in his Factory Bill of 1843 and achieved their withdrawal. Strong hostility to any state financial aid to education by Edward Baines Jr and his supporters during the 1840s and later led to some divergence from other dissenter reformers, but all voluntaryists continued to resist any kind of state intervention in education which might give advantages to the Established Church or challenge freedom of religious opinion.

For ardent dissenters even free trade in corn had a religious aspect to it. Many ministers were keen advocates of the Anti-Corn Law League; some saw the 'natural' operation of free commerce as a feature of God's arrangement of the world. More directly, as an outgrowth of their hostility to the church and contributing to it, they took aim at the landlords who benefited from the corn laws; they saw them as a major social and political support for the religious establishment as well as selfishly increasing the poverty of the lower classes who inhabited the towns where many of the dissenters had their chapels.[8]

The separate religious tendencies in antislavery thus exhibited either particular reform interests within the larger reform complex or approached collaborative activity from somewhat different perspectives. Most of the major reform agitations none the less were undertaken by coalitions of these different groups. Prison and penal reform efforts over many years provide examples. The network of reformers and humanitarians in which John Howard was the most widely-known proponent of institutional reform in regard to prisons crossed religious and intellectual lines. He drew in Quakers, Baptists and Rational Dissenters, many of whom also adopted an antislavery stance. They included Richard Price, John Aikin, the reformer-physician and tutor at the Warrington Academy, John Fothergill, the Quaker physician and philanthropist, as well as Samuel Whitbread. Fothergill in turn was part of a group of institutional medical reformers including the Manchester abolitionist and prison reformer, Thomas Percival, a Rational Dissenter. Fothergill's friend and biographer was the antislavery Dr John Lettsom who investigated and wrote about conditions in Newgate in 1795. By 1813 a Quaker group including Allen and William Forster visited Newgate and Allen encouraged Elizabeth Fry in her work in the women's prison. Mrs Fry engaged Buxton's sister Anna in her reorganisation of the conditions of the female prisoners.

Leadership of the movement for a more rational and humane penal code which gave priority to a reduction in the number of capital offences was taken up by Sir Samuel Romilly, a utilitarian in his outlook. But his parliamentary interventions were sustained mainly by Allen and other Friends who formed a society for penal reform and prison discipline in about 1808. They published information on capital punishment and co-ordinated their activities with Romilly, petitioning parliament in 1811 when Romilly made further progress in getting parliamentary repeal of the death penalty for a number of offences. Allen also took up, through a revived Prison Discipline Society in 1817, the problem of juvenile delinquents and the need for national standards for prison conditions and prison discipline. His close collaborators were Thomas Fowell Buxton and Samuel Hoare as well as the utilitarian James Mill. Wilberforce spoke critically in parliament on Newgate conditions and Buxton argued the need for regular outside visits of inspection, charging local authorities, as did Allen, with failing in their supervisory capacity. Joseph John Gurney also became involved when he accompanied his sister Mrs Fry in 1818 on a tour of prisons in the north and Scotland.

When Mackintosh assumed parliamentary leadership on the penal reform question in 1819 he received then and in following years parliamentary support from Buxton and later Wilberforce. In the country, Allen and other Quakers, and in 1821 Clarkson, initiated petitioning against a penal code based on 'no fixed principle of justice or gradation of crime'. They deprecated on grounds of both religion and the disrespect the law brought upon itself its 'unnatural severity and disregard of life'.[9]

Although Friends were closely identified with lunacy reform and the institution of 'moral treatment' this was also an area of collaboration. As will be demonstrated below (p.120), Unitarian physician reformers in Manchester, particularly John Ferriar, introduced a new asylum regime. When the issue of the treatment and housing of the insane reached parliament Wilberforce became a member of the 1807 parliamentary committee and antislavery evangelicals maintained a regular interest in the issue, culminating in Shaftesbury's role in the 1844–5 debates which produced the legislation requiring the housing of the pauper insane and instituting a permanent national inspectorate.

The temperance movement, 'escape from the Drunken House of Bondage', also appealed to antislavery reformers of all religious tendencies. When temperance took an organised form in the late 1820s some antislavery evangelicals adopted an anti-spirits policy in line with the British and Foreign Temperance Society; none the less the older generation of abolitionists did not always incorporate this change into their outlook. A few years later amongst middle-class antislavery people Quakers such as Joseph Eaton of Bristol and Samuel Bowly of Gloucester were early adherents of the more militant phase associated from the mid-1830s with teetotalism.

Joseph Sturge in Birmingham also entered active temperance work as a teetotaler at about the same time; the same is true of a number of provincial Friends listed as abolitionists in Harrison's biographical analysis of temperance reformers. The main initiative for teetotalism, however, came from working men, many of whom were dissenters and some of them also publicly identified with antislavery. Joseph Barker, in his various religious as well as his infidel guises, was one, as was the antislavery Chartist Henry Vincent who established a teetotal Chartist movement in 1840–1. Many of these teetotalers joined the prohibitionist United Kingdom Alliance after its foundation in 1853. The Rev. Patrick Brewster, William Lovett and other Chartist abolitionists were amongst this number, though doubt about its teetotal credentials also allowed Lord Brougham in. So significant was this influx of radical working men that in the 1860s, according to Harrison, it helped shape the UKA's support of franchise extension.[10]

The interrelationship of antislavery with other projects of reform within a community can be amply illustrated for the earlier part of the period – the late 1780s and first half of the 1790s – by considering Manchester. The expanding town's precocity in mass antislavery petitioning, its sizeable subvention to the London committee of 100 guineas and its role in prompting other towns to action indicate an antislavery dynamism. Closer examination makes it plain that anti-slave trade activity was only one element in an impressive culture of reform. There was a core leadership primarily of Unitarians but taking in a latitudinarian Anglican, Thomas Walker, the chairman of the anti-slave trade committee, having an intellectual centre in the Literary and Philosophical Society founded in 1781 and pressing a programme through an interlocking set of committees. The leaders of this reform culture were also able to find support on occasion from evangelical elements in the town's population.

The Literary and Philosophical Society was the intellectual and social base for the Manchester reformers. Its most prominent figures in the 1780s and 1790s shared intellectual perspectives through their religious commitments; in 1785 of forty-three members fifteen were trustees, ministers or closely related to trustees of the Cross St Chapel, the home of intellectual Rational Dissent. A significant number of members of the Literary and Philosophical Society were doctors or laymen with Warrington Academy and/or Edinburgh educations. Thomas Percival, Thomas Barnes, Thomas Butterworth Bayley as leaders of intellectual culture in Manchester were also instrumental in the establishment of the first British College of Arts and Sciences in 1783 and then, as the Warrington Academy came to an end, in 1786 the Manchester Academy, the origin of Manchester College. Percival was its first president, Barnes its first principal and their closest associates strong supporters. The leading physician–intellectuals of the Lit. and Phil. held positions at the Infirmary; similarly Percival's protégé, John Ferriar, was a directing force at the Asylum while Bayley and Percival were both active in the construction and improvement of the internal regimes of prisons. The Manchester Academy became an institution in which antislavery was part of the texture of life.[11]

The interlocking character of the committee structure of the reform culture can easily be demonstrated. The anti-slave trade committee in Manchester was established on 27 December 1787 with thirty-one members and a secretary. Four of its members had been founder members of the Lit. and Phil. in Thomas Percival's house in 1781; seven more had become Lit. and Phil. members between 1781 and 1787; a further four joined the Lit. and Phil. during the first phase of anti-slave trade agitation 1788–92 and one of these was Thomas Walker. Thus by 1792 fifteen members out of thirty-one of the 1787 committee were linked to the Lit. and Phil. The committee of the Infirmary in 1790 which initiated a controversial expansion and reform policy contained physician members of the abolition committee as well as lay figures such as Thomas Walker, George Philips, Barnes and Bayley. Even as late as 1796 at the time of the founding of the Manchester Board of Health to deal with the problem of fever amongst the manufacturing poor and to plan a more ambitious but largely unfulfilled programme of sanitary, housing and factory reform, continuity with the abolition committee of 1787 is discernible. Six members of the Board of Health in 1796, apart from at least three antislavery doctors from the Infirmary, had been on the abolition committee; five members of the Board, plus the Infirmary physicians, had been members of *both* the abolition committee and the reforming Infirmary committee of 1790.

Antislavery took its place as part of a culture of reform in Manchester whose prominent leaders and whose collective strength were tested by a number of sharp struggles. Despite, for example, Percival's contacts not only with the London abolition committee but also Joseph Priestley and French abolitionists including Mme Necker over the slave trade, he and his colleagues found some of their fellow townsmen unimpressed. The mill-owning Peel family, pillars of the

Tory establishment around the old manorial institutions and the collegiate church, came out in opposition to the petition effort and Lawrence Peel was the main organiser of the anti-abolition petition from Manchester. This was significant in coinciding with the efforts of the reformers for the repeal of the Test and Corporation Acts which local Tories also opposed and followed on from the experience of Walker in confronting opposition by the Peel group over his campaign against the fustian tax of 1784 and in resisting lower tariffs under the 1786 French treaty. Similar alignments emerged over the Infirmary in 1789–90. The reformer–physicians and their allies amongst the trustees wished to expand the institution particularly to separate out- or home-patients from others so as to reduce the possibility of contagion and to add new staff appointments to permit much more extensive home-visiting. Opposition came from the two long established surgeon families associated with the Infirmary, the Halls and the Whites, who also adopted conservative political positions. But the whole drive towards this kind of work, towards a social medicine focusing particularly on the manufacturing poor, was not only helped to victory in 1790 by a serious outbreak of fever, it was an approach by which Percival had already alienated Sir Robert Peel through an attack on the conditions of millworkers after the spread of fever in one of Peel's mills in 1784. The struggle at the Infirmary was presented by the reformers as a campaign to provide the best available treatment in the public interest and, characteristic of the outlook of Percival and Ferriar, to advance medical knowledge through the evidence provided by a much larger number of patients.

Ferriar's role at the Manchester Lunatic Asylum did not encounter this kind of opposition though he characteristically insisted on a break from the practices of older asylums by his concern for skilled handling of the inmates by a trained staff under professional medical direction. Since, in the same way as the Tukes at York, Ferriar tried to work not through physical restraint or coercion but the 'management of hope and apprehension . . . small favours, the show of confidence and apparent distinction' a sympathetic and alert pragmatism from an intelligent staff was essential. Only in that way could the inmates attain self-control through internal change.

The reform group could not however have got as far as it did if it had not been able to find support in the community at large. Though they were Rational Dissenters or latitudinarian Anglicans they were able to engage Methodist and other evangelical support for antislavery, for expansion of the Infirmary and for the Asylum. This was in some cases probably to do with the on-going dynamic of reform and opposition to it sketched above, and on some issues the refusal of supporters to see the matter as in any way 'political' but rather 'philanthropic'. As in the antislavery movement nationally, so the separate elements of the reform coalition in Manchester were not required to have an identical view of the world in order to work together.[12]

Sheffield antislavery reformers in the 1820s and 1830s, like their Manchester predecessors, exhibited a multiplicity of reform commitments and also contributed to the large body of writing issued by activists. The reform culture of Sheffield however was also distinctively different from the earlier Manchester formation. Evangelical religion was at its centre, it had little connection with radical politics and in the antislavery context there was some ambivalence about Sturgeite militancy in the later 1830s. The reformist literature, both poetic and in pamphlet form, was shaped by evangelical and humanitarian feeling rather than having the cooler, quasi-scientific tone of the Manchester reformers a generation earlier.

The core of reform activity probably lay in the friendship of James Montgomery and Samuel Roberts which began in the early years of the century. Both were strongly evangelical and pursued intertwined literary and reform careers, though their backgrounds were very different. Montgomery, born in Scotland, moved to Sheffield about 1790 and eventually took over Joseph Gales' radical paper, suffered a term of imprisonment for his activities as a radical editor but thereafter moved away from radical politics; he owned and edited the *Iris*, however, through to 1825. Roberts worked in his father's silver-plating business and started up on his own in the 1780s. By the early nineteenth century he had done sufficiently well to devote himself virtually full time to reform and literary activities. An early associate of Montgomery was the dissenter manufacturer Joseph Read of Wincobank Hall whose female relatives animated women's involvement in antislavery in the town from the mid-1820s. The cause also drew in evangelical dissenting ministers, some leading members of the cutlery trade such as the Master Cutler in the early 1830s, W. Ibbotson, and members of prominent professional families, notably Fairbank family members of the clan of land surveyors and civil engineers. Female relations filled the committee places of the Ladies' Anti-Slavery Society.[13]

By the 1820s some of the male reformers had long experience of acting together in good causes. About 1806 a female member of the

Fairbank family prompted Roberts, Montgomery, their evangelical friend, and later South Sea missionary, George Bennett and others to form a society to aid climbing boys. Montgomery was an early poetic opponent of the slave trade and was joined in antislavery activity and writing by Roberts. As was to be expected, support for the flourishing Sunday school movement in Sheffield was a common interest while there was great attraction in a Bible Society in which 'all names and distinctions of sects are blended till they are lost . . . in missionary work, though divided, they are not discordant'. Montgomery and Roberts collaborated to raise £320 for Moravian missions in 1823, Montgomery having become a Moravian. Roberts took up an interest in the situation of the gypsies and saw them as a suitable case for evangelisation. Promotion of secular education and science was compatible with this outlook; several of the reformers were members of the Literary and Philosophical Society after its establishment in 1822 and Bennett sent botanical specimens to the Lit. and Phil. during his years in the South Seas. Montgomery was also a prominent supporter of the Mechanics' Library, advocating useful, scientific literature and opposing popular romances and novels. In the 1830s Roberts became nationally prominent for his fierce campaigning against the new Poor Law.

This last fact did not indicate a stepping outside of the normal bounds of the evangelical reform perspective. It was one of the rare occasions in Britain, claimed Roberts, when a human law was 'directly opposed to and subversive of the most holy, immutable laws of God' and was the product of a declension in public life as well as the destruction of the old paternalist social order of the countryside with 'all the advantage of constant residence of the Squire at the Hall'. Roberts also transposed the familiar evangelical argument against slavery's destructive impact on the life of the family to the situation of climbing boys who were unprotected by law and removed from, and often 'sold', by their parents. This conservative strain found other expressions in Montgomery's case, particularly as the character of the middle-class reform complex changed in the 1830s. He was hostile to dissent's growing militancy against aspects of the religious establishment and had supported the levying of a church rate in Sheffield to help pay for a church building programme. He also distanced himself from aspects of Sturge's agitation against apprenticeship, particularly from criticism of the failings of missionaries, and had placed part of the blame indirectly on the 'over-zealous amongst the anti-slavery class' for the Jamaican insurrection. By 1837 his biographers describe him as holding a conservative position without being a party man. Unsurprisingly, therefore, though a theoretical free trader, Montgomery felt alienated by the agitational tone of the local Anti-Corn Law Society.[14]

The moralising of British society which antislavery reformers attempted had its counterpart internationally, undertaken by many of the same people in the generation after 1815. The most obvious example of this was missionary work which sprang from the conviction amongst the godly that it was their duty to make over the heathen to Christianity whether they were in the towns and countryside of India or Britain. Clapham evangelicals – Wilberforce, Thornton, Venn – helped establish in 1799 what later became the Church Missionary Society and by the 1820s the extensive lines of missionary activity were well known to and extensively supported by religious reformers of an evangelical persuasion inside and outside the Church.

Although some of the institutional bases of the mission work supported by abolitionists were laid earlier – in addition to the CMS there was organisation of Wesleyan foreign missions from 1787, the Baptists created their Missionary Society in 1792 and the Congregationalists in 1795 – the fullest expression of this impulse occurred after the wars. As such it coincided with a confident sense throughout British society that much of the world could and should be made subject to British influence in moral and religious as well as economic senses. The object was to 'augment the sum of human felicity'.

How this might best be achieved produced much agreement but also some characteristic differences of emphasis amongst different groups of reformers and some changes over time. Claphamites, with the leading role taken by Charles Grant, became a powerful presence in the early nineteenth century in the court of the East India Company and succeeded in getting the requirement to permit mission work in India inserted into the new charter of the company in 1813. The younger Grant and the younger James Stephen twenty years later, in drafting the Charter Act of 1833, explicitly set out the objective of Christianising and Anglicising India. The meaning of this evangelical project, however, needs to be carefully understood. It did not simply signal moral legitimation of commercial expansion and economic exploitation by the British. The Claphamites had no doubt of the cultural and technical backwardness of Hindus in the early nineteenth century and believed the Indians 'may well do homage to the genius of the nation to whom they have submitted'. This created a situation in which missionaries could 'recommend' Christianity. Along with Britain's commercial and technical superiority, with 'the Bible in one hand and the loom in the other' missionaries enabled Indians to see that 'far from perishing as they do in the shade of their superstition, art and science flourish under the wing of Christianity'. The main emphasis however was on missionaries as disseminators of education and piety through the English language. No doubt industry and commerce would consequently develop but commercial expansion to the benefit of British traders in India was not a prime objective; since open commerce would challenge the position of the East India Company through which the Claphamites operated it was unlikely that they would place much reliance upon it. When James Cropper and Liverpool Friends in the late 1820s engaged in support for mission work in India they too focused on education, especially on female schools in the Calcutta area.[15]

The cooler, more rationalist approach of Unitarian reformers produced a somewhat different perspective. Equally with the evangelicals the *Monthly Repository* had no doubt of the superior cultural and religious state of the British to the heathens whom they encountered. Yet that ought to mean that attempts to *civilise* them should normally take precedence. Like Christians (and mechanics) in England they had to be able and free to distinguish truth from error and thus 'a considerable degree of civilization and of social and mental improvement is absolutely necessary for the reception of Christianity'. The desire to achieve large numbers of conversions placed effect before cause.[16]

Despite these differences, however, it is clear that all kinds of antislavery reformers supportive of missions equated them with humanitarianism in the sense of providing a framework of individuals and institutions with links to the religious publicity machine in Britain to provide some improvement and protection for the indigenous populations of areas in which Europeans had intervened. By the end of the 1830s a specialised reform organisation, the Aborigines' Protection Society, had emerged whose antecedents were both missionary and antislavery. Protective activities before and after the foundation of the organisation were an example of cross-denominational co-operation amongst abolitionists.

But here we encounter a paradox. While abolitionists and missionaries might be called upon to safeguard the interests of indigenous populations against some obvious kinds of exploitation, it was the opening of far-flung territories to British influence which both made that protection imperative and gave new opportunities for missionary penetration. Missionary enthusiasm by abolitionists could provide a temporary halo for enterprises which to sceptics appeared ill-considered or downright regressive. Buxton's Niger expedition in the early 1840s seemed so to critics, but here also may be noted John Angell James' great support for missionary work in the Chinese Empire despite the opening up of China by means of the opium trade. And in the 1850s Shaftesbury's undiscriminating endorsement of American missionaries intent on converting the infidel Turk brought embarrassment to the BFASS when it became apparent that the antislavery credentials of their sponsoring body were not impeccable.

Time also brought a much closer connection in the eyes of reformers of commercial expansion with Christianisation as well eventually with emancipation than was true in the early nineteenth century. Porter has quoted Samuel Wilberforce's conviction in 1860 that the British had been given the providential task of spreading the gospel throughout the world and God 'had given us our commerce and our naval supremacy' to do it. To trace the course of this convergence of trade and religion and its part in antislavery it is necessary to return at least to the 1820s; it will here be argued that it can only be understood within the context of the rise of free trade abolitionism.[17]

Pamphleteering by members of the Liverpool Anti-Slavery Society in the early 1820s in favour of removing the tariff advantages enjoyed by West Indian sugar producers in the British market signalled a resumption of abolitionist preoccupation with commercial policy as a way towards their objectives. Cropper and Hodgson picked up a theme touched on in scattered writings by Priestley and Anderson at the end of the 1780s. Rapidly in the 1820s the demand for equalisation of duties gained wider support amongst provincial abolitionists – in Birmingham for example – and a spokesman in the Commons in the ideological free trader and member of the African Institution committee, William Whitmore.

Whatever the contribution of this argument to the antislavery persuasion for equal competition as dissolving the inefficient system of bondage, Cropper confronted apprenticeship in the mid-1830s by articulating the necessity of full free trade to make free labour a reality. Free labour could only deliver prosperity if it promoted the commitment of the labourer to his work and that would not happen unless irrational restrictions on the trade of the consumables the freedman produced were removed. Apprenticeship of the freedmen would moreover soon slide back into *de facto* slavery, unless free trade in sugar were established. If the planters kept their artificially high prices in the British market they would return to their old oppressive ways through deploying vagrancy laws against the ex-slaves. Only the labourers' willingness to work efficiently to meet the competition of a free market would stop their former owners from treating them badly. Thus, before the full emancipation of 1838, there was a strand of antislavery which prepared many abolitionists for support of a wider free trade movement.[18]

That took the form of support by antislavery Quakers, dissenters and Unitarians – as has been suggested in chapter 4 Anglican evangelicals now ceased to be very prominent in what was becoming a more liberal reform complex – for the Anti-Corn Law League (ACLL) with particular emphasis on its supposed international ramifications. Cobden took care to present the free trade movement to his abolitionist correspondents as a movement with 'moral weight', dissenting ministers flocked in large numbers to League meetings and MPs with antislavery credentials supported Cobden in the lobbies even when free trade motions gained only a handful of votes in the early 1840s.

Moreover, from their American abolitionist contacts and their existing concern with conditions within the various parts of the British Empire some abolitionists most active in the League in the early 1840s saw a process of internationalising free trade, initiated by removal of the Corn Laws, as a key to advances in the United States, India and possibly parts of Africa. Harriet Martineau had noted in her *Society in America* that the productive lands of the old north-west in the United States could supply foodstuffs for the industrial regions of England if it were not for the Corn Laws. It was an idea publicised by the American abolitionist Joshua Leavitt who envisaged the British taking more corn and less cotton from the United States and thereby weakening the power of the slaveholding cotton planters of the South. Sturge as well as Cobden corresponded with American reformers on the possibilities. At the time of the 1843 Anti-Slavery Convention in London Leavitt, Amos A. Phelps, James C. Fuller and other Americans discussed possibilities with free trade abolitionists in England; yet both the BFASS and the ACLL were unwilling as organisations to endorse a policy intended to shift the balance in trade with Britain in favour of the North. Despite Sturge's interest, the committee of the BFASS hesitated, perhaps, one critic suggested, because they saw such a policy as requiring too overtly a political intervention by them. As to the ACLL, textile manufacturer supporters were as much interested in a guaranteed cotton supply as they were in cheaper corn; without an equal certainty of a sufficient and regular alternative source of supply projects for rechannelling international commerce for moral ends were chimerical.[19]

This was one problem which faced reformers who would have liked to be able to harmonise their abolitionist and their free trade principles as the basis for a popular resurgence in the antislavery movement, promising benefits to the working population at home and a practical means of affecting a foreign system of slavery. The second problem was that posed by the advantage that West Indian and other colonial free-labour sugar had in the British market through tariff discrimination over slave-grown sugar, primarily from Cuba and Brazil. The abolitionists who inaugurated the British India Society on 6 July 1839 had a vision with India at its centre of how to deal with the first problem. If reforms were undertaken in India and the subcontinent brought more fully into the system of international trade, widespread benefits would accrue. In the BIS Joseph Pease of Darlington was the key figure; his interest in India went back several years. Initially he had worked in the 1830s for the abolition of slavery in British India and was instrumental in committing a number of provincial emancipation societies in the apprenticeship period to Indian abolition and reform. Largely through Pease's influence George Thompson began to speak on India in the late 1830s; the committee of the Aborigines' Protection Society took India up; at the celebratory 1838 Birmingham meeting O'Connell, Sturge and Lushington all raised reform and development in India. Pease's Quaker affiliation engaged William Allen and the Friends' reform network and free traders also had their interest aroused. Not only had Joseph Pease been a firm opponent of the Corn Laws since 1815 but he propounded the possibilities of the development of cotton and sugar in India to undercut the crops grown by slaves in the Americas. By the early 1840s he was claiming, primarily on estimates of much cheaper labour in Bengal than in the slave societies of the Americas, that East Indian sugar in bond could be got at a third of the current sugar price on the British market. He calculated the cost of Indian cotton at one-sixth of American and proclaimed his faith that, if free-labour production had been in open competition with slave labour, bondage would have ceased to exist as uneconomic even without emancipationist legislation.

The British India Society gained parliamentary support from Brougham, Lushington, Hawes and other antislavery people. This was unsurprising since the meetings of the late 1830s addressed by Thompson on India gave a prominent place to the demand for emancipation in territories ruled by the East India Company, territories which had fallen outside the 1833 Act. Yet it was seen as only the first step towards creating a prosperous Indian economy also requiring a reasonable settlement of the burdensome land tax, the grant of uncultivated land in sufficient blocks to Indians on leasehold terms to encourage cultivation of crops which competed with slave-grown produce and to encourage their sale in the British market by imposing minimal duties. The expectation was that this would also create a growing prosperity in India and thus a market for a much larger quantity of British goods. These hopes encouraged support by BIS abolitionists of the ACLL and in the early 1840s a specific sharing of Thompson's time and energies between the two organisations.[20]

Whether or not to follow their free trade inclinations and support the opening up of the British market to all sugar on equal terms became a harsh dilemma for significant numbers of abolitionists in the early 1840s. The issue was a live one at the time of the World Anti-Slavery Convention of 1840 when it had been resolved to hold the line against the importation of slave-grown sugar since to do otherwise would be to maintain foreign slavery and the slave trade, perhaps to develop it. The question of loyalty to the BFASS as the premier antislavery organisation also arose since its 1839 constitution committed it 'to promote the adoption of fiscal regulations in favour of free labour'. Sturge held the majority of leaders in the BFASS to what they saw as essentially a moral stand which required fiscal discrimination against slave-grown produce. Implicit in this position was the demand that the British people live up to their national antislavery professions. The troubling corollary was that these abolitionists found themselves aligned with their old planter enemies whom they still suspected of seeking to oppress the freedmen and against some of their old colleagues.

Antislavery reformers who stuck to a consistent free trade position were perhaps influenced by Cobden's intervention at the 1843 Convention and as much by the sense that things were moving in their direction. They reacted against even a tacit alliance with the planters and saw themselves as the friends of the working population of Britain. Equalisation of the sugar duties was 'necessary as an act of justice to the people of this country' since it would lower prices in

128

Britain and improve the standard of living of the population. This notion of justice beginning at home was squared with antislavery internationalism by the conviction that in the long run free labour would prove to be cheaper than that of slaves and thus the West Indies and the freedmen would survive and become more efficient in doing so.

At the 1843 Convention the proposition in favour of the unrestricted import of produce into Britain, whether from slave or free labour, was not voted upon and officially the BFASS proclaimed the 1840 decision stood. A free trade group came out publicly in opposition and a committee formed to proclaim its view chaired by George Thompson. The group tried to get discussion at the 1844 annual meeting of the free trade proposition and consideration of the constitutional clause favouring fiscal regulations in favour of free labour but the BFASS committee refused. Analysis of the signatories of the free trade address based on the 1843 Convention proposition of Thomas Spencer of Bath, W.T. Blair of Bath and G.W. Anstie of Devizes is inconclusive. Overwhelmingly they were provincial rather than metropolitan reformers; there was a West Country element, including the three main proponents; Joseph Pease and Thompson had already closely aligned themselves with the ACLL through its alliance with their BIS. The group also included Unitarians, Quakers and evangelicals. Yet according to calculations of its opponents the links of the group to *institutional* antislavery were not strong. Of the forty-four, at the time of their signature only fourteen were subscribers to the BFASS; it is of course quite likely that others had earlier had an institutional affiliation. Seemingly twenty-four had attended the 1843 Convention, fifteen had not done so, though apparently appointed delegates, and five had not been delegates. It can be no more than speculation that some of the free traders were merely making use of the antislavery meeting and the division it generated to dramatise their claims that free trade was of great benefit to ordinary free-born Englishmen. If this was so they were showing only a secondary concern with Afro-Caribbean freedmen.[21]

The majority of members of local auxiliaries seem to have accepted the BFASS position; Sturge and his supporters maintained strong opposition from 1843 to 1846 against equalisation and even after they were defeated by the Sugar Acts of 1846 and 1848 which produced equal treatment for colonial and foreign, free-grown and slave-grown sugar by 1854, they supported motions to restore discrimination in favour of West Indian producers. Yet it was not all or nothing for the Sturgeites. One of their chief opponents in the debate at the 1843 Convention expressed a common view in not disputing their desire to exclude slave-grown sugar but their wish to do it by legislative intervention. Both while the struggle against equalisation went on and after its establishment there was some attempt to revive a voluntary free-produce movement. Here Sturge and some other abolitionist Friends intersected with the antislavery strand concerned with India, though the BFASS leaders had not been active in Pease's organisation before it ceased operations in 1843. The group looked to India for free-grown cotton and possibly sugar and in 1846 also hoped to find American free-labour produce. Clarkson in the last months of his life showed support and there was some provincial interest. Despite Cobden's conviction that these efforts were 'delusive' they did intersect with the interest of John Bright and some Manchester cotton manufacturers in the late 1840s and early 1850s in the development of cotton growing and railway transport in India. This elided with Bright's criticism of the constitutionally irresponsible government of the East India Company (criticism shared by abolitionists like Sturge and Thompson) and his optimism that it would have an antislavery effect in the American South. These hopes bore little fruit before the exigencies of the American Civil War but they continued to illustrate the range of ambition fostered in reform circles by Britain's imperial and international role.[22]

A feature of that large ambition, closely related to the involvement with free trade and also taken up by some antislavery reformers was the desire to achieve international peace and devise means of maintaining it. Cobden flattered Sturge in 1846 with the hope that the main moral consequence of international free trade 'will be that the whole of the civilized world will become *quakers* in the practice of peace and mutual forbearance'. Certainly the peace movement in the sense of an organised peace society had Quaker antislavery origins in 1816. The Society for the Promotion of Permanent and Universal Peace originated in a meeting at the house of William Allen, though part of the impetus came from the wealthy antislavery ironfounder from Neath, Joseph Price. The organisation became a propagandist body rather than an activist pressure group, circulating publications including Clarkson's *An Essay on the Doctrines and Practice of the Early Christians, as they relate to war*, constantly reprinted and referred to in both British and American peace circles in later decades.

This society adopted a longer-term perspective, essentially educational, distinct from the more immediate peace petitioning which occurred during the Revolutionary and Napoleonic Wars, but which in turn was often led by liberal Rational Dissenters who had good anti-slave trade credentials. The post-war movement was also different in being managed primarily by Quakers and evangelicals. The clear connection between peace and antislavery remained evident in both individuals and the columns of the *Herald of Peace* in the 1820s and 1830s; it was not however a connection the Anglican evangelical element in antislavery often accepted. Thomas Clarkson was an exception and in his arguments for the settlement of international disputes by arbitration a transitional figure who both summoned up the rhetoric of eighteenth-century radicalism and looked forward, like Cobden and Sturge in the next generation, to the significance of the middle class. Wars were the product of that aristocratic sentiment 'Honour, another name for pride, ambition' and the result 'Robbery and Murder and a heart-aching and impoverished population'. It was the middle class he believed who had the most to suffer from wars and the extension of government; it was precisely this group which by the 1840s was the best lever for raising public opinion on the peace question in the view of Sturge and Cobden.[23]

By the early 1840s two factors gave at least temporary direction to a new phase of the peace movement. British and American reformers had developed extensive contacts which promoted overlapping discussions between them on antislavery, peace and temperance. In the summer of 1843 in London there were even successive international antislavery, peace and temperance conventions; a number of Anglo-American reformers attended all three. The second factor was the way in which peace was linked to the free trade movement.

The 1843 peace convention adopted the American William Jay's plan for international arbitration between states in dispute and an international deputation including English and American abolitionists tried to give it momentum by unsuccessfully pressing it upon Sir Robert Peel. This kind of plan was not new but the methods some English reformers and their American allies began to adopt were a departure from earlier propaganda and petitioning. Sturge and the antislavery Chartist O'Neill in 1842 tried to disrupt army recruiting activities by distributing peace propaganda as recruiting teams visited various towns. Public meetings also featured in efforts to rouse opinion against revival of the militia and increases in the naval estimates. Popular mobilisation as a tactic was natural to a provincial radical like Sturge and from 1846 he also welcomed American collaboration through the efforts of the 'learned blacksmith', Elihu

Burritt. Burritt espoused the value of friendly addresses between British and American towns (on English Quaker prompting) when Anglo-American relations were in a parlous state in 1845–6 and came to Britain where he devised the League of Universal Brotherhood. Sturge worked with him and drew in reformers in the antislavery tradition – Miall, Thompson and others. The League extended the idea of friendly addresses to 'Olive Leaves', brief articles on peace sent to the foreign press and then to addresses directly to governments. The next step in the aftermath of the upheavals of 1848 was the calling of a series of peace congresses between 1848 and 1853 in a number of European cities in the organisation of which Sturgeite radicals worked with some difficulty with elements of the more staid old-style proponents of peace like Samuel Gurney. The congresses hoped to put international pressure on governments not to use force; Sturge in particular made himself notorious in some quarters by leading delegations to statesmen for that purpose over the Schleswig-Holstein problem in 1850 and to the tsar in the period of tension before the outbreak of the Crimean War. This was (unsuccessful) 'people's diplomacy'.

The Sturgeites, although the collaboration was sometimes under strain, also worked with Cobden and Bright whose parliamentary efforts were to advance voluntary arbitration, phased disarmament and the international free trade which would give states an interest in them. Sturge and his supporters had the role of activating 'religious sentiments against the barbarous system' and although Cobden distanced himself from the reformers' utopianism over total disarmament, a Congress of Nations and direct intervention by peace advocates through delegations to contending powers, these different peace men maintained co-operation from the later 1840s onwards, though at the time of the Crimean War and after it was a collaboration in the adverse conditions of a triumphalist Palmerstonian Britain.[24]

The revolutions of 1848 must have made some impression on most educated people in England. But they allow the student of antislavery a useful illumination of the more general ideological stance of abolitionists because the upheavals could plausibly be seen as about the freedom of oppressed people and the role of violence in political change. Many abolitionists from the different religious groups had strong hopes of the upheavals, from the evangelical Scoble's expectation that enlarged civil and religious liberties would improve the moral quality of relations between states to celebration by more

132

radical figures at blows struck against political despotism and anticipation of a new liberal era. Yet there was also fear of French excesses by both William James and J.B. Estlin in Bristol and by the latter a conscious measurement of European revolutionary efforts, and scepticism of them, by the unquestioned British ideal of constitutional monarchy. With the defeat of liberal nationalism in Europe abolitionists in touch with the largely Unitarian circle of the radical lawyer, W.H. Ashurst, developed existing or began fresh contacts with revolutionary exiles from Italy and were involved in the foundation of the Society of the Friends of Italy in 1850. In addition to the Ashurst family antislavery sympathisers included Mrs Nichol, William Shaen and George Armstrong, the latter providing Mazzini with Garrisonian contacts in the United States. In provincial Sheffield the evangelical Rawsons were taken with the dramatic harangues of Gavazzi. Kossuth too, initially criticised for his muted abolitionism while in the United States, associated with the Nichols and Armstrong amongst others in the early 1850s.[25]

Doubts about 1848 and its results were stronger amongst Sturgeite abolitionists involved in the Peace Congress movement. Their hostility to the use of force by both revolutionaries and counter-revolutionaries alienated European liberals as an example of Quaker naïveté and separated them from many of their normal reformer allies in England both in 1848–50 and at the time of their campaign against the Crimean War which appeared to their critics as an opportunity for European subject peoples to throw off Russian autocracy.[26]

An even clearer contrast was between antislavery responses to the situation of the subject peoples of Europe and the Irish and Indians within the Empire. The Dublin abolitionists Webb, Allen and Haughton all recognised and understood the widespread resentment in Ireland at the political arrangements of the Union and the appalling conditions of much of the population but had differing views as to the virtues of O'Connell's Repeal movement as a way forward. In England the polarities were stark. The conservative evangelical Charles Stuart saw nothing to be done for the majority of the Irish population mired in Catholicism and misled by demagogues; the only feature of the situation in the 1840s which merited approval was the patient and prepared attitude of the British government. In contrast Elizabeth Pease praised the beginnings of the Repeal campaign as likely to offer a grand historical example of how to bring a people to freedom without bloodshed. Perhaps Estlin's attitude was characteristic of many reformers; he recognised the real grievances of the Irish but none the less adopted the patronising assumptions of the English ruling class believing the Irish 'a most indolent, uncivilized and intractable population to manage'. Repeal would thus constitute 'an act of the greatest cruelty'.[27]

BIS and other free trade abolitionists interested in India had ample criticisms of East India Company rule. The criterion of good government to be insisted upon by Christian reformers was defined by Joseph Pease solely as the prosperity and happiness of the Indian population. It was the objective of the fiscal and free trade reform programme they promoted, amounting to a remodelled British rule in India but not a step towards withdrawal of control. In the 1850s antislavery proponents of evangelisation approved forceful suppression of the Mutiny. Even the Sturgeite pacifists, critical of Company misgovernment as the cause of conflict and involved in a campaign against a policy of 'vengeance' by the British, assumed continued British rule. 'All', in George Thompson's words 'have an interest in the preservation of India in this country.'[28]

The spread of reforms in which abolitionists became involved was sufficiently extensive to provoke questions as to how and why they saw these activities fitting together. It will be suggested that the mentality of many reformers was shaped by a number of related oppositions: the human agent and the environment; the individual and the institution; the reformation of the person and the maintenance of good order; response to change and attachment to stability. They were preoccupied with finding ways, institutional and non-institutional, of combining these seeming opposites, bringing to bear the changing cultural resources available to them.

A useful starting point is an article in the *Philanthropist* in 1812 which proclaimed the success of the anti-slave trade reformers as a vindication of the power of 'benevolent and humane' attitudes. Progression of other projects of betterment, such as reform of the penal code, required the intervention of an 'enlightened public' combined with parliamentary initiative and had to accommodate both concern for the victims of unreformed practices and 'the general welfare of civil society'. In the example of reform of the penal code, especially through reduction of the number of capital offences, the article proposed that a correct balance could be struck by imposing solitary confinement in a penitentiary as a penalty in place of the death penalty. This allowed for the importance of deterrence, possible compensation for the victim of crime (a dead felon clearly did not), repentance by the perpetrator in his lonely meditation and thus a punishment more weighted to fit the crime. Change of this kind, like abolition, demonstrated the possibility of reform within the system, refuting the charge frequently made at that period of 'all innovation as dangerous to the community and [which] represents every attempt at improvement as ineffectual to answer the desired ends.'[29]

From these clues it is possible to describe a type of the reform mentality in which abolitionists shared as they took part in the complex of reforms within Britain and internationally. Often reformers seem to have begun their engagement with victims, subject to harsh and brutal treatment and regarded as less than fully human by those who exercised power over them. This was equally true of slaves in the Middle Passage and on the plantations, prisoners in the unreformed gaols, the insane in the madhouses, poor children in the hovels and workplaces or the sick poor. In each case a necessary step to improvement was the recognition of the essential humanity of these victims rather than their animality, an animality which required the equation of control with physical restraint or brutalisation. The acceptance of the humanity of victims, as was argued in the earlier chapter on ideology (pp.22–3), could take the form of recognising that all men, women and children were God's creatures for whose souls He was concerned. The performance of the humane as a product of the recognition of the human was thus in part the effect of the development of evangelical themes in theology. Even sinners in their sinfulness declared their humanity since sin itself was universally present. The impulse to reform had one source, in other words, in the urge to encourage self-order in individuals who appeared to lack it, either because they seemed evil or were ignorant of what was required.

The reform mentality recognised, however, that victims had bodies as well as souls which were abused and were the locus of pain and other human feeling. Acquaintance with the writings of reformers on the conditions of victims brings this home vividly; the parallel bodily circumstances of different categories of victim were sometimes made explicit. Thomas Pringle, secretary of the Anti-Slavery Society, in quoting from his friend Dr Walsh evidence of the physical brutalities of Brazilian slave society indicated analogous circumstances and implied the need for similar responses.

I never walked through the streets of Rio that some house did not present to me the semblance of a bridewell where the moans and cries of the sufferers and the sounds of whips and scourges within announced to me that corporal punishment was being inflicted.

It was also in the course of the eighteenth century, in the decades when evangelicalism began its rise, in Laqueur's speculative but plausible argument, that 'humanitarian narratives' of various kinds took form. They validated themselves through their detail and focused upon the body. The narratives of reformers describing a slave ship or a madhouse or a bridewell/gaol or early factory and, above all, the physical and bodily circumstances of persons within them can be categorised as such humanitarian narratives. Through the body as the point of abuse and pain the narratives equally with autopsies or case histories could, in Laqueur's suggestion, act 'as the common bond between those who suffer and those who would help'. They were a stimulus to action not least because they implied a system of causation which could not only complement the evangelical impulse but might particularly affect those with relevant knowledge and specialised technical and professional skills. This was a partial explanation of the prominence in the later eighteenth and earlier nineteenth centuries of the physician–reformer.[30]

As victims then, individuals were seen from the later 1700s as redeemable or improvable. But the reform mentality did not see them simply as individuals subject to the power of other individuals and to be reformed purely personally. They were also subject to the deleterious effects of environments – poverty, poor housing, lack of education, loss of family perhaps. In addition, or alternatively, victims already caught up in the institutional nexus of plantation or prison had to face the destructive impact of unreformed institutional regimes. These were perceived not only as not helping reformation but as contributing to the *spread* of sin, disease or criminality and thus, far from aiding the 'welfare of civil society', actually undermining it. The redemption or improvement of the individual depended not only on his own agency through growing control of self but on alteration of environments including institutional environments to provide conditions more conducive to the striving for self-control or order within the self.

Sunday schools were in effect new institutions in the late eighteenth century intended to draw the children of the lower classes into a morally healthful environment for at least one day of the week and perhaps provide them with a moral framework through the ability to read and absorb religious works so that they became capable of appreciating the circumstances of their lives and acting responsibly with some degree of perceived choice. Penitentiaries organised upon the principle of solitary confinement were proposed and implemented as transformations of or clear departures from the gaols of the eighteenth century with their criminal subcultures, indiscriminate mixing and exploitation by the turnkeys. Asylums likewise were intended to contrast with madhouses and to do so not only in their physical lay-out but through the flexible development of 'moral treatment' which was intended to encourage the supposed natural recuperative powers of the inmates towards developing self-restraint and rational behaviour. Those infirmaries too, as in Manchester, which became centres of reformist activity by physicians moved towards regular attention of the sick poor, separate wards to control contagion and firm discipline over habits and cleanliness to promote responsibility in individual patients.

All of these reformed regimes were posited on the assumption that inmates were capable of reflection guided by discipline towards guilt and redemption or towards assertion of their morally informed wills in a fashion which marked their improvement. Equally, reformation could only be expected if limits were accepted to their conduct by those who ran the new or reformed institutions; otherwise the balance between individual and environment would degenerate towards old tyrannies. As the history of prisons and mental institutions makes clear this regression did often happen. Without self-discipline by the managers of institutions, helped by the establishment of codes of rules and independent inspection, the planting of the seed of the sense of order which could flower through the growing capacity of moral self-management by inmates would not occur. Thus Buxton judged that Elizabeth Fry had turned the female prison at Newgate from a 'Hell on Earth to a place in which even some of the lowest had been transformed by repentance'. She devoted considerable attention, as did the Tukes at the York Retreat, to trying to find appropriate people to run the institutions.[31]

A balanced interrelationship between individual moral development and institutional discipline thus remained central in the reform mentality to the reformation or improvement of 'victims'. The further requirement to defer to the welfare of the whole society, including its security, is evident in the prominence of the role of labour in the workings of reformatory institutions. Buxton measured

137

Mrs Fry's success at Newgate by comparing it to a 'well-regulated Manufactory'. Asylum reformers aimed to create 'a hive of industry' so that to enter one was like encountering 'some vast emporium of manufacture; labour is divided, so that it may be easy and well performed and so apportioned that it may suit the tastes and powers of each labourer'. It was significant as an ideal though not often as an accomplishment. While such labour was clearly seen as part of the process of individual reform by encouraging self-control and self-possession and, if it avoided dullness, also stimulating to the mind, it was also an aspect of institutional discipline. More speculatively, it demonstrated the body and potentially the mind as being active, no longer the location of victimisation and thus both symbolically (if unconsciously) and actually labour was a preparation for re-entry into the world of work as part of a normal not deviant role in society.[32]

In another way, reformers showed their concern for the security and welfare of society by adding the role of guardian of society to that of manager, carer or teacher in their institutions. John Angell James required Sunday school teachers to pay 'discriminating attention to the different capacities and tempers of the children', on occasion to offer rewards, but also punishment, including corporal punishment in extreme cases, so long as it was proportionate to the offence. Chastisement had to be presented to the children as for their own good and consistency in this approach would produce the beneficial result of 'submission if not reformation'.[33]

An additional way of illustrating the reformers' need to balance the welfare of society against the improvement of individuals is through looking briefly at ideas about and expressions of institutional architecture. As a Suffolk magistrate in the 1780s the political reformer and anti-slave trade supporter Capel Lofft consulted his fellow reformer Dr John Jebb about the 'polity and construction' of a gaol and house of correction. After Jebb's comments were published Thomas Percival of Manchester took issue with him on one important point. Both were concerned to see a construction which preserved the health of the inmates while preventing the spread of contagion to the population outside as well as preventing opportunities for escape. Jebb and Percival both believed diseases spread largely by 'noxious vapours' and Jebb argued that walls above the level of the inhabited surface of the prison were incompatible with sufficient ventilation to disperse bad air. He therefore advocated that high walls be built within a deep ditch around the gaol. Percival opposed this in terms of its impracticality as a solution for gaols in towns but also, after characteristically carrying out experiments in his own yard surrounded by high walls, he found that breezes, sunshine and rain acted to dilute any contagion and still ensured the physical security of the prison. Percival was later involved in planning, with T.B. Bayley, the new prison at Manchester.

With the development of separate confinement as something of an orthodoxy prisons were built with the intention of keeping individuals as separate from each other as possible, even to the extent of separate exercise yards for separate wings and masks to prevent individual recognition. In Mrs Fry's chapel at Newgate separate boxed seating maintained the isolation of prisoners from each other while they focused on the preacher. It was a detailed architecture of control believed to be conducive to individual repentance but also a security against disorder within the prison and potential disorder outside.

At the York Retreat the Tukes placed considerable importance on the physical lay-out of buildings and grounds. They believed extensive and attractive grounds to be crucial to the right sort of environment for recuperation and the main building had no window bars though it did have strong doors and frames. Yet although concern for physical security – and consequent reassurance of the outside world – was clearly less than in prisons, it was present. Exercise courts were walled off, though they were also built at the bottom of a slope so that inmates could appreciate the surrounding countryside.[34]

Does the type of mentality sketched in the preceding pages suggest a sufficient family resemblance in the assumptions underlying various reforms to offer part of the explanation as to why abolitionists often engaged in several of them? At first glance there seem to be some features of antislavery which set it apart from the other activities. Its objects of concern were physically distant if we think of slaves in ships or on the West Indian plantations. Nor was the plantation as an institution on a spectrum from 'open' to 'total' or 'closed' as near the 'total' end as the penitentiary (though the slave ship may have been) or as near the 'open' end as the Sunday school. Yet there was enough in common for reformers to experience a sense of familiarity. While the slaves were physically distant from those who wished them well this was not true for Granville Sharp and his associates dealing with slaves in Britain or for those abolitionists who spent some time in slave societies. Also, the social distance between reformers and the 'victims' they dealt with in other reforms was comparable to the physical distance involved in antislavery. In each case the 'victims' were clients in an inferior position.

The desire to open up the lives of slaves to Christianity and thus to provide them both with the opportunity for salvation and the moral instrument to assume greater responsibility for themselves and their families was a fundamental ground of the hostility of reformers to the slave trade and slavery. Reformers held a similar attitude to those they tried to reach through Bible and Tract Societies and Sunday schools at home and by support of missionary endeavour abroad. The plantations on which the slaves worked were moreover not only obstacles to the evangelisation of the slaves, they were in effect treated by reformers as institutional regimes requiring progressive improvement. The capacity for authoritative intervention was of course initially much less than in social institutions within Britain. The fading expectation after 1807 that self-interest would cause slaveholders to improve conditions was underlined by the lack of any more direct instrument for change which would help the physical and moral amelioration of the slaves. Pressure for registration was in part a step towards more specific rules for the plantations which, after 1823, were to emanate from the Colonial Office or colonial legislatures. The failure of that policy in turn meant a decisive attempt to shift the balance between discipline and individual autonomy or self-discipline within the plantation by means of emancipation, but *not* an abandonment of the perspective or the institution. During the period of apprenticeship the stipendiary magistracy, however imperfectly it operated, may be seen as the rough equivalent of inspectorates which examined prisons, asylums or the schools run by the religious school societies. Moreover, the welfare of the colonial societies in which the plantations operated was perceived by reformers quite as much as by government officials or estate owners after emancipation to depend upon the productive labour of a workforce more of whose discipline would now have to be self-imposed.

In addition to these resemblances of fundamental assumption and approach between antislavery and other reforms it is revealing that the rhetoric of antislavery provided a language of documentation and persuasion in dealing with other contemporary social evils. The situation of factory children brought fierce denunciation from Sadler and Oastler in terms of their slavery. True it was denunciation which took on an ambivalent tone in regard to colonial slavery. Oastler savagely commented on the horrors of child labour uncovered in a supposedly Christian and philanthropic society where 'the tears of innocent victims' wet 'the very streets which receive the droppings of an "Anti-Slavery Society" '. None the less, in a less double-edged way, Wilberforce was sympathetic to the plight of factory children, seeing in them a parallel with West Indian slaves; some early reformers who became committed to women's rights were abolitionists and saw parallels in their two commitments, while the free trade movement's rhetoric of liberty came easily to the lips of antislavery reformers and with an added moral resonance. A similar transcendence of enslavement by reformation was close to the centre of the dramatic rhetoric of temperance.[35]

It was commonplace, moreover, in the first half of the nineteenth century for reformers explicitly to connect different social evils either causally or as part of a more general moral declension and thus to indicate that efforts to reform one evil ought to lead on to others. Crime was repeatedly linked to drunkenness and when supporters of antislavery such as Brougham turned to temperance they were also apt to show a concern over crime, prisons or the legal system. Similarly Raikes tried to direct his Gloucestershire Sunday schools towards temperance, thus providing an ethos in which religion was more likely to flourish amongst the labouring class. By the 1830s the British and Foreign Temperance Society which had many antislavery supporters was extremely expansive in the claims it made for its areas of operation. Temperance was thought to promote self-improvement not only as a way out of poverty but to encourage enterprise and commerce. Here the perspective of temperance reformers intersected with that of the free trade movement; enterprise and commerce provided firm foundations for improved relations between states and made international peace more likely.[36]

One final indication not merely of the compatibility of antislavery with a number of other reform movements but of the ease of multiple engagement by reformers was the similarity of the *processes* of reform activity across the spectrum of movements as indicated in the *Philanthropist* article. Organisationally from Bible and Tract Societies to antislavery, temperance, peace and ACLL auxiliaries, reform movements had much in common in propagandising and implementing policy locally through associations affiliated to a national committee and in focusing opinion through petitions or other pressure group activities on government or parliament. This was combined with or, in some instances like lunacy reform where local auxiliaries were not developed, largely taken over by a practised process centred on parliament of investigation by committee, legislative proposals and parliamentary debate.

There were none the less limits to the extent to which all the reform energies of abolitionists could be harmoniously combined within the middle-class complex of reforms as so far defined. These limits became particularly clear from the 1830s onwards in the changed context of reform already discussed in chapters 3 and 4. Many dissenter abolitionists began to devote an increasing proportion of energy to religiously sectarian objectives. Not only was this likely to strain relations with those Anglicans who remained active in antislavery but it provoked tensions within dissenter groups. 'Weighty Friends' like the Gurneys prevented the Quakers as a body from pursuing attacks on the religious establishment, yet individual Quaker reformers like the Sturge family did so. Many Unitarians, themselves in conflict with evangelical dissenters over chapel property, refrained from supporting the movement against Anglican privileges, and this was true even of some reformers like J.A. James within evangelical dissent. The growing prominence of sectarian militancy amongst many reformers gave something of a religious and class colouring to the free trade movement which helped mobilise support but put the movement beyond the loyalties of many of the older generation of particularly Anglican supporters of antislavery. The peace movement in the years of its dominance by Cobden and Sturge had similar problems, without the popular attraction of the material promises of free trade; it produced alienation of more conservative peace men such as Samuel Gurney. The mutual respect, let alone co-operation, of peace reformers had also come under strain when the perfectionist American strand of non-resistance associated with members of the Garrisonian wing of antislavery won over a small number of adherents in Britain and was preached by Henry Clarke Wright during his British stay in the mid-1840s. At the international as well as the domestic level of middle-class reform the limits of the reform front were clarified or, to put it another way, by the 1830s there was a shift in the centre of gravity of the reform complex which reflected changes in the composition of reform alliances.[37]

At the heart of the outlook of reformers was the need to strike a balance between encouraging self-discipline and responsibility in individuals and imposing discipline and good order on potential deviants. The different reformers were always liable to locate the balance at different points along a spectrum from individual autonomy to tight control of the individual to guarantee social order. A number of questions arise: were abolitionists in middle-class reform efforts directing their efforts only to specific categories of people or did they attempt reformation of the whole of society? Were they prompted primarily by a defensive anxiety to control threats to moral order and social stability or did they show an optimism about the likely improvement and good sense of the objects of their good will? Given the difficulty of reformers ever securing complete success on their own terms over an obdurate and complex reality, how did they respond to changing situations?

The evangelical project undertaken by both a minority of Anglicans and by dissenters to provide moral and religious education through Bible Societies, Tract Societies, Sunday schools and religious-based schools was managed with a strong desire to save souls and strict observance of the duty to produce orderly behaviour. The *Christian Observer* acknowledged the scriptures were opposed to oppression 'of monarchies, of aristocracies and democracies; as well indeed of mixed governments, for even these may become the tyrants of the people', yet exceptions to the rule of obedience 'broad and unlimited' to established authority were not likely to occur. Any criticisms of addresses issued for the enforcement of morality and religion in the best interests of the nation were 'calumnies'. In the particular case of Sunday schools James rejoiced that 'by an unconstrained election, the lower classes of the community have chosen their better instructed neighbours as the guardians of their children's minds and manners'.[38]

Although in theory this evangelical conservatism could be qualified by the priority the pious were bound to give to the laws of God rather than the laws of the state if the two ever seemed to be in conflict, a more precise definition of the approaches of evangelical reformers requires them to be situated in the contexts and crises as they developed at different times. Through the intersecting influence of the numerous voluntary associations which they sustained, the growing body of the evangelical middle class (including Quakers of an evangelical tendency) who were beyond 'anxieties of poverty and free from the solicitudes and enmities of the great' hoped, for example, during the social crisis of the war years to absorb and muffle the discontent of the labouring poor. Their efforts in Spitalfields provide an example. Both Buxton and William Allen were employers in the district and, with the aid of associates who included the antislavery Samuel Hoare and Peter Bedford, set up a soup kitchen to meet the desperate circumstances of the local silk-weavers thrown out of work by wartime interruptions of raw material supplies. They also organised a supply of subsidised food funded in part by contributions raised by the reformers. These measures appeared necessary to the survival of the labourers, let alone their sense of self-respect. But the reformers were also determined to maintain discipline by imposing a moral test. The subsidised food was only available to those who gave evidence of keeping good order within their families, showed that they were searching for work and kept clear of alcohol. Only these paragons acquired a ticket of eligibility. Both Anglican and dissenter schools were also established on the 'principles of piety and virtue', their character hinted at in the words of Allen's *Philanthropist* which recommended 'firmness, promptness and decision attendant on military order interwoven into the school discipline', yet to be conducted without severity.[39]

To create and maintain awe of authority was obviously a major intention of the mechanisms devised in Spitalfields, but they were based upon some compassion and betrayed a delicacy over appearing purely repressive even or especially in a dangerous quarter during dangerous times. Over the longer term different sorts of abolitionists involved in promoting institutional means of reform outside times of acute crisis showed different intensities of desire to discipline those they wanted to reform. Close to one end of the spectrum was Elizabeth Fry and her evangelical allies at Newgate. Though it was intended to elicit the consent of prisoners for what was done to them as prefiguring their recognition of their own guilt and the rightness of their punishment, what happened to them amounted to discipline through humiliation and close surveillance. Decoration and attractive clothing of any kind were forbidden, the hair of the women was cropped short and their activity during work-time closely scrutinised through a monitorial system. Separation by category of prisoner and periodic individual isolation further concentrated pressures on the prisoners.

Sunday schools drew in rapidly increasing numbers of pupils during the first half of the nineteenth century and came to be run by a variety of reformers with differing emphases as to the role and character of the schools. Raikes, in the late eighteenth century, was primarily concerned to end the potential for disorder in poor children running wild on the Sabbath and to provide them with some rudiments of religion through giving them the ability to read uplifting material. The evangelical priorities were even more abundantly evident in John Angell James' advice to Sunday school teachers in 1816. Conveying the ability to read was to do no more than the task of ordinary day schools. If teachers were to add to the basic knowledge children could acquire by reading 'habits of order, industry and morality' in order to form the characters of the children and to 'rise into life our orderly, industrious and sober race' the desirable result would be the 'peace, comfort and safety of the community'. Even so this fell short of the ultimate objective of Sunday schools of giving the religious knowledge and deep-rooted impressions and habits which would save the children's souls. The content of the education James envisaged was reading, with some spelling to help with the absorption of biblical revelation and then work on the catechism and memorising hymns.[40]

The different views held on whether the Sunday scholars should be taught to write were most revealing of the different balances struck between individual development and social discipline. James' conclusion that it was unnecessary to teach writing was an example of a widespread, though not universal, conviction amongst evangelicals, including abolitionists. In contrast, the Rational Dissenter William Turner in Newcastle argued for both writing and reading in the schools as early as the 1780s; by the 1820s the reality was that more and more of the schools were teaching writing. When Joseph Sturge promoted Sunday schools along with a girls' Lancasterian school and a Mechanics' Institute he advocated a 'ready subordination' but within a context of encouraging self-improvement and a widening of horizons.

It can be concluded then that many religious reformers betrayed anxiety about moral declension and social volatility, seeing it as their duty to counter them. But they also mostly steered clear of simple repression through prosecution or intimidation. They prominently embraced the theme of moral and social discipline and deployed powerful institutional resources to achieve it, but ultimately they looked to its final accomplishment through internalisation by individuals. Thus one side of the reform complex in which abolitionists were engaged amounted to an effort to renovate society morally and secure its stability by resting it upon the consent of a population 'sharing' many of the values of those with different levels of authority over them. It was also the case that this side of reform was most likely to be the product of the evangelical tradition (including Anglicans, dissenters and most of the activist Quakers) within the interwoven traditions of reform.[41]

The more rationalist tradition within antislavery was likely to engender reformers who showed greater optimism about the ability of people to follow enlightened ways without excessive restrictions or disciplinary pressures except for the truly recalcitrant. The *Monthly*

Repository reformers could manifest sharp distaste for the activities and style of life of the upper classes. In a similar frame of mind Dr James Currie in Liverpool urged the liberally educated middle class 'to check the insolence of wealth, to control the arrogance of rank, to strengthen and expand the charities of our nature'. By contrast, violent upheaval from the lower class was only to be anticipated 'at a very singular crisis of society' and thus they should not be regarded so harshly. Social cohesion was to be maintained by extending enlightenment rather than through force. Popular education under the Lancasterian system without religious indoctrination could be cheap and effective. 'It is the growth of knowledge which terrifies our elderly country squires, village clergymen who left college half a century ago and ancient maids who never felt a wish to read more than the Common Prayer Book with the Apocrypha.' It was a stance which looked with favour on reform by self-help and initiative in leadership by the knowledgeable - what Currie called 'the genius of the pen'. The Manchester case study earlier in this chapter (p.118–21) revealed less an anxiety about social control within the reform culture than a project by an Enlightenment coterie to modernise the institutions of their community and in most cases to provide greater access to them while offering services based on skill and the advancement of knowledge. The theme of self-improvement is apparent in Unitarian abolitionist support for the Society for the Dissemination of Useful Knowledge and Mechanics' Institutes and for self-dependence, in the interest in free enquiry and the attraction of liberal economics.

This last point leads to the other aspect of the rationalist reform outlook; self-dependence as an objective could in some cases minimise the imperative of conscious social benevolence. Priestley tended to scepticism about forms of charity which underlined the dependent status of the recipient and believed the bracing independence encouraged by *laissez-faire* economics much preferable; other Rational Dissenters and Unitarians saw the alternatives less starkly. It was also the case that initiative by the knowledgeable tended to optimistic belief in the quasi-scientific management of environment and, indirectly, personality, as at the Manchester Asylum where John Ferriar emphasised 'the management of hope and apprehension' conveying a concern with both 'ascendancy' and 'gentleness of manner and kindness of treatment'. There is no doubt that a kind of imposition was here intended, though justified in quasi-scientific rather than social or primarily moral terms. On the whole though it is reasonable to conclude that the rational religious tradition promoted an outlook amongst reformers which gave more room to the subjects of reform to take part in the selection of the terms and the direction in which they should develop than did the evangelical tradition.[42]

To make this judgement is not, however, to conclude that only the strand of rational religion in antislavery created abolitionists who can be characterised as liberals, especially if due emphasis is placed on the period from the 1820s onwards and if liberalism is understood both as *laissez-faire* economics and in broader terms as well. The inclination of abolitionists of different religious backgrounds to adopt the assumptions and arguments of liberal political economy in the 1820s in their attacks on slavery has been noted. Elements of that tendency outside the question of slavery can, however, be detected earlier. Wilberforce as a member of the parliamentary committee on the woollen textile industry in 1806 supported the majority recommendations to dispense with protective regulations which aided the smaller clothiers in favour of opening the trade up to free competition and by extension creating a free market in labour in the industry. He appears to have believed that this would contribute to greater prosperity even if at the cost of some painful dislocation in some parts of the industry. But this did not mean that he had permanently set aside his moral paternalism even on labour questions since he accepted the need for some safeguards to protect child labour. A similar view was strongly advocated by the evangelical Sir Thomas Bernard through the reports of the Society for Bettering the Condition of the Poor because he believed that child labour in the factories, increasingly not supervised by parents, dissolved the family bond, employers doing too little to find a substitute form of moral discipline. More strikingly, the experience of seeing the conditions of child labour in the mills drove the Rational Dissenter Thomas Percival to sharp criticism of factory regimes, although, initially, he had anticipated the mill as an instrument of education as well as discipline. He joined evangelicals in supporting government regulation of factory labour by means of the first Factory Act of 1802. The advance of the idea of a free market in labour by the 1830s was, however, plain in the opposition of evangelical dissenters such as the Baineses to Factory Acts and the Ten Hours Movement as well as antislavery Unitarians, the Strutts and Bowring to Ashley's 1833 Factory Bill. There was, in other words, no unified attitude amongst abolitionists to regulation of the labour market, though most of them became more likely in later decades to oppose any regulation of the market except to protect child labour.[43]

A related issue which has exercised historians is the attitude of abolitionists to the New Poor Law of 1834, particularly as it may be seen as in part devised to create 'self motion' in individuals by establishing such austere conditions in workhouses, with the denial of outdoor relief, that they were pressed into the labour market. At the parliamentary level in 1834 antislavery supporters were divided; Eltis calculates that a majority of antislavery MPs either supported the New Poor Law or abstained. Those who opposed it were the more politically radical, Daniel O'Connell and the Irish. Yet there were also some notable antislavery figures in the country who opposed the new system. The Sheffield evangelical, Samuel Roberts, campaigned vigorously against it yet significantly lamenting the absence of support for his position from all but a handful of dissenting ministers. In the Unitarian camp a minority only came out in opposition but it included both the Leeds reformer the Rev. Charles Wicksteed and his radical antislavery Manchester colleague, John Relly Beard, who believed in regulation on behalf of the poor as an intermediate necessity on the way to the complete freedom guaranteed by morality and benevolence. This continued a critical radicalism found in earlier years in Robert Aspland's *Monthly Repository*. The objective of abolitionists in this tradition was to establish as the core of the social values of different interacting groups the value of interdependence, 'Union of all the necessary parts to an achievement is the thing meant and that "union" to set one element against another is truly "division".'[44]

Initially freedom of trade seemed to present fewer complexities to abolitionists than a free labour market. The overlap between antislavery and the ACLL in its early years is well known. Once again, however, although the broader antislavery constituency in the country probably remained loyal to the free trade campaign, a substantial number of reformers active in antislavery organisations found themselves demanding modification of free trade so far as sugar from slave economies was concerned. But the sharp divisions of the mid-1840s were not permanent and the substantiality of division can be exaggerated. Both sides believed themselves to be adopting a moral stance. The free traders saw a duty to British workers in reducing their cost of living and thereby encouraging greater social harmony. However, they and their opponents could agree that ultimately the spread of free commerce would bring prosperity and peace. Joseph Sturge and the majority within the BFASS gave a more immediate and specific moral priority to protection of the West Indian freedmen and discouragement of slavery in Cuba and Brazil and of the slave trade to those areas. But they could sound as hard-headed as the free traders in pointing to the waste of expense in maintaining an anti-slave trade squadron while contemplating a policy which would encourage the slave trade; Buxton, on this issue in alliance with Sturge, deployed this argument.

What was finally in contention was a matter of priorities in the shorter and longer term, although by the 1840s neither the Sturgeite moral radicals nor their critics fundamentally questioned the framework of liberal political economy. The Sturgeites offered a limited because temporary qualification. They accepted that open markets whose demands were met by free labour were their final objective. They were prepared for open competition on equal terms between West Indian and foreign free-labour sugar and expected that this would lead to improvements in productive efficiency in the West Indies. They were prepared for universal competition in the sugar market when the conditions of the competitors were roughly equal. To this end a system which distinguished between all free-labour (British and foreign) and all slave-grown sugar to the advantage of free labour would encourage slaveholders to convert, thus creating the conditions for universally free markets. The Sturgeites were appealing in the mid-1840s for a temporary maintenance of fiscal intervention by the liberal state to bring about the circumstances for the equal competition which would permit the cessation of that intervention. Long after the extensive deployment of the axioms of liberal political economy within the antislavery movement therefore elements within the movement continued to seek some limits to their full implementation.

Though they were minority voices within the antislavery constituency as a whole they were sometimes able to command local organisational majorities. They were also voices from different traditions spanning Shaftesbury's evangelical paternalism, Roberts' provincial missionary evangelism and the marginal and radical Quaker or Unitarian aspirations to class conciliation and to laying firm foundations for an eventually self-regulating liberal society. Study, observation and experience convinced these abolitionists that too many people still suffered and therefore it was too soon to move to an unfettered economic liberalism as the solvent of social and moral problems. Had they believed in the complete liberal solution they would have been confessing the virtual redundancy of the roles they had previously filled.

In taking the discussion of liberalism beyond its economic content the question arises of the commitment of abolitionists to pluralism, particularly religious pluralism in the sense of equality of legal status for religious groups. The drive to secure the removal of legal disabilities from non-Anglicans goes back beyond the beginning of our period and was later followed by resistance to Anglican financial claims on non-Anglicans and finally a phase in which increasing numbers of nonconformists pressed for religious disestablishment. There are, however, some complexities to the story. The efforts to repeal the Test and Corporation Acts between 1787 and 1790 provoked as firm an opposition by the Anglican minority who were abolitionists as amongst their more conservative colleagues. Trans-mutation of this hostility into grudging acceptance of repeal by the 1820s occurred amongst many Anglican reformers, but Catholics posed a different problem for them and for dissenters. In the late 1780s it was mainly some of the more radical Rational Dissenters who stood out publicly for repeal of civil disabilities against Catholics as well as Protestant dissenters; the Priestley mob in 1791 had a point in shouting 'No Popery'. William Roscoe took a similar position in the Commons in 1806-7. In the 1820s it was Unitarians like Lant Carpenter who pressed the importance of Catholic Emancipation in his correspondence with Lord Holland as perhaps even more urgent than repeal of the Test Act. In contrast the Claphamite *Christian Observer* showed recurrent hostility to Catholics, for example over their supposed unwillingness, should a hierarchy be allowed to be established, to accept the constitutional right of royal veto in the appointment of bishops. Granville Sharp to the end of his life remained harshly anti-Catholic; he regarded Catholics as already being entirely free to engage in worship in their own way and thus joined the Protestant Union in 1813 to oppose the true purpose of Catholic Emancipation which he interpreted as to gain political rights for Catholics. During the 1820s many Wesleyans and evangelical dissenters refused to collaborate with Catholics in pressing for religious equality. Enmity of this kind was the product of history and Protestant mythology. Paradoxically perhaps the refusal to support emancipation for Catholics was justified by abolitionists as much as by other Englishmen on the ground that Catholicism was 'utterly subversive of the principles of genuine liberty' and owed allegiance to a foreign despotism. This conviction remained in some antislavery circles long after Catholic Emancipation.

The force of anti-Catholicism contributed to the ironic intertwining of devotion to liberty with emotional intolerance in abolitionist responses to rising nationalisms primarily of a liberal character in the Europe of the 1840s and 1850s. Amongst the Unitarian liberals and radicals and radical Quakers who were advocates of Italian and Hungarian freedom there was a plain continuity between their domestic political outlook and their internationalist liberalism in opposition to authoritarian imperial governments. Difficulties arose when some of them looked at Ireland. Harriet Martineau could not abide O'Connell and the Repeal movement and Estlin frankly opposed it by 1848 as 'more injurious to the Irish than the English'. Partly, we may speculate, these liberals and radicals could not equate Britain with the governments of Austria and Russia; if not the unblemished home of freedom the British system was open enough, they believed, to inform English opinion on Irish issues and secure the reform of abuses. But Estlin was not alone in betraying traces of an ethnocentric disdain towards the Irish in terms of their excitability, improvidence and dependency. The sub-text was that too few of them exhibited good, middle-class, Protestant virtues.

Many evangelical abolitionists however framed their outlook on the nationalist question much more overtly in anti-Catholic terms, particularly after they had been stirred up by the Maynooth controversy and the establishment of the Catholic hierarchy. Garibaldi came to be seen as an opponent of papal oppression. So too did Elizabeth Rawson's hero, Gavazzi, who drew large evangelical audiences to hear 'scurrilous anti-papist propaganda'. The money he raised later for his efforts in Italy to establish a 'primitive, apostolic, evangelical christian church' and sustain the nationalist impulse drew upon the contemporary missionary enthusiasm in England. Appropriately the Rawsons combined admiration for Gavazzi with raising funds for Protestant missions in Italy. With these attitudes evangelicals found the Irish situation a confirmation of many of the factors antithetical to moral and material progress. The best they could do was to support Hibernian Societies that aided those Irish who had had the good fortune to escape their homeland.[45]

One other dilemma faced abolitionists embroiled in the larger reform complex: what should be their attitude to the state? It was an important issue because it focused the ambivalence many of them showed about the balance between moral and social discipline and individual autonomy. It is also a useful question for the historian in resuming the issue of liberalism from yet another angle over a number of decades. The efforts at moral reform undertaken primarily by evangelicals in the late eighteenth and early nineteenth centuries so far as Claphamites were concerned ought to involve voluntary action rather than state regulation in order to develop individual moral responsibility on the part of those they were trying to improve. It was this preference which underlay Claphamite distaste for the prosecutory zeal of some members of the Vice Society; outward regulation did not reach the sinner's conscience. Wilberforce, Henry Thornton and Macaulay also resisted the sometimes deceitful methods the zealots of the Vice Society used to gather evidence for prosecutions. The Rational Dissenters' *Monthly Repository* also opposed judicial intervention against immoral behaviour in the belief that it would be directed largely against the lower classes.

More complex problems like the poverty of labourers and their families could not be left to voluntary exhortation. Nor did the committee of Bernard's society, a roster of evangelicals and evangelically-inclined Quakers, intend that the society would itself raise funds and distribute them to cases needing assistance. It defined its role as investigation and the accumulation of evidence. It encouraged parishes to provide relief and stimulate both personal benevolence and moral and social discipline in the localities. This could best be achieved on the part of 'benevolent individuals'

> by a *personal inspection* into their [the poor's] real situation, by watching over the administration of those funds which are raised by the authority of parliament and by discriminating between the honest, industrious and peaceable sufferer and those pests of society who are eager to avail themselves of every opportunity to create disturbance.

Active benevolence and inspection were a refinement and supplementation of local administration, an aid to its moral and disciplinary efficiency rather than a replacement. The Spitalfields Association for the Relief of the Poor directed by abolitionists performed in this way in one locality.[46]

Thomas Clarkson represented a more overt suspicion of the state. Over many years he criticised the growth of state offices, sinecures and pensions and the stimulus to the elaboration of the state apparatus created by wars. The main counterweight he saw in the 'national virtue' which abolitionists and other reformers managed to encourage. This perspective was one shared by religious liberals such as Priestley who feared the power of the state as a danger to pluralism of opinion. It was an outlook which promoted educational reform so long as it stopped short of a state system of education, though rigorous moral education of criminals through penitentiaries was permissible. Similar anti-statist libertarian tendencies can also be discerned in Romilly's opposition to a paid police force, though he was prepared to see a professionalisation of personnel in penitentiaries. This kind of suspicion of state power was not, however, quite the same thing as that which surfaced in the debates over education from the early nineteenth century and in which so many abolitionists took part. Amongst nonconformist antislavery supporters of the British and Foreign School Society the fear was more particularly of the effect of the Established Church's link to the state on the content of education and was the product less of intellectual liberalism than the development of denominationalism. By the 1830s William Allen was in favour of a national system only if religious education was based on scripture without any sectarian emphases and it was overseen by a board of education representative of all religious denominations backed by an inspectorate. In the 1840s, however, both Congregationalists and Unitarians broke from the British society on voluntaryist grounds.[47]

The advance of *laissez-faire* economic doctrine also had its effect on how reformers envisaged these changes occurring. It reinforced the extreme voluntaryism of a Baines who believed that for the state to substitute its powers for individual striving towards improvement was to 'deprive [men] of their virtues'. And, as earlier discussion has suggested, interventionism in the form of moral limits to *laissez-faire* was usually not the mark of a fundamental revolt against non-statist preferences but a temporary or limited qualification. Where reformers did support legislation in the area of moral reform – as in Buxton and Wilberforce's support for the RSPCA – it did not constitute a concession to centralisation. It may more appropriately be seen as exemplary or symbolic and where there was active enforcement of law protecting animals it was through local voluntary associations. Or, in the case of the African Institution a reversal of complementary functions between voluntary agency and state took place whereby the Institution monitored and gathered information on slave trading practices and government repaired legislative loopholes and developed enforcement policies which took account of briefings from abolitionists.[48]

What the preceding discussion suggests is that while widely divergent doctrines about the state could be enunciated by different reformers – at an earlier date the elder James Stephen represented the statist alternative to the voluntaryists of the 1840s – as things actually developed a case-by-case approach to reform according to circumstance was the usual result. Where reformers had devised physically enclosed institutional solutions, or revisions of institutions – penitentiaries, asylums, regulated factories – experience and circumstances produced somewhat more bureaucratic and centralised practices, but they tended to emerge in a piecemeal way and over an extended period of time. The abolitionist-dominated Prison Discipline Society, for example, continued to refer to the virtues of local administration of prisons under magistrates in the 1820s but simultaneously recognised that similar standards required national legislation nationally enforced. Piecemeal reform legislation, however, did not provide the full mechanisms required until the 1840s. Similarly, abolitionists between 1807 and 1838 adjusted their stance on what Whitehall should be doing according to both their changed perceptions of circumstances in the West Indies and what they believed the British government could be brought to do. Few of them displayed an unblemished or unseeing consistency throughout.[49]

6

ANTISLAVERY, RADICALISM AND PATRIOTISM

The present chapter is intended to complement the account in the last of antislavery's connections with middle-class moral and social reform and philanthropy. Its purposes are to 'place' antislavery through the outlooks and activities of its constituent elements, of individuals and groups by their relation to both intellectual and popular political radicalism. This can only be accomplished in a manageable space by selecting phases of radicalism from the late eighteenth century to the mid-nineteenth; the focus of the discussion will therefore be from the late 1780s to 1807 and the years of early Chartism in the late 1830s and early 1840s.

The account will inevitably reveal divergences between individual abolitionists but also some, though a far from complete, correspondence between the different intellectual–religious traditions in antislavery and different levels of commitment to political liberalism and radicalism. As in other chapters, these themes are anchored in brief narratives of reform networks in different localities. Inescapable too, especially in the 1790s and early 1800s, is a consideration of the contested claims to patriotism. Earlier parts of this book have indicated the antislavery movement as a whole met the West Indian charge that its actions and objectives undermined the national interest by claiming the true national interest lay in the reform cause which, moreover, enhanced Britain's moral authority in the world at large; abolitionists were thus the true patriots. Yet at the moments of national and social crisis the nature of patriotism seemed both simpler and more complex. Amongst abolitionists, beneath the moral certainty that their pet reform was an enhancement of national virtue, there were deep and divisive anxieties about how far political reform was compatible with the national security and the social stability few wished to deny constituted the core of patriotic concern. The discourses of patriotism, drawing from different though overlapping traditions, inevitably became part of the culture of antislavery and underlined both the coherences and contradictions of the movement. In the following discussion the contradictions will be more apparent; conflicting notions of patriotism appear as a counterpoint to the theme of differential involvement in radicalism.

The earlier chapter on antislavery ideology underlined the frequently underestimated contribution of Rational Dissent and its allies, especially those who came from liberal Anglicanism, in propounding a distinctive case against the slave trade in the late 1780s and early 1790s. The intellectual and moral assumptions which underpinned this antislavery similarly encouraged a position and activities against discrimination potentially or actually suffered by non-Anglicans and promoted justifications and pressure for political reform. The result was a co-operation with patrician Whig liberalism and later, under the influence of the French example, sometimes more risky associations with artisan radicals by a minority of Rational Dissenters. In the case of some Rational Dissenter abolitionists of the late 1780s there was a considerable prehistory of agitation and argument on behalf of closely intertwined religious and political grievances. On the ecclesiastical front, hostility to the requirement of subscription to the Thirty-Nine Articles which was liable to be enforced in the universities or on entry into various public offices and even the infrequently enforced legislation against anti-Trinitarian views kept many Rational Dissenters aware of their vulnerability to the demands of Anglican orthodoxy. Even though subscription was not made effectively universal dissenters knew that the religious establishment could call upon the powers of the state. The legal and institutional interdependence of the church and the state, proclaimed as crucial by defenders of the *status quo*, logically led dissenters and their sympathisers to connect religious and political reform.

Both at the parliamentary level and amongst reformers in the country there was considerable overlap between hostility to the slave trade and support for the efforts to repeal the Test and Corporation Acts in the years 1787 to 1790. In many cases both coincided with advocacy of parliamentary reform, often through the Society for Constitutional Information in the 1780s. At the widely noticed dinner of the Revolution Society at the London Tavern in 1788, attended by liberally minded men from all over the country, both Anglicans and dissenters, parliamentarians and provincial reformers, the toasts juxtaposed parliamentary reform, repeal of the religious tests and the abolition of the slave trade. The assembly embodied the association of liberal and even more radical dissenters with patrician Whig reformers like Stanhope.[1]

While tactically there was some reorientation towards the religious tests issue after the failure of Pitt's parliamentary reform proposals in 1785, the third defeat of the repeal proposals in 1790 swung the attention of this kind of reformer back to parliamentary change as a priority. But whether they gave priority at any moment to the religious or the political question liberal reformers could draw on a richly articulate tradition linking, in John Disney's words, 'the progressive improvement of civil liberty' with the circumstances in which individuals rationally determined their own choices and by discussion and debate pursued the truth as they saw it. At the level of raising intellectual issues this approach placed question marks against as many established institutions and practices as individuals or groups had the temerity to confront. Before and during the American Revolution Joseph Priestley and Richard Price not only opposed British policy but indicated the need for government to observe a utilitarian ethic and accommodate to natural rights. Freedom of speech and the press were both necessary to the 'progressive improvement of civil liberty', indeed an aspect of its substance.

Although only a minority of Rational Dissenters and liberal Anglicans drew out the implications of this basic stance into a radical critique of the religious and political establishments, they cannot be dismissed as simply exhibiting the coterie radicalism of intellectuals. The same channels of influence in the country which gave them a practical role to play in antislavery also transmitted the broader critique which, in concert with the experience of obduracy from supporters of the *status quo*, helped to radicalise opinion in some places by the beginning of the 1790s. A personally cohesive network of ministers and intellectuals linked to affluent local and sometimes more generally influential congregations was able to exploit outlets for publication. To develop an instance mentioned earlier, Joseph Johnson of St Paul's Churchyard published Priestley, Price, Erasmus Darwin, Mrs Barbauld, Dr Aikin and others who combined antislavery with a radical political temper and established the pages of the *Analytical Review* as a place of sharp-edged discussion. The congregations themselves were joined by multiple lines of communication through family, marriage, friendship and intellectual and business connections. In particular localities at particular times this meant that radical notions secured some grounding in the community and a hearing, though under progressively greater difficulties by 1792. Moreover in the 1780s the Society for Constitutional Information (SCI) had drawn together liberal provincial and metropolitan reformers in the Church of England and Rational Dissent in favour of the Quaker antislavery petition of 1783 and thus linked it to their critical political position. As will become apparent, local equivalents of the SCI had a similar effect.[2]

In communities where religious liberals took a prominent part in both antislavery and criticism of religious and political establishments they laid themselves open to counter-attack. The onslaught came from supporters of the *ancien régime* but also from some evangelicals who were allies on antislavery. Rising anxiety about French influence, Paineite doctrines and political radicalism, which loomed the more threateningly as it mobilised and expressed the convictions of toughly militant artisans, converted early sympathy for the French Revolution into a badge of political unreliability. The more politically radical abolitionists in consequence faced hostility from overtly loyalist antislavery elements and found themselves kept at arms length by more moderate reformist allies. Some were forced into isolation, silence or, in some cases, exile.[3]

Before such community and intra-abolitionist tensions became manifest, the London committee between autumn 1787 and spring 1788 showed itself perfectly willing to accept support and look for aid from political reformers. The minutes of the committee record letters from Major John Cartwright, William Frend and Capel Lofft in late 1787 and at the beginning of the next year Frend met the committee to pay over money subscribed for the anti-slave trade campaign in the University of Cambridge. In May the committee appointed a group to lobby MPs in favour of Pitt's resolution requiring the Commons to discuss the slave trade early in the next session and included Thomas Walker of Manchester whose lobbying expertise clearly overbore any doubts the committee might have had as a result of his developing radical politics. Moreover to this group 'Major Cartwright is requested to give his assistance'.

There is other evidence that more or less prominent individuals in the early stages of antislavery could acceptably combine it with reformist politics. Granville Sharp targeted British policy towards America and the slave trade, slavery and the corruptions of the parliamentary system as all expressions of arbitrary power to be opposed. After joining the SCI he pressed tracts upon his old contact

158

Wilkes 'to promote the measure of a *more equal Representation in annual Parliaments* '. Amongst Quakers Davis has also noted the influence of the Fothergill brothers and especially of Dr John Fothergill whose antislavery had a radical quality suggested by his support for Priestley and impact on younger doctor–reformers such as John Coakley Lettsom.[4]

If the experience of abolitionists in different communities is scrutinised up to the period of intensified conflict over political radicalism in 1791–2, the specifically religious impetus in the politics of challenge to the *ancien régime* is seen to have been central. It is true that, for example, in Nottingham and Norwich where Anglicans did not normally attempt exclusive control in local politics the issue of religious disabilities was not a conspicuous impetus to demands for political reform. Perhaps more frequently, as Ditchfield has noted of Lancashire, the question engendered bitterness. This was not only because the efforts to repeal the religious tests failed but was also the result of the agitation reinforcing the political as well as the religious divisions in communities, divisions which often set some abolitionists against both those who opposed them over the slave trade and evangelicals sympathetic to antislavery. It was easy for liberally educated Rational Dissenters to question the legitimacy of the national political order as well as the local exercise of power in both incorporated and unincorporated towns as they strove to achieve equality of rights and status.[5]

In contrast to Nottingham and Norwich, dissenter demands for the removal of their civil disabilities in Liverpool and Manchester were crucial to a broader radicalism and reactions against it. At the end of the 1780s Liverpool had a solidly Anglican, virtually self-perpetuating and pro-slave trade corporation. Manchester was unincorporated but its leading dissenters were kept out of local manorial offices which, with the exception of the one-year tenure of the borough-reeve's office by the radical Anglican Thomas Walker, were filled by the Anglican Tory group associated with the collegiate church. The dissenter reform and philanthropic network in Manchester discussed in the last chapter (p.118–21) was in part a compensation for a *political* inferiority forced on its members in their community. In Liverpool the antislavery circle of William Roscoe, William Rathbone IV, Dr James Currie, Edward Rushton, the Revs Shepherd, Smith and Yates was composed mainly of dissenters of an enlightened tendency and with one or two others they were bound together by cultural interests including a literary antislavery. Already cohesive, they took up agitation in promoting resolutions at a public meeting against the Test and Corporation Acts and, in an attempt to achieve greater accountability of MPs, a resolution to support only parliamentary candidates willing to pledge opposition to religious disabilities. In Manchester public activity directed to sustaining a third application for relief of dissenters which was to be defeated in parliament in March 1790 began in the previous May with a public meeting in which Manchester abolitionists were prominent. This began a process of forming local committees and a Lancashire and Cheshire county committee on which Liverpool and Manchester abolitionists met. Meetings in various Lancashire towns in late 1789 and early 1790, the selection of delegates for a national gathering in London and the choice of a committee of correspondence revealed the radicalism which sustained the campaign against religious disabilities and the divisions which it provoked. After a meeting at Warrington on 4 February 1790 Independents and Baptists determined, with Samuel Fletcher of Bolton taking the lead, to pursue repeal separately; they expressed resentment at the dominance of the Rational Dissenters or 'Presbyterians' and took exception to the radical gloss which Thomas Cooper of Manchester gave to the campaign. More important for the present argument, other antislavery liberals were unhappy at such an evident association with radicalism. Ditchfield reports James Currie as insisting on moderation to remove the impression of exciting rather than diminishing prejudice, while Thomas Percival was opposed to radical zeal in the campaign 'with the hope, perhaps in a more enlightened or tranquil period, the claims which were denied such a requisition might be granted as a *boon*'.[6]

Of what did this divisive radicalism consist? Cooper in particular went beyond demands for the repeal of the Test and Corporation Acts to aspire to a completely non-confessional state in which all penal statutes arising out of religious difference would be abolished. This squared with the increasing prominence of the language of natural right employed by the more radical dissenters in relation to repeal. It was also consistent with the general radical political ideas which Cooper had already published. He asserted that the right to govern was derived entirely from the consent of the governed and considered, with explicit commendation of Mary Wollstonecraft, that the governed included women. The way in which women were treated and educated indicated men's assumption of 'the right of making them our Slaves through Life' since the essence of slavery was the government of a person without his or her consent. The right to exercise consent, directly or indirectly, was necessary and fundamental to the object of government which was the happiness of the governed. It was an argument against slavery in its legal as well as its metaphorical senses and neatly integrated antislavery, political radicalism, opposition to the subjection of women and claims to civil and religious equality. Cooper's passionate optimism convinced him

> the structure of political oppression . . . begins now to totter: its day is far spent: the extension of knowledge has undermined its foundations, and I hope the day is not far distant when . . . one stone of the fabric will not be left upon another.

This also constituted the intellectual framework for the Manchester Constitutional Society when it was established in October 1790 with the radical abolitionists to the fore – Thomas Walker, Thomas Cooper, Samuel Jackson, George Philips, Matthew Falkner and Samuel Birch especially. Thus even before radicalism and its problematical connection to events in France became a major subject of scandal and concern in Manchester the radical core of abolitionists had staked out religious and political positions which provoked Anglican and Tory counter-meetings but had also begun to cause anxiety to more moderate antislavery dissent.

Although Currie in Liverpool doubted that Cooper's militancy was an asset to the anti-Test campaign he himself favoured some measure of parliamentary reform at the beginning of the 1790s and some of his associates showed greater political zeal in action and programme. Rathbone took the lead in attacking the exclusivity of the Tory Anglican corporation in 1790–1. In October 1790 he was involved in the memorial sent by prominent freemen complaining to the mayor and bailiffs of the method of filling vacancies on the council. At the start of 1791 over a thousand freemen petitioned calling for the Common Hall to select new councillors and at the subsequent meeting which chose councillors Rathbone demanded a proper audit of the town's books. This was the beginning of a long struggle with the corporation over the closed nature of town government which by 1792 was to intersect with a broader political radicalism and opposition to it. The broader radicalism was encouraged not only by the early phase of the revolution in France but by a sustaining interchange of ideas within the Roscoe circle leading recurrently to publication, though care was taken to avoid a public stance on the slave trade for fear that it would be counter-productive.

However, Rushton in particular became known for his radical politics and Rathbone and Roscoe as parliamentary reformers.[7]

Antislavery in Birmingham took shape in late 1787 when a private meeting raised 100 guineas for the London committee. In January 1788 a committee was formed drawing together the Anglicans Spencer Madan and John Riland with the Rational Dissenters Joseph Priestley and William Russell, the Friend Charles Lloyd and the industrialist Samuel Garbett. The abolitionists promoted a public meeting to discuss a petition against the trade and prepared for it by securing sermons in its favour from churches and meeting houses. The petition condemned the trade in principle but left parliament to decide on specific action. Money quotes Priestley at this stage as being optimistic about Birmingham antislavery as 'zealous and unanimous'. But inter-denominational church–dissent collaboration in the town was fragile. A similar alliance to promote Sunday schools had failed to hold together. Open support by Priestley and especially Russell for the efforts to repeal the Test and Corporation Acts in 1787 and 1789 prepared the way for Russell's initiative with other Rational Dissenters in mobilising Birmingham dissent to send delegates to the general gathering in London during the third attempt at repeal. When a Midland District organisation was formed in January 1790, parallel-ing the Lancashire and Cheshire committee, William Russell emerged as the secretary and treasurer of the executive committee. Even after the defeat of Fox's proposal in the Commons on 2 March 1790 the case continued to be pressed in the Birmingham area. Before the Commons' decision the Anglican abolitionist Madan had linked religious agitation to undesirable politics by announcing that 'Presbyterian principles are unquestionably republican.' The evangeli-cal Riland had a long history of hostility to complaint about the privileged position of the Church of England and shared Madan's view that religious liberalism was a form of infidelity likely to encourage republicanism since the authority of church and state reinforced each other. Certainly neither Russell nor Priestley dis-guised their hope for political change; Russell belonged to the SCI in the 1780s and Priestley, though neither a complete democrat nor a social egalitarian, hoped for parliamentary reform. His attempts to recruit for the Warwickshire Constitutional Society in the spring of 1791 and his known sympathy for what was happening in France were factors in the riots of which he was the most prominent victim.[8]

Cambridge was also a place in which political tensions fused with evangelical–Rational Dissenter divisions despite a shared antislavery outlook. The university and the town were both predominantly Tory at the time of the emergence of organised antislavery and the evangelical Isaac Milner, Wilberforce's religious mentor, assumed the role of spokesman for ecclesiastical and political authority, qualified only by his abolitionism. The other source of antislavery in the town and the university was Rational Dissent whose representatives diverged sharply from Milner and in the case of William Frend came into direct conflict with him. The rationalistic Baptist minister Robert Robinson made opposition to the slave trade a feature of his circle which included George Dyer, schoolmaster, scholar and Robinson's future biographer and William Frend. Both the religion and politics of this group were unorthodox. Robinson tended to Unitarianism and Frend resigned his Anglican curacy in 1787 and campaigned for the removal of the subscription requirement for BAs at the university. Frend's open confession of Unitarianism led to his removal from his tutorship at Jesus College and drew him, already locally notorious, to the Robinson group. Hostility to the religious tests was shared by the group and Frend propagandised amongst the undergraduates. They were at the centre of the Cambridge Constitutional Information Society which, according to Dyer, became 'a very large body of freeholders of liberal sentiments' intent on parliamentary reform. These activities focused growing hostility on Frend, the attack on him eventually being managed by Milner, but his stoutly defended religious principles brought admiration and support from another former Anglican antislavery Unitarian, Theophilus Lindsey, and from Priestley.[9]

The absence of support amongst Anglican evangelical abolitionists for the claims of dissenters and their extension in many cases into demands for significant political reform are explicable at two levels. By the time of the contest over Fox's repeal resolution of 2 March 1790, decisive for a whole generation, supporters of established political and ecclesiastical authority betrayed growing anxiety over the possible influence of events in France. Despite the minority and frequently resented role of evangelicals within the church, with few exceptions they identified themselves with its existing status and opposed any external challenge to it. In general they were as prepared to be mobilised by the anti-repeal agitation which was prevalent in the month before the Commons debate as other Anglicans. In the debate itself not only was Pitt hostile to Fox's argument for 'the Universal Rights of Human Nature', but Wilberforce and Dolben, author of the recent reforming measure concerning slave trade vessels, both touched on fear of the French Revolution which they suggested proponents of repeal supported. When Burke delivered his speech in defence of the *status quo* his attack touched on Robert Robinson as well as the radical sentiments against church tithes and the Anglican liturgy reported to him as having been voiced by Cooper and others.

Harmony with non-evangelical establishment opinion on this question was perfectly consistent with Wilberforce's hope that one day 'the whole machine of civil life would work without obstruction or disorder and the course of its movements would be like the harmony of the spheres'. If that was to be attained it would be by making effective use of existing British institutions rather than overturning or radically transforming them when through them 'the highest station was rendered only the more efficaciously operative in the wider diffusion of happiness among the humbler ranks of society'. Fellow evangelicals Thomas Gisborne and Hannah More also advocated the purifying moral and religious leadership of the professional classes within the existing social and political order. Despite Wilberforce's support for Pitt's earlier reform proposal, by 1791–2 there was no hint that any of the evangelical abolitionists shared the conviction of Cooper or the Quaker Williams Allen that substantive political change was required to create the conditions for progress against the slave trade.[10]

The spectrum of abolitionist attitudes to political change apparent by 1791 presaged severe difficulties in the following years for antislavery activists who were also politically radical. They had to accommodate to an increasingly hostile political climate, withdraw from public activity or face persecution. The result was submergence of the politically radical end of the antislavery spectrum. The worsening environment for radical abolitionists was the product of the way in which events in France were translated into political argument and action in Britain with the effect of intensifying the emergent divisions already discussed.

The starting point for elucidating this next phase of antislavery's relation to political radicalism is the response to Burke's *Reflections*. Capel Lofft, a moderate political reformer who was also a contact of the London committee, justified his welcome of the early stages of the revolution by defining its liberal character as corresponding largely to celebrated English liberties. In doing so he was sounding a note struck by Clarkson in his journal entries during his visit to France beginning just after the fall of the Bastille. The young antislavery Whig lawyer

Mackintosh similarly claimed the values of 1688 for the French. If in practice in Britain truly free government required an extension of representation, the system in France had been much worse, based on an 'illegitimate inequality of orders dominated by an exclusive corporate spirit'. Freedom was advancing there by bringing forward the commercial and manufacturing 'middle rank among whom almost all the sense and virtues of society reside'. More generally the continued vindication of free discussion and advocacy of change within the subculture of Rational Dissent placed liberally-minded abolitionists in opposition to efforts to block change and exclude some positions from a hearing.[11]

Resistance to Burke's view of events in France, and thus to his view of the world, did not mean an unqualified embrace of Paine, even by abolitionists more politically radical than those just discussed. Certainly Walker and Priestley associated with Paine on occasion in 1791. Cooper confessed to the younger James Watt that *The Rights of Man* made him even more 'politically mad . . . I regard it as the very jewel of a book'. He underlined his belief in equality of political rights both in his writings in the Manchester *Herald* and in a pamphlet response to Burke. Yet, as Claeys points out, neither Mrs Barbauld nor William Frend accepted as appropriate for Britain Paine's view of the activities of government. Nevertheless, the radical assertion of a fundamental equality of rights for all legitimated the linking of abolition with the drive for political change at home.

It was not to be expected that evangelical exponents of abolition would see French liberty in any of these ways. Hannah More's *Village Politics*, extensively distributed with government support, through the figure of the downright blacksmith, Jack Anvil, combined hints of criticism of the higher ranks with a sturdy defence of the constitution (the castle). Some ('my lady') wanted the castle pulled down and rebuilt 'in her frippery way' (a clear allusion to the French). She was refused by her husband 'so now and then they mend a little thing . . . but no pull-me-down works'. True 'our great folks' could set a better example in going to church but 'they'll answer for that in another place'.

Suitably convinced, Anvil's interlocutor, Tom Hod, destroys his copy of Paine. By 1792 some of the more feverish responses to the supposed dangers of radical constitutional change appear to have made the willingness of evangelicals to criticise the moral and religious failings of the upper classes a pretext for their High Church and other critics to lump them with all other kinds of abolitionists in the 'Old Jewry Society'. They were denounced as dangerously motivated by 'Fanaticism and False Philanthropy', promoting constitutional reform through which 'they saw the means of establishing such a Government as best suited their wild ephemeral theory'. Cooper's activities and the conduct of the Society of the Friends of the People were charged as justifying 'classing the promoters of Abolition and the Republicans together'. Developments within local communities from 1791 onwards scarcely confirmed this simple equation. [12]

By 1791–2 members of the Roscoe circle in Liverpool had moved beyond antislavery, religious equality and a challenge to the closed corporation to enter the more general political debate. Roscoe followed earlier pro-French poetic effusions with a sharp reply to Burke while Shepherd in 1792 published a verse epistle to his political radical friend Edward Rushton and took up Burke's contemptuous reference to the 'swinish multitude'. None the less, some differences of emphasis were apparent even amongst such a closely-knit group. Currie's generally more cautious approach has been noted; the group as a whole appears to have made less public show of its French sympathies after the Priestley riots. Rathbone engaged in debate with the mayor over a proposed loyal address in 1792 and was publicly supported by Roscoe but some of the Liverpool reformers apparently thought this behaviour rash. Certainly the majority at a public meeting supported the loyalist position and in November of that year the corporation distributed thousands of copies of resolutions aimed locally at 'Jacobins'. In response Rathbone and Roscoe produced an address of grievances at a public meeting. Feelings, however, were running high and Rathbone was jostled by a Tory mob shortly afterwards on the same day an anti-radical riot occurred in Manchester, 10 December 1792. The outbreak of war with France further restricted the appeal of the reformers. Writings critical of the war in 1793 by Rathbone, Roscoe and Currie (writing as 'Jasper Wilson') only revealed how little support there was for such a stance in the town; Wilberforce, who knew of Currie's authorship, expressed strong disapproval of his plea for negotiations with the French. Not surprisingly members of the reform circle seem increasingly to have withdrawn into less exposed humanitarian activity and private interests. Currie and Shepherd considered removal to America and Roscoe's French enthusiasm ebbed. Abolition was not again raised as a public issue in Liverpool before 1804. There remained in this dark period a willingness by Rathbone to help organise a petition against the government's Two Acts in 1795 and on Roscoe's part continued advocacy of peace negotiations, though public outlets for such arguments were becoming more restricted by 1797. In essence, however, the radical edge of Liverpool antislavery was blunted after 1793.[13]

The radical tone of one element of Manchester antislavery became even more provocatively evident in 1791-2. When the Priestley riots occurred in Birmingham Walker, Cooper and Samuel Jackson tried to persuade their fellow members of the Literary and Philosophical Society to express sympathy for Priestley and when they failed, they all resigned. The same group and others of their antislavery associates in the Manchester Constitutional Society committed themselves to some Paineite positions. The Constitutional Society promoted part I of *The Rights of Man* and Cooper abridged it for easier assimilation. The radicals congratulated Paine on his writings and within this ethos George Philips published *The Necessity of a Speedy and Effectual Reform in Parliament* (1792). From 31 March 1792 the radicals had their own *Herald* newspaper to advocate their ideas; in its columns they placed opposition to slavery as well as the slave trade alongside parliamentary reform and sharp criticism of British institutions, often written by 'Sidney' who was Cooper.

The antislavery committee of 1792, as Hunt points out, contained as members ten radical and moderate reformers from the 1787 committee. It had lost some Tories and of those who stayed on potentially the most influential were the editors of the *Mercury* and the *Chronicle*, James Harrop and Charles Wheeler. But neither was active; they printed notices of meetings but paid no attention to antislavery in their editorial columns. In practice amongst committee members the radical drive of Manchester antislavery created tensions not with Tory supporters but with moderate Whiggish reformers. When at a dinner in November 1792 the toast to the universal abolition of slavery was offered Percival and Bayley seem to have drawn back from what they saw as a utopian stance. They were the more likely to have done so after the controversies in which some of the radical abolitionists had become embroiled in the spring and summer of 1792. Cooper and his friend James Watt Jr (employed by Walker's firm to drum up foreign business) being in Paris in April were charged by the Manchester Constitutional Society with demonstrating the radicals' internationalism by taking an address to the patriotic societies in France; the Jacobin Club reciprocated and the visitors met Robespierre. In the accents of Paine to the Americans in 1776 Manchester radicals proclaimed the French Revolution the cause 'of all Mankind'. The tone was maintained in stressing the illumination the French had provided 'upon the true principles of Politics and the natural Rights of Man' which further taught that the time had come to replace national rivalry with international fraternity. The event provoked controversy when Burke raised it in the Commons. The Constitutional Society issued a statement, probably composed by Walker and Cooper, describing their objective as purification of the constitution by parliamentary reform defined as changes in representation in the Commons, a shortening of parliaments and a lessening of the existing excessive influence of the peerage. As to events in France, the radicals welcomed them without justifying everything done in the revolution's name or claiming that similar measures should be imposed in Britain. Cooper soon attacked the May 1792 proclamation in the king's name against seditious writings and produced a full reply to Burke's attack on English Jacobinism in pamphlet form.[14]

The abolitionist radical's assimilation of Paineite ideas was apparent in his assault on the power of hereditary orders in government as 'leeches of the community' and as contradicting the principle that abilities and virtue rather than birth should produce the reward of influence. He proclaimed the inutility of monarchy in government and added conventional radical Whig or commonwealthman strictures against the tendency of governments controlled by hereditary orders to enter wars, create expensive establishments and threaten liberties with standing armies. Yet it is important to note that the Constitutional Society never gave open support to Paine's republicanism and Cooper was careful to accept, despite his near-republicanism in theory, that not only did Britain have a constitution which Paine had been inclined to deny, but that in practice reform of the Commons to make it truly representative would remove objections to the British system of government as derived from the existence of privileged orders. He was none the less radical in his understanding of 'effectual reform' and proper representation.

> I would have the Man whose Stake in the Community consists of Life and Liberty and Labour, with a Penny in his Pocket, to have an equal voice in the Choice of Legislators by whose Laws that Stake is to be protected with another Man who has Life and Liberty and Labour with a hundred thousand Pounds in his Pocket.

Despite these political positions, however, the Manchester antislavery radicals had limited contacts with the developing democratic societies of artisans. Thomas Hardy of the London Corresponding Society (LCS) was strongly antislavery and wrote to Walker about co-operation in the common cause. The Constitutional Society, however, set a subscription beyond the reach of most artisans. When in late 1792 popular and potentially violent church-and-king activity threate-ned the radicals Walker gave the use of his house for meetings to more plebeian Reformation and Patriotic Societies but it is doubtful that the middle-class radicals were intimately involved with them.

Necessarily also in combating the proposed Loyalist Association about to be formed on 11 December 1792 Cooper appealed to the mass of the population to reflect on the Pitt government's course towards war and the place of a Loyalist Association in fostering support for war against France. He argued that the people could not benefit from conflict; taxes would remain high and the markets abroad for manufactures would be cut off. Poverty for the small producer and unemployment were likely to follow. After the Loyalist meeting led to attacks on the shop of the abolitionists Falkner and Birch where the *Herald* was produced and then on Walker's house, Walker continued to assert his determination 'to enlighten the People respecting their just rights' and to see the poorer classes 'better lodged and better fed and *better instructed* '. Purification of the system of representation and of the constitution as a whole as his objective marked him out, he claimed, as one of the nation's 'most sincere well-wishers'. Persecution of radicals merely stained the British character.[15]

The anti-radical violence of December 1792 was, none the less, a turning point. Local Loyalists, including Nathan Crompton, a Tory merchant who had been a member of the 1787 Manchester anti-slave trade committee, seem to have gained the upper hand. In spite of Walker's earlier prominence in the town his enemies eventually forced him to face a trial on a charge of sedition. In the dock with him at Lancaster in April 1794 was the radical abolitionist Samuel Jackson; when they and their fellow accused were acquitted they were congratulated by antislavery associates, Fox, Stanhope and Thomas Clarkson. But Manchester no longer harboured a union of antislavery and radicalism. Public antislavery activity had ceased before the trial. In its aftermath Walker concluded that local civil and ecclesiastical authorities were hostile to 'reformation' but, more seriously, that religious dissenters whose abolitionist and reform energies had seemed so important earlier 'have as a body fallen short of their own principles' and as 'professionally temperate men have been the first deserters from and have uniformly done mischief to the rights of the people'. In response to Pitt's introduction of the Two Bills against sedition in late 1795 some of the old abolitionist group – George Lloyd, Samuel Greg, Thomas Percival – joined Walker and his brother Richard in petitioning against the proposed restrictions on speaking, writing and meetings but significantly the Manchester Loyalists' petition in support of the measures gained more signatures.

The radical circle was dispersed; Cooper emigrated to Pennsylvania to join Priestley in 1794, George Philips drew back into a respectable Whiggery and Walker himself, his business ruined, declined into relative obscurity. The moderate reform elements which had for a period been allied with the radicals in antislavery and the pursuit of religious equality often continued their philanthropic work but distanced themselves from all suspicion of political radicalism. Bayley as a senior magistrate was active in the later 1790s to preserve order and reported to the Home Office on support for the United Englishmen. By 1800 at a time of scarcity of provisions he held responsible for threats against parliament 'the Democrats who wish to create a general Outcry against the War and the Ministry'. Percival's politics had always been to 'enlarge [the constitution's] boundaries' as to civil and religious privileges 'for the security of what is so invaluable by the reformation of abuses'; political improvements should go 'in a gentle pace'. The development of the French Revolution reinforced his aversion to innovation based on 'philosophic fancy' which promoted violence and licentiousness. As 'a temperate and constitutional Whig' to the end of his days he regretted 'the permanent injury which has been sustained to the cause of political reformation in all parts of the world' by the turn of events in France.[16]

In Birmingham the divisions opened up in 1790–1 between leading antislavery figures over the Test Act agitation and its political implications were confirmed and extended by subsequent events. Before being driven from the town by the riots against him Priestley responded to Burke in a pamphlet which seemed partially to substantiate the charges made by Madan and Riland linking the claim for religious equality to political radicalism, though not republicanism. He sketched a glorious prospect opening for the world, prefigured by the American example and carried forward by the doings of the National Assembly in France which pointed towards a millennium grounded in true religion, philosophy, 'good sense and the prevailing spirit of commerce'. Government would become concerned only with what the general good required, leaving men undisturbed in as many of their natural rights as possible 'and no more interfering with matters of religion'. He promised a continued assault upon the corruptions of Anglicanism evidenced in the preferment system derived from the Crown's link to the Church of England and a parallel campaign for equality for taxpaying dissenters through representation in a reformed parliament.

By late autumn 1791 the elder James Watt reported fierce party conflict in the town reflecting an ironic relation between theory and practice in which 'the professed Aristocrates are democrates in practice, that is encouragers of the Mob' but 'the democrates are those who have always contended for a police and good government of the town, therefore are in fact aristocratic'. With the further development of loyalism the 'democrates' were thrown very much on the defensive by 1792. Riland asserted *The Rights of God* against the influence of Paine, denouncing the idea of absolute rights as both blasphemy and treason. Loyalist demands for public professions of loyalty led William Russell as spokesman for dissenter radicals after Priestley's departure to declare for the Hanoverian succession and the principles of 1688 but bravely to call for parliamentary reform as a remedy for abuses which had appeared in the past century. Russell also opposed sedition but stressed the importance of press freedom and insisted that measures should only be taken against overt illegal acts. Robinson has also noted the increasing political diffidence of James Watt Jr in 1792–3 from the time of the August–September massacres in France onwards. Claiming to speak as well for his friends amongst the English democrats he argued that they had wanted reform of abuses in the English constitution in order to avoid the kind of Jacobin government the French had got by late 1793. The English radicals had preached 'the doctrine of gradual reform, but never that of riot and subversion of order has been inculcated'. It was a position which in the circumstances necessitated a virtual repudiation of artisan or labouring-class militancy. The democrats had directed their appeal 'to the thinking and sensible part of the nation'; their enemies had not been able to demonstrate 'their ever having attempted to tamper with the lower order of people'. On the contrary 'the establishment of lawless riot is to be expected . . . from those who dread to see abuses put an end to'. However, the intellectual political radicalism associated with Russell and Priestley's New Meeting was not entirely dissipated in the following years but it was not again linked to any organised form of antislavery in the town.[17]

In Cambridge in the early 1790s divisions between the components of antislavery, evangelical and Rational Dissenter, became acute. On one side they arose from an attempt to crush the linked heterodoxies in religion and politics associated with Frend and the circle of which Robinson had been the centre until his death in 1790 and on the other the championing of religious equality, parliamentary reform and peace which in Benjamin Flower's *Cambridge Intelligencer* involved sharp criticism of Wilberforce for his support of the war and illiberal measures by Pitt's government. As the controversy generated by Burke's *Reflections* developed Frend urged the establishment of more Constitutional Societies across the country on the Cambridge model. He was however careful not simply to advocate imitation of French ideas and forms. Rather than taking the new French constitution for a model he tried to reinvigorate arguments for parliaments of shorter length and elected by voters gradually expanded in numbers; vigorous reform within the existing framework of British institutions was the way forward. Reform had also to include loosening the connection of church and state and of the clergy's dependency on the Crown as well as removing religious discrimination in public office; Frend claimed that the result would be a steady attachment to authority by those helped in this way. It was in the interest of the ruling powers to see these changes happen to avoid worse. Consequently he sweepingly dismissed the common contention that the time was not ripe.

Frend's writings and activities and continued membership of the university even after the loss of his college tutorship provoked the growing ire of Isaac Milner and other conservatives. Eventually in 1793 Milner presided over proceedings and secured Frend's expulsion from membership of the university, though at the cost of suffering Frend's wounding irony before a large audience. It brought Milner the satisfaction of believing, he told Wilberforce, he had ruined 'the Jacobinal party as a University thing'. Flower's *Intelligencer* now became the forum for advocating antislavery within the context of radicalism in the town and more widely through its national circulation. The paper's consistent support for abolition of the slave trade accompanied an editorial defence of Catholic Emancipation, press freedom and freedom of speech as well as fierce argument for a peace rather than war policy towards France. This last objective was fundamental to Flower's and several of his correspondents' outspoken denunciations of Wilberforce and the evangelicals who supported Pitt's policy. Wilberforce became 'the evangelical statesman with his bloody votes'. Even when conceding the need to aid the evangelicals on antislavery petitioning the paper suggested evangelicals did not work wholeheartedly enough. By early 1796 Flower brought together his disgust at lack of progress in parliament against the slave trade with his opposition to the illiberal effects of the war at home, opposition which he had shown in his prominent participation in late 1795 at a meeting against the Treason and Sedition Bills and his promotion of a petition against them; he charged that the whole slave trade issue had been put off so that Pitt and Wilberforce could concentrate on 'forging additional fetters for their countrymen at home'. Flower's stance on the war in particular attracted widespread hostility then and in later years. It was a difficulty general to antislavery radicals and in Flower's case it marginalised him.[18]

Glimpses of the circumstances of some antislavery radicals and their response to them in the mid-1790s and the following several years can be obtained from another angle: their claims to patriotism and how these claims placed them in relation to conservative forces and other abolitionists not identified as radicals. As chapter 2 indicated, all manner of abolitionists in the early years of the campaign against the slave trade were prepared to argue against the West Indians that the true national interest lay in abolition. They were also happy to celebrate the love Britons had of liberty and gladly assumed that it was Britain's patriotic duty to set an example to Europe and the world by antislavery work in her own sphere. In this sense a form of patriotism was a binding force within early antislavery. It was moreover able to coexist alongside clear differences of emphasis over the precise relation between devotion to one's own country and concern for the rest of mankind. The evangelical James Ramsay's antislavery flowed from feeling in 'the old classical mode that respected friends and native land' and deprecated 'the theoretical, lifeless notions of universal benevolence that can never be reduced to practice because the objects of them, the rivals and enemies of their country can never be within their reach'. Price's and Priestley's perspectives denied country and world as polarities; Price's 'love of country' acknowledged the need to seek the good of one's own country in the first place but did not assume that virtue and wisdom were restricted to it. His and Priestley's antislavery reflected expectations of a more general enlightenment which would bring the end in Priestley's words of 'national prejudice' and lead to the establishment of 'universal peace'. Granville Sharp had struck a similar balance, though in different language. True self-love depended on our attitude to our neighbours; true patriotism was manifested in universal benevolence; duties as 'Citizens of the World . . . should always regulate and limit [patriotism] by the eternal Rules of natural Equity and Justice.' Moreover, in its more radical formulations by the 1780s the rhetoric of patriotism made the defence and extension of liberty a central theme and deplored the 'slavery' threatened by unreformed political institutions.[19]

In the 1790s, however, it rapidly became more difficult to find much political space for radical patriotism and thus for radical abolitionists to combine their antislavery with it. This resulted both from the growing hostility in Britain to political radicalism as such and the vulnerability of abolitionism to attacks as a consequence of the slave revolution in the French Caribbean colony of St Domingue, an event widely perceived as a disaster arising out of French revolutionary principles which at the same time threatened to destroy Britain's West Indian empire.

The willingness of some provincial abolitionists to identify themselves with calls for radical constitutional and political change in the early 1790s and the temporary association of the odd national abolitionist with radicalism, notably Clarkson, laid them open to implicit and explicit charges of unpatriotic behaviour. The Liverpool and Manchester reformers encountered this; Dundas warned Wilberforce after Clarkson attended a reform meeting at the Crown and Anchor that 'He could not have done a more mischievous thing to the Cause you have taken in hand.' At the extreme, abolitionists were presented as alien figures, 'the JACOBINS of ENGLAND', who were either dupes or directed and divorced from 'an honest and enlightened Public' whose 'Common Sense and Humanity' would decide truly, i.e. against antislavery radicalism.[20]

Evangelical abolitionists wanted none of this. On occasion, orthodox Tory Anglicanism charged evangelicals and Methodists with promoting discontent and thus becoming necessary targets of zealous anti-Jacobinism. The grain of truth here was that they *were* morally dissatisfied with the *status quo*, including the manner and outlook of the upper classes. Kiernan and Newman have plausibly argued that the Claphamites, Hannah More and their supporters could thus campaign to purify the nation while taking advantage of the French Revolution to associate not only liberal and radical ideas with the traditional French enemy but decadent aristocratic cosmopolitanism with the same source. Patriotism became a weapon not only in the struggle to define the moral and religious character of the nation but to give class boundaries to its centre of gravity. The supposed taste in the culture of educated aristocrats for 'speculative philosophy' was presented as making them as alien and potentially infidel as dissenter intellectuals. Anti-aristocratic, anti-radical and anti-French sentiment was thus subsumed in a firm patriotism by evangelical abolitionists as Britain entered the crisis of the Revolutionary Wars.[21]

There were some abolitionists in the tradition of Rational Dissent who insisted throughout on their moderation. Percival, for example, was as concerned in some of his writings as any evangelical to sustain the moral health of the family and develop virtue in the next generation. It was claimed that he never favoured 'faction or discontent' though he also urged that just authority best secured itself by allowing 'the calm investigation of the principles upon which it is founded'. But in the circumstances of the mid- and later 1790s he easily proclaimed his patriotism and 'always held in view the fundamental principles of legitimate authority'. Thus necessary and proper order emerged again as the basis for the alignment of the kind of moderate liberal reformer represented by Percival and Bayley with evangelicals and expressed in part through a common patriotism; both the Manchester men subscribed to and Bayley took a position in the Volunteers.[22]

The difficulty some initially pro-French Revolution radical abolitionists had in curbing their universalist or internationalist convictions contrasts with the resort to patriotism. The problem emerged acutely when news of the great slave revolt in St Domingue reached Britain. From early November 1791 the Jamaican Assembly through their agent in London, Stephen Fuller, and the Society of West Indian Merchants and Planters kept up a drumbeat of propaganda and near-continuous pressure on government and parliament to protect the British West Indies against the threat posed by developments in the French colony. The West Indians detected

> a mutinous Disposition . . . industriously promoted by Communications between mischievous and misguided Persons in this Country and in France, subversive of that Subordination on which entirely depends the Welfare of the Negroes themselves and every other Inhabitant of the West-India Colonies.

The planters claimed that the nature and extent of discussions on the slave trade in parliament were being misrepresented to the slaves, though amongst themselves Fuller and his associates seem to have concluded that the anti-slave trade committee, having sown the seeds of rebellion in St Domingue, intended a similar harvest in Jamaica. In effect the abolitionists were thought by their enemies in the West Indian interest to have been revealed in the commission of treason, though nothing like detailed evidence was ever attempted. It was treason essentially prompted by French principles; antislavery zealots in Britain were trying 'to put an end to the distinction between the white man & the black, the master & the labourer, to give up all the wisdom, the joy & benefits of society and to bring mankind to one universal level'.[23]

It is not surprising that when St Domingue and its effects were debated in the Commons on 2 April 1792 Wilberforce distanced himself from the black uprising; so too did Fox. But a few radical abolitionists refused to adopt a defensive posture when the revolt provoked some discussion in the country. Roscoe announced that the slaves were right to use force against slavery which itself substituted force for right. Another northerner, Percival Stockdale, saw the revolution of the slaves putting the world the right way up: '*We* are the savages; the Africans act like *men* . . . their revenge is the *Act* - of NATURE and of GOD.' Such sweeping universalism left no room for patriotic considerations. Clarkson, however, in his 1792 pamphlet on the upheaval was more interested in denying that the anti-slave trade committee had provoked the events. By claiming that the slave trade had undoubtedly provided the materials for the revolt by pouring in thousands deeply resentful of their treatment 'as creatures of another species' he was able to argue that the revolt made it the more urgent for the campaign against the British trade to be carried to a successful conclusion in the interests of Britain and the West Indian proprietors. Yet he too saw the slaves in St Domingue as vindicating 'the unalterable Rights of Man'.[24]

The anticipation of the dawn of general enlightenment entertained by dissenter intellectual radicals such as Price and Priestley and, Marilyn Butler has forcefully argued, the resort to a universalist rhetoric of liberty and right which assumed an international rather than a patriotic colouring, appeared extremist to a good deal of English opinion after 1792 as preoccupation with a possible war mounted. The effect was increasing isolation unless radicals in this tradition were able to adjust their tone to take account of the anxieties of their own nation. The major effort to do so took the form of developing a critique of the war policy of Pitt's government; it was undertaken by liberal and some more radical reformers, many of them abolitionists, who became known as the Friends of Peace.

Such a connection was not surprising. Soon after the outbreak of war in 1793 the waging of it was registered in sermons as one of the 'national sins' and coupled with the maintenance of the slave trade.

National virtue demanded the cessation of both. The common ground of anxiety over the nation's fate if nothing were done brought some evangelical and liberal and radical dissenters together against war. Amongst Anglican evangelicals Wilberforce, until his support for the Two Acts of 1795, continued to be seen as a channel through which critics of the war could have their views conveyed to the prime minister and government. It was a view derived from Wilberforce's antislavery and other modest reform credentials of earlier years and temporarily strengthened by his advocacy of peace negotiations at the end of 1794. The first phase of peace petitions and addresses largely managed by liberal religious circles followed on this intervention, including an initiative by a cluster of the old Manchester Constitutional Society abolitionists. Currie revealed to William Smith, no doubt remembering his own clash with Wilberforce in 1793 over the anti-war letter he had published as 'Jasper Wilson', that the evangelical leader had 'at last' found wisdom. 'Would to God he had never sanctioned the war.' Its supporters exemplified irrationality, embodying 'prejudice, passion and pride' which 'form an almost insuperable barrier to honest and avowed conviction'.[25]

Yet ultimately the most striking thing about the anti-war agitation for a student of the culture of antislavery it that, far from continuing the antislavery alliance into a period when antislavery itself largely disappeared as a public issue, it underlined the developing divergence between Anglican evangelicals and many evangelical dissenters on one side and liberal and radical dissenters and some Quakers on the other. An important way in which this divergence and their increasingly beleaguered position was expressed by the liberals and radicals took the form of their proclaiming adherence to the national interest truly understood and as patriotically sustaining Britain's national identity as the home of liberty. 'Peace', Currie announced, 'can not be restored to Europe till the wealth of England has run off in showers of blood'. Roscoe complained that the government's war policy had 'reduced us to the necessity of submitting to a mode of taxation which a few years ago would have revolted the feelings of every Englishman'. The greedy absorption of resources by the war must issue in the material ruin of the people. More fundamentally, however, the war policy had created 'a system which has already brought destruction & disgrace on all our allies' and created at home a war interest whose enrichment threatened the independence of the people and posed the possibility of political despotism. By contrast with the administration the Friends of Peace saw themselves as champions of true order and proper independence, particularly embodied, as Currie expressed it, in the useful and productive employment and moral integrity of the middle ranks of society. This was the perspective which mobilised liberal and radical abolitionists against the sedition bills in late 1795 and against the support of Pitt on the issue by evangelicals represented prominently by Wilberforce.[26]

Flower stridently denounced evangelicals for not focusing on truly national sins and thus associated those of them who proclaimed the war 'just and necessary' with 'slave traders, borough jobbers, church pluralists, prime ministers'. What they had in common, he charged, was concern only with 'pecuniary interest'. Moreover, real friends of the constitution who only wanted its purification were faced by politicians, friends of Wilberforce and Thornton, who employed informers and by the charge from evangelicals that they were 'disaffected persons'. Frend who, like Flower, spoke for the remnants of what had been the radical end of the earlier antislavery spectrum, supported funds for the defence of some of these 'disaffected' charged with high treason in a pamphlet and articles in the *Intelligencer*, was also close to the artisan radicals of the London Corresponding Society by the mid-1790s, and attacked the war as provoking scarcity and popular disorder.[27]

Liberal and radical abolitionist dissenters, in difficult circumstances, thus contested the claims of pro-war elements to a monopoly of patriotic virtue. The circumstances, however, became ever more difficult with developing fears of French expansion in the later 1790s and great anxiety at the prospect of a French invasion, then and in the following few years. In these crisis times radical patriotism had to try to maintain political space against, in Linda Colley's terminology, a 'state-sponsored nationalism', which, as its immediate alien 'other', focused on France. Some of those who most eagerly lent their support to the claims of the warring state were drawn from evangelical abolitionists and, in their local communities, moderates of the Bayley and Strutts of Belper variety. The essence of British patriotism so far as Wilberforce was concerned in 1803 was to be found in 'true Christians' who could agree 'in the grand fundamentals of Religion' whatever their sect and who could reverse 'the decline of Religion and morality'. Hannah More translated the requirement of moral discipline in the nation into an attempt to chivvy the poor into martial ardour by reminding them of what they would forfeit in the event of a French invasion; loss of house and garden and orchard; of employment, wife and child; of British laws which preserved property and rights.

If the 'squire should oppress
I get instant redress
My orchard's as safe as his park, sir.

The heritage of law and liberty was under grave threat; a successful invasion by Napoleon would turn Britain into a prison and her people into slaves.[28]

In this fashion more conservative evangelical patriots deployed their antislavery convictions to push the question of liberty to the fore and assume some of the ground claimed by a more radical patriotism. Such a context and such a critical moment made it hard for antislavery radicals not to accommodate to the state. Frend rallied to the flag in a pamphlet of 1804 on patriotism; so too did Cartwright. Both posed a true patriotism which spread sentiments conducive to the public welfare against a false variety nurturing 'most sordid and self-interested views'. Just as in the early days of the French Revolution French patriots had resisted 'confederate despots' so now a deeply-rooted British patriotism based on liberty had to stand against Napoleonic despotism. Thus Frend's argument conceded the need for unity in crisis but maintained a refusal to accept the implied exclusivity of the more conservative evangelical patriotism and state-sponsored nationalism.

Within three and four years legislation was enacted to end the British slave trade. And it was seen as a national achievement by abolitionists which reflected well on the country. Yet it is also apparent, within the context of a discussion of antislavery and patriotism, that the distinctive emphases, evident even when at their narrowest in 1803–4, remained. The very success of conservative patriotism in defining British identity largely in terms of the heritage of liberty and repudiation of despotism which brought slavery in its train, reinforced the sense of the immense distance of Britain from slavery in all its forms. As the home of freedom it became ever more difficult for Britain to remain embroiled in the business of trading and dealing in slaves. When, in the summer of 1805, Clarkson offered his impressions of the revival of antislavery feeling in the country he found 'all ranks of people were warm in the cause and desirous of lending their aid'. A conservative version of abolition as a national and patriotic project was formulated at this time by Robert Raikes, the proponent of Sunday schools, as a by-product of his concern with

Christianity and commerce. He believed that 'a large portion of political liberty' in the state, which British possessed, was the necessary foundation for a commerce which could alone bring sufficient prosperity to the 'savages' who were the concern of the missionary and to the populace at home to make them receptive to Christianity. Religion in its turn prevented the benefits of commerce running to 'luxury and licentiousness' and forbade trade which involved 'the exercise of either force or fraud, of rapine or injustice'. The slave trade was thus of no advantage because contrary to the principles of Christianity. At home the political liberty characteristic of Britain and requisite for commerce to flourish posed the potential danger of popular tumult; only religious instruction could constrain men from becoming 'the instruments of seditious zeal and furious fanaticism'. Britain's special heritage of liberty was therefore understood as requiring both abolition abroad and rigorous moral order at home.

The evangelical antislavery *Christian Observer* argued essentially in the same tradition about the time of abolition. Britain in 1805 exhibited a pious 'patriotism . . . in multiplying the resources of the needy and in disseminating whatever information may increase economy and comfort in the retreats of poverty'. This was to the benefit of future generations as well as the present and illustrated religion's 'powerful tendency to produce internal harmony and general cooperation for the public good'. Such patriotic satisfaction was augmented by the evidence that Nelson's victory at Trafalgar gave 'as an indication of divine favour' to the country. Yet although 'like the Israelites of old' the British seemed 'the appointed depositories of the true faith' there remained acute anxiety that 'the blood of Africa still cleaves to our skirts'. The imperative of abolition was the greater the more there was evidence of God's favour. Exultation at a 'truly providential success' was therefore the inevitable reaction when abolition was completed in 1807. It was a 'happy presage of our future destinies as a nation' and the abolitionists had been largely instrumental in redeeming the nation 'amidst the aboundings of iniquity'.[29]

This was a kind of antislavery patriotism, indeed a kind of thinking, which owed nothing to the doctrine of the rights of man. The *Christian Observer* explicitly laid such a philosophy at the door of 'those of the Unitarian school, men accustomed to speculate in their closets on the theory of government'. Liberty was best passed on not by theorising, but in the British fashion under a constitution which was balanced but through which 'weight was *permanently* given to popular opinion'. However, those abolitionists within the tradition of liberal religion and radical dissent did not entirely give up the claim to a distinctive patriotism. True, an abolitionist like William Wood of the Mill Hill Chapel, Leeds, who had been influenced by Priestley, spoke of benevolence, including a fierce hostility to the slave trade, as 'Universal', treating 'men as the children of the Universal Parent' and not as Britons or Frenchmen; the columns of the *Monthly Repository*, none the less, more often promoted a liberal patriotism. Raikes was chided for sneering at 'patriots' who wanted a reform of parliament; critics of the war, Roscoe and Flower amongst them, were thought to have demonstrated patriotism as well as courage in exposing 'our national guilt'. Theirs was a patriotism which did not celebrate the present so much as try to engender improvement and greater happiness in society in the future. By 1806–7, however, with the exception of Frend, it could not be confused with the radicalism associated with Burdett's contemporaneous campaign in the Westminster election. In Roscoe's view Burdett had been carried across the line which had to be drawn 'between the firm, consistent and temperate friends of liberty and those who allow their feelings on this subject to mislead their judgement'. The cause of liberal progress would be injured less by disunity with radicals than 'any association with crude, inexpedient or injudicious designs'. Whitbread, speaking as an antislavery Foxite, took a similar view. The political space within which abolitionists of the middle social ranks had tried to combine antislavery with political radicalism, notwithstanding their claims to be true patriots, had, for the time being, become extremely limited.[30]

The first half of the 1790s had been a time when artisan radicals had expressed antislavery views and when there had been an articulate radical wing to middle-class antislavery. Some links existed between the two but, in general, collaboration had been rather limited. The relation of the abolitionist Thomas Hardy and some of his comrades in the London Corresponding Society to intellectual antislavery radicals in the SCI was not representative of a more general link elsewhere in the country, despite contact in Manchester between Walker's circle and artisan radicals in the Revolution Society. Ironically, the momentum of anti-Jacobinism rode over the limited character of the connection and drove antislavery radicals, some of whom anyway were reassessing their outlook, on to the defensive, into quiescence, towards a more moderate reformism or a partial, patriotic accommodation to the state.

Some recent historical writing has argued that by the 1830s there was a much more direct relationship between antislavery and working-class radicalism. Walvin and Drescher, drawing especially on evidence of mass petitioning for emancipation in the years before 1833 and again in 1837–8 against the continuation of apprenticeship, have identified antislavery as a cause hugely supported by the working class, including many radicals, as well as the religious and philanthropic elements of the middle class. Antislavery was a mass rather than merely a class cause. Drescher has added a twist to the argument by indicating that some abolitionists, responding to sharpening class lines consequent upon working-class disappointment with the terms of the 1832 reform, began to deploy the language of antislavery to describe and analyse such issues as child labour and factory reform which were of particular concern to working people. Working-class radicals in turn adopted the language.[31]

These arguments have led to a stress on the willingness of some abolitionists to align themselves with predominantly working-class agitations both on social and economic questions and in pursuit of political claims in the early Chartist years. Drescher and Fladeland especially imply a natural and increasingly radical continuity in the 1830s and 1840s between liberation of the slaves and attempted liberation of the working classes. While there is some evidence which clearly points in this direction it will be argued in the rest of this chapter that the situation was much more complex. It is necessary to underline again that comprehension of antislavery requires avoidance of any initial assumption of an integrated and largely homogeneous movement but rather analysis of the different antislavery elements in their attitudes and relation to working-class radicalism. Moreover, an alliance requires acceptance on both sides; working-class spokesmen manifested a variety of attitudes to both emancipation and the reformers who were identified with it. Finally, the demands codified in the Charter were political but some spokesmen foreshadowed the solution of deep social and economic grievances with the attainment of the six points. It is by no means certain that all of even those abolitionists sympathetic to working-class political aims appreciated or accepted their most radical implications.[32]

It is easy enough to find working-class radical and Chartist spokesmen employing the language of antislavery in the late 1830s and early 1840s but it was a language which embraced a range of issues and pointed to different conclusions. Bronterre O'Brien spoke of wages slavery within the developing factory system of industrial capitalism. Similarly Peter Murray McDouall in 1841 wrote a series of articles in his *Chartist and Republican Journal* on 'The White Slaves of Great Britain'. The disappearance of the handloom weaver, he declared, exemplified the destruction of independence, family economy and control of the pace and nature of work, which was the situation of 'the factory slave'. At his trial in 1843 O'Connor likewise denounced 'the purse-proud *liberal masters* ' under the factory system for their brutality towards their slaves. McDouall concluded that if he had a choice between factory and chattel slavery 'I would rather be the slave of the West Indies and possess all the physical benefits of real slavery than be the white factory slave of England and possess all the hardships of an unreal freedom.' O'Brien went further and attacked the fatal effects of emancipation. Under wages slavery 'the master employs and supports his slave only when he needs him; in the other [form of slavery] he supports him whether he had work for him or not . . . Emancipation enables the master to get more labour and to pay less for it'. He therefore denounced abolitionists, and especially the Anglican evangelical element, for giving the impression that 'outside of the blacks there was no slave under British rule'. Buxton, a 'smooth-tongued rogue', appears to have struck him with his evangelical religious sensibility as particularly likely to produce the kind of cant which diverted attention from wrongs nearer home.

O'Brien appeared hostile to emancipation itself; more often the issue was probably the abolitionist priority of slave emancipation over working-class grievances, putting the West Indies before the West Riding. It was a similar perception which underlay disruption of antislavery meetings by Chartists even after apprenticeship had ended. In Norwich in November 1840 it was West Africa and the proposed Niger expedition which claimed priority. A meeting to be addressed by Buxton and J.J. Gurney was taken over by 200 Chartists claiming to be worse slaves than the Africans carried across the Middle Passage whose fate was to be tackled by the Niger plan. In 1840-1 a number of other antislavery meetings were similarly disrupted. The Charter, these incursions announced, came before everything else, was a precondition for all political and social progress.[35]

By 1840 the evangelical and Quaker circle around Buxton reciprocated the hostility of the working-class radicals. Samuel Hoare spoke in tones of class disdain of Chartists as weak, uninfluential and ignorant but nonetheless betrayed anxiety about their capacity for mischief. Katherine Fry's response to the disruption of the Norwich meeting was to underline the unacceptable nature of Chartist demands by referring to 'three notorious socialist women . . . amongst the most vocal of the agitators'. After consultation with the sheriff, the abolitionists had tried to keep away any poorly dressed people from the meeting and resolved to hold another gathering of guaranteed respectability through allowing admission by ticket only.[34]

None the less it has long been a commonplace amongst scholars that some prominent working-class activists were strongly anti-slavery and more open to collaboration with middle-class reformers than O'Brien in the early 1830s or O'Connor. Lovett, others of the London Working Men's Association and Collins perceived black and white slavery in similar terms and desired to end both. In 1839 Scots Chartists showed support for blocking free trade in slave-grown produce. In return some of them clearly hoped for aid in gaining their political objectives.

Here too the language of antislavery is quite common. But the relation of this language to the practice and achievement of organised antislavery is more problematical than Drescher has suggested. In the years adjacent to the antislavery victories of the 1830s it is reasonable to suppose that the terms of antislavery rhetoric and analysis assumed an additional resonance as they were applied to other issues. Yet the image of legally free labour as, in certain circumstances, a form of enslavement was by no means new in the 1830s. In the case of radical critics of 'factory slavery' it was also language sometimes used *against* abolitionists, illustrating the expansive and protean character of such language. Similarly the use of slavery to indicate primarily *political* exclusion is familiar in the late 1830s as when the London Democratic Association in 1838 declared 'the oppressed have no voice in the formation of the laws that rule their destiny – the masses are socially – because they are politically slaves'. Once again, however, this is not new. As in the economic employment of the term there are eighteenth-century precedents both pre-dating and in the very early years of organised antislavery activity. Such an extensive history of this particular form of discourse suggests not only that its sources are not simply in abolitionism but also that its protean character may be a sign of its increasing conventionality.[35]

The response of middle-class antislavery reformers to the democratic political claims of Chartists was as varied as the attitudes

ANTISLAVERY, RADICALISM AND PATRIOTISM

of working-class radicals towards them. Drescher has noted Anglican evangelical criticism of the involvement of political radicals in the push to achieve the 1833 emancipation legislation and Buxton disclaimed all radical political tendencies. Joseph John Gurney, perhaps the leading figure within the evangelical tendency in Quakerism, was hostile to Chartism's politics which was to be expected in light of his views on American democracy experienced at first hand in the late 1830s. Democracy, he wrote back from the United States, was no good unless it was also a theocracy; he particularly disliked what he saw as the habit of oppressive popular violence in the democratic system. Edward Baines is an example of a prominent antislavery evangelical dissenter who saw the situation in a broadly similar way. After 1832 he was sure that the middle-class electorate had to be preserved from being overwhelmed by the uneducated mass and for many years was opposed to universal or complete suffrage proposals and even to household suffrage. Both William Howitt and Elizabeth Pease by contrast, coming from liberal Quaker environments, reacted positively, though not entirely without ambivalence, to 'moral force' Chartism of the Lovett variety. Howitt even expressed a clear preference for Chartists over the 'Millocrats' of the Anti-Corn Law League. More usually, as in the case of Pease, George Thompson and other British Garrisonian abolitionists of the 1840s, the hope was that abolition of the Corn Laws and working-class political advance could be pursued simultaneously.[36]

There are two main reasons why, apart from Joseph Sturge and his Birmingham associates to be treated below (p.187–95), British sympathisers with Garrison's radical brand of American abolitionism constituted the most visible group of abolitionists actively sympathetic to the 'moral force' tendency in Chartism. Garrison and some of his closest colleagues, though severely critical of the operation of many American institutions, paradoxically were strongly marked by the style of thought of American republicanism with its stress on the necessity to sustain forces capable of offsetting the drive of rulers towards despotism. Garrison, Phillips and Lucretia Mott translated that perspective to the British scene, which they all observed during their visit in 1840, by urging their abolitionist friends to become 'chartists, repealers and ultrademocrats'. Associating with Garrison reinforced the alienation of these British reformers particularly from the more conservative evangelical reformers who were least likely to favour the Chartists. Religious heterodoxy made political heterodoxy more likely. Thus Pease and her father had links with the Rev. Patrick

185

Brewster whose social religion expressed in his *Chartist Sermons* led to a year's suspension from his pastorate in Paisley. They were also in contact with the radical solicitor William Ashurst and his largely Unitarian circle in London. Other radical antislavery figures such as Henry Solly and Joseph Barker had both Garrisonian and Unitarian connections and proclaimed their Chartist sympathies.[37]

It is revealing none the less that Thompson and Pease had to work through their ambivalences about Chartism, especially in the difficult years 1841–2. Thompson as an active lecturer for the ACLL was clearly troubled by Chartist hostility to the League and as to Chartists had to be convinced that 'a double honour awaits him if he will take up their cause'. Pease initially feared that Chartists were trying to dictate the ground on which abolitionists should stand, though she declared her sympathy for their grievances and principles. But in the critical summer of 1842 she was deeply anxious over the prospects for social order. She hoped the Corn Law campaign could accompany working-class political advancement by radicalising the middle class into a recognition of the obduracy of aristocratic power and the perception that their own freedom depended upon the 'political liberty and equality of the people'. The class collaboration for change which this implied she thought necessary to avoid widespread disorder and a threat to property, particularly if the government attempted to use military force against the people. Yet she remained uncertain how much of a threat mob violence posed. Probably, she concluded, the people as a whole, while driven by desperation, yet offered less danger than 'the few wicked & reckless who will mix themselves with the rest, may do serious damage and endanger life as well as property'. Pease and her father helped distribute Chartist literature in Darlington and she concluded with nervous humour to the Phillipses 'so I've a right to expect protection – have I not?!!!'

All of these British Garrisonian radicals and many of the Sturgeites in the Complete Suffrage campaign had concluded, whatever their personal anxieties, that class legislation was the fundamental source of evil in society. It is easy, however, to exaggerate the significance of abolitionist links to Chartism. The range of response to Chartism exhibited by antislavery reformers underlines the conclusion that there was no single set of abolitionist answers to working-class grievances. Mass support for abolitionism in the 1830s (which died away after 1838) coexisted with sympathy, ambivalence and much hostility amongst abolitionists towards claims for greater autonomy and greater influence by spokesmen for the masses. Above all, efforts by abolitionists in the early Chartist years to work with Chartists achieved very little.[38]

So far the relationship between abolitionists and working-class radicalism has been analysed largely in terms of categories of attitude and the different components of the antislavery movement. The final phase of the chapter will attempt a more textured sense of the striving by an abolitionist minority for class collaboration with working-class radicals by focusing on the shaping of the Complete Suffrage movement within Birmingham, its difficulties and the unsuccessful effort to generalise that experience to build a national campaign for radical political change.

Contemporary reformers in the Birmingham area associated with the Birmingham Political Union convinced themselves that they had led the popular movement which had brought about parliament's acquiescence in its own reform in 1832. At the heart of this conviction of large national influence was celebration by Thomas Attwood and his colleagues of a strength deriving from the union in the town of the middle and lower classes. Joseph Sturge and two of his brothers joined the BPU in 1831 just as it was supposedly about to attain its greatest influence. The union of the classes was based, the leadership of the BPU proclaimed, on a unity of interest of all the 'productive classes', a term which included both manufacturers and workers. The myth of class collaboration bringing success was a powerful one in Birmingham and even to outsiders the attempt to repeat the trick through a complete suffrage campaign which drew together middle-class radicals and the more respectable elements in Chartism appropriately drew its impetus from Birmingham.[39]

The relation of social, ideological and political factors was, however, more complex than this suggests. Despite the proclaimed success of the alliance of the classes it was the evident dissatisfaction with the 1832 settlement of working people in Birmingham which contributed largely to the re-emergence of the Political Union between 1837 and 1839 and the pragmatic adjustment of Attwood and his associates to a programme of universal suffrage which they had earlier opposed. This was a response to a distinctive working-class radicalism, apparent as early as the 1820s and even then committed to universal suffrage. By the late 1830s the radicalism was increasingly channelled through trade societies and separate class organisations, themselves in part a product of changes in the local economy towards a greater amount of factory organisation in various trades, downward pressure on wages and fear of unemployment or underemployment. Developing economic conflict with employers and resentment at the exclusion of working-class representatives from a share in the leadership of the BPU rendered the hold of a 'unity of interest' ideology precarious. In addition, by the beginning of 1839 a number of Attwood's associates amongst the middle-class radicals had other sources of power and influence in the town. The campaign for the incorporation of Birmingham achieved success in 1838 and in December elections occurred which put more than a dozen members of the BPU council into municipal office. Unlike their erstwhile working-class allies they had ceased to be excluded and as they took power the middle-class radicals withdrew from the BPU, which was wound up in March 1839. By the spring and summer the former BPU leaders P.H. Muntz and Scholefield took the initiative in having some local radicals prosecuted and called in outside detachments of police during the period of the Chartist Convention in the town to control rioting crowds in the Bull Ring. The claims of these middle-class radicals to lead a union of classes bound together by common interests had collapsed.[40]

One of the strengths, however, of middle-class radicalism in Birmingham up to the late 1830s was that the bankers, manufacturers and businessmen who took the lead in the BPU had been able to draw in another element of the town's middle class; this was the group characterised by the recent biographer, Alex Tyrrell, of Joseph Sturge as exponents of a 'moral radicalism'. Their outlook was much more explicitly shaped by non-Anglican religious loyalties; a number were indeed ministers. Their conviction of the possibilities of class harmony through class collaboration did not arise from any socio-economic analysis and they had no evident attraction to Attwood's currency theories, but their presence in the BPU appears to have had some effect. Attwood and his associates adopted an antislavery position which they maintained even after 1833 and they found common ground with religious reformers over factory regulation and opposition to the financial claims of the state church. The abolitionist William Boultbee was an active member of the BPU council in the early 1830s; influence in the same direction came from the radical antislavery Catholic priest Father T.M. McDonnell who had been on the local antislavery committee since 1826. The alliance continued after the first phase of the BPU when Charles Sturge worked with members of Attwood's group in the Reformers' Registration Society to maintain the reform vote and took part in discussions about the revival of a political union.[41]

The religious reformers thus shared a number of specific objectives with the Attwood group and the more general aspiration to class collaboration. But by 1835 the approach to such class collaboration began to diverge in emphasis from the BPU approach. A more distinctive moral radicalism was given voice in a new weekly paper, the *Reformer* and its successor, the *Philanthropist*. In addition to opposition to West Indian apprenticeship, support for freer trade, the ballot and further franchise reform, the moral radicals directed their views at the aspiration to respectability of the working class in advocating temperance and offering 'proper animadversions' against 'prize fights and all low and brutal excitements of the people, together with all contrivances to encourage the sensual and depress the rational faculties'.

This was also a matter of patriotism. The duty of Christian reformers to eradicate corruption wherever it was found was also that of the patriot who 'will be swiftest to discern every improvement that can be added' to his country's system without either sliding into revolution or restricting himself to his own country. 'All sincere and disinterested patriots . . . expect that glorious period when justice shall have established the universal fraternity of amity and peace.' Programmatically moral radicalism thus comprehended antislavery, peace, religious voluntaryism 'and reform of every abuse from the throne to the poor house'. In consequence by the time of the revival of the BPU in 1837 both the stress of Attwood on purely political change along with his pet panacea of currency inflation and his comparative lack of concern with the other issues which attracted the attention of the moral radicals was a source of tension between the two groups. Moreover, the *Philanthropist* concluded at the end of 1837, the Political Union no longer commanded the support it had in 1832; it lacked the influence to turn the ministry out and was suspected simply of hoping for something better from the Tories.[42]

With the collapse of the Attwood–working-class alliance by 1839 the moral radicals were potentially placed to establish a new union of the classes. There is little doubt that the Sturgeites assumed that they would lead any such alliance. 'We are not of the opinion that Universal or Household Suffrage is out of the reach of the Working Classes; but we think that for them to get it, they must possess more judgement than they have at present.' With the strong reaction of the law against Chartist rioting in the Bull Ring, Birmingham in July 1839 Joseph Sturge took the initiative in urging commutation of death sentences and, facing the threat of legislation to put police in

Birmingham under a commission appointed by the Home Secretary, he led the opposition out of a 'christian duty' to 'prevent encroachments upon the liberties of his country' and as part of the requirement he felt 'to advocate the rights of the poorest individuals in the community to all the religious, civil and political privileges of the wealthiest in the land'. His closest collaborator in the campaign was his fellow radical abolitionist Captain Moorsom. At least from this point on he had good contacts with Birmingham Chartists and good reason to know that his initial interest in a literacy franchise or household suffrage was not enough for the Chartists. Reflection on what he saw during his American visit of 1841 appears to have induced his acceptance of working-class suffrage and confirmed his movement towards a working-class alliance. He floated the idea to a few sympathetic fellow members of the Anti-Corn Law League in the autumn of 1841 and looked to the kind of constituency within the middle-class which the Birmingham moral radicals had always tried to cultivate. 'I have turned my attention seriously to getting that part of the religious philanthropic public who do not commonly mix in politics to take the subject up and the result has been most encouraging.'[43]

Perhaps one reason for this sense of encouragement was the contemporaneous emergence of a 'new move' Chartism amongst just the kind of respectable spokesmen of the working class most likely to appeal to Sturge and his religious radicals. They had turned away from O'Connor's National Charter Association to Arthur O'Neill's Chartist church in Birmingham, to John Collins (who received a hero's welcome in Birmingham on his release from gaol in 1840) and his plans jointly with William Lovett to work for political rights through education and also to Henry Vincent's teetotal Chartism, immediately encouraging to the temperance reformers amongst the moral radicals. By the spring of 1842 Sturge and a provisional committee had called a conference in Birmingham to establish a movement for extension of the suffrage which drew together moderate Chartists and sympathetic middle-class radicals.

A characteristic shared by elements of both groups was their abolitionism. Almost all members of Sturge's Birmingham circle had been active in antislavery. Their potential allies amongst the Chartists had not been those who had attacked the limited sympathies of abolitionists in the 1830s. The one notable exception was Bronterre O'Brien who seems to have revised his attitude by 1842 to the worth of working with middle-class elements who were anyway, unlike

Buxton, not Anglican evangelicals. Slightly more than 100 delegates attended the conference in April 1842 on complete suffrage; a prominent clutch of them had gone to the 1840 World Anti-Slavery Convention or would go to the 1843 Convention. Yet the familiarity of these figures to the student of abolitionism and the known antislavery sympathies of working-class participants at Birmingham should not lead to the supposition that an altogether homogeneous point of view was to emerge. Despite the rather different approach to class collaboration evolved by the moral radicals as compared with the Attwood group, they, no more than Attwood earlier within the BPU, were able to avoid the issue of power relations within their reform organisation.[44]

The creation of the National Complete Suffrage Union (NCSU) occurred after a number of earlier inconclusive moves towards class collaboration. The Birmingham conference thus had to be quite carefully prepared. ACLL supporters were informed of a suffrage resolution thought by Sturge and his associates to be suitable for parliamentary discussion and at a preliminary meeting in February 1842 the substance of the Charter was adopted as the basis for further discussion. The preliminary report to the conference indicated awareness amongst the middle-class radicals of the need for conciliation on their part. They announced it as a misconception that a memorial embodying principles agreed in the preliminary discussions 'was intended to defeat the People's Charter'. They acknowledged more concessions had to come from enfranchised opinion than from the non-electors and their spokesmen. None the less the imprint of the formed outlook of moral radicalism, and antislavery as part of it, is clear in the minutes and record of the conference. The commonplace language of 'political slavery' was widely used and a proposed pattern of operation through correspondents, lecturers and missionaries, tracts and pamphlets as well as propaganda in religious periodicals such as the *Nonconformist* and the *Eclectic Review* was reminiscent of the operations of antislavery. The points of the Charter were accepted but they were tied to a repudiation of physical force and an exclusive reliance on 'a moral agency [that] goes far to establish its victories from the reach of general change'. The political exclusion and consequently unjust legislation against which the conference committed itself had effects which Miall and others saw primarily in moral and religious terms. 'Political slavery' of those without constitutional rights places 'their conduct, their movements, their social and domestic enjoyments and even their religious convictions subject in

191

considerable measure to the control of others'. The special grievances fostered by partial legislation included 'a vast system of ecclesiastical despotism', 'absurd and unjust restrictions' on commerce and, in an incorporation of elements of the traditional rhetoric of radicalism contesting 'Old Corruption', the conference denounced a system of taxation only lightly touching the rich which allowed governments to engage in warfare and bring the country to the edge of 'irremediable ruin'. 'Sobriety and temperance' as well as earnest propaganda were recommended for the proper conduct of the movement.

Much of this the Chartist members of the conference did not dissent from but signs of future difficulties emerged. Bronterre O'Brien and John Collins forcefully insisted that representation was a fundamental right derived from membership of society. Lovett argued that acceptance of the principles of the Charter without its name made the unity of classes less likely since the Charter had become the legislative textbook of millions. Miall and Spencer in particular voiced the unease of some of the middle-class radicals that the Chartists were trying to dictate the terms of the alliance and the issue was left open for another conference.[45]

None the less there was nothing inevitable about the failure of collaboration, at least between the kind of working-class radicals in Birmingham and present at the conference and the Sturgeites. By the spring of 1842 complete suffrage associations existed in many large towns. Although Crawford's parliamentary motion for 'full, fair and free representation' was heavily defeated, NCSU missionaries spread out across the country; the programme was taken to a series of by-elections, most notably through a rousing but unsuccessful campaign at Nottingham on behalf of Sturge which drew in both local and more distant Chartists. Working-class reformers favourable to class collaboration saw the April conference as evidence that 'TRUTH WILL PREVAIL'. They argued the good effects of the Charter in terms which overlapped significantly with the programmatic elements of moral radicalism. 'The great body of the middle classes', the *Question* proclaimed hopefully, 'have discovered that the Corn Laws can only be repealed through the People's Charter.' It would also scatter the drones, pensioners and sinecurists who had battened on to an exclusive political system, reduce burdensome taxes and make the Church of England become dependent upon the voluntary support of its members rather than legal privilege granted by the state. An inclusive political order would bring peace; sobriety and self-respect would raise the moral character of the people and, having renewed herself, 'England will become a renovator of the world'.

The chance to build the NCSU on this substantial common ground was destroyed by the effects of the social crisis of the summer of 1842. It has been noted that even as radical an abolitionist as Elizabeth Pease was highly ambivalent about the widespread strikes and disturbances of the period. Many middle-class people had their fear of the crowd increased by these events. Even O'Neill, the pastor of the Chartist Church in Birmingham, while urging the strikers to abstain from violence, urged civil disobedience and was arrested as an agitator. Sturge and the NCSU council initially supported civil disobedience but this alienated some middle-class supporters. At this point the Sturgeites probably recognised their isolation. Evangelical ministers and clergymen in Birmingham such as James and Marsh who had been abolitionists and engaged in moral reform had no time for more overtly political activities, particularly not in collaboration with supporters of the Charter. The BFASS never gave institutional sanction to Sturge's activities in this field and the council of the ACLL distanced itself from him. The Sturgeites concluded that they were in danger of losing the 'feeling of the more liberal minded electors of the middle class' and thus went to the reconvened NCSU conference in December 1842 determined to push through a Bill of Rights rather than the Charter as the basis for policy. The effect was only to unite Lovett and O'Connor and their supporters in defence of the name of the Charter and to cause Sturge and his middle-class associates to withdraw, preserving as allies amongst the prominent Chartists only Vincent, O'Brien and O'Neill. The divergence was underlined by a Sturgeite declaration which contrasted the predicted alienation from suffrage reform of thousands by associating it with 'anarchy and confusion' if the Charter took priority and the expectation of the middle-class radicals in the NCSU of creating 'an independent and enlightened public opinion'. The organisation continued to proclaim both the pivotal role in a class society of the middle class and the conviction that progress required the overthrow of 'aristocratical dominion' which in turn necessitated adult male suffrage. Over the next two or three years, however, except to an extent in Birmingham, the complete suffrage campaign failed to hold together middle- and working-class radicals; the Charter retained the loyalty of most working-class activists.[46]

It was never very likely that the O'Connorite wing of Chartism would embrace the moral radicalism which informed the outlook of the middle-class leaders of the complete suffrage campaign.

Supporters of O'Connor's National Charter Association responded to an appeal which placed greater stress on the rhetoric of class, a sense of economic exploitation, a politics more often 'rough' than 'respectable' in type. More critical to the success of their immediate hopes was the failure of the Sturge circle to carry most of the respectables with them. They were unable to bridge within an emerging national organisation the kind of gulf which was evident in Birmingham in the final stages of the BPU in 1838–9 between the different class elements. It was John Collins who had symbolised the determination of the working-class radicals to gain some measure of equality in the leadership of radical agitation when he was promoted as a Birmingham delegate to the Chartist convention alongside members of the Attwood group. Collins again spoke in 1842 in the same terms: 'If ever the middle classes united with them again it must be upon the principle of equality.' This was behind the demand in debate within the complete suffrage campaign not only for the points but the name of the Charter; it symbolised 'equal rights for all men . . . equal justice for all men'.[47]

Antislavery and complete suffrage constituted elements of a comprehensive moral radicalism which was both a matter of legislative enactment and the cultural reproduction of moral and religious values. The Sturgeites anticipated the development of a more harmonious society in conditions in the urban and industrial centres by the 1840s which no longer allowed plausibility to an ideology of class collaboration derived from a supposed unity of interest of the productive classes. Yet neither in Birmingham nor within the national campaign for complete suffrage could the moral radicals escape the contradictions of such a cultural and political project. Experience in the 1830s suggested that class collaboration, even with working-class elements most inclined to it, required middle-class radicals to accept that they could not achieve it without visible acknowledgement of the substantial equality of esteem as well as rights of working people. But to accept a working-class role which manifested equality was to anticipate one of the main ends to which moral radicalism was directed and thus to encounter fears elsewhere in the middle class of the *present* unfitness of workers for equal collaboration. Not to concede substantial equality was to expect a client working-class radicalism taking its cue from, and assimilating the outlook of, middle-class leaders. In the circumstances of the early 1840s all but a small minority of working-class radicals saw insufficient benefit in appearing to accept such a relationship. Equally, the Sturgeites were implicitly forced to recognise the social limits of their project.

One final point arises from this moral radical and complete suffrage phase of antislavery radicalism. There is some room for argument about how completely emancipation was seen, even at the time of its enactment, as a national achievement in which all classes could take a patriotic pride. But whatever the situation in the mid-1830s, by the early 1840s a common antislavery, however clothed in patriotism, was no mark of consensus on other questions; it does not seem to have been central to the outlook even of those working-class radicals who gave it their support and certainly did not predispose them to accept middle-class leadership.

7

THE ANGLO-AMERICAN CONNECTION

I have been deeply affected by the many proofs I have already
had of the uncompromising zeal and deep devotion of the
friends of abolition in this country. You have *begun well*. Your
object is righteous. It is approved in heaven. Your motives are
pure. Your labours and sacrifices demonstrate it. Your *means*
have so far been wise and good.

(George Thompson to George Benson, 7 October 1834)

I never appealed to Englishmen in a manner calculated to
awaken feelings of hatred or disgust or to inflame their
prejudices towards America as a nation, or in a manner
provocative of national jealousy or ill-will; but I always appealed
to their conscience – to the higher and nobler feelings of the
people of that country, to enlist them in this cause . . . But it is
asked, 'What good will this do?' or 'What good has it done?'
'Have you not irritated, have you not annoyed your American
friends and the American people rather than done them good?' I
admit that we have irritated them. They deserve to be irritated.
(Speech by Frederick Douglass to the American Anti-Slavery
Society, New York, 11 May 1847)[1]

English abolitionists maintained a fluctuating but frequently strong
concern about American slavery throughout the decades covered by
this study. They and their American collaborators were most
extensively and vigorously active in the years between the passage of
the emancipation law in Britain and the period of the liberation of the
American bondsmen and their initial settlement as freedmen. Within
this period the decade from the mid-1830s to the mid-1840s was the

196

highpoint of transatlantic abolitionism as a functioning international enterprise. In these years it overshadowed in the minds of many abolitionists preoccupations with slavery and its aftermath elsewhere within the British empire and outside it. American slavery as an object of concern even matched anxiety over the evil of the international slave trade.

Also, from the 1830s Anglo-American abolitionism became a major component of the larger transatlantic internationalism of middle-class Protestant benevolence alongside temperance and the search for international peace. Activism was rooted in a widespread confidence that the English-speaking peoples shared a set of common religious and moral perspectives to the benefit, if most could be brought to perceive it, of their own societies and the rest of the world. The 1830s and early 1840s especially were the confident years of English abolitionists; they had triumphed and, as George Thompson's tone in the letter quoted at the head of the chapter suggests, they felt able to tutor their American brethren. As spokesmen and activists for antislavery became more attached to the liberal side in British politics some of them were aware of a further reason for working to overthrow American slavery; if American democracy was to offer an attractive image of the more popular political order towards which reformers wanted to move Britain it was urgent the stain of slavery be removed from American life.

It was, however, a mark that the pre-Civil War highpoint of transatlantic abolitionism had been passed by the mid-1840s that Frederick Douglass, whose travels to Britain made him as well-known for a period in reform and benevolent circles on this as on his own side of the Atlantic, had to argue for the worth of the British reformers' critical attention towards the United States. Why Elizur Wright's confidence in 1835 that 'Moral force cannot be bounded by geographical lines, rivers or oceans. The cry of foreign interference cannot stop it' was lost and how it was connected to the activities Anglo-American abolitionists undertook will be the subject of the second half of this chapter. The first part sketches not only the range of connections and activities across the Atlantic from Granville Sharp onwards but suggests why it was plausible for abolitionists in England to believe that their culture of reform was part of a continuum with the Americans'.[2]

Some aspects of the range of activities English abolitionists directed towards American slavery have already been indicated. If we begin no earlier than Sharp's correspondence with Anthony Benezet, Benjamin Rush and other early American antislavery reformers, the history of supplying information on slavery and the slave trade and the progress of the cause was a long one. From the 1770s also slavery in America prompted remonstrances from Britain through the supply of English abolitionist writings in book, pamphlet and periodical form. In later years American reformers appreciated antislavery contributions to the great British reviews which had prestige and a select circulation in America. They hoped that 'the deep indignation of the civilized world against a slave-holding republic' would thus become apparent to leaders of the South. American reformers themselves were intended to receive reassurance as to the rightness of their convictions and behaviour when, for example, the *Emancipator* in New York covered in full the public debate on American slavery between George Thompson and his southern opponent Breckinridge in Glasgow in 1836 and stressed the conclusion that Thompson in his militant antislavery was truly representative of opinion in Britain unlike the circumspect ministers of religion who had visited the United States. Despite divisions over the desirability of public remonstrance, by the 1830s and 1840s elements within religious denominations pressed their American counterparts to take an antislavery stance and worked to exclude from British denominational pulpits any American ministers not clearly identified as abolitionists. Some of these measures arose from expressions of Anglo-American solidarity at the London conventions of 1840 and 1843.[3]

Financial support for antislavery projects in the United States occupied part of the energies particularly of women reformers. From the 1830s onwards British female abolitionists sent consignments of fancy work across the Atlantic, the sale of which was to raise funds for American antislavery bodies. Goods for the Boston Bazaar of the American Anti-Slavery Society each year became a focus for the work of British Garrisonians in the 1840s and 1850s, at one time engaging the efforts of 300 people in Bristol. It was an alienating disappointment when in 1858 Maria Weston Chapman announced that the Bazaar would in future only accept cash. Finance was provided for antislavery Oberlin College when John Keep and William Dawes manifested their active abolitionism on tour in Britain in 1839–40 and friends of Frederick Douglass sent money to help him establish and then maintain a newspaper. Most dramatically, the enthusiasm attendant on Mrs Stowe's visit of 1853, after the success of her novel and various London stage adaptations of it, was able to be translated into raising a national Penny Offering for her discretionary use on behalf of antislavery.[4]

Anglo-American collaboration was also prompted by particular issues which arose both within the religious and philanthropic world with which abolitionists were intimately engaged and in the more unfamiliar spheres of international diplomacy, Anglo-American governmental relations and the metropolitan–colonial connection. The attempt of the American Colonization Society to secure support in Britain for what it presented as a benevolent project to secure release of enslaved blacks in the American South, and to translate them to Liberia as a beach-head of Christian enlightenment, provoked in 1833 and 1840 within British antislavery vigorous onslaughts, with American allies, on these pretensions. When it became known that after the Disruption of 1843 the Free Church of Scotland, in order to establish itself, had taken money from slaveholding donors in the American South the demand that the money be returned was voiced through joint British and American agitation in England as well as Scotland, especially in 1845-6. The latter year also saw the aspiration to an Anglo-American, or even world-wide Evangelical Alliance contested by Anglo-American reformers because the organisation did not unambiguously exclude slaveholders from its founding convention in London, and could not agree on a clear antislavery stance.

Anglo-American diplomatic relations remained in a rather volatile state for much of the generation before the Civil War but this did not deter transatlantic antislavery co-operation from interventions over British recognition of the Texas Republic and then to try to arrest the annexation of Texas to the United States. A similar joint determination was demonstrated in efforts to secure the permanent freedom of American fugitive slaves escaping to the West Indies or Canada; both the interpretation of article X of the Anglo-American Treaty of 1842 and its implementation in colonial courts were targets for pressure and publicity in this campaign.

This plethora of activities was built, especially by the 1820s and 1830s, on an increasingly dense network of antislavery organisational, religious and personal links across the Atlantic. The relative cohesiveness of the network lay in the consciousness and expectation of common intellectual and religious assumptions which were only fully tested, and in some respects found wanting, by years of experience.

Communication between individual English abolitionists and antislavery bodies and American antislavery organisations had a long, though patchy, history before the turn to America as a major priority in the post-1833 period. Correspondence linking, on the English side, Sharp, Richard Price, Thomas Percival of Manchester, John Lettsom and Josiah Wedgwood with Benezet, Benjamin Rush, Benjamin Franklin and John Jay resulted in Sharp becoming a corresponding member of the Pennsylvania Abolition Society and the New York Anti-Slavery Society and Price of the Pennsylvania Abolition Society. Through William Dillwyn the recently established Anti-Slave Trade Committee in London opened a correspondence with the Philadelphia and New York societies in 1787. The Philadelphians supplied useful information on the good effects of manumission on slaves which was employed by William Dickson to challenge pro-slave trade propaganda on African inferiority. Samuel Hopkins in Rhode Island was encouraged by Sharp to prompt American free blacks to go to Sierra Leone and American abolitionists looked forward to future useful co-operation. American reformers were thus saddened by the decline in English abolitionist activity by the mid-1790s. Revival of that activity in the following decade, however, had an American dimension. The committee of the PAS promoted the sale of Clarkson's *History* as did the American Convention for the Abolition of Slavery, partly in the hope of influencing American legislators. The African Institution tried to enlist American antislavery organisations in enforcing abolition laws on illicit slave traders of both nations. In 1809 Zachary Macaulay argued for reciprocal rights of search and enforcement and in later years the English reformers supplied detailed information to American abolitionists and officials of American citizens who were evading the American anti-slave trade law. The American Convention also raised with English sympathisers the problem of finding a suitable asylum for blacks manumitted by their owners but prevented by laws in the southern states from staying there as free men and women. This led to Anglo-American discussion of colonisation projects which in its capacity to divide reformers will be discussed below (pp.206–9).[5]

Regular communication between both institutions and individuals within denominations sustained a sense of common outlook and common endeavour incorporating antislavery work. While such intimacy also on occasion revealed differences on aspects of antislavery or divergences which could have adverse effects on the campaign against bondage, the connections were of the kind to give hope that limits could be set to any conflict. Davis' account of the transatlantic network binding the Society of Friends as abolitionists, and well established by the later eighteenth century, indicates how effectively the testimony of John Woolman and Anthony Benezet was transmitted to English Quakers through publication, communication between the Philadelphia and London Yearly Meetings, personal acquaintance and the efforts of William Dillwyn of Pennsylvania who helped engage the commitment of many of the Friends who formed the core of organised antislavery in the 1780s. Expectation of maintaining the strength of antislavery was also stimulated amongst reformers through visits to the United States by Friends whose sometimes quiet testimony was thought insufficient by their critics but who tended to assume they were speaking to co-religionists already inclined to abolitionism: Anna Braithwaite in the 1820s, Jonathan and Hannah Backhouse between 1830 and 1835, J.J. Gurney at the end of the decade, Sturge in 1841–2. Unfortunately such assumptions were not always correct by the 1840s when many American Quakers adopted a quietist stance, squeamish about co-operating with non-Friends in antislavery and alienated by Garrisonian radicalism. The importance of the denominational link was nevertheless underlined even in an example of failure in Indiana in the mid-1840s. The Quaker hatter from Rhode Island, Arnold Buffum, succeeded in breaking through the passivity on slavery of Indiana Friends and some of them set up a library of antislavery literature; the result was a rupture with other Quakers. The London Yearly Meeting decided in 1845 to send out a delegation to heal the breach in Indiana; it consisted of William and Josiah Forster, George Stacey and John Allen, all good antislavery men. They were unable to persuade the antislavery dissidents that reunification without sacrifice of principle was possible. According to Lewis Tappan the delegation had been persuaded that in the American context where some abolitionists were infidels it was improper for Friends to become too actively engaged. Yet the intervention from England was as important as its failure in illuminating some of the assumptions framing Anglo-American abolitionism.[6]

The evangelical dynamic at the heart of the growth of Methodism and then the Congregationalists and Baptists in England bore a strong resemblance to the energies released in the Second Great Awakening which had such a powerful impact on the major denominations in the United States. John Angell James, even more of a substantial figure in Congregationalism and in evangelical 'united front' efforts than he was in antislavery, had firm links with American evangelicals, including revivalists, whose efforts he believed might produce abolitionist conclusions. The abolitionist, one-time editor of the *Anti-*

Slavery Reporter and prominent Baptist, J.H. Hinton, also assumed the likelihood of antislavery advance arising from revivalism and exhibited admiration for American ministers. Both of them were powerful voices within their denominations for strong fellowship with co-denominationalists in America. Although, as will be argued later, the evangelicalism of Methodists, Congregationalists and Baptists made them hostile to Garrison and his unorthodox American ideas when they encountered them in Britain, so far as fellow evangelicals from America were concerned English nonconformists followed the strategy of bringing friendly pressures to bear. Drawing on Wesley's own antislavery, Methodists in England, sometimes through touring ministers and certainly in correspondence, urged support for liberation of the slaves as an expression of a fundamental unity. Baptist and Congregationalist delegations to America were criticised at home for insufficient antislavery witness, but in the case of the Congregationalists Reed and Matheson their return home resulted in a moderate remonstrance against slavery to their denomination in America. More vigorously, a group of antislavery Baptists around Thomas Price issued in the mid-1830s a paper, *Slavery in America*, and through the *Baptist Magazine* tried to sever all denominational links with slaveholders in America. John Angell James expressed acute concern when he realised his earlier assumption that American revivalism produced abolitionism was faulty and he was mainly responsible at the 1840 London Convention for the resolution imposing religious ostracism on slaveholders. James was also a prime mover to create a largely Anglo-American Evangelical Alliance at a convention in London in 1846. Some attempt was made to avoid inviting slaveholders but, to make sure, as controversy rose in evangelical circles Hinton moved the exclusion of slaveholders.[7]

Such measures of purification were also an indication when undertaken by Unitarian abolitionists of a similar process of using common religious loyalties to advance antislavery. There were, however, some differences in the case of liberal Christians. As indicated in chapters 4 and 5, one characteristic of liberal Christianity was an attachment to a congregational autonomy which paralleled devotion to individual religious enquiry. Inevitably the result was a comparative slowness in constructing denominational organisations, continuing wide variation of attitude within Unitarianism over antislavery as well as religious matters and thus some difficulty in mobilising broad support for remonstrating with American colleagues. The late eighteenth-century antislavery of Richard Price and

Joseph Priestley was of no great significance to American antislavery and anyway preceded by many years the crystallisation of the Unitarian denomination in New England in the 1820s. Despite the contribution, widely noted in the early years of the Anti-Slavery Society, of the Unitarian missionary in Jamaica, Thomas Cooper, to antislavery propaganda, most antislavery Unitarians taking a public stand adopted a moderate gradualist tenor. Nor did the wide attention given in England to the antislavery views of William Ellery Channing – in favour of a gradual process of compensated emancipation – do anything to modify Unitarians' outlook when they turned their attention to American slavery. Some spoke favourably of the American Colonization Society until they recognised that the motives of colonisationists were not primarily antislavery and that its measures were too small-scale to have any serious effect on southern bondage. In the end, however, most of those English Unitarians who demonstrated a strong and continuing concern over American slaves developed links with the more radical Garrisonian wing of American abolitionism. One reason for this was that, as victims of sharp attacks from the evangelical mainstream of nonconformity in the 1830s and 1840s, liberal Christians felt particularly alienated and isolated. For those of them who reacted not by retreat but by counter-attack their very isolation made projects of reform somewhat easier; when it came to American allies they were more likely to have a natural sympathy for the abolitionists who were charged with 'infidelity' by evangelical opponents. Paradoxically too, though it might be hard to move the denomination as a whole to a clear stand on American abolition, the continuing looseness of the Unitarian connection in England imposed few restraints on local congregations or regional groupings who chose a radical path. Since, however, this predisposition towards the more heterodox American reformers was given active form primarily by the controversies surrounding the 1840 convention and the translation of American divisions to the British antislavery scene, the busiest phase of transatlantic Unitarian antislavery contributed less to evidence of an Anglo-American continuum than to tensions within the reform world.[8]

Individual friendships within and outside particular religious denominations were especially significant as focal points for dissemination of argument and co-operative action, or at least proposals for action. This was exemplified in the long and increasingly warm correspondence of Sharp and Benjamin Rush. They regularly supplied each other with publications for use in their own communities and

Sharp suggested plans for gradual emancipation with an eye both to the prosperity of masters and slaves and to meet fears about the unfitness of blacks for freedom. Some similarities of function and perhaps social position also made some transatlantic friendships central to the later history of Anglo-American reform. Joseph Sturge's link to Lewis Tappan in New York became the linchpin of the moderate mainstream of antislavery. Elements of Sturge's career have already been analysed but it can be noted here that his role in tirelessly organising reform and benevolence was similar in character to the work Tappan undertook. The axis they created was at the core of anti-Garrison abolitionism in Anglo-American antislavery especially in the 1840s.[9]

Early dramatic expression of transatlantic hostility to American slavery as well as later dissent from the evangelical mainstream of reform also had friendship near its centre, particularly the comradeship of George Thompson and William Lloyd Garrison. Thompson's stormy visit to America in 1834–5 when he encountered threatening mobs sealed a bond maintained ever afterwards, whatever Garrison's occasional criticisms of his friend. Garrison too was a victim of the mob's anger and both of them were socially rather marginal men committed to agitation as a career and both had uncertain futures. In Thompson's words 'As the soul of Jonathan was knit to the soul of David, so is my soul to your soul. Your joys, sorrows, perils, persecutions, friends and foes are mine.'[10]

Thompson's tour was only the most notorious of many visits in both directions with specifically antislavery objectives which confirmed mutual convictions in reform circles, until the American divisions of 1840 were translated to Britain. Thereafter, tours tended to underline divergencies within the antislavery movement. Until that turning point, however, after the experiment of emancipation was begun in the West Indian colonies, American abolitionists of all kinds appreciated news of developments there, particularly if brought directly by English abolitionist visitors. In 1837 Lewis Tappan brought together in New York Dr William Lloyd who had just come from the Caribbean, Thomas Harvey, Sturge's companion during his influential investigation of apprenticeship and the Americans Thome and Kimball who had also studied the West Indian situation. In August 1839 John Scoble addressed large meetings in Philadelphia, New York, Boston and elsewhere on his conclusions about the new free-labour system in the islands with results 'highly beneficial to the cause of emancipation'.[11]

The whole structure of Anglo-American connections rested upon a reiterated conviction of a common Christian duty to banish wickedness. As early as the crisis of the American Revolution Sharp and Rush had agreed that both countries were about to 'expiate their guilt' and that in the case of Britain the nation was suffering a just punishment from God

> for the enormous Wickednesses which are openly avowed and practised throughout the British Empire amongst which the Public Encouragement given to the Slave Trade by the Legislature at home and the open Toleration of Slavery and Oppression in the Colonies abroad are far from being the least.

The achievement of emancipation promised an Anglo-American purification of the world and as a first step Britain's moral energies were perceived as being released to drive on 'the Saviour's chariot' in America.[12]

Under the aegis of the BFASS abolitionists tried to draw together the kinds of connections they had developed and embody their sense of a world-wide human family in calling World or General Anti-Slavery Conventions in 1840 and 1843. They were in reality largely Anglo-American in membership and despite accumulating information on slavery in many parts of the world devoted a good deal of attention in resolutions, admonitions, memorials and remonstrances to American slavery and the relation of American religion to it. Even the less impressive size of the 1843 meeting did not depress the aspirations of some delegates. A spokesman from the Congregational Union declared 'We are not merely Britons, but cosmopolites. We go to the east and to the west, to the north and to the south, to seek for misery and to endeavour to relieve it.' The American Joshua Leavitt similarly stressed the universal character of reform intentions and hoped that the convention's effect in Britain would be to encourage the public to act 'as it affects the destinies of the world'.[13]

Yet the conventions also revealed a clear counterpoint to these broad visions; they registered some disenchantment with the possibilities of transatlantic abolitionism. To understand why this was so it is necessary to go back into the 1830s. Initial optimism of English and American reformers that they would successfully execute their duty through collaboration was premised upon the British accomplishment of 1834 being both a stimulus to American opinion in promising the triumph of free labour everywhere and relevant as to methods, having 'written out the demonstration of the problem as if with letters of light on the blue vault of heaven'. There was some recognition in England, however, of the difficulties created by the federal political system for translating moral power into effective antislavery politics in America. And from various sources English abolitionists began to realise and be informed that their experience diverged from what American abolitionists were undergoing. In Britain reformers had succeeded on a tide of favourable opinion against a system in distant colonies whose slaveholding elite knew that ultimately they could not do without the support of metropolitan power. By contrast, as Harriet Martineau influentially expressed it in 1838, 'The primary abolitionists of the United States have encountered with steady purpose such opposition as might here [in Britain] await assailants of the whole set of aristocratic institutions at once, from the throne to pauper apprenticeship.' By 1840, assimilating this experience, some American reformers began to feel the limits of comprehension of their British colleagues and thus of their guidance. Henry Stanton questioned whether his British audience could know what it was like to stand under fire. Had the power of circumstance rather than moral power produced West Indian emancipation? By 1843 Leavitt was defining a much more modest role for the British than that voiced by Thompson in the quotation at the head of this chapter. 'If England will take care of her own interest, her own laws, her own subjects, her own commerce, her own diplomacy, her own peace, we ask nothing more – the antislavery cause goes alone.' Far from accepting British patronage, increasingly in the 1840s American reformers bemoaned the feebleness of the antislavery spirit in England. There was a developing tendency to underline American cultural and political autonomy even as Douglass still spoke for the value of Christian rebuke by outsiders. Abolitionists in Britain in turn betrayed reduced confidence in the value of their efforts against American slavery. Whether Garrisonian or anti-Garrisonian by the 1850s abolitionism often seemed a matter of tradition without a vital flame; all that could be done was to continue performing one's duty.[14]

Central to this waning of confidence on both sides about the value of the transatlantic link was the mixed outcome generated by joint activity. In the buoyant days of the early 1830s British and American reformers took on the pretensions of the American Colonization Society to antislavery support made through its agent Elliott Cresson during a tour of Britain. They believed that they succeeded in destroying the claim of colonisationists to constitute an alternative to American abolitionists in the eyes of the British public. That was substantially true, but even in this case there was evidence of difficulty in the Anglo-American reform relation. Cresson was in Britain between 1831 and 1833 to raise money for his organisation – he ultimately transmitted more than £2,000 to the United States – and his tour overlapped in part with Garrison's first visit of 1833. The presence of the two Americans became the occasion for Anglo-American collaboration in polemics against the colonisationists, revealing cross-currents of dissent within the antislavery movement in England.[15]

The attack on the project of colonisation was stimulated by the presence of Charles Stuart who had returned from the US in 1829 and who was convinced of the pro-slavery character of the American Colonization Society. His opposition was complemented by abolitionists such as Buxton and Joseph Phillips, both in touch with Garrison who had published his own indictment of the colonisationists in 1832, and above all by James Cropper. Between them these critics articulated the charge which thereafter pursued colonisationists; that their prime object was to perpetuate slavery not to end it. Critics agreed that not only was it impractical to suppose that sufficient blacks could be transported to Africa to make serious inroads into the slave and free black population, but slavery and the slave trade could only be sustained if a portion of the black population were siphoned off. That would maintain the value of slaves who remained and make slave trading worthwhile; thus in any way to aid an organisation committed to the removal of blacks was to maintain slavery. Critics were confirmed in this conclusion when they noted how interested colonisationists were in removing free blacks from America as a disturbing influence and against their wishes.

Cropper, however, and the American Arnold Buffum too, had to devote efforts, publicised in the antislavery press in both countries, to countering the less hostile views of the Colonization Society embraced by Thomas Clarkson, for a period by William Wilberforce and also by other respectable reformers such as J. Perronet Thompson, J.S. Buckingham, R.D. Alexander and Thomas Hodgkin. In part these dissenting judgements arose from a different focus of attention; Clarkson and the others were concerned less with the effect of the colonisation of blacks on slavery in America than with the civilisation of Africa. For this purpose the planting of colonies in West Africa could set an example to the indigenous population, provide civilising institutions and orderly ways of living into which Africans could be drawn and undermine the attractions of the slave trade by introducing

207

profitable market relations in legitimate trade goods through outside merchants. It should also be said that Clarkson was plainly less impressed with the likely impact of colonisation on American slavery; the slave population was simply too large, the emancipation of American slaves would require other plans.[16]

When we seek an explanation for this partial divergence of opinion two possibilities suggest themselves. In some cases, notably those of Clarkson and the initially uncertain Wilberforce, older abolitionists had long had an interest in British colonisation ventures in Africa – especially Sierra Leone. As Hodgkin pointed out in defence of the American colonisationists in 1840, such schemes went back to the days of Granville Sharp and they had been promoted by the Clapham Sect and others for reasons identical to those Clarkson gave for expecting a beneficial effect on Africa from the Liberian settlement. Clarkson, on the assumption that manumitted slaves were to be transported to Africa or Haiti, had been in correspondence with the Colonization Society from its earliest days. His activities from this perspective could be seen as a continuation of the good work in Africa begun by British antislavery people half a century before.

The second possibility has to do with the strength of the transatlantic Quaker network. Part of Cresson's persuasiveness to some British reformers lay in the fact that he was a Friend and recommended by Roberts Vaux, one of the most prominent of the older generation of philanthropists and abolitionists amongst Philadelphia Friends. In addition R.D. Alexander, Clarkson's Quaker Friend in Ipswich, had been in sympathetic correspondence with colonisationists in Philadelphia who had clearly given the impression that funds would lead to manumissions of slaves and their earning of a free livelihood in Liberia. Testimony of emigrants was printed in London and circulated under the auspices of the Female Anti-Slavery Society; in 1831 the Meeting for Sufferings decided to provide money to buy the freedom and transport to Liberia of slaves nominally held by trustees on behalf of one of the American meetings in a state in which manumission was not permitted.

It is not surprising then that some British reformers saw virtue in a colony of American blacks in West Africa and were more inclined to take the antislavery professions of colonisationists seriously than was Garrison. When Clarkson and Alexander discussed his charges against the colonisationists with Garrison they were not satisfied with some of his replies. They were of course less familiar with the American situation than Stuart and perhaps less aware of the sharp conflict between colonisationists and immediatists than Cropper or Buxton. Essentially, however, they were responding to a different sense of antislavery history in which African projects, in an era in which gradual improvement only in the situation of blacks had been anticipated, had seemed an important way forward.[17]

Meetings and counter-meetings on Cresson's mission and the activities of the American Colonization Society punctuated the summer of 1833 in England. Garrison took a prominent part in the polemics, underlining the anti-immediatist character of the Colonization Society even when faced with the horrors of American slavery. In July 1833 leading British abolitionists signed a protest against the Colonization Society damning it with Southern origins and asserting their increasingly commonplace conviction that the slave trade would be ended only by the destruction of slavery itself and for that purpose settlements such as Liberia were of little use. Charles Stuart, in particular, kept up the attack on colonisationists throughout the 1830s and American abolitionists continued to encourage such attacks. Yet the different ways in which colonisation could be seen in the two countries became a problem again at the end of the decade when Buxton formed his Civilization Society which was approved of by Stuart and was claimed by Ralph Gurley of the Colonization Society, both before and during his visit to Britain in 1840, to be pursuing a policy very similar to that of the colonisationists. In 1832 Buxton had told Garrison that he saw some use for Liberia but that it was no way to extinguish slavery in the US in a reasonable time and he had signed the protest in 1833. With American encouragement Buxton clarified his position at the 1840 Convention. Clarkson also came out publicly against Gurley's organisation, claiming to have been misled about its antislavery character in 1833; he did not, however, repudiate the value of settlements as such. The luckless Gurley was also refused the sanction of the BFASS committee and by 1841 the influence of his organisation had been substantially blocked in Britain, though the process had revealed that different assumptions and antislavery histories could produce misunderstandings even amongst men of good will and common conviction.[18]

Despite the conflicts within antislavery in Britain, originating in a hardening of religious divisions and intensified by the impact of fragmentation in the American movement from 1840 onwards, transatlantic collaboration continued on issues internal to the world of religion and reform. Without it ever being entirely the case links were, however, much more likely to be between 'moderates' in both countries and Garrisonians in both countries. In the cases of the controversies over the acceptance of money from southern Presbyterians by the Free Church of Scotland and slaveholders' involvement in the Evangelical Alliance, collaboration produced very limited results and revealed that the other side of the common sentiment encouraged by Anglo-American denominational bonds was fear of the disruptive effect of antislavery on religious life. In the Free Church campaign when abolitionists demanded the return of tainted money to the South it was the supporters of Garrison in Britain who were mainly active alongside the American radical, Henry C. Wright, and Garrison himself in his visit of 1846. The BFASS and Tappan's American and Foreign Anti-Slavery Society, however, took a similar view of the 'Wee Frees" ties to the South and so highly did the Garrisonian committee of the Glasgow abolitionists regard the Tappanite address to the Free Church commissioners visiting the United States that they had 500 copies of it printed and distributed at the door of the Free Church assembly. None the less the Free Church did not return the southern money and the only gain made by the campaign was to polarise opinion within the Free Church sufficient for the establishment of the Free Church Anti-Slavery Society convinced that slaveholding necessarily involved 'heinous sin'.[19]

It has been noted earlier that both J.A. James and J.H. Hinton were active in bringing together a convention in 1846 to form a World (in practice an Anglo-American) Evangelical Alliance and in trying to guarantee its antislavery stance. During the preparations for the convention the BFASS addressed the British section arguing that acceptance of an evangelical confession of faith and sustaining slavery were incompatible since Christians had to plead the cause of the oppressed. The Tappanites later sent over a widely distributed remonstrance on similar lines. When Hinton tried to resolve the issue at the convention itself by proposing the total exclusion of slaveholders, after an earlier move to add a statement of facts on slavery to the objects of the Alliance had been withdrawn as a result of American protests, the result was still inconclusive. A special committee considering 'social ends' in general expressed the hope that no branch would admit slaveholders but more American protests caused the issue to be dropped. The difficulties experienced by some evangelical abolitionists are indicated by Wardlaw's attempt to avoid a ban on individuals while condemning slavery as an institution. An Anglo-American Garrisonian campaign, combined with attacks on the Free Church and employing Garrison, Wright, Frederick Douglass,

James N. Buffum and George Thompson at meetings in the north, Scotland, Dublin and, after Garrison's departure, at Exeter Hall, took up where the 'moderates' had left off. Eventually the British section of the Alliance, while refusing to pronounce on the personal Christianity of an individual slaveholder, excluded all slaveholders from member-ship, in practice a largely empty gesture. The campaign had been none the less something in which evangelical abolitionists wishing to maintain the purity of church and ministry and Garrisonians, hoping to underline the normal role of the church as 'a bulwark of slavery' had both been able to take part. But abolitionist efforts had not been able to hold the Alliance together and use it against slavery in America. Reformers had to recognise that a common evangelical faith did not necessarily accord the highest priority to antislavery witness amongst all British evangelicals on any priority at all amongst many American evangelicals. It was the American delegates in particular at the convention, even those who were personally antislavery, who resisted the abolitionist test. Too much was asked of the religious bond; in a foreign context the abolitionist test was, moreover, offensive to a prickly national sentiment amongst the Americans.[20]

Such a 'nationalist' factor was also present when Anglo-American abolitionists intervened in international diplomacy in resistance to possible British recognition of Texas and later the Lone Star Repub-lic's annexation to the United States. Successive British governments, though professedly antislavery, turned out to be inadequate in pursuing the overthrow of slavery internationally. The reformers underestimated government unwillingness to arouse American natio-nal resentments and failed sufficiently to recognise the power of other priorities than antislavery in policy-making. When Texas broke away from Mexico in 1836 its future depended upon a number of variables: the capacity of Mexico to reconquer Texas, the balance of Texan parties as between independence and annexation to the United States, the attitude of the Americans to annexation and the extent to which Britain or France or both offered Texas links which added attraction to the prospect of maintaining an independent republic. Not until 1842 did Mexico show any serious signs of attempting subjugation of Texas and, while the US extended recognition in March 1837, in part because annexation had been refused to the Texans, there was no unanimity amongst the rebels as to their future and the British and French were relatively slow to define their position. All this meant that there was plenty of time for both American and British abolitionists to intervene. American reformers saw Texas as a danger area in which slavery might be extended to a region from which it had supposedly been banished by Mexican decree in 1829. John Quincy Adams, perhaps supplied with information by the veteran antislavery campaigner Benjamin Lundy who had visited the area in 1830–1, spoke out on precisely this issue in Congress. In 1837 Lundy published a fierce blast against Texas alleging that its loss to Mexico would 'open a vast and profitable SLAVE MARKET'. Amos A. Phelps co-ordinated a lecturing and petitioning campaign to coincide with the discussion of Texas in Congress and British abolitionists were prompted to spread information on what was now seen as a southern plan to extend slavery through Texas.

Sturge proclaimed the main motive for Texan independence as slavery expansion but the issue had been pre-empted by George Thompson, continuing his role as messenger of brutal American realities on return from his controversial visit. At a series of meetings in England and Scotland in late 1836 and early 1837 he combined attacks on West Indian apprenticeship with exposure of the Texas issue. He deployed arguments first used by Americans and quoted from Adams' anti-Texas speeches. By 1839 Scoble drew together the familiar moral arguments and published them as a justification for Britain refusing recognition to Texas, supplementing them with optimistic arguments about the commercial potential of Mexico to Britain, denial of the likelihood that Texans would act seriously against the slave trade in return for recognition and claimed that Britain's moral status as an emancipating power forbade treating with the promise-breaking Texans whatever the content of their diplomatic sweeteners.

Continued reliance on the arguments of Lundy and Adams, however, suggested a staleness in the British campaign. Tappan was appealed to and suggested Stephen Pearl Andrews, a perennial optimist 'peddling schemes of humanity and collecting subscriptions for perfecting the human race', as a source of information who knew Texas well. Sturge, probably influenced by Andrews' line of reasoning and aware that Mexico was unlikely to reconquer Texas, shifted the basis of the abolitionist case to the British government to one of offering recognition as part of an arrangement to achieve abolition as a permanent feature of Texas. In November 1839 an antislavery deputation to Palmerston produced the assurance that he was unwilling 'to do anything by which the influence of Great Britain could become accessory to the extension or perpetuation of slavery' and this may have given some hope to reformers. At any rate provincial antislavery opinion joined the efforts of the committee of the BFASS to try to get an abolitionist *quid pro quo* for recognition. Like Lundy and Birney in the United States, British abolitionists began to think about inducements to engage Texan *interests* in a process of abolition, but mostly set aside ideas for free-labour colonisation as tainted by the whole controversy over such settlements as encouraging emancipation. At the 1840 Convention American delegates gave staunch support to the campaign against recognition unless on antislavery terms, but shrewdly a message from the American Unitarian abolitionist Channing, largely ignored by the reformers, challenged the basis of British government interference.

I can conceive of hardly anything more disastrous than an attempt on the part of the English government to put down slavery here. Such effort would identify slavery with our national pride and would rouse I fear a national spirit for its support.

The predicted response began to emerge even when the interference was in the still-independent Lone Star Republic. Despite continued pressure after the convention, when Palmerston granted recognition to Texas as an aspect of the signature of three treaties in November 1840, although one of the treaties committed Texas to abolition of the slave trade and acceptance of the right of search of suspected slavers, abolitionists in Britain and the United States reacted with anger as to a defeat. There was little evidence that even the inadequate antislavery element in the recognition agreement had arisen from abolitionist efforts. Eventually Channing and Tappan found hope in recognition as a basis for antislavery influence from Britain in Texas but the outcome could only have reduced confidence in the value of Anglo-American abolitionist co-operation and in the antislavery priorities of the British government.

The antislavery organisations in both countries now turned to trying to get British intervention to preserve the independence of Texas as a lesser evil than American annexation which American reformers told their British colleagues could tip the political balance against the free states. In the second half of 1841 Aberdeen succeeded to the Foreign Office when Peel's Conservative government came in; his and the government's antislavery posture was as clear as that of their predecessors. Equally, however, antislavery was a principle which would have to be reconciled with Aberdeen's concern for rapprochement with France after the enmity provoked by Palmerston and his desire to settle outstanding problems with the Americans. These departures from previous policy were not fully grasped by abolitionists and their mistakes in dealings with government to prevent annexation arose in part from failure to absorb their implications.

Both American and British abolitionists believed that British recognition of Texas, although for some time yet permitting an element of mediation between Mexico and Texas, made it a British duty to work against American annexation and their task to press the duty on government. The elements in the diplomatic situation were complex and changing. While it is doubtful whether there were leading figures in consistent contention within Texas over the alternatives of independence or annexation there were conflicts, for example, between President Sam Houston and the Secretary of State, Anson Jones; Jones wanted to reopen talks with Washington while remaining on reasonable terms with Britain and France in case their aid was necessary in getting recognition by Mexico of an independent state. Houston may not have been unambiguously in favour of annexation throughout and was looking for as good a bargain as possible. The Americans were concerned with only two possibilities: either Texas remained independent and, so far as the South saw it, a way had to be found to guarantee that slavery within the union was not threatened; or Texas joined the union and steps had to be taken to avoid conflict with Mexico. The limits of British policy were different. Preference was probably for a strong independent Texas without slavery; alternatively, Texas would have to be encouraged to accept something less than formal recognition by Mexico but which amounted to *de facto* independence. Britain did not want Texas to be absorbed by the United States and did not believe that Mexico could reconquer the territory.

Anglo-American abolitionist co-operation to put pressure on the British government to give substance to its anti-annexationist preference led to a process by which the reformers learned the limits of the government's antislavery diplomacy. Disruption of Anglo-American relations which had been put on a firmer basis by the Treaty of Washington of 1842 was excluded; failure finally to persuade the Mexicans to recognise Texas and the Texans to take it as the basis for maintaining independence, failure even to prevent annexation, could be borne if British efforts along with France had done something to repair Anglo-French relations. Texas was a card in a larger diplomatic game the British government was playing, not an opportunity for it to act on its professed (and genuine) antislavery principles.

The reformers did not, and could not afford, to recognise such complexities. In the early days of the Peel administration an antislavery deputation found, as they reported to the Tappanites in New York, no 'very friendly feeling towards Texas' in the Foreign Office. The New York group tried to impart a sense of urgency to the BFASS, claiming that annexation would make slavery permanent in the United States and 'the curse would probably be spread over Mexico and perhaps far beyond it'. If necessary slaveholders would promote war with Mexico to secure annexation. Much of the correspondence across the ocean consisted of a reciprocal keeping up to date and American reminders that the record of British emancipation made the country 'the bulwark of liberty'. American prompting did influence the assumptions on which abolitionists in Britain came to operate. Texas was increasingly seen within the perspective of the danger of continuing American expansionism which encouraged greater urgency amongst British reformers. The solution would have to be an independent, free-labour Texas since, despite speculation about a successful Mexican invasion in 1842, by 1843 reformers were sure that the Mexicans could not reassert their sovereignty. To get this result Texans needed financial inducements and the British government should be encouraged to provide them, especially as reformers came to believe that the policy would receive the support of a growing antislavery party in Texas.

Information supplied by Tappan's group to the BFASS encouraged the belief that slavery was being weakened in Texas by migration to southern states and that there was a growing undercurrent of feeling against slavery in the republic. This last conclusion probably came from Stephen Pearl Andrews who was in contact with Tappan. At this juncture 'a million pounds sterling loaned on land securities, contingent upon the abolition of slavery' might well bring success. These hopes and assumptions came together at the 1843 Convention in London where Tappan and some of his leading colleagues were present. Despite the possibilities of American expansionism the American delegate Joshua Leavitt thought that even Texan slaveholders might recognise their interest in Texan independence and the consequent attraction of free labour which would increase the value of their lands. But he also feared that these possibilities and any antislavery sentiment in Texas would be undermined if Americans were able to have their anti-British prejudices roused; this was the reverse side of the benefit of transatlantic collaboration. Tappan in convention debate hoped for a British government guarantee to any British capitalists who raised a loan for Texas provided Texas gave up slavery; in return for emancipation he wished Britain to press Mexico to grant recognition. The next stage of collaboration was an Anglo-American deputation to meet Lord Aberdeen after which the reformers rose to heights of optimism, the English Quaker George Stacey even telling the convention that the government had precisely the same aims in view as the assembled reformers. It was the case that in both Texas and Mexico British representatives pressed a linkage of recognition and emancipation at this time but the second facet of the plan intended to produce movement on the issue – British financial inducements to Texas – made no progress. Tappan was told by the abolitionist banker, Samuel Gurney, who specialised in handling American investment opportunities, that 'Bankers would not adventure and the government would decline.' Despite this, a second Anglo-American deputation to Aberdeen on 12 July 1843 made the proposed financial inducement the centrepiece of its argument for British action. The minister was accommodating to worries about annexation but would not consider either a government loan to Texas or, a few days later, 'facilities equivalent to a loan'. Thereafter reformers prompted Brougham to raise Texas in the Lords, and they sent addresses to both Sam Houston in Texas and the Mexican dictator Santa Anna. At what seemed the most opportune period abolitionists had thoroughly aired the question but British policy had taken no new direction.

The likelihood of abolitionists having any serious influence thereafter grew less. It became apparent that the existence of a Texas antislavery movement was chimerical. As the Tyler administration in the United States actively pressed annexation, the slowness of transatlantic communication and a shortage of accurate information handicapped any further action by reformers. They also became more conscious that their own interventions might simply contribute to mobilising support for the annexationists who were increasingly playing on anti-British feeling. By early 1844 Tappan's main hope for holding off the incorporation of Texas was a widespread fear that it would fracture the union. At this stage British policy clearly put as its first priority Anglo-French co-operation to warn off the Americans combined with pressure on Mexico to recognise Texas immediately. It was a priority which also caused the disappearance of emancipation in Texas from the agenda so as to make the Texans more receptive to any offer by Mexico. Ashbel Smith in London reported back to Texas that Aberdeen now 'regretted the agitation of the abolition of Slavery in Texas'. But there was no evidence that either Britain or France was prepared to go beyond a concerted expression of displeasure at possible annexation combined with the hope that Mexico would act in time to offer any Texans still wanting independence an alternative. The almost inevitable result was the conclusion of annexation. The abolitionist response, in Tappan's words, was of religious hope, which was a confession of worldly failure. 'How small is our faith that we do not see the hand of God in *every* event. He will cause the policy of wicked men to turn against them and foil Satan of his prey.' [21]

The other issue which brought Anglo-American abolitionists into contact, and ultimately into some conflict with the British government was their desire to secure an absolute guarantee that American fugitive slaves escaping to the 'free air' of British territory in the West Indies or Canada should never be returned. The basis for their argument was the natural right to liberty but initially, in so far as British ministers protected fugitives, it was through an assertion of British national sovereignty. Thereafter reformers experienced difficulty in squaring freedom for fugitives with American and colonial judicial interpretations of the extradition clause of the Webster–Ashburton Treaty of 1842. Though in practice freedom nearly always prevailed, right up to the outbreak of the American Civil War reformers were aware that they had not established the natural right to liberty as the basis of government policy or colonial judicial action. As John Scoble lamented, 'The merits of the case are left untouched.' [22]

The argument then has been that by the early 1840s, despite antislavery contacts between British and American reformers stretching back to the years before organised antislavery began in England and although some similarities in religious developments in the two countries, cemented through personal and denominational connections, promoted common convictions about the evil of the slave trade and slavery, the value of Anglo-American co-operation and the true depth of a transatlantic reform culture were brought into question. Scepticism about the value of the link arose from divergences in the experience of British and American abolitionists which rendered optimism based on the British precedent increasingly irrelevant. Practical success seemed largely to elude reformers when they did co-operate, whether over issues internal to the world of religion and reform or through efforts to influence the British government to act against slavery in North America. Even such comparative successes as the onslaught on the American Colonization Society in Britain, which anyway preceded the failures, revealed the significance of different antislavery histories and perspectives in the two societies.

How deep was mutuality of sympathy and understanding is the question posed and answered ambiguously by the impact of American abolitionist divisions on antislavery in Britain. Those divisions, in producing some organisational conflicts in a declining movement in Britain, reinforced tensions growing out of a hardening of religious lines discussed earlier (p.94–8). The last part of this chapter is thus complementary to the final section of chapter 4 in pursuing the expressions of fragmentation in antislavery and illuminating the limits imposed on the understanding by English reformers of attitudes originating in America. Yet the ambiguity of the answer lies in the conclusion that deep and sympathetic links remained, particularly between the radical minority wings of antislavery in both countries. In being the major focus of Anglo-American antislavery attitudes from 1840 onwards William Lloyd Garrison dramatised the coexistence of both alienation and admiration in the relationship as the initiative inevitably moved to the Americans.

American abolitionists who later became bitterly critical of each other had worked together relatively harmoniously during much of the 1830s when attempts at moral suasion of the population complemented some kinds of political action and calls to the federal government to act against slavery where it fell within its jurisdiction. Yet increasingly Garrison and his closest associates read their experience as agitators as rendering worthless their reliance on political and religious leadership to weaken slavery. Mass petitioning to Congress in the mid-1830s achieved little but a 'gag' rule against discussion of future antislavery petitions; abolitionist propaganda was unconstitutionally blocked in the South; the concern of many southerners to annex Texas appeared to be 'for the express purpose of extending slavery and the slave trade'. The Slave Power seemed to be taking over American government. Nor did the Garrisonians sustain their initial belief in the leadership of evangelical ministers of religion; they seemed so cautious about risking unpopularity with their congregations and conflict within their denominations that the radicals perceived them as betraying their antislavery leadership role. This reading of experience was supplemented by doctrine in the case of Garrison and others. In part under the influence of the perfectionist communitarian John Humphrey Noyes, Garrison became convinced that the acceptance of Christ permitted perfection since Christ spoke through the regenerate individual. Moral suasion would take time to apply to the whole of society but it was the sole road to perfection. Perfectionism also entailed the Garrisonians universalising their reform interests while recognising, some of them concluded, that human government, like slavery, disrupted man's relations with God. Their aim was to bring men 'under the dominion of God, the control of an inward spirit, the government of the law of love, and unto the obedience and liberty of Christ'. Love and self-control were to replace the coercion upon which all governments relied. Moreover, all those truly regenerate individuals, including women, committed to destroying slavery and all the sins of the world were to be equal partners in the great enterprise.[23]

These developments created tensions with more conventional evangelical abolitionists which produced organisational division in Massachusetts in 1839 and resulted in the Garrisonians assuming control of the American Anti-Slavery Society at the May meeting in 1840. It is therefore not surprising that it was amongst antislavery evangelicals that there emerged the earliest signs in England of hostility to Garrison and alignment with his evangelical critics who joined Tappan's breakaway group, the American and Foreign Anti-Slavery Society. By 1840 Josiah Conder and John Angell James were both critical of Garrison's attachment of other 'extremist' causes to abolition and the Congregational Union in that year denounced American 'fanaticism' as bringing disrepute upon the abolitionist cause. Billington suggests correctly that the American the Rev. Nathaniel Colver's intervention with British evangelicals was crucial here, an assessment shared by Garrisonians at the time. It was Colver who encouraged antislavery Baptists to work with anti-Garrisonians at the 1840 Convention and who focused the attention of British evangelicals on Garrison's 'infidelity' in questioning the status of the Sabbath and the Bible and harshly challenging the church and the ministry.

By the time that American delegates arrived in London for the World Anti-Slavery Convention British abolitionists were aware of the other main sources of division amongst Americans. They received news of opposition from anti-Garrisonians to the radicals' insistence on the equal public role of women in the movement and were encouraged by the American and Foreign Anti-Slavery Society to reject 'no human government' doctrines and urge political action on abolitionists as individuals. By such means the anti-Garrisonians, largely evangelicals, presented themselves as using the normal means of social action but in a more vital fashion.[24]

At the 1840 Convention American divisions over the role of women prompted the initial separation of British reformers into supporters and opponents of Garrison when women delegates from the United States were denied seats on the floor of the convention. The instigation of party alignments amongst the British was taken further by tours of part of the British Isles after the convention by Garrison, his American critics (often accompanied by committee members of the BFASS) and, after Garrison's return home, John A. Collins, a zealously polemical agent of the radical Massachusetts Anti-Slavery Society.

By the autumn of 1840 it was clear that leading members of the BFASS, and particularly the future secretary, John Scoble, had aligned themselves with the anti-Garrisonians. They initially took no notice of Collins in Britain and when he approached them denied sanction for his fund-raising activities and refused financial help themselves as a committee. In Scotland Charles Stuart tried to arouse evangelicals against Garrisonian radicalism and 'infidelity'; abolition had been associated with the extraneous cause of women's rights and the doctrines, horrifying to Stuart, of anarchism, as well as hostility to the Sabbath and 'a regularly educated and supported ministry'. His British as well as his American critics were convinced that Garrison's peculiarities retarded the progress of abolitionist opinion.

In the early months of 1841 the British antislavery public was subjected to a barrage of argument over American divisions and the position of the BFASS. In reply to charges against Garrison both British and American sympathisers circulated counter-arguments. In essence antislavery collaboration was seen as based on agreement on the sinfulness of slavery and the necessity for immediate emancipation; it was beyond sectarian and other differences which were irrelevant to the cause. Garrison himself intervened to rebut Colver's charges of infidelity and to declare that he believed the variety of religious affiliation amongst British abolitionists was a source of strength.

Collins' controversial tour also had the effect of translating differences over American abolitionists into institutional schisms in British antislavery and provided reinforcement for existing provincial suspicions of metropolitan reform leadership. In Ipswich abolitionists were divided over a meeting encouraged by a local Unitarian minister which Collins addressed in order to attack the 'new organisationists'.

Richard Allen on behalf of the Hibernian Anti-Slavery Society in Dublin, which had a history independent of and prior to the BFASS, carried on a critical correspondence with the London committee about its treatment of Collins; despite efforts by the BFASS to maintain a sense of common objectives the Irish group concluded that Collins had been done an injustice and that the London committee had sown the seeds of division by its commitment to Tappan's American and Foreign Anti-Slavery Society. Thereafter the Dublin group remained sceptical of the motives and activities of the BFASS leaders.

It was not surprising that Elizabeth Pease and her father Joseph in Darlington, who agreed with Collins' conviction that 'English abolitionists are in sectarian straitjackets' gave him constant support, advising on and encouraging the publication of *Right and Wrong among the Abolitionists of the United States*. When Collins and the black abolitionist Charles Remond addressed antislavery supporters in Darlington, however, a motion to censure the BFASS committee was headed off by Elizabeth Pease's cousins, the Quaker minister John Pease and his brother, the MP Joseph Pease. They saw the London committee as 'guardian of the antislavery cause'. The longest and sharpest struggle of antislavery factions promoted by Collins' presence was within the Glasgow Emancipation Society in which the party sympathetic to Garrison led by the joint secretaries John Murray and William Smeal contended with a group of evangelical ministers of whom the most prominent was Dr Ralph Wardlaw. The issues of whether to declare support for the 'old organisation' in America (the AASS rather than the AFASS), Garrison's religious 'ultraism' and women's rights all became part of the struggle. The Scots supportive of Collins also tended to a *political* radicalism shunned by most of the ministers. Thus a public meeting which supported Collins also passed a Chartist motion on the suffrage. The Wardlaw group made explicit their agreement with the BFASS over the exclusion of women from the 1840 convention and dissented from the 1840 annual report of the Glasgow Emancipation Society in terms similar to those voiced by Joseph Sturge who objected to criticism of the BFASS and insisted his name as an honorary member of the society be removed. The radical group were prepared to withdraw co-operation from the London committee. Eventually the radicals prevailed and for some years Glasgow became one of the two (along with Dublin) main outposts in the British Isles of Garrisonian loyalists.[25]

The effects of this painful rending of antislavery were various.

Reformers loyal to the BFASS after 1840–1 largely avoided publicly reopening polemics with either American or British Garrisonians. In more private meetings and correspondence Scoble and Charles Stuart guided their contacts away from the radical wing in Britain. The BFASS and provincial groups like Sturge's in Birmingham exchanged information with the Tappan group and sent resolutions and addresses to America. New competition within Anglo-American abolitionism, however, emerged especially clearly in rival claims on Clarkson's influence and opinions. Recognising the veteran reformer's stature in both countries American delegates joined BFASS colleagues in pressing him to write on American questions for circulation in the United States. He produced strong condemnations of southern planters and pro-slavery clergy and later a remonstrance on the treatment of free blacks.

His American writings of the earlier 1840s were channelled through the anti-Garrisonians, Tappan, Sturge and Gerrit Smith, but in 1844 he was pressed by the Garrisonian, Maria Weston Chapman, to contribute to the *Liberty Bell* in Boston and by H.C. Wright to provide material. Both also urged their disunionist views upon Clarkson. He tried to avoid identification with any particular American party, he claimed, and Tappan advised him to make clear his distance from the radicals when he produced his contribution. However, no more than a month before Clarkson's death in late 1846 Garrison with Frederick Douglass and Thompson visited him at his house and secured from him a document supporting disunion which had become the most notorious feature of the American radicals' position. After Clarkson's death Garrison insisted on publishing these views to the consternation of his Anglo-American opponents and with a triumphant flourish against 'the sectarian *surveillance* under which soi-disant abolitionists of the school of the British and Foreign Society attempted to keep him [Clarkson]'.[26]

Apart from this contest to acquire Clarkson's sanction, however, the two wings of antislavery largely operated in parallel in England. Antislavery sentiment amongst Unitarians had been pushed in the direction of the radicals by the perceived oppression of women through their exclusion from the 1840 Convention, and their paper, the *Inquirer*, beginning publication in July 1842 under an old Liverpool abolitionist friend of William Roscoe, William Hincks, for several years pursued a pro-Garrison line. Glasgow and Dublin radicals accepted the rightness of the disunionist position because they believed the American constitution 'expressly binds the nation to protect slaveholders'. Partly stimulated by the visit of Samuel May Jr in 1843 Unitarians in the West Country, Glasgow and Dublin sent antislavery addresses to their fellow believers in America. Their sympathies, encouraged by Harriet Martineau, were clearly towards Garrison. In 1840 Garrison had established friendly relations with a number of English middle-class radicals apart from the liberal Quakers and Unitarians already mentioned; the early feminist Anne Knight of Chelmsford, William Ashurst, the radical lawyer who began to write for the *Liberator*, the journalist–reformers, William and Mary Howitt, John Bowring, scholar and politician. They and the provincial radical outposts formed the network which maintained the Garrisonian minority for much of the 1840s and 1850s.[27]

It is clear that Garrison personally commanded great admiration. He appealed to the utopian in Richard Webb who compared him and Wright in their reputation amongst 'wealthy easy-going antislavery people in England' as 'not much better than Rousseau and Voltaire in . . . estimation'. Consequently he hung a portrait of Garrison in his drawing room with one of Lucretia Mott; they 'are looked on as flags of defiance to the whole society'. Garrison's American republican plainness made him fierce about 'silver slipper' abolitionism in England because he saw it as a gesture made by people essentially hostile to freedom who were determined to thwart necessary radical reforms at home. He was hostile to an 'overgrown monarchy and a bloated aristocracy' and sharply critical even of genuine reformers who 'complimented' the royal family. The figure who emerged in English eyes was likely to attract only a small minority but to be especially cherished by them. The Garrisonians in Britain thus became quite close knit in feeling though geographically scattered. There was much of the sense of a gathering of friends at the establishment of the Anti-Slavery League in London in August 1846; sectarianism was excluded by the rule that anyone who subscribed to the principle of the sinfulness of slavery and the need for immediate abolition was able to become a member. Dr Estlin conducted Garrison around a sympathetic Unitarian network after the establishment of the League and the American reciprocated their 'hearty approval'. It was this close network, and Estlin's money, which made possible continued support for the Garrisonian outlook in the 1850s through the publication of the *Anti-Slavery Advocate*.[28]

Even so Garrison's total conviction of his rightness and the uncompromising perfectionist thrust of his outlook sometimes went beyond what his admirers in Britain could accept. He illuminated the tensions produced by cultural divergences and personal temperament even within a close-knit group. Even Webb could not swallow the Garrisonian denunciation of the 'new organisationists' of 1840 as pro-slavery 'though their views on all subjects may not be so far darting as those of our old organisation friends'. James Haughton's liberalism was offended by conviction so fierce as to become intolerance. Elizabeth Pease agonised over the questioning of the Sabbath and the doctrine of non-resistance, hoping to balance freedom of discussion against the need 'to keep questions independent which are so in reality'. Estlin's similar anxieties about association with 'moral force' Chartism were frankly expressed in terms of the gap to be perceived between reform platforms in England which were 'much narrower than with you', drawing together people who generally thought alike in politics and religion and Garrison's commitments to universal reform and a broader popular base. Estlin concluded that the American simply offended 'higher circles' and though his radicalism appealed to some he had not grasped that the 'lower & lower middle classes do not have sufficient personal interest in the subject [American abolition]'. Yet when confronted by common critics from within the mainstream of middle-class Quaker and evangelical reform the bonds of friendship held.[29]

The criticism by other antislavery reformers reinforced the role of religious differences in tensions within antislavery in England and elsewhere in Britain. Controversy encouraged interventions by American Garrisonians and their American opponents which had the effect of maintaining divisions in British antislavery even when local abolitionists were trying to come together. Ceasing to be a Friend in the mid-1840s on her marriage outside the Society, Elizabeth Pease aided Joseph Barker in his journalistic propagation of radical and eventually free-thought notions. Barker himself knew and was influenced by H.C. Wright when he was in Britain, worked alongside Douglass, offered public support to Garrison and exchanged letters with Theodore Parker. Billington has also brilliantly explored the attraction to Garrison expressed in radical, secularist and liberal Christian papers in Britain by George Jacob Holyoake, F.R. Lees and Charles Clarke. With such advocates Garrison became even more of a target for evangelical animus. More conservative Unitarians also resisted attempts to commit the British and Foreign Unitarian Association (BFUA) to a strong stand against American slavery and it was not until 1851, at a separate meeting during its annual gathering, that abolitionist Unitarians succeeded in passing and sending off to

American co-denominationalists resolutions hostile to the recently passed American Fugitive Slave Law. So controversial had Garrison become as early as 1846 that he was boycotted in several places by English abolitionists during his visit.[30]

Maria Weston Chapman was present at the BFUA discussion of 1851 and she influenced the Bristol and Clifton Ladies' Anti-Slavery Society to adopt a Garrisonian position in 1851–2 and distance itself from the Broad Street committee of the BFASS. On the other side of the American divide the ex-slave clergyman J.W.C. Pennington influenced the establishment of a new association in Glasgow at the beginning of the 1850s by persuading women reformers in the city that charges of 'infidelity' against Garrison were just. At the same time the Edinburgh Ladies' Anti-Slavery Society withdrew from supplying the Boston Bazaar for similar reasons. The presence of the Garrisonian militant, Parker Pillsbury, in Britain in the middle years of the 1850s further contributed to continued divisions; he was present at the Manchester anniversary meeting in 1854 and then at the conference on antislavery unity in London in November. His main contribution was to demand full recognition of the American Anti-Slavery Society, in effect a complete retraction of their previous views by BFASS abolitionists. Pillsbury and his allies had much to do with George Thompson's failure to smooth over differences by advocating a general resolution of sympathy for all American abolitionists given his understanding from private conversations that in future there would be no refusal by the BFASS to work with other abolitionists on the grounds of their religious or political opinions.[31]

Much of this, coming from the accumulated bitterness of years, was probably incomprehensible to most people outside the dwindling membership of antislavery organisations. It constituted the antithesis of the earlier commitments to an international culture of reform based on common convictions. In the last years before the outbreak of the American Civil War one further issue central to American abolitionism which had received only limited attention earlier in Britain re-emphasised party lines amongst British antislavery reformers: was the American constitution to be understood as antislavery in tendency, thus permitting honest engagement in antislavery politics? By the mid-1850s the BFASS offered support to Gerrit Smith's Radical Abolitionist Party which interpreted the constitution as permitting federal power to be used directly against slavery in the states; in addition they welcomed the early progress of the Republican Party while holding back from any unqualified endorsement. Smith's organisation had no general influence in the United States and the controversy was distant from general antislavery opinion, and probably the understanding of many reformers in England. Its significance was dramatised by Frederick Douglass who had long broken from the Garrisonians and who was in Britain in 1860. The form of the dramatisation was a public debate with George Thompson in Glasgow. Thompson had been a severe critic of the constitution ever since his experiences of 1835 and had been loyal to Garrisonian disunionism based on the constitution's pro-slavery character from the time of its enunciation in the early 1840s. Again the presence of a prominent American abolitionist was the occasion, though not the simple cause, of renewed internal division in antislavery. Moreover, rejection or acceptance of Douglass constituted acceptance or rejection of the whole political course taken by American antislavery in the 1850s.[32]

At the beginning of the American Civil War developments made one final ironic comment on the earlier aspirations for an Anglo-American movement. Although opinion was not unanimous in either BFASS or amongst British Garrisonians about how the North ought to respond to southern secession, there was considerable support across the spectrum of abolitionism for letting the southerners go. Supporters of disunion in earlier years thought this perfectly logical and some BFASS supporters looked to recognition of the Confederacy as a *quid pro quo* for southern suppression of the illegal slave trade. Pacifist distaste for the use of military force also played its part. This substantial measure of agreement amongst abolitionists in Britain, however, occurred as many American abolitionists, whatever their previous convictions, gathered behind Lincoln's administration in a system purified by the secession of most slaveholders. They committed themselves to war to end slavery and reunite the republic. The ironic divergence was one more demonstration of the difficulty of translating aspiration and feeling conviction into a working system of international co-operation.[33]

8

CONCLUSIONS

This book has attempted to map a culture of antislavery which incorporated understandings of and responses to the process of industrialisation, but which also extended beyond such preoccupations. The more the culture has been analysed in this extended way, the more appropriate it has seemed to characterise antislavery as constituting a series of changing *alliances*. The alliances necessarily had strong integrating features but were at the same time composed of distinct elements with divergent attitudes and emphases. This is especially apparent if due recognition is given to antislavery Rational Dissenters and Unitarians whose significance has often not been appreciated. Heterogeneity of religious and intellectual tradition, and of attitudes on a range of issues, create complexities for the interpretation of antislavery, exemplified in abolitionist activists, as facilitating the hegemonic class interests of a developing industrial bourgeoisie. Equally, from such a perspective, any simple alternative reading of abolitionists as predominantly advancing on a broad front the values of freedom and independence and thus defining the core of a general movement of improvement and liberalisation, is problematic.[1]

Consideration of the articulated and implied *intentions* of abolitionist reformers makes it apparent that they tried to combine in various proportions attachment to moral and social order through disciplinary mechanisms with the promotion of greater self-possession and more autonomous behaviour. Despite the fact that most abolitionist activists were not industrial employers or especially close to them, the outlook of many of them could be compatible with the presumed perspective of the industrial middle class on social discipline. But there were differences amongst abolitionists on particular questions which had more general implications for the contradictory character of reform culture.

227

Disputes over the content of education revealed divergences over its purposes. Was the importance of education in the extent to which it would culturally reproduce the values of the reformers themselves and a deference appropriate broadly to the dynamic equilibrium of existing social and economic relations? Or was it significant as a way of encouraging the accomplishment of aspirations and, perhaps unintentionally, thus prompting resistance to aspects of the abolitionist reformers' and industrialists' outlook? Many reformers embraced the value of self-determination but within a powerful consciousness of the need for good order. Contradictions within individual abolitionists as well as divergences between different groups were the likely result.

The existence of divergence as well as convergence amongst abolitionists questions the implicit model in much historical writing of 'the antislavery movement' as a largely integrated phenomenon. There are reasons also for questioning it as a *continuous* phenomenon. There was a striking continuity in its national leadership from the 1780s to the 1820s, but it is not clear that this was true to the same extent in local reform communities. Even if it were, there is evidence of the difficulty reformers had in re-animating popular support in communities which had previously demonstrated it. Nor was there always a smooth change of gear from the objective of abolition to emancipation to the removal of apprenticeship. Moreover, as chapter 4 has argued, by the 1830s the type of abolitionist leader underwent a change nationally and in the localities, while rank-and-file support from the 1820s onwards drew crucially on evangelical dissenters as never before. The history of antislavery thus demonstrates significant discontinuities as well as evolution.

There was a recurrent element in the culture of antislavery which embraced abolition and emancipation as a key to a *desirable* discontinuity in the moral world. At different periods and envisaging different forms of quasi-millennial change, some abolitionists looked to a wholesale transformation of the moral and institutional texture of Britain and perhaps the world. At the beginning and during the early years of the French Revolution, antislavery radicals, liberal and latitudinarian in religion, most evidently evinced such hopes, even confidence. Antislavery was seen as part of an irresistible international wave of enlightenment which was set fair to produce rational and purified government, social and economic relations in conformity with the natural order and universal peace and harmony. This confidence was crucially sapped, however, as it became dependent upon the actual historical fate of the French Revolution. These expectations were paralleled by, but in contrast with, the aspirations of some later, post-1815 abolitionists. They were more evidently shaped by the evangelical impulse to Christianise the world, an impulse congruent with the increasing certainty of English reformers that Britain's international influence had never been greater. The anticipated universalising of antislavery blended with missionary expectations, the growth of religious and reform ties with Americans and the belief that, although the power of the British state only needed to be applied directly in a few areas of policy, British influence was sufficient to create the appropriate framework for Christian endeavour and an eventual time of jubilee world-wide.

Heterogeneity within the middle-class reform community was none the less combined with a recognition by just about all abolitionist reformers of limits which can best be described as class limits. Although reformers influenced by the evangelical current were probably somewhat more likely than religious liberals to feel and act on the need for social control of the populace possessing as they did a more vivid and immediate sense of evil, it is probable that very few abolitionists were free of anxiety on this account.

More specifically, despite being periodically involved in stimulating popular antislavery mobilisations, abolitionists observed limits in their attitudes to and relations with artisans and workers both within antislavery and in their capacities as more general reformers. Indeed the implicit model of the class relationship they expressed in antislavery may have been part of the problem. Of course, some abolitionists were more favourable to popular claims in the 1790s and 1830s and 1840s than others. Nevertheless the radicalism of a minority of abolitionists in the late eighteenth century was predominantly of an intellectual kind, with limited practical and organisational connections to artisan democrats. In the 1820s and 1830s there was paradoxical evidence of abolitionist attempts to enlist social deference to promote community support through exploiting social hierarchy, at least in the filling of the 'dignified' offices of antislavery organisations and in using working men for street canvassing work deemed unsuitable for middle-class reformers. Moreover, many of the minority of antislavery radicals in the Chartist years were troubled by mixed feelings over developments in the working-class movement. All of them avoided any public sanction of popular disorder and found themselves closest to Chartists who stressed their Christianity and promoted education as a major path of working-class advancement. They were naturally happiest when they saw opportunities for convergence of attitudes and behaviour between themselves and working-class spokesmen.

In those same years when middle-class reform circles conventionally presented emancipation as further evidence of Britain's national identity as the embodiment of liberty, this formulation of freedom was challenged by some working-class spokesmen. It was a challenge which, implicitly and sometimes explicitly, queried the unproblematic virtue of the abolitionist project. Even when this was not so, the conflict over the National Complete Suffrage Union suggested distrust amongst antislavery working-class spokesmen of middle-class abolitionist reformers as guarantors of working people's rights and liberties. The issue revealed the ambivalence of even many of the more radical abolitionist reformers, less about political rights for working men than about their determination to cease to be dependent on middle-class reformers in gaining those rights.

Although the relation between antislavery culture and class has been a major focus of this book, it is worth stressing at this point that recent valuable work employing gender and race as ways of exploring aspects of the culture of antislavery have suggested analogous tensions and complexities in antislavery to those exposed by looking at class. Often they arose in relation to women and blacks, as in the case of working men, over conventional white, middle-class, male abolitionist beliefs about appropriate roles for these groups and the sometimes limited but generally expanding conception of what they could and should do held by members of the groups themselves. Such evidence and conclusions have to be incorporated to provide a fully comprehensive analysis of the structuring of antislavery culture.[2]

How abolitionists understood the free labour market is one way of taking the issue of class in the culture of antislavery further and at the same time opening up the problem of how far the development of that culture expressed, or positively advanced, the emergence of a liberal society.

In one sense, by definition, antislavery advanced free labour. Yet abolitionists recognised that a large swathe of potential and actual members of both British and colonial labour markets required, for a variety of reasons, that their labour be regulated. This was because various categories of potential and actual labourers were in some sense deficient in the requirements for full participation in an unregulated market. Ideally such a market had to work without extra-economic coercion but in a relatively disciplined fashion because the ethic of regular work had been internalised by the majority who had to labour. Properly performed work resulting from this ethic was deemed central to an orderly but liberal society. However, imprisoned criminals, asylum inmates, plantation slaves in the amelioration period and apprentice freedmen in the years after emancipation were believed by abolitionist reformers to require careful induction into the free but regular labour ethic. Many were perceived as being redeemable from the effect of their past experiences but only if, for a longer or shorter transition period, their labour was not completely free. On this general conclusion there were few differences between abolitionist reformers, at least until the eve of emancipation – and then in reference to the slaves. Some reformers believed that the slaves would only become productive free labourers if completely free to adopt the ethic of regular work.

On labour in factories, as chapter 5 indicated, there was fairly continuous support from abolitionist reformers for *protective* regulation of child workers who by reason of age and strength were seen as unfit to enter an untrammelled labour market. In the earlier stages of antislavery, reformers of different religious backgrounds supported some government regulation of factory labour more generally. By the 1830s, however, on adult factory workers the balance amongst reformers had swung very much towards as unregulated a labour market as possible. Amongst reformers an increasingly anachronistic strand of moral paternalism was represented by Ashley's 1833 Factory Bill but by that date there were few signs that many were prepared to contemplate that the reality of unequal power within a free labour market might not produce the best results for everyone.

What these evolving attitudes indicated was that abolitionist reformers did not in their outlook and practical behaviour draw an absolutely unambiguous line between free and unfree labour from the beginning of organised antislavery. They were aware that some environments were destructive enough to require those who had suffered them to have special provision to make them fit inhabitants of the world of work. Their ideal increasingly was freedom in the labour market but its difficulty of attainment was highlighted not only by the condition of servitude but by other social categories whose members fell short of the requirements for a liberal but disciplined economy.

So far as free trade, the other major economic ingredient of a liberal society, was concerned the overwhelming majority of abolitionists ultimately became free traders, with some of them wanting limited modifications to benefit the colonial sugar economies and ease their transition after emancipation. The spread of free-trade doctrines amongst abolitionists coincided with general recognition of Britain's emergence as the predominant economic and political influence in the world and the knowledge that freer trade was generally in the country's interest. Free trade in sugar as a weapon against the West Indians could thus be presented as conducive to the national interest. The earlier difficulties involved in presenting legitimate trade from West Africa as of greater benefit to the nation than the trade in slaves had no later parallel; as liberal political economy displaced the mercantilist assumptions which had provided the intellectual and policy framework for sustaining the slave trade, it offered a coherent and comprehensive policy rationale which threw the enemies of the abolitionists on to the defensive. It is not surprising, therefore, that despite the attention paid in the historical literature on antislavery to industrialisation and its effects, abolitionists themselves showed more immediate preoccupation with *commerce* as an instrument of reform. This was true in advancing both antislavery and some of their other reform interests. Had they been able to achieve their reform objectives by substituting legitimate trade for the slave trade, or redirecting the flow of commerce to weaken the position of slaveholding classes, this would have had an impact on manufacturing, but not uniformly for the good. Cotton textile manufacturers, for example, could well have been alarmed at efforts to find free-labour sources of cotton if they undermined the continuing sufficiency and quality of raw cotton supply.

There may be relevance here in the recent argument that the development of the international market in the eighteenth century produced an extended sense of causality and thus, eventually, by revision of moral conventions a widespread sense of humanitarian responsibility. But it is too unspecific to account for English abolitionists' concern with commerce as an instrument of moral policy. As an explanation it omits the religious dynamic necessary for organised action and the qualitative leap in awareness amongst English reformers of Britain's world economic role after 1815. The argument flattens out the multiform origins of 'the humanitarian sensibility' and its chronologically differentiated modes of operation.[3]

The discussion can now turn to the political dimensions of the emerging liberal society and antislavery's relation to them. In so far as abolitionists from an early point sought to link antislavery and patriotism it can be argued that they helped the general association of liberty with the character of the nation to the benefit of liberal politics. Yet the contest over versions of patriotism before 1807, in which abolitionists engaged with each other as well as with pro-slavery opponents, indicates how difficult it could be in the crisis years of war and fragile peace for antislavery patriotism to have broader liberalising effects, particularly in the form of the spread of *political* rights. And it has already been argued that by the 1830s too close an identification of British love of liberty with slave emancipation did not suit the demands of significant working-class spokesmen for a radical extension of political rights. Nor did the claims to patriotism of the Birmingham 'moral radicals' help to overcome the tensions between them and their potential working-class radical allies in the early 1840s.

Even if this had not been so, as chapter 5 has indicated, the political role and character of the state often provoked a strong vein of scepticism amongst abolitionists drawing on different sources. Evangelicals often expressed a distaste for particular manifestations of 'Old Corruption', seeing them as the opposite of exemplary behaviour by the political elite. Radical abolitionists drew on the hallowed rhetoric of the Commonwealthman tradition which implied more systemic change but in neither case was much progress achieved in transforming the framework or practice of government, with or without the involvement of abolitionist reformers, before the late 1820s. By then, however, the theme that the state ought to be purified had become implicitly linked to the assault on slavery. When abolitionists tried to present slaveholders as moral outsiders whose sectional interests were moreover antithetical to the national interest, they were also indicating that slaveholders were entitled to no claims on the state because the state must not pander to immoral interests. In reality the political forces supporting the West Indians were powerful enough to bring about a compromise with compensation and apprenticeship as its products. This recognition that slaveholders did have claims which the state could not ignore was a source of hostility to compensation, scepticism amongst some abolitionists about apprenticeship and a source of distrust of the parliamentary regime for the provincial militants who led the anti-apprenticeship campaign. The quasi-alternative through which reformers could try to continue the process of change was 'opinion', but they were aware that it was subject to short-windedness and volatility.

Pluralism as an aspect of an emerging liberal society, particularly religious pluralism, provoked considerable anxiety amongst some abolitionists. Their concern with a proper moral order in society created tension with the religious pluralism which actually existed, however inadequately that pluralism was recognised. When it was the basis for claims for full legal equality it raised fears of a greater crystallisation of disunity and the promotion of disharmony in practice. At one level the cause of antislavery was none the less a counter to this fear particularly prevalent amongst Anglicans. It not only brought people together on the common ideological ground of moral purification and the pursuit of true order but, in requiring their practical co-operation over a long period, could be seen as contributing positively to a more harmonious society. Yet when the issue was specifically that of religious equality abolitionists were as divided along the same lines as the larger society. Right through to the 1820s Anglican evangelical abolitionists were hostile to the claims of dissenters, evangelical and liberal. Catholic claims until the same period were thought insupportable by all except Rational Dissenters and Unitarians; evangelicalism, whether Anglican or nonconformist, was a source of hostility to liberal Christians for even longer. The main factor here was the obverse side of the evangelical impulse to make over society and the world. To make over came close to meaning trying to create a morally homogeneous society and world. Thus the acquisition of influence by non-evangelicals could be perceived as a threat and had to be resisted at the cost of discrimination against some religious groups.

It is clear then that, recognising the heterogeneous character of abolition activists (active beyond the signing of mass petitions), they adopted attitudes and pursued policies amenable to the ideological hegemony of industrial capitalist employers but also, a minority of them, supportive to a limited extent of forces actually and potentially disruptive of that hegemony. The overall judgement must be, and more so as time went by, that the balance was on the side of the hegemony of capitalist values. That is not, however, the end of the discussion.

If antislavery ultimately pointed in the direction of capitalist values, that did not mean its unproblematic association with liberal values in their broadest sense. Nor did it necessarily indicate that antislavery contributed fundamentally to the complex transformation British society underwent in the years covered by this book. Setting aside the fact that historians are far from agreed that capitalist values did unambiguously triumph in this period and leaving aside the variety of possible relationships between *ideological* hegemony and the structures governing the actual distribution of power in a society, more immediately there is little evidence that abolitionists primarily intended to facilitate such an ideological hegemony.[4]

More seriously, if the problem is posed in terms of the *effect* of antislavery, whether intended or not, there is a good case for concluding that historians of antislavery have proposed greater general influence for it than is warranted. Much of the period of opposition to the slave trade coincided with the critical war years with the result that antislavery was practically rendered subordinate to the preservation of the nation and its liberty. These were understood in terms of the *status quo*, without entirely eliminating the radical critique of the political order offered by a small minority of abolitionists.

In the political styles they adopted, abolitionists command respect for their effectiveness. However, as demonstrated in chapter 3, it was their success rather than their novelty which gave them what exemplary influence they had on reformers in other fields. They did not significantly expand the repertoire of political practice though they did something to render previously radical practices respectably reformist.

From the 1820s the increasingly formidable drive towards emancipation was part of a large-scale process of reorganisation of both the constitutional framework – the repeal of the Test and Corporation Acts, Catholic Emancipation, the Reform Act, the Municipal Reform Act – and of the framework of social and commercial policy – the factory legislation, the New Poor Law, repeal of the Corn Laws, the equalisation of the sugar duties. It was part of the process because many abolitionists supported some or all of these changes and shared in the reform mentality which aided their achievement. In practice too the political and legislative struggle to gain emancipation revised the relationship between the metropolitan government and the colonies. But it is hard to argue that in the absence of antislavery any of the listed changes would have been prevented (except perhaps the equalisation of sugar duties) or that their significance would have been different. There had been a long history of concern on all of the non-commercial issues independent of antislavery. No doubt there was a relatively short-run, though unmeasurable, fillip to other reformers brought about by popular mobilisation for and the achievement of emancipation, but this should not be exaggerated. Antislavery was rather symptomatic of important changes taking place in English culture and to some degree paradigmatic for reformers. But primarily it should be seen as a constituent, not a shaping force, of the complex mutations and reorganisation of many facets of life in Britain and its empire in the later eighteenth and the first half of the nineteenth centuries.[5]

NOTES

1 APPROACH AND CONTEXTS

1 W.E.H. Lecky, *A History of European Morals*, 2 vols, 6th edn, London, 1884, II, p.153; Frank J. Klingberg, *The Anti-Slavery Movement in England*, New Haven, Conn. and London, 1926; Reginald Coupland, *The British Anti-Slavery Movement*, London, 1933 and 1964; C.H. MacInnes, *England and Slavery*, London, 1934 are some examples.

2 Eric Williams, *Capitalism and Slavery*, London, 1944, new edn, 1964; David Brion Davis, *Slavery and Human Progress*, New York and Oxford, 1984; Seymour Drescher, *Capitalism and Anti-Slavery*, London, 1986.

3 Ronald Walters, *The Antislavery Appeal*, Baltimore and London, 1976 provides an example of the 'culture' approach to American abolitionism but seen in a static fashion and without the dimension of class.

4 Alan D. Gilbert, *Religion and Society in Industrial England. Church, chapel and social change, 1740-1914*, London, 1976, part I and part II, chs 3 and 4.

5 Deborah M. Valenze, *Prophetic Sons and Daughters. Female preaching and popular religion in industrial England*, Princeton, NJ, 1985, pp.19-29.

6 Elizabeth Isichei, *Victorian Quakers*, Oxford, 1970, pp.xxv, xxi, 166-7, 173-85.

7 R.K. Webb, 'The Unitarian Background', in Barbara Smith (ed.), *Truth, Liberty, Religion. Essays celebrating two hundred years of Manchester College*, Oxford, 1986, esp. pp.8-17; Gilbert, op. cit., pp.40-1; John Seed, 'Gentlemen Dissenters: the social and political meanings of Rational Dissent in the 1770s and 1780s', *Historical Journal*, 28, 2, June 1985, esp. pp.301-5.

8 N.F.R. Crafts, 'British Economic Growth, 1700-1831; a Review of the Evidence', *Ec. Hist. Rev.*, 2nd ser., XXXVI, 2, May 1983, pp. 177-99; Maxine Berg, *The Age of Manufactures. Industry innovation and work in Britain 1700-1820*, London, 1985.

9 Ralph Davis, *The Industrial Revolution and British Overseas Trade*, Leicester, 1979, esp. pp.92-3, table 40, 88-9, table 38, 13-14, 16; Seymour Drescher, *Econocide: British Slavery in the Era of Abolition*, Pittsburgh, 1977, pp.16-25.

10 P.J. Cain and A.G. Hopkins, 'The Political Economy of British Expansion Overseas, 1750-1914', *Ec. Hist.Rev.*, 2nd ser., XXXIII, 4, Nov. 1980, esp. pp.471-3; Cain and Hopkins, 'Gentlemanly Capitalism and British Expansion Overseas I The Old Colonial System, 1688-1850', *Ec. Hist. Rev.*, 2nd ser., XXXIX, 4, 1986, pp.523-4.

11 Boyd Hilton, *Corn, Cash, Commerce. The economic policies of the Tory government 1815-1830*, Oxford, 1977, pp.176-84; Cain and Hopkins, 'Political Economy', op. cit., pp. 482-3; G. Ingham, *Capitalism Divided ? The City and Industry in British Social Development*, Basingstoke, 1984, pp.113-16.

12 Cain and Hopkins, 'Political Economy', op. cit., pp.475-8; Ingham, op. cit., pp.97, 259 note 4.

13 Ralph Davis, op. cit., pp.88-9, table 38, 90-1 table 39, 43-4, 110-25 tables 57-64.

14 ibid., pp.110-25, tables 57-64 (corn, palm oil).

2 ARGUMENT AND IDEOLOGY

1 Elizabeth Isichei, *Victorian Quakers*, Oxford, 1970, pp.18-25; Anne Cropper, *Extracts from the letters of the late James Cropper, transcribed for his grandchildren by their very affectionate mother and aunt*, n.p., n.d. [1850], pp.14-15; John Kent, *Elizabeth Fry*, London, 1962, p.21.

2 Isichei, op. cit., pp.4-6; David E. Swift, *Joseph John Gurney: Banker, Reformer and Quaker*, Middletown, Conn., 1962, pp. 118-128.

3 Marginal comment in Thomas Clarkson's hand on Matt.III v.2, Clarkson family Bible, Clarkson Papers, box 2, Atlanta University (hereafter Clarkson-A).

4 Written on 30 June 1822, Stephen Papers BL Add. Mss. 46443; Clarkson marginal comment on Matt.XXII, v.14, Clarkson Bible, box 2 Clarkson-A.

5 Granville Sharp, *The Just Limitation of Slavery in the Laws of God*, London, 1776, pp.34-40; Haddon Willmer,'Evangelicalism', Hulsean Prize Essay, unpub., University of Cambridge, 1962, pp.141-3.

6 Isichei, op. cit., p.26; John Seed, 'Unitarianism, political economy and the antinomies of liberal culture in Manchester, 1830-1850', *Social History*, 7, 1, Jan. 1982, p.3; R.K. Webb, *Harriet Martineau. A Radical Victorian*, London, 1960, p.68 quoting W.J. Fox; J.E. Cookson, *The Friends of Peace. Anti-War Liberalism in England, 1793-1815*, Cambridge, 1982, pp.4-6.

7 Society of Friends, *The Case of our Fellow Creatures the Oppressed Africans*, London, 1783.

8 W. Agutter, *The Abolition of the Slave Trade considered in a Religious Point of View*, London, 1788; Peter Peckard, *Justice and Mercy recommended, particularly with reference to the Slave Trade*, Cambridge and London, 1788, esp. pp.21-30.

9 Thomas Clarkson to Comte de Mirabeau, 8 Dec. 1789, CN38 Clarkson Papers, Huntington Library, San Marino, Ca. (hereafter Clarkson-Hunt.).

10 Rev. Raymond Harris, *Scriptural Researches on the Licitness of the Slave Trade*, Liverpool, 1788; William Hughes, *An Answer to the Rev. Mr.*

NOTES

Harris's 'Scriptural Researches', London, 1788, pp.4–33; William Roscoe, *A Scriptural Refutation of a Pamphlet lately published by the Rev. Raymund Harris*, London, 1788, pp.7ff.; H. Dannett, *A Particular Examination of Mr. Harris's Scriptural Researches*, London, 1788, pp.iii–iv.

11 Caroline Robbins, *The Eighteenth-Century Commonwealthman*, Cambridge, Mass., 1959; H.T. Dickinson, *Liberty and Property. Political Ideology in Eighteenth-Century Britain*, London, 1977, chs 6 and 7; J.G.A. Pocock, *Virtue, Commerce and History*, Cambridge, 1985, part III.

12 James Anderson, *Observations on Slavery*, Manchester, 1789, pp.3–8; Joseph Priestley, *A Sermon on the Subject of the Slave Trade*, Birmingham and London, 1788, p.16; R. Robinson, *Slavery Inconsistent with the Spirit of Christianity*, Cambridge and London, 1788, pp.24–5; Thomas Cooper, *Letters on the African Slave Trade*, Manchester, 1787, p.4.

13 Anderson, op.cit. pp.8–11; Joseph Priestley, *Lectures on History and General Policy, to which is prefixed an Essay on a Course of Liberal Education*, Birmingham, 1788, pp.377–8.

14 Robert Norris, *A Short Account of the African Slave Trade*, London, 1789; Paper *c.* 1792 in Liverpool Papers, BL Add. Mss. 38416, ff.261–5.

15 M. Kerr, *Reflections on the Present State of the Slaves in the British Plantations*, York and London, 1789; Anon., *Thoughts on Civilization and the gradual Abolition of Slavery in Africa and the West Indies*, London, 1789, esp. pp.9–11.

16 [Thomas Clarkson] *A Summary View of the Slave Trade*, London, 1787, pp.9–11; Joseph Priestley, *A Sermon on the Subject of the Slave Trade*, pp.26–7; Peter Peckard, *Am I Not a Man? and a Brother?*, Cambridge and London, 1788, pp.91–2; James Ramsay, *An Inquiry into the Effects of Putting a Stop to the African Slave Trade and of Granting Liberty to the Slaves in the British Sugar Colonies*, London, 1784, pp.16–24.

17 Insertion in newspapers of conclusion in Abolition Committee Minute Books II, BL Add. Mss. 21255, p.100; Vindex, *Old Truths and Established Facts*, n.p., 1792; Clarkson, op. cit., pp.12ff.; Ramsay, op. cit., pp.7–9; Anderson, op. cit, pp.12–17.

18 Thomas Clarkson, *The True State of the Case respecting the Insurrection at St. Domingo*, Ipswich, 1792; Thomas Cooper, *Considerations on the Slave Trade and the consumption of West Indian Produce*, London, 1791.

19 Priestley, op. cit., pp.33–4; David Brion Davis, *The Problem of Slavery in the Age of Revolution, 1770–1823*, Ithaca, NY and London, 1975, pp.310–12; Samuel Bradburn, *An Address to the People called Methodists*, Manchester, 1792, p.12; Anna Letitia Barbauld, *Epistle to William Wilberforce Esq.*, London, 1791, p.12; Robinson, op. cit., pp.8–9.

20 *Parliamentary Hist.*, vol. xxix, cols 1055–1158 (2 April 1792); *Substance of the Debates on a resolution for abolishing the Slave Trade which was moved in the House of Commons 10 June 1806 and in the House of Lords 24 June 1806*, London, 1968 (first published 1806).

21 B.W. Higman, 'Slavery and the Development of Demographic Theory in the Age of the Industrial Revolution', in James Walvin (ed.), *Slavery and British Society, 1776–1846*, London, 1982, pp.177–8, 180–1; Davis, op. cit., pp.414–17; *Substance of the Debates . . . 1806*, pp.78–9 (Fox); W.

Wilberforce to J.J. Gurney, 21 Feb. 1818, Ms. Eng. 183(13) Boston Public Library, Boston, Mass.
22 Joshua Steele to Marquis of Lansdowne, 18 Oct. 1793, Lansdowne Papers, vol. 88 ff.129–30, William L. Clements Library, University of Michigan, Ann Arbor, Michigan; William Dickson, *Letters to Thomas Clarkson*, London, 1814; Thomas Clarkson, 'Mr. Steele's Plan for the Manumission of Slaves', *c.* 1814, Clarkson Papers, VII, BL Add. Mss. 41267A, ff.76–8; M.G. Lewis to Clarkson, 25 July 1815, Clarkson BL Add. Mss. 41267A, ff.79–80.
23 Davis, op. cit., pp.418–20. *Seventh Report of the African Institution, 1813*, London, 1813, pp.16–17, *Sixteenth Report of the African Institution, 1822*, London, 1822, pp.43–5. *First Report of Committee of Newcastle Upon Tyne Society for promoting the Gradual Abolition of Slavery throughout the British Dominions*, Newcastle, 1825, p.3.
24 James Cropper to Zachary Macaulay, Clarkson BL Add. Mss. 41267A, f.112; *Seventeenth Report of the African Institution, 1823*, London, 1823, xiv–xxi, xxviii–xxix; Thomas Clarkson to Lord Liverpool, 3 May 1823, Liverpool Papers, BL Add. Mss. 38416, f.391.
25 *An Address to the Public on the State of Slavery in the West India Islands. From the Committee of the Leicester Auxiliary Anti-Slavery Society*, London, 1824, p.3; *First Report of the Suffolk Auxiliary Society for the Mitigation and Gradual Abolition of Slavery*, Ipswich, 1825, p.6; *The First Report of the Female Society for Birmingham . . . for the relief of British Negro Slaves*, Birmingham, 1826, pp.12–3; *Concluding Report of the Sheffield Female Anti-Slavery Society*, Sheffield, 1833, pp.3–4; *Proceedings of the General Anti-Slavery Convention 1840*, London, 1841, pp.47–55; Josiah Conder to Mrs M.A. Rawson, 7 May 1838, Wilson–Rawson Papers, MD2021, Sheffield Central Library, printed in M.A. Rawson (ed.), *Hymns for Anti-Slavery Prayer Meetings*, London, 1838.
26 James Walvin, 'The Public Campaign in England against Slavery, 1787–1834', in David Eltis and James Walvin (eds), *The Abolition of the African Slave Trade*, Madison, Wis. and London, 1981, pp.71–2; James Cropper, *Letters Addressed to William Wilberforce M.P.*, Liverpool, 1822; Adam Hodgson, *A Letter to M. Jean-Baptiste Say on the comparative expense of free and slave labour*, Liverpool, 1823; *An Address to the Public . . . Leicester Auxiliary Anti-Slavery Society*, op. cit., pp.12–13; Josiah Conder, *Wages Or the Whip. An Essay on the comparative cost and productiveness of Free and Slave Labour*, London, 1833.
27 *Substance of a Speech delivered by Joseph John Gurney, Esq. at a Public Meeting of the Inhabitants of Norwich*, London, 1824, pp.13ff.; *Speeches delivered in the Town Hall of Beverley*, Beverley, 1824, pp.5–6; James Kennedy LLB, *An Address to the Inhabitants of Hull and Its Neighbourhood*, Hull, 1823, pp.3ff.; Thomas Clarkson, *The Argument that the colonial slaves are better off than the British Peasantry, answered from the Royal Jamaica Gazette of June 21, 1823*, Whitby, for the Whitby Anti-Slavery Society, 1824, pp.4–17. James Cropper to Zachary Macaulay, 10 May 1822, Clarkson Papers, vii, BL Add. Mss. 41267A, ff.104–6.
28 James Cropper, op. cit.; James Cropper, *A Letter addressed to the*

Liverpool Society for promoting the abolition of slavery, Liverpool, 1823; James Cropper, *Relief for West Indian Distress*, London, 1823.

29 Kennedy, op. cit., pp.9–11, 14–5; *Speech . . . Gurney*, op. cit., pp.9–11; *A Report of the Speeches at a County Meeting held at the Castle of Leicester*, Leicester, 1826, pp.21–3; *Speeches . . . Beverley*, op. cit., pp.11–12; *Proceedings of a Public Meeting held at the Town Hall Chester*, Chester, 1823, pp.6–15; *First Report . . . Newcastle*, op. cit., pp.4–5; *Speech . . . Gurney*, op. cit., p.2; *Speeches . . . Beverley*, op. cit., p.12; *An Address from the Liverpool Society for the Abolition of Slavery*, Liverpool, 1824, p.15.

30 *The Negro's Friend or the Sheffield Anti-Slavery Album*, Sheffield, 1826.

31 *Seventeenth Report of the African Institution, 1823*, London, 1823, pp.xxxi–xxxvi; Zachary Macaulay to Thomas Fowell Buxton, 11 Nov. 1823, Macaulay Papers, MY430, Huntington Library; *Speeches . . . Beverley*, op. cit., p.16; *Speech . . . Gurney*, op. cit., pp.5, 7, 8; Birmingham Anti-Slavery Society Minute Book 1, 7 March 1832, Birmingham Reference Library.

32 Elizabeth Heyrick, *Immediate not gradual abolition*, London, 1824; David Brion Davis, 'The Emergence of Immediatism in British and American Antislavery Thought', *Mississippi Valley Historical Review*, XLIX, 2, Sept. 1962, pp.209–30; Anon., *Reasons for preferring immediate to what is called gradual emancipation*, n.p., n.d. [1830], pp.1–10; *Speech of T.C. Granger Esq. at a meeting of the inhabitants of the City of Durham*, Durham, 1830, p.4. This is a perfect example of what Davis, following Tillich, has called *kairos*. David Brion Davis, *Slavery and Human Progress*, New York and Oxford, 1984, pp.128–9.

33 Printed Letter of Instructions from Anti-Slavery Society Office, Temp Mss. Box 101/6, Friends' House Library, London; *The Times*, 23 Sept. 1833. Buxton quoted in an editorial.

34 Rev. Thomas Cooper to Rev. S.S. Toms, 4 Aug. 1818, 2 April 1820, Clarkson Papers, VI, BL Add. Mss. 41266, ff.257–60; *Speeches . . . Beverley*, op. cit., p.31; *Speeches . . . Gurney*, op. cit., p.4; *Speeches . . . Beverley*, op. cit., p.11; *A Report . . . County Meeting, Leicester*, op. cit., p.9.

35 *Parliamentary Debates (PD)*, 3rd ser., 9, 1 May–19 July 1823, cols 263–360 (15 May); *PD*, 3rd ser., 3, 4 March–22 April 1831, cols.1408–1469 (15 April); *PD* 3rd ser., 17, April–May 1833, cols. 1193–1262 (14 May).

36 *Final Report of the Sheffield Female Anti-Slavery Society*, Sheffield, 1833, p.7; *An Appeal to the Christian Women of Sheffield from the Association for the Universal Abolition of Slavery*, Sheffield, 1837, pp.3–8; *Report of the Proceedings at Birmingham on the 1st and 2nd of August in commemoration of the Abolition of Negro Apprenticeship in the British Colonies*, Birmingham, 1838.

3 MAKING ABOLITIONISTS

1 James Walvin, 'The Propaganda of Anti-Slavery', in Walvin (ed.), *Slavery and British Society 1776-1846*, London and Basingstoke, 1982, p.60; Thomas Cooper, *Letters on the Slave Trade*, Manchester, 1787, preface;

Thomas Clarkson to Zachary Macaulay, 4 April 1823, Macaulay Papers MY 140, Huntington Library; ASS Minute Book, 9, 16 April 1823, B. Emp. Mss. S20 E2/1, Rhodes House Library (hereafter RH), Oxford.

2 Gwynne E. Owen, 'Welsh Anti-Slavery Sentiments, 1790-1865', MA thesis, University College of Wales, Aberystwyth, 1964, pp.16-17. Howard Temperley, *British Antislavery 1833-1870*, London, 1972, appendix B, p.271; Correspondents from Devizes, Cork, Chelmsford, Liverpool to Thomas Pringle, 22, 23, 24 Aug., 1 Sept. 1831, B. Emp Mss. S18 C1/4, 6, 12, 15, R.H.

3 R.D. Alexander to Thomas Pringle, 13 March, 28 March 1828, B. Emp. Mss. S18 C1/1 and 2, RH; ASS Minute Book, 1 Dec. 1829, B. Emp. Mss. S20 E2/3, RH; Henry Brougham to Zachary Macaulay, n.d., 31 Jan. 1825, n.d., B. Emp. Mss. S18 c 106/59, 61, 68, RH; Joshua Leavitt to Joseph Sturge, 5 July 1839, in Annie H. Abel and Frank J. Klingberg (eds), *A Sidelight on Anglo-American Relations 1839-58*, Lancaster, Pa., 1927, p.55.

4 George Harrison to Thomas Harrison, 30 Jan 1821, Temp. Mss, 101/3 Friends' House Library, London (hereafter Friends); *Fifteenth Annual Report of African Institution, 1821*, London, 1821, p.27.

5 Seymour Drescher, *Capitalism and Antislavery*, London, 1986, p.78; Richard Ball to Robert Stokes, 8 Sept. 1837, B. Emp. Mss. S18 C2/16, RH.

6 John Feather, *A History of British Publishing*, London, 1988, pp.131-3; C.J. Mitchell, 'Provincial Printing in Eighteenth Century Britain', *Publishing History*, XXI, 1987, pp.5-24; Feather, op. cit., pp.118-19.

7 Calculations based on entries in Margaret Canuly and David Knott comp., *Catalogue of the Goldsmiths' Library of Economic Literature, vol.I, Printed Books to 1800*, Cambridge, 1970; Canuly, Knott and Joan M. Gibbs comp., *vol II, Printed Books 1801-1850*, Cambridge, 1975. Not all antislavery works published in particular years are listed but the lists are sufficiently extensive to allow comparative and proportionate conclusions.

8 Thomas Clarkson to Thomas Were Fox, 28 Aug. 1807, HM 35525, Huntington Library; Clarkson to Fox, 28 Oct. 1807, Clarkson Papers, 18E, Duke University Library, Durham, NC; Paul Edwards (ed.), *Equiano's Travels*, London, 1967 edn, pp.xi-xii.

9 Minute Book of Meeting for Sufferings Slave Trade Committee, 23 July 1784, 30 Dec. 1784, LO51.66, Friends; Thomas Clarkson to Zachary Macaulay, 30 March 1823, MY 139, Huntington Library; Glasgow Emancipation Society (hereafter GES), *Third Annual Report*, Glasgow, 1837, pp.100-15.

10 Douglas Hall, *A Brief History of the West India Committee*, Barbados, 1971, pp.4-6, 10-12, 13-14; F.E. Sanderson, 'Bibliographical Essay. Liverpool and the Slave Trade: a guide to sources', *Trans. Historical Society of Lancs and Cheshire*, 124, 1973, pp.161-5; W.L. Burn, *Emancipation and Apprenticeship in the British West Indies*, London, 1937, p.100 note 1.

11 E.M. Hunt, 'The North of England Agitation for the Abolition of the Slave Trade', unpub. MA thesis, University of Manchester, 1959, pp.38-44.

12 *Report of the Committee of the African Institution read to the general meeting on 15 July 1807*, London, 1811, pp.1-4; Thomas Fowell Buxton to

NOTES

Hannah Buxton, 30 Jan., 1 Feb. 1821, in Patricia Pugh (ed.), *Calendar of the Papers of Sir Thomas Fowell Buxton*, n.p., 1980, pp.263–6, 175–8.

13 Thomas Clarkson to Thomas Fowell Buxton, 25 Sept. 1833, CN75, Clarkson–Hunt.

14 GES, *Fourth Annual Report*, Glasgow, 1838, pp.10–11.

15 David M. Turley, ' "Free Air" and Fugitive Slaves', in Christine Bolt and Seymour Drescher (eds), *Anti-Slavery, Religion and Reform*, Folkestone, 1980, pp.163–82; chapter 7 below.

16 Hall, op. cit., p.9.

17 David Brion Davis, *Slavery and Human Progress*, New York and Oxford, 1984, p.115; Hunt, op. cit., pp.43–4; James Walvin 'The Public Campaign against Slavery, 1787–1834', in D. Eltis and J. Walvin (eds), *The Abolition of the Atlantic Slave Trade*, Madison, Wis., 1981, p.70; George Stephen, *Anti-Slavery Recollections*, London, 1971 edn, p.158.

18 GES Minute Book, pp.35–6, Smeal Collection, Mitchell Library, Glasgow; *Emancipator* (New York) 15 Dec. 1836, 19 Jan. 1837; correspondents from Liskeard, Stroud, Canterbury, Leek, Raithby to Robert Stokes, March-June 1835, B. Emp. Mss S18 C2/6, 9, 37, 103, C3/9, RH (reluctance); correspondents from Hull, Exeter, Canterbury to Robert Stokes, 5 June 1835, 27 July 1837, 5 Sept. 1837, B. Emp. Mss. S18 C2/64, 68, C3/36, RH (revival); BFASS Minute Book I, 26 July, 27 Dec. 1839, pp.57, 137–9, B. Emp. Mss. E2/6, RH; GES Minute Book, 6 Dec., 12 Dec. 1833, pp.2, 30–4, Smeal Collection, Glasgow; Edward Baldwin to Elizur Wright, 17 Oct. 1837, Elizur Wright Papers, Library of Congress (hereafter LC).

19 Thomas Clarkson, *History of the Abolition of the Slave Trade*, Vol I, London, 1968 edn, e.g. pp.415ff.; *Speeches delivered in the Town Hall of Beverley at a public meeting convened by The Right Worshipful The Mayor for the purpose of petitioning Parliament to Abolish Slavery in the West Indies*, Beverley, 1824; *First Annual Report of the Swansea & Neath Auxiliary Anti-Slavery Association*, Swansea, 1826; *Report of the Committee of the Manchester Society for the furtherance of the Gradual Abolition of Slavery*, Manchester, 1827; *Report of the Agency Committee of the Anti-Slavery Society*, London, 1832; George Stephen, op. cit., p.158.

20 Brian Keith-Lucas, 'County Meetings', *Law Quarterly Review*, 70, 1954, pp.109–13; Hunt, op. cit., pp.24–9; Drescher, op. cit., p.214 note 35; Henry Jephson, *The Platform*, vol. 1., London, 1892, pp.319–20.

21 Herbert Butterfield, *George III, Lord North and the People*, London, 1949, pp.187–9; Albert Goodwin, *The Friends of Liberty. The English Democratic Movement in the Age of the French Revolution*, London, 1979, pp.28, 360–1; Drescher, op. cit., p.223 note 3; George Stephen, op. cit., p.10; Davis, op. cit., p.185; James Cropper to Joseph Sturge, 16 April 1828, in Anne Cropper (ed.), *Extracts from the letters of the late James Cropper, transcribed for his grandchildren*, n.p. [1850], pp.65–6.

22 *Report . . . Agency Committee*, op. cit., pp.8ff.; George Thompson to Jenny Thompson, 23 Sept. 1831 (Rochester). Thompson to Thompson, 8 July 1832 (Sheffield), Raymond English Deposit, John Rylands University Library, Manchester.

23 F.E. Sanderson, 'The Liverpool Abolitionists', in R. Anstey and P. Hair (eds), *Liverpool, the African Slave Trade and Abolition*, n.p., 1976,

pp.207–11; Thomas Clarkson to Zachary Macaulay, 7 Dec. 1823, MY 144, Macaulay–Hunt. George Thompson to Jenny Thompson, 16 Feb. 1833, Raymond English Deposit, Rylands; GES Minute Book, 8 June 1836, Smeal Collection.

24 Colin Leys, 'Petitioning in the Nineteenth and Twentieth Centuries', *Political Studies*, III, no.1, 1955, pp.45–63; *British Sessional Papers, House of Commons, Parliamentary Papers*, LXXXIII, 1852–3, pp.104–5; Drescher, *Capitalism and Antislavery*, op. cit. pp.217–19, notes 54–6; John Brewer, *Party Ideology and Popular Politics at the Accession of George III*, Cambridge, 1976, p.194; Butterfield, op. cit., p.217.

25 Calculations based on comparison of lists of places petitioning in *Eighth Report of the African Institution, 1814*, London, 1814, pp.40–7 (1814), 51–67 (1792).

26 Thomas Clarkson to Zachary Macaulay 30 March, 8 June, 1823, MY 139, MY 143, Hunt.; Roger Anstey, 'Religion and British Slave Emancipation', in Eltis and Walvin (eds), op. cit., pp.40–7; Joseph Sturge to Thomas Pringle, 20 March 1828, B. Emp. Mss. S18 C1/60, RH; ASS Minute Book, 1 Sept. 1830, B. Emp. Mss. S20 E2/3, RH; Seymour Drescher, 'Public Opinion', in James Walvin (ed.), *Slavery and British Society, 1776–1846*, London, 1982, pp.35–6.

27 Priscilla Buxton to Sarah Maria Buxton, 16 May 1833, Thomas Fowell Buxton Papers, B. Emp. Mss. S444 vol. 2, pp.273–88; Leys, op. cit., pp.48–53; Elizabeth Isichei, *Victorian Quakers*, London, 1970, p.190.

28 Thomas Cooper, *Supplement to Mr. Cooper's Letters on the Slave Trade*, Warrington, 1788, p.5; F.E. Sanderson, 'Bibliographical Essay', op. cit., p.159; William Wilberforce to Principal Robertson, 25 Jan. 1788, Robertson–Macdonald Mss. 3943 ff. 30–1, National Library of Scotland; Campbell Haliburton to Archibald Fletcher, 1 April 1791, MacGregor Papers GD50/235/4, Scottish Record Office, Edinburgh; Printed letter from Campbell Haliburton, 23 July 1792, MacGregor Papers GD50/235/6, SRO; Thomas Clarkson to Henry Taylor, 20 June 1813, HM 33546, Hunt.; James Cropper to Zachary Macaulay, 12 July, 21 Oct. 1822, Clarkson Papers vii BL Add. Mss. 41267A, ff. 108–9, 128–9.

29 Frederick B. Tolles, *Quakers and Atlantic Culture*, London, 1960, pp.44, 53–4; Minute Book, Slave Trade Committee of Meeting for Sufferings, 7 May 1784, 22 Dec. 1790, LO51.66, Friends; Hunt, op. cit., pp.32–8; J.M. Norris, 'Samuel Garbett and the early development of industrial lobbying in Great Britain', *Ec. Hist. Rev.*, 2nd ser., vol 10, 1957–8, pp.450–60; William Wilberforce to Thomas Fowell Buxton, 23 March 1826, B. Emp. Mss. S18 C106/7; James Cropper to his wife, 24 May 1831, in Anna Cropper, op. cit., pp.77–8; Birmingham ASS Minute Book 1, 15 Dec. 1835, 26 Jan. 1836, Birmingham Reference Library.

30 Brewer, op. cit., p.194; Goodwin, op. cit., p.91; Drescher, *Capitalism and Antislavery*, op. cit., p.90; Samuel Bowley to Thomas Pringle, 2 May 1831, B. Emp. Mss. S18 C1/9, RH; Drescher, 'Public Opinion', pp.30–1; William Smeal to Robert Stokes, 15 Sept. 1837, B. Emp. Mss S18 C3/62, RH; BFASS Minute Book I, 4 June 1841, B. Emp. Mss. E2/6; Correspon-

dents to Robert Stokes, 25 July, 18 Sept., 7 July, 29 Aug. 1837, B. Emp. Mss. S18 C2/29, 30, C3/76, 77, RH.
31. Goodwin, op. cit., pp.26-7, 350.
32 Birmingham ASS Minute Book 1, 27 Dec. 1830, Birmingham Reference Library; Davis, op. cit., pp.200-3; Thomas Fowell Buxton to Lord Althorp, 24 May 1832, Thomas Fowell Buxton Papers, B. Emp. S444, vol 3, pp.29-30, RH; Buxton to Mr. East, 15 Oct. 1832, Thomas Fowell Buxton Papers, B. Emp. S444, vol. 3, op. cit., pp.31-4, RH; Alex Tyrrell, *Joseph Sturge and the Moral Radical Party in Early Victorian Britain*, London, 1987, pp.55-7; Birmingham ASS Minute Book 1, July 1833.
33 Birmingham ASS Minute Book 2, 14 Oct., 25 Oct. 1837; Temperley, op. cit., p.39; Thomas Fowell Buxton to Josiah Forster, 3 Nov. 1837, in Patricia Pugh (ed.), *Calendar of the Papers of Thomas Fowell Buxton*, n.p., 1980, vol. 16, pp.159 e-m; *Birmingham Journal*, 30 Dec. 1837; Tyrrell, op. cit., pp.78-81; Birmingham ASS Minute Book 2, 19 April, 4 July 1838.
34 Joseph Sturge to Amos A. Phelps, 2 Oct. 1841, Phelps Papers, Boston Public Library; Patrick Lipscomb, 'William Pitt and the Abolition Question: A Review of an Historical Controversy', *Proceedings of the Leeds Philosophical and Literary Society*, xii, June 1966-April 1968, pp.87-128; David Eltis, *Economic Growth and the Ending of the Transatlantic Slave Trade*, New York and Oxford, 1987, pp.104-5; Davis, op. cit., pp.172-4; George Stephen, op. cit., pp.7-8; *Fifth Report of the African Institution, 1811*, London, 1811, pp.3-9, *Fourth Report, 1810*, London 1814, pp. 1-7, 15; *Sixth Report, 1812*, London, 1812, pp.19-20; *Third Report, 1809*, London, 1814, pp.28-31.
35 *Sixth Report of the African Institution, 1812*, London, 1812, pp.11-14; Davis, op. cit., pp. 176-7; Thomas Clarkson, Paper [1815?], CN 56, Clarkson-Hunt.; W.L. Burn, op. cit., pp.78-9; Betty Fladeland, 'Abolitionist Pressures on the Concert of Europe, 1814-1822', *Journal of Modern History*, 38, 1966, pp.355-73.
36 Richard Cobden to Joseph Sturge, 3 Jan. 1854, Sturge Papers BL Add. Mss. 43722, f.8; John Bright to Joseph Sturge, 11 Oct. 1857, Sturge Papers, BL Add. Mss. 43845, ff.50-3. Douglas H. Maynard, 'The World's Anti-Slavery Convention of 1840', *Mississippi Valley Historical Review*, XLVII, 3, Dec. 1960, pp.452-71; *Proceedings of the General Anti-Slavery Convention called by the committee of the British and Foreign Anti-Slavery Society . . . 1840*, London, 1841; *Proceedings of the Convention called by the Committee of the British and Foreign Anti-Slavery Society*, London, 1843.
37 Drescher, *Capitalism and Antislavery*, op. cit. pp.79, 216 note 46; Thomas Clarkson to Lucy Townsend, Aug. 1825, Antislavery Eng. Mss. 741(20) [R63635], Rylands; James Cropper to ?, 14 July 1827, in Anna Cropper, op. cit., pp.61-2; Minute Book, Sheffield Ladies' ASS, 10 July 1827, Antislavery Eng. Mss. 743, Rylands; Louis Billington, 'British Humanitarians and American Cotton, 1840-1860', *Journal of American Studies*, 11, 3, Dec. 1977, pp.313-34; John R. Procter to G.W. Alexander, 14 Sept. 1848, B. Emp. Mss. S18 C104/83, RH.

4 BEING ABOLITIONISTS

1 Thomas Clarkson, *History of the Abolition of the Slave Trade*, 2 vols, London, 1808 (repr. 1969), vol. 1, p.25.

2 Noel Annan, 'The Intellectual Aristocracy', in J. H. Plumb (ed.), *Studies in Social History*, London, 1955, pp.244–5; Leonore Davidoff and Catherine Hall, *Family Fortunes. Men and women of the English middle class 1780–1850*, London, 1987, pp.83–5.

3 Annan, op. cit., pp.245–6; Joseph Foster, *Pease of Darlington. With notices of the Families of Robson, Backhouse, Dixon and others, being the descendants of Joseph Pease of Shafton in the Parish of Felkirk, Yorkshire*, printed for private circulation; 1891, George Thompson to Jenny Thompson, 7, 8, 9 Oct. 1831, Raymond English Deposit, John Rylands University Library, Manchester.

4 Annan, op. cit., p.246; J. E. Cookson, *The Friends of Peace. Anti-war Liberalism in England 1793–1815*, Cambridge, 1982, pp.9–13, 22–4; R.K. Webb, *Harriet Martineau*, London, 1960, p.57; Clyde Binfield, *So Down To Prayers: Studies in English nonconformity, 1780–1920*, London, 1977, pp.41–3, 37–8.

5 Davidoff and Hall, op. cit., pp. 160, 43; Annan, op. cit., p.273.

6 Binfield, op. cit., pp.109–10; Davidoff and Hall, op. cit., p.128.

7 James Stephen Papers, vol. II, BL Add. Mss. 46444, pp. 2–3.

8 Clarkson, op. cit., vol. 1, pp.222–30; Clarkson Papers, vol. VII, BL Add. Mss. 41267A, ff. 200–1; Anne Cropper (comp.), *Extracts from the letters of the late James Cropper transcribed for his grandchildren*, n.p. [1850], pp. 20–1; Hannah Buxton to Anna Gurney and Sarah Buxton, 10 May 1833, Thomas Fowell Buxton Papers, B. Emp. Mss. S444 vol. 2, p.255, RH; William Wilberforce to George Stephen, 20 May 1833, Edwards Letters, Historical Society of Pennsylvania, Philadelphia.

9 Ralph Wardlaw, DD, *The Jubilee: A Sermon preached in West George Street Chapel, Glasgow, Friday August 1st 1834*, Glasgow, 1834, pp.20–31; *Sixteenth Report of the African Institution, 1822*, London, 1822, pp.xxvi–xxviii.

10 Douglas Charles Stange, *British Unitarians against American Slavery, 1833–65*, Rutherford, NJ and London, 1984, pp.23, 32, 39–41, 51; Mrs M.A. Rawson to Committee and Friends, n.d. [late 1837, early 1838], Antislavery Papers 742 (51) [R63635], Rylands.

11 *Report of the Committee of the Society for the Mitigation and Gradual Abolition of Slavery throughout the British Dominions read at the General Meeting of the Society, held on 25th day of June 1824*, London, 1824, pp.2–3, 46–62, 65–70, 70–1, 79, 85.

12 Clarkson, op. cit., vol 1, pp. 27–9, 80–179, 256–7; Prince Hoare, *Memoirs of Granville Sharp Esq.*, 2 vols, London, 1828 edn, vol. I, pp.xxvi–xxvii, II, pp.255–60, 203–6; Clarkson, op. cit., vol. 1, pp.272–3. *Sixteenth Report of the African Institution, 1822*, London, 1822, p.xxvi.

13 Hoare, op. cit., vol. I, pp.139–40; Clarkson, op. cit., vol. 1, p.8, vol 2, pp.583–4.

14 Thomas Clarkson to Charles Sturge, 19 July 1841, Sturge Papers, BL Add. Mss. 43845, f.6; Thomas Clarkson to ?, 7 March 1841, B. Emp. Mss. S18

NOTES

C107/4, RH; Thomas Clarkson to Thomas Thompson, 5 May 1823, Ms. Eng. 183(43), Boston Public Library (BPL); *Fifth Report of the Female Society for Birmingham*, Birmingham, 1830, p.10.

15 Journal of Anna Gurney and Sarah Maria Buxton, 1 Aug. 1834 and following, Thomas Fowell Buxton Papers, B. Emp. Mss., S444, vol. 13, pp. 111-23, RH.

16 Birmingham Anti-Slavery Society Minute Book, vol. 2, 1 Aug. 1838, 29 June 1839, Birmingham Central Reference Library.

17 Mary Clarkson to 'Mother', 12 June 1840?, Clarkson Papers, vol. VII, BL Add. Mss. 41267A, ff. 176-7; Benjamin Robert Haydon, Description of the Picture of the 1840 Convention, Clarkson Papers, vol. VII, BL Add. Mss. 41267A, ff.242-7, esp. f.246; Alex Tyrrell, ' "Woman's Mission" and Pressure Group Politics in Britain (1825-60)', *Bulletin of the John Rylands University Library*, 63, 1, 1980, pp.194-230; *Proceedings of the Convention called by the Committee of the British and Foreign Anti-Slavery Society*, London, 1843, preface.

18 David Newsome, *A Parting of Friends*, London, 1966, esp. pp.9-16; Richard Brent, *Liberal Anglican Politics*, Oxford, 1987, pp.261ff.; Elizabeth Isichei, *Victorian Quakers*, Oxford, 1970.

19 George Thompson to Jenny Thompson, 20, 22, 28 Sept. 1831, Raymond English Deposit, Rylands; Richard Webb to Elizabeth Pease, 4 Nov. 1840, Garrison Papers, BPL; Richard Webb to Maria Weston Chapman, 20 Nov. 1841, in Gloria Clare Taylor (ed.), *British and American Abolitionists, An Episode in Transatlantic Understanding*, Edinburgh, 1974, pp. 156-7.

20 Henry Thornton to John Clarkson, 23 Nov. 1792, Clarkson Papers, vol. I, BL Add. Mss. 41262A; R.I. and S. Wilberforce, *Life of William Wilberforce*, 5 vols, London, 1838, esp. vol. I; Thomas Clarkson, *Strictures on a Life of William Wilberforce by the Rev. W. Wilberforce and the Rev. S. Wilberforce*, London, 1838, pp.62, 65-73, 74; Sara Coleridge to Catherine Clarkson, 4 Sept. 1838, HM 31457, Huntington Library, San Marino, Ca.; H. C. Robinson, *Exposure of the Misrepresentations contained in the preface to the Correspondence of William Wilberforce*, London, 1840, pp.3-9.

21 Catherine Clarkson to William Smith, 26 July, 12 Aug., 18 Aug., 9 Sept. 1834, William Smith to Catherine Clarkson [Aug. 1834], Thomas Clarkson to Robert Wilberforce, [Aug. 1834], William Smith Papers, 18H, Duke University Library, Durham, NC; Clarkson, op. cit., pp.12-13, 16-19, x-xiii (Brougham), 52; Thomas Fowell Buxton to William Smith, 5 Sept. 1832, William Smith Papers, 18H Duke; Thomas Clarkson to William Smith, 28 June 1833, William Smith Papers, 18H Duke.

22 James Stephen, *Essays in Ecclesiastical Biography*, 2 vols, London, 1849, vol. II, pp.244-7; George Stephen, *Anti-Slavery Recollections*, London, 1971 edn, pp.85-7.

23 James Stephen, op. cit., vol. II, pp.324, 382-3; George Stephen, op. cit., pp. 5, 18-19, 46-8, 78-83.

24 George Stephen, ibid., pp.92-8, 76-7, 114-27, 200-3, 160-1.

25 Ibid., pp.2-3, 149-52, 210-13.

26 For full discussion of the impact of American abolitionist divisions see chapter 7 below. Thomas Fowell Buxton to Thomas Clarkson, 11 Dec. 1838, Clarkson Papers, f.4, Moorland–Springarn Collection, Howard University Library, Washington DC; Joseph Sturge to Gerrit Smith, 31 July 1839, Gerrit Smith Papers, George Arents Research Library, Syracuse University, Syracuse, NY; Catherine Clarkson to Mary Clarkson, 3 July 1840, Clarkson Papers, vol. VII, BL Add. Mss. 41267A, f.218; Thomas Clarkson to J.M. Trew [1841?], CN49 Clarkson–Hunt.; J.J. Gurney to Thomas Clarkson, 29 Oct. 1840, Clarkson Papers, vol. VII, BL Add. Mss. 41267A, ff. 224–6.

27 Brent, op.cit., pp. 275–6; Mary Clarkson to Catherine Clarkson, 23 June 1840, Clarkson Papers, vol. VII, BL Add. Mss. 41267A, ff. 198–9.

28 Elizabeth Pease to John A. Collins, 24 Dec. 1840, Garrison Papers, BPL; *Liberator* (Boston), X, 24 July 1840; Richard Webb to John A. Collins, 7 Jan. 1841, Garrison Papers, BPL; *Anti-Slavery Advocate*, 1, Oct. 1852, 5, Feb. 1853.

29 Richard Webb to Elizabeth Pease, 26 May 1844, James Haughton to Maria Weston Chapman, 18 July 1844, in Taylor (ed.), op. cit., pp.220–2.

30 C. Duncan Rice, *Scots Abolitionists, 1833–1861*, Baton Rouge, La., 1981, pp. 126–46; Henry Wigham to W.L. Garrison, 17 Nov. 1852, in Taylor (ed.), op. cit., p.390; David M. Turley, 'Relations between British and American Abolitionists from British Emancipation to the American Civil War', unpub. Ph.D thesis, Cambridge, 1970, pp.342–4.

31 Ibid., pp.349–50, 351–7; Christine Bolt, *The Anti-Slavery Movement and Reconstruction. A study of Anglo-American co-operation, 1833-1877*, London, 1969.

5 ABOLITIONISTS AND THE MIDDLE-CLASS REFORM COMPLEX

1 M.J.D. Roberts, 'The Society for the Suppression of Vice and its Early Critics, 1802–1812', *Historical Journal*, 26, 1, 1983, pp.160–6, 173–4; Ian Bradley, *The Call to Seriousness: the evangelical impact on the Victorians*, London, 1976, pp.96ff.; Ford K. Brown, *Fathers of the Victorians: the Age of Wilberforce*, Cambridge, 1961, pp.86–8; *Christian Observer*, 7, 3, March 1808, p.203; Thomas Clarkson to Zachary Macaulay, 14 Oct. 1822, MY 136, Huntington Library.

2 Thomas W. Laqueur, *Religion and Respectability: Sunday Schools and working-class culture, 1780–1850*, New Haven, Conn., 1976, pp.25–8, 34–5; John Roach, *Social Reform in England, 1780-1880*, London, 1978, pp.51–2; Ford K. Brown, op. cit., pp.88–90.

3 Ibid., pp.235–242; David Owen, *English Philanthropy, 1760-1960*, Cambridge, Mass., 1964, pp.93–4; Thomas Fowell Buxton to Hannah Buxton, 27 Nov., 29 Nov. 1816, in Patricia Pugh (ed.), *Calendar of the Papers of Sir Thomas Fowell Buxton Bt.*, London, 1980, pp.183–90.

4 John Pease, *Address of J. Pease to Friends in America*, New York, 1845, pp.9–10; *Philanthropist*, 1, 1, 1811, esp. pp.1–2; Isabel McKenzie, *Social Activities of the English Friends in the first half of the nineteenth*

century, privately printed, New York, 1935, pp.11–15, 34–40, 53–60, 71–2, 80–1, 87–91; Thomas Clarkson to William Allen, 4 July 1811, Temp. Mss. Box 4/6(4), Friends' House Library, London; *Philanthropist*, 2, 1, 1812, pp.57–108; Alex Tyrrell, *Joseph Sturge and the Moral Radical Party in Early Victorian Britain*, London, 1987, p.155.

5 Anne Cropper (comp.), *Extracts from the letters of the late James Cropper, transcribed for his grandchildren by their very affectionate mother and aunt*, n.p. [1850], pp.15, 92–3, 125, 133; Boyd Hilton, *Corn, Cash, Commerce. The economic policies of the Tory government, 1815–1830*, Oxford, 1977, pp.57, 86; McKenzie, op. cit., pp.92–4; David Martin, 'Land Reform', in Patricia Hollis, (ed.), *Pressure from Without in Early Victorian England*, London, 1974, pp.133–4.

6 Andrew T. Scull, *Museums of Madness. The social organization of insanity in nineteenth century England*, Harmondsworth, 1982, p.56; Samuel Tuke, *Description of the Retreat (1813)*, London, 1964 edn, introduction by Richard Hunter and Ida Macalpine; Anne Digby, *Madness, Morality and Medicine. A study of the York Retreat, 1796–1914*, Cambridge, 1985, part I.

7 G.M. Ditchfield, 'Repeal, Abolition and Reform: a study in the interaction of reforming movements in the parliament of 1790–6', in Christine Bolt and Seymour Drescher (eds), *Anti-Slavery, Religion and Reform: Essays in memory of Roger Anstey*, Folkestone, 1980, pp.101–18; William Smith to Lord Holland, 14 July 1820, Holland House Papers, BL Add. Mss. 51573, ff. 217–18; Lant Carpenter to Lord Holland, 25 May 1828, 24 Dec. 1828, Holland House Papers, BL Add. Mss. 51592, ff.163, 167–8; J.E. Cookson, *The Friends of Peace. Anti-war Liberalism in England, 1793–1815*, Cambridge, 1982; Douglas Charles Stange, *British Unitarians against American Slavery 1833–65*, Rutherford, NJ, 1984, pp.32–7; Betty Fladeland, *Abolitionists and Working-Class Problems in the Age of Industrialization*, London and Basingstoke, 1984, pp.46–8; R.S. Fitton and A.P. Wadsworth, *The Strutts and the Arkwrights. A study of the early factory system*, Manchester, 1958, pp.178–80, 184; S.A. Steinthal to S. May, 29 Sept. 1854, in Clare Taylor (ed.), *British and American Abolitionists: an episode in transatlantic understanding*, Edinburgh, 1974, p.411; M.J. Shaen (ed.), *William Shaen*, London, 1912, pp.7–9.

8 Clyde Binfield, *So Down to Prayers: Studies in English Nonconformity, 1780-1920*, London, 1977, p.84; David M. Thompson, 'The Liberation Society', in Hollis (ed.), op. cit., pp.211–23; Derek Fraser, 'Edward Baines', in Hollis (ed.), op. cit., pp.194–7.

9 Michael Ignatieff, *A Just Measure of Pain. The Penitentiary in the Industrial Revolution*, London, 1978, pp.50, 58–60, 146–8; McKenzie, op. cit., pp.160–4, 175–82, 201–3, 168–70; Thomas Clarkson to C.N. Warren, 6 March 1821, Clarkson Papers 18E, Duke.

10 Scull, op. cit., pp.56, 59; Richard Webb to Elizabeth Pease, 4 Nov. 1840, in Clare Taylor (ed.), op. cit., p.119; Elizabeth Isichei, *Victorian Quakers*, Oxford, 1970, pp.236–7; Brian Harrison, 'The British Prohibitionists, 1853-1872. A Biographical Analysis', *International Review of Social History*, XV, 1970, pp.376–7, 427, 448, 463; Brian Harrison, 'Religion and

Recreation', in Brian Harrison, *Peaceable Kingdom: Stability and Change in Modern Britain*, Oxford, 1982, pp.126–7, 136.

11 V.A.C. Gatrell, 'Incorporation and the Pursuit of Liberal Hegemony in Manchester, 1790–1839', in D. Fraser (ed.), *Municipal Reform and the Industrial City*, Leicester, 1982, pp.25–9; J.V. Pickstone and S.V.F. Butler, 'The Politics of Medicine in Manchester, 1788–1792: Hospital Reform and Public Health Services in the Early Industrial City', *Medical History*, 28, 1984, pp.227–49; G.M. Ditchfield, 'Manchester College and Anti-Slavery', in Barbara Smith (ed.), *Truth, Liberty, Religion. Essays celebrating two hundred years of Manchester College*, Oxford, 1986, pp.187–224.

12 *Society for the . . . Abolition of the Slave Trade*, Manchester, 1788; *Complete List of the Members and Officers of the Manchester Literary and Philosophical Society from its institution on February 28th 1781 to April 28th 1896*, Manchester, 1896, pp.8, 9, 16–39; Charles Webster and Jonathan Barry, 'The Manchester Medical Revolution', in Barbara Smith (ed.), op. cit., p.182, note 64; Pickstone and Butler, op. cit. On Percival and Bayley see *The Works Literary, Moral and Philosophical of Thomas Percival MD*, 2 vols, London, 1807; W. Magee (ed.), *Biographical Memories of the late Thomas Percival, M.D., F.R.S. & C.*, Manchester, 1804; Thomas Percival (ed.), *Biographical Memoirs of the late Thomas Butterworth Bayley, Esq., F.R.S. of Hope Hall near Manchester*, Manchester, 1802.

13 John Holland and James Everett, *Memoirs of the Life and Writings of James Montgomery*, 6 vols, London 1855 and 1856, vols 3, 4 and 5; Samuel Roberts, *Autobiography and Select Remains*, London, 1849; Anti-Slavery Papers 742 (53) R63635; Minute Book, Sheffield Female ASS, 1825–33, Papers 743 R63635, John Rylands University Library, Manchester; *The Sheffield Directory and Guide*, Sheffield, 1828; Thomas W. Hall, *The Fairbanks of Sheffield 1688 to 1848*, Sheffield, 1932.

14 Roberts, op. cit., pp.54, 101–4; Holland and Everett, op. cit., vol. 3, p.19, vol. 4, pp.33, 93–5; Colin Holmes, 'Samuel Roberts and the Gypsies', in Sidney Pollard and Colin Holmes (eds), *Essays in the Economic and Social History of South Yorkshire*, Barnsley, 1976, pp.233–46; Samuel Roberts, *The Rev. Dr. Pye Smith and the New Poor Law*, London, 1839, pp.5, 6, 9; Samuel Roberts, *A Cry from the Chimneys or an integral part of the abolition of slavery throughout the world*, London, 1837, pp.11ff.; Holland and Everett, op. cit., vol. 4, pp.242–3, vol. 5, pp.242, 265–7.

15 *Eclectic Review*, I, Oct. 1805, in Andrew Porter, 'Commerce and Christianity: the Rise and Fall of a Nineteenth-century Missionary Slogan', *Historical Journal (HJ)* 28, 3, 1985, pp.599–605; Bradley, op. cit., pp.75–88; *Christian Observer*, 8, 2, Feb. 1809, pp.83–4, no.4, April 1809, pp.220–5; James Cropper to Joseph Sturge, 27 Oct. 1828, 2 April 1829, in Anne Cropper, op. cit., pp.66–7.

16 *Monthly Repository*, II, 1807, p.607.

17 Brian Stanley, ' "Commerce and Christianity" ': Providence Theory, the Missionary Movement and the Imperialism of Free Trade, 1842–1860', HJ, 26, 1, 1983, pp.77–80; BFASS Minute Books, III, 3 Nov. 1854, B. Emp. Mss. E 2/8, RH; Porter, op. cit., pp.611–13.

18 For Liverpool abolitionists' pamphlets of early 1820s see chapter 2 above;

Birmingham ASS Minute Book, I, 4 April 1827, Birmingham Reference
Library; Hilton, op. cit., pp.150-1, 274-5; James Cropper to Joseph
Sturge, 16 May 1835 to 10 Nov. 1837, to Sturge, 3 Dec. 1837, in Anne
Cropper, op. cit., pp.116-17, 143-7.

19 Richard Cobden to Joseph Sturge, 28 Jan. 1841, BL Add. Mss. 43656, f.2;
T.P. Martin, 'The Upper Mississippi Valley in Anglo-American Anti-
Slavery and Free Trade Relations, 1837-42', *Mississippi Valley Historical
Review*, XV, 1928, pp.204-5; George R. Mellor, *British Imperial
Trusteeship, 1783-1850*, London, 1951, pp.140-1; John Curtis to R.D.
Webb, 14 Feb. 1842, in Clare Taylor (ed.), op. cit., p.165; Louis Billington,
'Some Connections between British and American Reform Movements,
1830-1860', MA thesis, University of Bristol, 1966, pp.147-8.

20 Joseph Pease, *On Slavery and its Remedy*, London, 1841; John Hyslop Bell,
*British Folks and British India Fifty Years Ago: Joseph Pease and his
Contemporaries*, London, 1891, pp.5-6, 11-15, 20-4, 77-87; George
Thompson to R.D. Webb, 15 Feb. 1839, in Clare Taylor (ed.), op. cit., p.45.

21 *Proceedings of the General Anti-Slavery Convention . . . 1840*, London,
1841, pp.376ff., 519; *Proceedings of the General Anti-Slavery Convention
. . . 1843*, London, 1843, pp.128-73 (pp.144-7 for Cobden); George
Thompson to BFASS Committee, 15 May 1844, Emp. Mss. S24 J 111,
pp.9-10, RH.

22 Tyrrell, op. cit., pp.141-2; Rev. Thomas Spencer, in *Proceedings . . . 1843*,
pp.132-3; Thomas Clarkson to Manager of Free Produce Association of
Philadelphia, 1 May 1846, Rhoads Papers, Quaker Collection, Haverford
College, Haverford, Pa.; John Murray to editor of *Anti-Slavery Reporter*,
17 Nov. 1845, B. Emp. Mss. S18 C 103/111, RH; Richard Cobden to
Joseph Sturge, 13 Jan. 1846, BL Add. Mss. 43656, f. 9-10; John Bright to
Joseph Sturge, 27 March 1853, BL Add. Mss. 43723, f.14.; see also chapter
3 above.

23 Richard Cobden to Joseph Sturge, 26 March 1846, BL Add. Mss. 43656, ff
13-14; Isichei, op. cit., pp.220-1; Thomas Clarkson, Mss. on African
Institution and c. [*c.* 1824], CN33, Clarkson-Hunt.; T. Clarkson, Memor-
andum on the state of the nation [*c.* 1843] CN80, Clarkson-Hunt.;
Richard Cobden to Joseph Sturge, 3 Jan. 1848, BL Add. Mss. 43656, ff.21-
2.

24 Lewis Tappan's Journal, 1 July 1843, Lewis Tappan Papers, Library of
Congress; Tyrrell, op. cit., pp.143-4, 162-72; Richard Cobden to Joseph
Sturge, 9 Oct. 1850, BL Add. Mss. 50131, f.210; Cobden to Sturge, 19 Jan.
1849, BL Add. Mss. 43656, f.90.

25 John Scoble to Le Hardy de Beaulieu, 8 Oct. 1848, Ms. Eng. 183 (110h)
Boston Public Library; William James to Samuel May, 24 March 1848, J.B.
Estlin to Samuel May, 7 April 1848, 30 Jan. 1849, in Clare Taylor (ed.), op.
cit., pp.321-4, 336; Anna M. Stoddart, *Elizabeth Pease Nichol*, London,
1899, pp.172-3, 182, 200-2; Shaen, op. cit., pp.11-13; George Armstrong
to Samuel May, 14 Aug. 1855, G. Mazzini to Armstrong, n.d. [1855], in
Clare Taylor (ed.), op. cit., pp.416-17.

26 Tyrrell, op. cit., pp.167-72, 209, 211-14.

27 R.D. Webb to E. Quincy, 16 Aug. 1843, 16/17 Oct. 1843, 2 Feb. 1844,
Richard Allen to Maria Weston Chapman, 6 Feb. 1844, James Haughton

to Maria Weston Chapman, 1 April 1847, R.D. Webb to ?, 3 Aug. 1849, in Clare Taylor (ed.), op. cit., pp.192-6, 199-203, 213-17, 311, 340; Charles Stuart to Theodore Weld, in Gilbert H. Barnes and Dwight L. Dumond (eds), *The Letters of Theodore Dwight Weld, Angelina Grimké Weld and Sarah Grimké, 1822-1844*, 2 vols, Gloucester, Mass., 1965 edn, vol. II, pp.980-1; Elizabeth Pease to Anne Warren Weston, 27 Jan. 1844, in Clare Taylor (ed.), op. cit., pp.211-13; J.B. Estlin to Samuel May, 26 May-9 June 1848, in ibid., pp.324-5.

28 Bell, op. cit., pp.49-52; Tyrrell, op. cit., pp.228-9.

29 *Philanthropist*, 2, 6, 1812, pp.202-6.

30 Despite the difficulties it poses the work of Michel Foucault is relevant here. See Michel Foucault, *Madness and Civilization. A history of insanity in the age of reason*, London, 1967; Michel Foucault, *Discipline and Punish. The Birth of the Prison*, Harmondsworth, 1979. Also Scull, op. cit., pp.64-5, 132-4. Thomas Pringle, 'Supplement to the History of Mary Prince by the editor', in Henry Louis Gates (ed.), *The Classic Slave Narratives*, New York and Scarborough, Ontario, 1987, pp.235-6; Thomas W. Laqueur, 'Bodies, Details and the Humanitarian Narrative', in Lynn Hunt (ed.), *The New Cultural History*, Berkeley and London, 1989, esp. pp.177-9, 182. For a suggested link to John Ferriar's reform activity, pp.189-90.

31 Ignatieff, op. cit., pp.60-1, 67, 144; W. Laqueur, op. cit., pp.5ff.; Scull, op. cit., p.143; Pickstone and Butler, op. cit.

32 Ignatieff, op. cit., pp.144-5; Scull, op. cit., pp.104-6.

33 John Angell James, *The Sunday School Teacher's Guide*, 2nd edn, Birmingham, 1816, pp.82-114.

34 Thomas Percival, *Works*, op. cit., vol. II, pp.453-4, 454-61; Scull, op. cit., illustration 3 opp. p.144. By 1814, however, Samuel Tuke thought that the construction of the Retreat should have allowed greater surveillance and concluded a panopticon would have been preferable. Tuke, op. cit., 'Introduction', pp.14-15.

35 Robert Gray, 'The languages of factory reform in Britain, c.1830-1860', in Patrick Joyce, (ed.), *The Historical Meanings of Work*, Cambridge, 1987, pp.147ff.; Brian Harrison, 'The Rhetoric of Reform in Modern Britain: 1780-1918', in Harrison, *Peaceable Kingdom*, op. cit., pp.379-80, 389-90.

36 Brian Harrison, 'The British Prohibitionists', p.414; Laqueur, op. cit., pp.234-5; Tyrrell, op. cit., pp.69-72.

37 Tyrrell, op. cit., p.68; Isichei, op. cit., pp.244-5; John Murray to Elizur Wright, 20 July 1837, Elizur Wright Papers, Library of Congress; Richard Webb to Elizabeth Pease, 4 Nov. 1840, Garrison Papers, Boston Public Library.

38 *Christian Observer*, 6, 3, March 1807, p.204; 5, 6, June 1806, p.381; 8, 12, Dec. 1809, pp.756-7.

39 R.J. Morris, 'Voluntary Societies and British Urban Elites, 1780-1850: an Analysis', *HJ*, 26, 1, 1983, pp.96-7, 110; *Philanthropist*, I, 1811, pp.3-5, 77-83; Ignatieff, op. cit., pp.164-6; F.M.L. Thompson, 'Social Control in Victorian Britain', *Ec. Hist.Rev.*, 2nd ser., XXXIV, 2, May 1981, pp.191-3.

NOTES

40 Ignatieff, op. cit., pp.143–4; Laqueur, op. cit., pp.229–31; James, op. cit., pp.39–62.

41 Laqueur, op. cit., pp.126ff.; Tyrrell, op. cit., pp.41–2; *Philanthropist*, I, 1811, p.7.

42 *Monthly Repository*, IV, 1809, pp.297, 347; James Currie to Dr Hector Macneill, 29 Oct. 1801, Ms. 5319, National Library of Scotland; Roy Porter, 'The Enlightenment in England', in Roy Porter and Mikulas Teich (eds), *The Enlightenment in National Context*, Cambridge, 1981, pp.10–12, 16–17; *Monthly Repository*, III, 1808, pp.509–10; William Stafford, *Socialism, Radicalism and Nostalgia. Social Criticism in Britain, 1775 1830*, Cambridge, 1987, pp.87–9; Digby, op. cit., pp.6–9.

43 John Smail, 'New Languages for Labour and Capital: the transformation of discourse in the early years of the Industrial Revolution', *Social History*, 12, 1, Jan. 1987, pp.5–6; R.J. Hind, 'William Wilberforce and the Perceptions of the British People', *Historical Research*, LX, 143, Oct. 1987, pp.321–35; Ignatieff, op. cit., pp.114–15; C.M. Elliott, 'The Political Economy of English Dissent, 1780–1840' in R.M. Hartwell (ed.), *The Industrial Revolution*, Oxford, 1970, pp.155, 158.

44 Eltis, op. cit., pp.21–2, 299 note 17; Elliott, op. cit., pp.158, 160–1, 163–4; Harriet Martineau to H.S. Tremenheere, 25 Jan. 1844, M.F. Hale Autograph Collection, vol. I, p.36, Ac. 10735, LC.

45 Linda Colley, 'Radical Patriotism in Eighteenth-Century England', in Raphael Samuel (ed.), *Patriotism. The Making and Unmaking of British National Identity, vol.1, History and Politics*, London, 1989, pp.182–3; *Christian Observer*, 9, 3 and 4, March, April 1810, pp.171–2, 248; Prince Hoare, *Memoirs of Granville Sharp Esq. composed from his own Manuscripts*, 2 vols, 2nd edn, London, 1828, vol. 2, pp.276–80; Bernard Porter, *The Refugee Question in Mid-Victorian Politics*, Cambridge, 1979, pp.39–40; Elizabeth Pease to Anne Warren Weston, 27 Jan. 1844, R.D. Webb to Maria Weston Chapman, 16 Nov. 1843; J.B. Estlin to Samuel May, 7 April 1848, in Clare Taylor (ed.), op. cit., pp.213, 206–7, 323; Elizabeth Rawson to Cecil [Wilson], 22 Feb. 1851, Wilson–Rawson Papers, MD 2475, Sheffield Central Library; Notes of Helen Wilson, March 1918, Wilson–Rawson Papers, MD 6041; Porter, op. cit., p.107; Basil Hall, 'Allessandro Gavazzi: a Barnabite Friar and the Risorgimento', in Derek Baker (ed.), *Church, Society and Politics*, Oxford, 1975, pp.345–6.

46 Bradley, op. cit., pp.126–31; Roberts, op. cit., pp.167–71; *Philanthropist*, 2, no.7, 1812, pp.229–38.

47 Thomas Clarkson, *The History of the Rise, Progress and Accomplishment of the Abolition of the African Slave Trade*, London, 1968 edn, p.581; Ignatieff, op. cit., pp.116–19; McKenzie, op. cit., pp.62–3, 82–4.

48 Patricia Hollis, 'Introduction', in Hollis (ed.), op. cit., p.3; Brian Harrison, 'Moral Reform', in Hollis (ed.), op. cit., pp.309–10.

49 David Brion Davis, *Slavery and Human Progress*, New York, 1984, pp.180–1; Gray, op. cit., pp.168–9; Ignatieff, op. cit., pp.168, 188–9.

6 ANTISLAVERY, RADICALISM AND PATRIOTISM

1 Albert Goodwin, *The Friends of Liberty. The English Democratic Movement in the Age of the French Revolution*, London, 1979, pp. 36-8, 54-5, 66-7, 73-4, 85-6; John Seed, 'Gentlemen Dissenters, the Social and Political Meanings of Rational Dissent in the 1770s and 1780s', *Historical Journal (HJ)*, 28, 2, June 1985, pp.299-325; J.E.Cookson, *The Friends of Peace. Anti-War Liberalism in England, 1793-1815*, Cambridge, 1982, ch. 1; John Gascoigne, 'Anglican Latitudinarianism and Political Radicalism in the Late Eighteenth Century', *History*, 71, 231, Feb. 1986, pp.22-38.

2 Cookson, op. cit, pp. 88-91, 125-6; R.V. Holt, *The Unitarian Contribution to Social Progress in England*, 2nd rev. edn, London, 1952, pp. 41-3; C.B. Jewson, *The Jacobin City. A portrait of Norwich in its reaction to the French Revolution, 1788-1802*, Glasgow and London, 1975; V.A.C. Gatrell, 'Incorporation and the pursuit of Liberal Hegemony in Manchester, 1790-1839', in Derek Fraser (ed.), *Municipal Reform and the Industrial City*, Leicester and New York, 1982, pp.16-60.

3 Ian Sellers, 'Unitarians and Social Change. Part I: Varieties of radicalism 1795-1815', *Hibbert Journal*, 61, 1962-3, pp. 16-22; Mark Philp, 'Rational Religion and Political Radicalism', *Enlightenment and Dissent*, 4, 1985, pp.35-46. Both Priestley and Cooper, the Manchester radical dissenter, migrated to the United States in 1794.

4 London Anti-Slave Trade Committee, Minute Book, vol. 1, 30 Oct., 22 Nov., 18 Dec. 1787, 1 Jan.1788, vol. 2, 6 May 1788, BL Add. Mss. 21254-5; Prince Hoare, *Memoirs of Granville Sharp Esq. composed from his own Manuscripts*, 2 vols, 2nd edn, London, 1828, vol.1, pp.118, 211-12, 284-90; Granville Sharp to John Wilkes, 12 Jan. 1780, BL Add. Mss. 30872, f.168; David Brion Davis, *The Problem of Slavery in the Age of Revolution 1770-1823*, Ithaca, NY and London, 1975, pp.230, 373-7.

5 Goodwin, op. cit., pp.155-8; G.M. Ditchfield, 'The Campaign in Lancashire and Cheshire for the Repeal of the Test and Corporation Acts, 1787-1790', *Transactions of the Historic Society of Lancashire and Cheshire (THSLC)*, 126, 1976, pp.109-10.

6 Ditchfield, ibid., pp.110-20; Goodwin, op. cit., pp.90-1; Ian Sellers, 'William Roscoe, the Roscoe Circle and Radical Politics in Liverpool', *THSLC*, 120, 1968, pp.47-8.

7 Thomas Cooper, *Propositions respecting the Foundation of Civil Government* (1787), reprinted in Cooper, *A Reply to Mr. Burke's Invective against Mr. Cooper and Mr. Watt in the House of Commons on the 30th April 1792*, London and Manchester, 1792, pp.78-88; E.M. Hunt, 'The Anti-Slave Trade Agitation in Manchester', *Transactions of the Lancashire and Cheshire Antiquarian Society (TLCAS)*, 1977, p.63; Goodwin, op. cit. pp. 143-5.

8 John Money, *Experience and Identity: Birmingham and the West Midlands, 1760-1800*, Manchester, 1977, pp.195-7, 219-23, 238 note 2; Margaret Canovan, 'Paternalistic Liberalism: Joseph Priestley on Rank and Inequality', *Enlightenment and Dissent*, 2, 1983, pp.23-37.

9 M.J. Murphy, 'Newspapers and Opinion in Cambridge 1790-1850',

NOTES

MA thesis, University of Kent, 1971, pp.21-3; Frida Knight, *University Rebel. The Life of William Frend (1757-1841)*, London, 1971, pp. 60-73, 104-5.

10 Knight, ibid., p.88; Ian Bradley, *The Call to Seriousness. The evangelical impact on the Victorians*, London, 1976, pp.15, 70; Goodwin, op. cit., p.96; Ditchfield, op. cit., p.127; Haddon Willmer, 'Evangelicalism 1785 to 1835', Hulsean Prize Essay, University of Cambridge, 1962, pp.143-5; *Seventeenth Report of the African Institution, 1823*, London, 1823, p.lv.

11 Goodwin, op. cit., pp 172-3; Gregory Claeys, *Thomas Paine. Social and Political Thought*, London, 1989, p.68; Journal of Thomas Clarkson's visit to France, 1789-90. unpaginated, box 1, Clarkson-A; Philp, op. cit., pp. 35-6, 39-42.

12 Goodwin, op. cit., pp.187-8; Frida Knight, *The Strange Case of Thomas Walker. Ten Years in the Life of a Manchester Radical*, London, 1957, pp.63-4; Claeys, op. cit., pp 124-5, 132-3, 113, 151-3; Marilyn Butler (ed.), *Burke, Paine, Godwin and the Revolution Controversy*, Cambridge, 1989, pp.181-2; [Truth], *A very new pamphlet indeed!*, London, 1792, pp.4-5.

13 F.E. Sanderson, 'The Liverpool Abolitionists', in R. Anstey and P. Hair (eds), *Liverpool, the African Slave Trade and Abolition. Essays to illustrate current knowledge and research*, Historic Society of Lancashire and Cheshire, Occasional Ser., vol. 2, 1976, pp.217-21; Betty Fladeland, *Abolitionists and Working-Class Problems in the Age of Industrialization*, London and Basingstoke, 1984, pp.27-8, 33-6; Sellers, 'Roscoe', pp.48-9, 51-3; Cookson, op. cit., p.124.

14 Goodwin, op. cit., pp.145-7, 201-3; E. Robinson, 'An English Jacobin: James Watt Jr. 1769-1848', *Cambridge Historical Journal*, XI, 3, 1955, pp.350-1; Pauline Handforth, 'Manchester Radical Politics, 1789-94', *TLCAS*, 66, 1956, pp.94-8; Hunt, op. cit., pp.70, 72 notes 86 and 87; Knight, *Walker*, op. cit., pp.74-5. 78-9.

15 Thomas Cooper, *A Reply to Mr. Burke's Invective against Mr. Cooper and Mr. Watt in the House of Commons on 30th April 1792*, London and Manchester, 1792, esp. pp.24-5, 61-5; Knight, *Walker*, op. cit., pp.92-104, 114-15.

16 Alan Booth, 'Popular Loyalism and Public Violence in the North-West of England, 1790-1800', *Social History*, 8, 3, Oct. 1983, pp.295-313; Knight, *Walker*, pp.158, 166, 172-3; John Bohstedt, *Riots and Community Politics in England and Wales 1790-1810*, Cambridge, Mass., 1983, pp.119-20, 80-1, 90; Goodwin, op. cit., p.437; Thomas Percival, *The Works, Literary Moral and Philosophical*, 2 vols, London, 1807, vol. 1, pp. clxxv-vi, ccxxxvi-vii.

17 Claeys, op. cit., pp.69-70, 163; Robinson, op. cit., pp.351 note 9, 352-5; Money, op. cit., pp.233, 224-5.

18 Knight, *University Rebel*, op. cit., pp.91-3; William Frend, *Peace and Union recommended to the associated bodies of Republicans and Anti-Republicans*, St Ives, 1793; Murphy, op. cit., pp.52-3, 55-8, 85-93, 101-9.

19 Thomas Clarkson to Lord Hawkesbury, 29 May 1788, Liverpool Papers ccxxvii, BL Add. Mss. 38416, f.94; Thomas Cooper, *Considerations on the Slave Trade and the Consumption of West Indian Produce*, London, 1791, pp.13-16; *Address Concerning the Slave Trade*, Glasgow, 1791, p.3, Draft,

James Ramsay Papers, BL Add. Mss. 27621, f.8; Richard Price, *A Discourse on the Love of Our Country, Delivered on Nov. 4 1789 at the Meeting-House in the Old Jewry*, London, 1789, pp.25-6; Joseph Priestley, *Letters to the Right Hon. Edmund Burke, Letter XIV*, Birmingham, 1791, extract in Marilyn Butler (ed.), op. cit., pp.88-9; Granville Sharp, *The Law of Liberty or Royal Law*, London, 1776, pp.16-17.

20 Booth, op. cit., pp.304, 306; Thomas Clarkson to Comte de Mirabeau, 13 Nov. 1789, CN35, Clarkson-Hunt.; Henry Dundas to William Wilberforce, 18 July 1791, 18H Wilberforce Papers, Duke; [Truth], *A very new pamphlet indeed!*, London, 1792, pp.3-4.

21 Gerald Newman, 'Anti-French Propaganda and British Liberal Nationalism in the Early Nineteenth Century; suggestions toward a general interpretation', *Victorian Studies*, June 1975, pp.385-418; V.G. Kiernan, 'Evangelicalism and the French Revolution', *Past and Present*, 1, Feb. 1952, pp.44-56.

22 [W. Magee], *Biographical Memoirs of the late Thomas Percival M.D., F.R.S. & C.*, Manchester, 1804, pp.14-16; Percival, *Works*, op. cit., vol.1, pp.lxxxv, lxxxix; Bohstedt, op. cit., p.115.

23. David Geggus, 'British Opinion and the Emergence of Haiti, 1791-1805', in James Walvin (ed.), *Slavery and British Society 1776-1846*, London, 1982, pp.123-4; Resolutions at a General Meeting of the West-India Planters and Merchants held at the London Tavern, 3 Nov. 1791, Fuller Letterpress, 1787-96, Duke; Stephen Fuller to Committee of Correspondence of Jamaica Assembly, 3 Jan. 1792, Fuller Letterpress, 1787-96, Duke.

24 Geggus, op. cit., p.127; Thomas Clarkson, *The True State of the Case Respecting the Insurrection at St. Domingo*, Ipswich, 1792, pp.2-4, 7-8.

25 Philp, op. cit., pp.43-4; Butler, op. cit., pp.4-5; Cookson, op. cit., pp.135-6, 128-9; Richard W. Davis, *Dissent in Politics 1780-1830. The Political Life of William Smith M.P.*, London, 1971, pp.110-11; James Currie to William Smith, 17 April 1795, Small Purchases, Ms. 5319, ff.113-15, National Library of Scotland.

26 Ibid.; William Roscoe to Lord Holland, 6 Dec. 1796, Holland House Papers, BL Add. Mss. 51650, f.47; Cookson, op. cit., pp.76-7.

27 Benjamin Flower, *National Sins considered in two letters to the Rev. Thomas Robinson*, Cambridge, 1796, pp.v-vi, 23-4, 48-9, 59; Knight, *University Rebel*, op. cit., pp.176, 180.

28 Linda Colley, 'The Apotheosis of George III: Loyalty, Royalty and the British Nation 1760-1820', *Past and Present*, 102, Feb. 1984; Marilyn Butler, 'Romanticism in England', in Roy Porter and Mikulás Teich (eds), *Romanticism in National Context*, Cambridge, 1988, pp.41-6; R.S. Fitton and A.P. Wadsworth, *The Strutts of Belper*, Manchester, 1958, pp.188-9; William Wilberforce, 'Advice Suggested by the State of the Times', in Frank J. Klingberg and Sigurd B. Hustvedt (eds), *The Warning Drum. The British Home Front Faces Napoleon. Broadsides of 1803*, Berkeley and Los Angeles, 1944, pp.177-9; Hannah More, 'The Ploughman's Ditty: being an answer to that foolish question, What have the poor to lose?', in Klingberg and Hustvedt (eds), op. cit., pp.188-90; Stella Cottrell, 'The Devil on Two Sticks: francophobia in 1803' and Hugh Cunningham, 'The

Language of Patriotism', in Raphael Samuel (ed.), *Patriotism: The Making and Unmaking of British National Identity, vol.1 History and Politics*, London and New York, 1989, pp.260-3, 63-4.

29 William Frend, *Patriotism; or the love of Our Country*, London, 1804; Thomas Clarkson's report, London Anti-Slave Trade Committee, Minute Book III, BL Add. Mss. 21256, p.115; [Raikes], *Christianity and Commerce*, London, 1806, pp.42, 55-6, 17-18, 27-9; *Christian Observer*, 4, 11, Nov. 1805, pp. 682-4; 4, 12, Dec. 1805, pp.776-7; 6, 2, 1807, p.124.

30 *Christian Observer*, 6, 3, March 1807, pp.201-3; *Monthly Repository*, III, 1808, p.399; VI, 1811, p.583; III, 1808, pp.107-9; Cookson, op. cit., pp.164-5; Knight, *University Rebel*, op. cit., p.244; William Roscoe to Lord Holland, 13 Nov. 1806, Holland House Papers, BL Add. Mss. 51560, ff. 89-90; Samuel Whitbread to Lord Holland, Holland House Papers, BL Add. Mss. 51576, f.9.

31 James Walvin, 'The Public Campaign in England against Slavery, 1787-1834', in David Eltis and James Walvin (eds), *The Abolition of the Atlantic Slave Trade. Origins and effects in Europe, Africa and the Americas*, Madison, Wis., 1981, pp.63-79; Seymour Drescher, 'Public Opinion and the Destruction of British Slavery', in Walvin (ed.), *Slavery*, op. cit., pp.22-48; Seymour Drescher, *Capitalism and Antislavery. British mobilization in comparative perspective*, London and Basingstoke, 1986, pp.143-7; Betty Fladeland, *Abolitionists and Working-Class Problems in the Age of Industrialization*, London and Basingstoke, 1984; Robert Gray, 'The Languages of Factory Reform in Britain, c.1830-1860', in Patrick Joyce (ed.), *The Historical Meanings of Work*, Cambridge, 1987, p.148.

32 Drescher, op. cit., pp.147-50; Betty Fladeland, ' "Our Cause Being One and the Same": Abolitionists and Chartism', in Walvin (ed.), *Slavery*, op. cit., pp.69-99.

33 Royden Harrison, *Before the Socialists: Studies in Labour and Politics 1861-1881*, London, 1965, pp.59-60; Neville Kirk, 'In Defence of Class. A Critique of Recent Revisionist Writing upon the Nineteenth Century English Working Class', *International Review of Social History*, XXXII, 1, 1987, pp.19-23; Fladeland, 'Abolitionists and Chartism', op. cit., pp.85-8.

34 Samuel Hoare to T.F. Buxton, 9-13 Jan. 1840, Buxton Papers, B. Emp. Mss. 5444, vol.19, pp.101 a-d, RH; Katherine Fry to Louisa Pelly, 19 Nov. 1840; Rev. Frances Cunningham to Rev. Robt. E. Hankinson, 19 Nov. 1840; Priscilla Johnston to Anna Gurney, 19 Nov. 1840; Edward Buxton to T.F. Buxton, 21 Nov. 1840, Buxton Papers, vol. 20, pp.37-45 a-h, RH.

35 Royden Harrison, op. cit., pp.58-9; Fladeland, 'Abolitionists and Chartism', op. cit., pp.81-2; L.C. Wright, *Scottish Chartism*, Edinburgh, 1953, p.78; Obadiah Hulme, *An Historical Essay on the English Constitution* (1771), pp.141ff., in H.T. Dickinson, *Liberty and Property. Political ideology in eighteenth century Britain*, London, 1977, p.222; Richard Price, *A Discourse on the Love of Our Country*, London, 1789, pp.40-1; *Manifesto of the London Democratic Association* (1838), in Gareth Stedman Jones, *Languages of Class. Studies in English working class history 1832-1982*, Cambridge, 1983, p.108.

36 Drescher, 'Public Opinion', op. cit., pp.37-40; E.N. Buxton (ed.), *Memoirs*

of Sir Thomas Fowell Buxton Bt., London, 1849, p.445; J.J. Gurney to T.F. Buxton, 18–23 Oct. 1837, Buxton Papers, vol. 16, pp.188–93; J.J. Gurney to John Henry and Anna Gurney, 23 Nov. 1837, Buxton Papers, vol. 17, pp.13–15, RH; D. Fraser, 'Edward Baines', in Patricia Hollis (ed.), *Pressure from Without in Early Victorian England*, London, 1974, pp.203–5; David Martin, 'Land Reform', in ibid., pp.145–6.

37 Editorial in *Liberator*, 23 Oct. 1840; David Turley, 'Moral Suasion, Community Action and the Problem of Power; Reflections on American Abolitionists and Government, 1830–1861', in Rhodri Jeffreys and Bruce Collins (eds), *The Growth of Federal Power in American History*, Edinburgh, 1983, esp. p.30; E. Pease to J.A. Collins, 12 May [1841]; E. Pease to Anne Warren Weston, 30 Dec. 1841, in Clare Taylor (ed.), *British and American Abolitionists. An episode in transatlantic understanding*, Edinburgh, 1974, pp.151, 159; Betty Fladeland, *Abolitionists and Working-Class Problems*, op. cit., chs 6 and 7; E. Pease to Wendell and Ann Phillips, 29 Sept./2 Oct. 1842, in Clare Taylor (ed.), op. cit., pp.183–4.

38 Lucretia Mott to E. Pease, 18 Feb. 1841, Garrison Family Papers, box 54, folder 1562, Sophia Smith Collection, Smith College, Northampton, Mass.; E. Pease to Wendell and Ann Phillips, 16 Aug. 1842; E. Pease to Wendell Philips, 31 Jan. 1843; R.D. Webb to Maria Weston Chapman, 2 Feb. 1843, in Clare Taylor (ed.), op. cit., pp.180–1, 185–7.

39 Carlos Flick, *The Birmingham Political Union and the Movements for Reform in Britain 1830–1839*, Hamden, Conn. and Folkestone, 1978, pp.45ff, 95–6; Clive Behagg, 'An Alliance with the Middle Class: the Birmingham Political Union and Early Chartism', in James Epstein and Dorothy Thompson (eds), *The Chartist Experience: Studies in Working Class Radicalism and Culture, 1830–60*, London and Basingstoke, 1982, pp.60–1, 67.

40 Behagg, op. cit., pp.61–73, 75, 79; Kirk, op. cit., pp.33–4.

41 Flick, op. cit., pp.75–6, 102, 112; *Reformer*, I, 4, 7 May; I, 5, 14 May; I, 7, 28 May 1835; *Philanthropist*, II, 93, 19 Jan. 1837; Alex Tyrrell, *Joseph Sturge and the Moral Radical Party in Early Victorian Britain*, London, 1987, p.44. The whole of Tyrrell's admirable study is valuable for a study of currents of reform in Birmingham.

42 *Reformer*, I, 9, 11 June 1835; *Philanthropist*, I, 31, 12 Nov. 1835; I, 43, 4 Feb. 1836; *Reformer* I, 1, 16 April 1835; *Philanthropist* II, 89, 22 Dec. 1836; II, 141, 21 Dec. 1837.

43 *Philanthropist*, II, 146, 25 Jan. 1838; Dorothy Thompson, *The Chartists. Popular Politics in the Industrial Revolution*, Aldershot, 1986, pp. 262–3; Tyrrell, op. cit., pp. 119–21.

44 Thompson, op. cit., pp.259–61; Alex Tyrrell, 'Personality in Politics. The National Complete Suffrage Union and Pressure Group Politics in Early Victorian Britain', *Journal of Religious History*, 12, 4, Dec. 1983, p.390; *Report of the Proceedings at the Conference of Delegates of the Middle and Working Classes held at Birmingham, April 5 1842 and three following days*, London, 1842, pp.2–3.

45 Fladeland, 'Abolitionists and Chartism', op.cit., pp.82–4; Thompson, op. cit., pp.263–4; Alex Wilson, 'The Suffrage Movement', in Hollis (ed.), op.

cit., pp.82–5; *Minutes of the Proceedings at the Conference of Representatives of the Middle and Working Classes of Great Britain*, Birmingham, 1842, pp.8–9, 10–12, 23–4; *Report . . . Conference*, op. cit., pp.23, 24–5, 27, 55–9, 45–6, 48, 52.

46 Wilson, op. cit., pp.86–93; *The Question, What Good Will the Charter Do? Answered by the Birmingham Christian Chartist Church*, Birmingham, n.d. [1842], unpaged; Tyrrell, *Sturge*, op. cit., pp.128–9; Leonore Davidoff and Catherine Hall, *Family Fortunes. Men and Women of the English Middle Class, 1780–1850*, London, 1987, pp.92–5; Thompson, op. cit., pp.266–9; *The Suffrage. An Appeal to the Middle Classes by one of themselves. Tracts of the National Complete Suffrage Union No.2*, 3rd edn, London, 1843, pp.3–12.

47 Behagg, op. cit., pp.81–2; *National Association Gazette*, 19 Feb. 1842, quoted in Thompson, op. cit., p.264.

7 THE ANGLO-AMERICAN CONNECTION

1 George Thompson to George W. Benson, 7 Oct. 1834, Garrison Papers, BPL; Philip Foner (ed.), *The Life and Writings of Frederick Douglass*, 4 vols, New York, 1950–5, vol. 1, pp.236–8.

2 Elizur Wright to Beriah Green, 19 March 1835, Elizur Wright Papers, Library of Congress (LC).

3 Prince Hoare, *Memoirs of Granville Sharp Esq. composed from his own manuscripts*, 2 vols, 2nd edn, London, 1828 vol. 1, pp.146–50, 168–72; John A. Woods (ed.),'The Correspondence of Benjamin Rush and Granville Sharp, 1773–1809', *Journal of American Studies (JAS)*, 1, 1, 1967, pp.1–38; David M. Turley, 'Relations between British and American Abolitionists from British Emancipation to the American Civil War', unpub. Ph.D thesis, University of Cambridge, 1969, ch. 1; *Emancipator*, 8 Sept., 27 Oct. 1836.

4 William Smeal to Elizur Wright, 22 July 1837, Elizur Wright Papers, LC; *Report of 23rd National Anti-Slavery Bazaar, 1856–57*, Boston, 1857, pp.8–9; Douglas Charles Stange, *British Unitarians against American Slavery*, Rutherford, NJ and London, 1984, pp.86, 154; Turley, op. cit., p.35; Foner, op. cit., vol 1, pp.278–9; Julia Griffiths to Lewis Tappan, 8 Aug., 3 Sept. 1857, Lewis Tappan Papers, LC; Benjamin Quarles, 'Sources of Abolitionist Income', *MVHR*, XXII, 1, June 1945, pp.63–76.

5 Michael Kraus, *The Atlantic Civilization: Eighteenth Century Origins*, Ithaca, NY, 1949, pp.148–58; Hoare, op. cit., vol. 2, pp.125–30; Thomas Clarkson, *The History of the Abolition of the Slave Trade*, 2 vols, London, 1808, 1968 edn, vol. I, pp.444, 461; Circular, 9 April 1808, Pennsylvania Abolition Society (PAS) Committee of Correspondence, Letterbook 1794–1809, pp.100–1 Am. S081, Historical Society of Pennsylvania (HSP), Philadelphia; PAS Minute Book, 1800–24, 15 March 1813, p.184, HSP; Zachary Macaulay to Benjamin Rush, July 1809, Holland House Papers, BL Add. Mss. 51820, ff.53–6; *Fourth Report of African Institution, 1810*, London 1814, pp.10–12; *Sixth Report of African Institution, 1812*,

London, 1812, pp.8–9; PAS Minute Book, 1800–24, 12 Jan. 1816, pp.234–5, HSP.

6 David Brion Davis, *The Problem of Slavery in the Age of Revolution, 1770–1823*, Ithaca, NY and London, 1975, pp.234ff.; Kraus, op. cit., pp. 144–5; Minute Book of the Slave Trade Committee of the Meeting for Sufferings, 25 Feb. 1785, pp.26–8, L051.66, Friends' House Library, London; Clarkson, op. cit., vol I pp.196–202; Clare Taylor (ed.), *British and American Abolitionists: an episode in transatlantic understanding*, Edinburgh, 1974. pp.21–2; David E. Swift, *Joseph John Gurney. Banker, Reformer and Quaker*, Middletown, Conn., 1962, pp.199ff.; Lewis Tappan to Joseph Sturge, 12 Sept., 13 Sept. 1845, Lewis Tappan Papers, LC; Henry Richard, *Memoirs of Joseph Sturge*, London, 1864, pp.230–1.

7 Richard Carwardine, *Transatlantic Revivalism: popular evangelicalism in Britain and America, 1790–1865*, Westport, Conn. and London, 1978, pp. 59, 63–4, 66–8, 103ff.; *Emancipator*, 18 Aug. 1836; Thomas F. Harwood, 'British Evangelical Abolitionism and American Churches in 1830s', *Journal of Southern History*, XXVIII, 3, Aug. 1962, pp.287–306.

8 Stange, op. cit., esp. pp.14, 48, 54, 58–9.

9 Richard, op. cit.; G.D.H. Cole, *Chartist Portraits*, London, 1965 edn, pp.164, 167–9; Anne H. Abel and Frank J. Klingberg (eds), *A Side-Light on Anglo-American Relations, 1839–1858 furnished by the Correspondence of Lewis Tappan and Others with the British and Foreign Anti-Slavery Society*, Lancaster, Pa., 1927.

10 George Thompson to William Lloyd Garrison, 22 Oct. 1835, Garrison Papers, BPL; George Thompson's Anti-Slavery Scrapbook, vol. III, Raymond English Deposit, John Rylands University Library, Manchester.

11 C. Duncan Rice, 'The Anti-Slavery Mission of George Thompson to the United States, 1834–1835', *JAS*, II, 2, 1968, pp.13–31; Lewis Tappan, Journal, 2 June 1837, 7 Aug. 1839, Lewis Tappan Papers, LC; Henry B. Stanton to [Amos A. Phelps], [Aug.] 1839, Phelps Papers, BPL; Henry B. Stanton to J. H. Tredgold, 23 Aug. 1839, B. Emp. Mss. S18 C10/68a, RH; *Emancipator*, 12 July 1838.

12 John A. Woods, op. cit., p.10; Elizur Wright to Beriah Green, 19 March 1835, Elizur Wright Papers, LC.

13 *Proceedings of the General Anti-Slavery Convention . . . 1840*, London, 1841; *Proceedings of the Convention . . . 1843*, London, 1843, pp.120ff., 14.

14 Anne Cropper to the Boston Female Anti-Slavery Society, 4 April 1837, in M.W. Chapman (ed.), *Right and Wrong in Boston*, Boston, 1837, pp.104–6; Harriet Martineau, *The Martyr Age of the United States of America*, Newcastle-upon-Tyne, 1840, p.2; *Proceedings . . . 1840*, p.126; *Proceedings . . . 1843*, pp.115–16; Beriah Green to Amos A. Phelps, 3 Nov. 1843, Phelps Papers, BPL; Lewis Tappan to Joseph Sturge, 31 March 1846, Lewis Tappan Papers, LC; *Anti-Slavery Advocate* 2, 13,17, Jan., May 1858.

15 Gilbert H. Barnes, *The Anti-Slavery Impulse*, Gloucester, Mass., 1957 edn, pp.36–7; *African Repository*, IX, 7, Sept. 1833, p.222.

16 James Cropper, *Letter to Thomas Clarkson*, Liverpool, 1832; Charles Stuart, *Prejudice Vincible*, n.p., 1832; Joseph Phillips to William Lloyd Garrison, 6 June 1832, Garrison Papers, BPL; *Abolitionist*, I, 6, June 1833

(Buxton letter to WLG, 12 Nov. 1832); I, 1, Jan. 1833; William Wilberforce to Thomas Clarkson, 10 Oct. 1831, Clarkson Papers, BL Add. Mss. 41267A, ff.142–3; William Wilberforce to Thomas Clarkson, 19 Jan. 1833, Ms. Eng. 183 (35), BPL; *African Repository*, VIII, 9, Nov. 1832.

17 *Proceedings . . . 1840*, p.490; Thomas Clarkson to Francis Scott Key, 18 March 1817, CN58 Clarkson–Hunt.; R.D. Alexander to William Manley, 4 Oct. 1831, Temp. Mss. 10/22, Friends' House Library; Thomas Clarkson to Crisp, 24 Oct. 1833, CN76 Clarkson–Hunt.

18 *African Repository*, IX, 7, Sept. 1833; John L. Thomas, *The Liberator. William Lloyd Garrison. A Biography*, Boston, 1963, pp.159–61; *Abolitionist*, 1, 10, Oct. 1833; Scoble, 29/30 Sept. 1840, in Abel and Klingberg (eds), op. cit., p.73 note 37; *Proceedings . . . 1840*, pp.244–5; James G. Birney to Lewis Tappan, 3 Sept. 1840, in Dwight L. Dumond, (ed.) *The Letters of James G. Birney, 1831–1857*, 2 vols, New York, 1938, vol. II, pp.597–9; Thomas Clarkson to William Lloyd Garrison, Sept. 1840, B. Eng. Mss. S18 c 107/108, RH.

19 Glasgow Emancipation Society (GES), Minute Book, pp.245–7, 257, 259, 268–9, 285–8; Henry C. Wright, *American Slavery Proved to be Theft and Robbery*, Edinburgh, 1845; *An Address to the Office - Bearers and Members of the Free Church of Scotland . . . from the committee of the Free Church Anti-Slavery Society*, Edinburgh, 1847; BFASS, Minute Book II, pp.407, 419, 504–5, 511, B. Emp. Mss. S.18, E2/7, RH; BFASS, Petitions and Addresses, II, pp.311–26, B. Emp. Mss. S18 E2/19, RH; G.A. Shepperson, 'The Free Church of Scotland and American Slavery', *Scottish Historical Review*, XXX, 1951, pp.126–43; Shepperson, 'Frederick Douglass and Scotland', *Journal of Negro History*, XXXVIII, 1953, pp.307–21.

20 BFASS, Memorials and Petitions, 1843–1853, pp.307–10, B. Emp. Mss. S18 E2/19, RH; Lewis Tappan to John Scoble, 1 Feb. 1847, in Abel and Klingberg (eds), op. cit., p.213 note 176; W.P. Garrison and F.J. Garrison, *William Lloyd Garrison: The Story of His Life as Told by His Children*, 4 vols, New York, 1885–9, vol. III, pp.164–8, 173ff.; William Lloyd Garrison to Edmund Quincy, 18 Sept. 1846, Garrison Family Papers, Sophia Smith Collection, box 1, folder 17, Smith College, Northampton, Mass.; GES, *12th Annual Report, 1847*, Glasgow, 1847, pp.8–9; GES Minute Book, 28 Oct. 1846, p.293, William Smeal Collection, Mitchell Library, Glasgow; J.F. Maclear, 'The Evangelical Alliance and the Antislavery Crusade', *Huntington Library Quarterly*, XVII, 2, 1978–9, pp.141–64.

21 A fuller diplomatic context for Texas as an Anglo-American antislavery issue as well as detailed references for the narrative on Texas are in Turley, op. cit., chs 2 and 3.

22 David M. Turley, ' "Free air" and Fugitive Slaves: British abolitionists versus government over American fugitives, 1834–61', in Christine Bolt and Seymour Drescher (eds), *Antislavery, Religion and Reform : essays in memory of Roger Anstey*, Folkestone, 1980, pp.163–82.

23 David Turley, 'Moral Suasion, Community Action and the Problem of Power: Reflections on American Abolitionists and Government, 1830–

1861', in Rhodri Jeffreys-Jones and Bruce Collins (eds), *The Growth of Federal Power in American History*, Edinburgh, 1983, esp. pp.28-9.

24 Louis Billington, 'Some Contrasts between British and American Reform Movements 1830-1860. With special reference to the Anti-Slavery Movement', unpub. M.A. Thesis, Bristol University, 1966, pp.121, 132-4; *British and Foreign Anti-Slavery Reporter* (BFASR), 15, 15 July 1840.

25 David M. Turley, 'Relations between British and American Abolitionists' op. cit., ch. 6, esp. pp.291-320; C. Duncan Rice, *The Scots Abolitionists 1833-1861*, Baton Rouge, La. and London, 1981.

26 Bristol and Clifton Ladies' Anti-Slavery Society, Minute Book, 27 Oct. 1841, Estlin Papers, Dr Williams' Library, Gordon Square, London; John Scoble to Amos A. Phelps, 16 May 1843, Phelps Papers, BPL; Lewis Tappan to Joseph Sturge, 26 Feb. 1845, Lewis Tappan Papers, LC; Thomas Clarkson to Lady Bunbury [1840-1], Clarkson Papers 18E, Duke; Gerrit Smith to Thomas Clarkson, 2 Nov. 1840, 3998, reel 21, pages 155-6, Gerrit Smith Papers, Syracuse University; Thomas Clarkson to Gerrit Smith, 20 Feb. 1844, 3998, reel 4, Gerrit Smith Papers; Thomas Clarkson to ?, 1 Sept. 1844, Anti-Slavery Papers, William L. Clements Library, Ann Arbor, Michigan; Lewis Tappan to Thomas Clarkson, 14 Sept. 1844, Clarkson Papers, Moorland-Springarn Collection, Howard University; Maria Weston Chapman to Clarkson, 1 Oct. 1844, CN44, Clarkson-Hunt.; Henry C. Wright to Clarkson, 2 Sept. 1845, CN193, Clarkson-Hunt.; 'Hints in case no union with Slave-holders should be resolved upon by the People', Clarkson Papers, VIII, BL Add. Mss. 41267A, ff.319-23; Abel and Klingberg (eds), op. cit., p.211 note 171.

27 Stange, op. cit., pp.58-60; GES, Minute Book, 2 Aug. 1844, 1 Aug.1845, pp.264, 275-7, Smeal Collection, Mitchell Library, Glasgow; Garrison to R.D. Webb, 1 Mar.1845, Garrison Papers, BPL; Billington, op. cit., pp.128-30; Samuel May Jr to George Armstrong, 9 Oct. 1843, George Armstrong to Samuel May Jr, 30 Oct. 1843, William James to Maria Weston Chapman, 1 Nov. 1843, in Clare Taylor (ed.), op. cit., pp.198, 203-5.

28 R.D. Webb to Sarah Poole, 30 Aug. 1840, Garrison Papers, BPL; Webb to ?, 8 July 1849, Webb to Maria Weston Chapman, 26 Feb. 1846, in Clare Taylor (ed.), op. cit., pp.338, 253-4; George Thompson's diary, 1846, 10-11 Aug., Raymond English Deposit, John Rylands University Library, Manchester: J.B. Estlin to Samuel May Jr, 1 Sept. 1846, Garrison to Samuel J. May, 19 Dec. 1846, in Clare Taylor (ed.), op. cit., pp.281, 304.

29 R.D. Webb to E. Pease, 4 Nov. 1840, E. Pease to John A. Collins, 17 Dec. 1840, Garrison to E. Pease, 1 June 1841, Garrison to E. Pease, 20 June 1849, Garrison Papers, BPL; J.B. Estlin to Marian Weston Chapman, 28 Feb. 1846, Estlin to Samuel May Jr, 1 Oct. 1846, in Clare Taylor (ed.), op. cit., pp.256-7, 291-2.

30 Billington, op. cit., pp.222-7, 305-13; *20th Annual Report of the Massachusetts Anti-Slavery Society*, Boston, 1852, pp.48-50; Stange, op. cit., pp.125-8.

31 Bristol and Clifton Ladies' Anti-Slavery Society, Minute Book, 1, 16, 18 Sept., 8 Oct., 13 Nov. 1851, 19 Feb. 1852; *Anti-Slavery Cause*, Glasgow, May 1850; *London Anti-Slavery Conference . . . held at the London*

NOTES

Tavern on 29 & 30 November 1854, London, n.d.; F.W. Chesson, diary, 30 Nov. 1854, Raymond English Deposit, John Rylands University Library, Manchester.

32 *Anti-Slavery Advocate*, 2, 40, April 1860; Foner (ed.), op. cit., vol. 2, pp.467–80.

33 *Anti-Slavery Advocate*, 2, 50, Feb. 1861; BFASS, Minute Book IV, 25 Jan., 5 April, 15 April 1861, B. Emp. Mss. S18, E2/9, RH. For some opposition to recognition of the Confederacy, GES, Minute Book, 29 April 1861, Smeal Collection, Mitchell Library, Glasgow.

8 CONCLUSIONS

1 David Brion Davis, *The Problem of Slavery in the Age of Revolution, 1770–1823*, Ithaca, NY and London, 1975; Seymour Drescher, *Capitalism and Antislavery: British Mobilization in Comparative Perspective*, London, 1986 contain the most effective arguments of the two positions.

2 See various essays in Jane Rendall (ed.), *Equal or Different. Women's Politics 1800–1914*, Oxford, 1987; Susan Mendus and Jane Rendall (eds), *Sexuality and Subordination*, London, 1989; Kenneth Corfield, 'Elizabeth Heyrick: Radical Quaker', in Gail Malmgreen (ed.), *Religion in the Lives of English Women 1760–1930*, London, 1986, pp.41–67. But the admirably full standard work on women abolitionists is now Clare Midgley, 'Women Anti-Slavery Compaigners in Britain, 1787–1868', unpub. Ph.D thesis, University of Kent, Canterbury, 1989. On black abolitionists and British antislavery, for context see Christine Bolt, *Victorian Attitudes to Race*, London, 1971. See the significance of the black American abolitionist connection in R.J.M. Blackett, *Building an Antislavery Wall: Black Americans in the Atlantic Abolitionist Movement*, Baton Rouge, La. and London, 1983; C. Peter Ripley (ed.), *The Black Abolitionist Papers, vol.1, The British Isles, 1830–1865*, Chapel Hill, NC, 1985.

3 Thomas Haskell, 'Capitalism and the Origins of the Humanitarian Sensibility. Part I', *American Historical Review (AHR)*, 90, 1, 1985, pp.339–61; Part 2, *AHR*, 90, 2, 1985, pp.457–566.

4 For the issues and flavour of the long-running debate on the character of social development in Britain see Perry Anderson, 'Origins of the Present Crisis', *New Left Review (NLR)*, 23, 1964; Anderson, 'The Figures of Descent', *NLR*, 161, 1987; Geoff Eley, 'Rethinking the Political: Social History and Political Culture in 18th and 19th Century Britain', *Archiv für Sozialgeschichte*, XXI, 1981, pp.427–57; Geoffrey Ingham, *Capitalism Divided? The city and industry in British social development*, Basingstoke, 1984; J.C.D. Clark, *English Society 1688–1832. Ideology, social structure and political practice during the ancien régime*, Cambridge, 1985; E.P. Thompson, 'The Peculiarities of the English', in R. Miliband and J. Saville (eds), *The Socialist Register*, 2, London,2 1965; David Nicholls, 'Fractions of Capital: the aristocracy, the City and industry in the development of modern British capitalism', *Social History*, 13, 1, Jan. 1988; Barrington Moore, *The Social Origins of Dictatorship and Democracy*, Harmondsworth, 1967, ch. 4. The terms of the discussion on ideological

hegemony in relation to abolitionism may be gathered from David Brion Davis, 'Reflections on Abolitionism and Ideological Hegemony', *AHR*, 92, 4, 1987, pp.797-812; Davis, 'Capitalism, Abolitionism and Hegemony', in B. Solow and S. Engerman (eds), *British Capitalism and Caribbean Slavery*, Cambridge, 1987, pp.209-27; John Ashworth, 'The Relationship between Capitalism and Humanitarianism', *AHR*, 92, 4, 1987, pp.813-28; Thomas L. Haskell, 'Convention and Hegemonic Interest in the Debate over Antislavery: A Reply to Davis and Ashworth', *AHR*, 92, 4, 1987, pp.829-78.

5 For clarification on this last section I am indebted to discussion with my friend and colleague, Hugh Cunningham.

BIBLIOGRAPHY

Place of publication London unless otherwise indicated.

MANUSCRIPT SOURCES

Alderman Library, University of Virginia, Charlottesville, Va.
  British Antislavery Movement Papers, 1821–87
Arnett Library, Atlanta University, Atlanta, Ga.
  Clarkson Papers
Birmingham Central Library, Archives Dept
  Birmingham Anti-Slavery Society: minute books Ladies' Society for the
  Relief of Negro Slaves: minute book, cash book, album, ledger
Boston Public Library, Boston, Mass.
  Garrison Papers
  Samuel May Jr Papers
  Ms. Eng. 183
  Phelps Papers
  Weston Family Papers
British Library, Students' Room
  Aberdeen Papers, Add. Mss. 43123, 43126, 43154, 43155
  Clarkson Family Papers, Add. Mss. 41262–7
  Cobden Papers, Add. Mss. 43656
  Committee for the Abolition of the Slave Trade: minute books, 3 vols,
  1787–1819, Add. Mss. 21254–6
  Egerton Mss. 2190
  Holland House Papers, Add. Mss. 51573, 51576, 51592, 51650, 51820
  Liverpool Papers, Add. Mss. 38416
  Palmerston Papers, Add. Mss. 48495
  Peel Papers, Add. Mss. 40489, 40553, 40584
  Poole Papers, 1765–1837, Add. Mss. 35344
  Ramsay Papers, Add. Mss. 27621
  Stephen Papers: Memoirs, 2 vols, Add. Mss. 46443, 46444
  Sturge Papers, Add. Mss. 43722, 43723, 43845, 50131
Clements Library, University of Michigan, Ann Arbor, Michigan
  Anti-Slavery Papers

Lansdowne Papers
Friends' House Library, London
  Anti-Slavery Correspondence, 1821–32
  Clarkson's Abolition of the Slave Trade: Illustrations, 3 vols
  William Dickson: Diary of a Visit to Scotland 5 January–19 March 1792 on
  behalf of the Committee for the Abolition of the Slave Trade, Temp. Mss.
  box 10/14
  Meeting for Sufferings, Committee on the Slave Trade: Minutes, 1783–92
  Meeting for Sufferings, Standing Committee to aid in promoting total
  abolition of slavery: minutes, 1820–33
Henry E. Huntington Library, San Marino, Ca.
  Clarkson Papers
  Macaulay Papers
John Rylands University Library, Manchester
  Raymond English Deposit: George Thompson Papers
  Rawson Family Papers
Library of Congress, Washington DC
  Sharp Letters, Misc. Mss. 165
  Tappan Papers
  Wilberforce Papers, Misc. Mss. 197
  Wright Papers
Mitchell Library, Glasgow
  Smeal Collection: Glasgow Emancipation Society minute books, subscrip-
  tion book, cash books, misc. letters
Moorland-Springarn Research Center, Howard University, Washington DC
  Clarkson Correspondence
National Library of Scotland, Edinburgh
  Glen Memorial Collection: letters to Robert Southey, Mss. 2529
  Paul Papers, Mss. 5139
  Robertson–Macdonald Papers, Mss. 3943
  de Rothesay Papers, Mss. 6161, 6209, 6228
  Small Collections, Mss. 3925, ff.201–11
  Small Purchases, Mss. 5319
Perkins Library, Duke University, Durham, NC
  Clarkson Papers
  Fuller Letterpress Book, 1787–96
  Smith Papers
  Wilberforce Papers
  Wilder Scrap Book
Rhodes House Library, Oxford
  Anti-Slavery Society: minute books, correspondence
  British and Foreign Anti-Slavery Society: minute books, memorials and
  petitions, correspondence
  Buxton Papers
Sheffield Central Reference Library
  Sheffield Literary and Philosophical Society: James Montgomery Letters
  Wilson–Rawson Papers
Smith College Library, Northampton, Mass.
  Garrison Family Papers, Sophia Smith Collection

Syracuse University Library, Syracuse, NY
  Gerrit Smith Papers
Dr Williams' Library, London
  Bristol and Clifton Auxiliary Ladies' Anti-Slavery Society: minute book
  Estlin Papers

PRINTED SOURCES

Official

Parliamentary Debates (PD), new ser., 9, cols 263–360, 15 May, 1823
PD, 3rd ser., 3, cols 1408–69, 15 April 1831
PD, 3rd ser., 17, cols 1193–1262, 14 May 1833
Parliamentary History of England, xxix, cols1055–1158, 2 April 1792
Substance of the Debates on a resolution for abolishing the Slave Trade which was moved in the House of Commons 10 June 1806, and in the House of Lords, 24 June 1806, London, 1806

Letters, journals etc.

Abel, Annie H. and Klingberg, Frank J. (eds), *A Side-Light on Anglo-American Relations*, Lancaster, Pa., 1927
Barnes, Gilbert H. and Dumond, Dwight L. (eds), *Letters of Theodore Dwight Weld, Angeline Grimké and Sarah Grimké, 1822–1844*, 2 vols, Gloucester, Mass., 1965 (orig. edn, 1934)
Bevington, Merle (ed.), *The Memoirs of James Stephen*, 1954
Blassingame, John W. (ed.), *The Frederick Douglass Papers*, ser. 1, vols 1 and 3, New Haven, Conn., 1979, 1985
Brett, R.L. (ed.), *Barclay Fox's Journal*, 1979
Cropper, Anne (ed.), *Extracts from letters of the late James Cropper*, n.p., 1850
Dumond, Dwight L. (ed.), *Letters of James G. Birney, 1831–1857*, 2 vols, Gloucester, Mass., 1968 (orig. edn, 1938).
Fergusson, Charles Bruce (ed.), *John Clarkson's Mission to America, 1791–1792*, Halifax, Nova Scotia, 1971
Foner, Philip S. (ed.), *The Life and Writings of Frederick Douglass*, 4 vols, vols 1 and 2, New York, 1950
Griggs, E.L. and Prator, Clifford H. (eds), *Henry Christophe and Thomas Clarkson. A Correspondence*, Berkeley and Los Angeles, 1952
Parker, C.S. (ed.), *Sir Robert Peel from his private papers*, 3 vols, vol. 3, 1899
Pugh, Patricia M., *Calendar of the Papers of Sir Thomas Fowell Buxton 1786–1845*, List and Index Society, special ser., 13, n.p., 1980
Ripley, C. Peter (ed.), *The Black Abolitionist Papers, vol.1 The British Isles, 1830–1865*, Chapel Hill, NC, 1985
Folarion, Shyllon, 'Letters of a Black Abolitionist', appendix I in Shyllon, *Black People in Britain 1555–1833*, 1977
Taylor, Clare (ed.), *British and American Abolitionists: an episode in transatlantic understanding*, Edinburgh, 1974
Tolles, Frederick B. (ed.), *Slavery and the "Woman Question", Lucretia Motts's Diary of her visit to Great Britain to attend the World's Anti-*

Slavery Convention of 1840, Friends' Historical Society, *Journal, Supplement*, 33, 1952

West India Association, *The Correspondence between John Gladstone, Esq., M.P. and James Cropper, Esq., on the Present State of Slavery in the British West Indies and in the United States of America*, Liverpool, 1824.

Wilberforce, R. I. and S. (eds), *The Correspondence of William Wilberforce*, 2 vols, 1840

Woods, John A. (ed.), 'The Correspondence of Benjamin Rush and Granville Sharp 1773–1809', *Journal of American Studies* (JAS), 1, 1, April 1967, pp.1–37

Newspapers and periodicals

African Repository, Washington, 1833, 1840
Anti-Slavery Advocate, Dublin, 1852–62
Anti-Slavery Watchman, Manchester, 1853–4
British and Foreign Anti-Slavery Reporter, 1839–60
Christian Observer, 1802–12
Eclectic Review, 1842
Economist, 1843–6
Edinburgh Review, Edinburgh, 1838–1843
Emancipator, New York, 1836–9
Empire, 1853–6
Liberator, Boston, Mass., 1831–40
London and Westminster Review, 1838–43
Monthly Repository, 1806–12
Nonconformist, 1842
Philanthropist, 1811–19
Philanthropist, Birmingham, 1835–8
Reformer, Birmingham, 1835

Pamphlets, broadsheets, addresses

An Address from the Liverpool Society for the Abolition of Slavery on the safest and most efficacious means of promoting the gradual improvement of the Negro Slaves in the British West India islands, Liverpool, 1824

An Address to the Inhabitants in general of Great Britain and Ireland relating to a few of the Consequences which must naturally result from the Abolition of the Slave Trade, Liverpool and London, 1788

Agutter, William, *The Abolition of the Slave Trade considered in a religious point of view*, 1788

[Allen, William], *The Duty of abstaining from the use of West India Produce*, 1792

Anderson, James, *Observations on Slavery; particularly with a view to its effects on the British Colonies in the West Indies*, Manchester, 1789

Anon., *Reasons for preferring immediate to what is called gradual emancipation*, n.p., n.d. [1830?]

Anti-Slavery Cause, Glasgow, 1850

An Appeal to Englishwomen, n.p., n.d. [1862/3?]

Barbauld, Anna Letitia, *Epistle to William Wilberforce, Esq., on the Rejection of the Bill for abolishing the Slave Trade*, 1791

Bradburn, Samuel, *An Address to the People called Methodists; concerning the evil of encouraging the slave trade*, Manchester, 1792

Burgess, Dr (late Bishop of Salisbury), *Considerations on the Abolition of Slavery and the Slave Trade upon grounds of natural, religious and political duty*, 1789

The Case of our Fellow-Creatures, the Oppressed Africans, respectfully recommended to the Serious Consideration of the Legislature of Great-Britain by the People called Quakers, 1783

Chesson, F.W., *The Anti-Slavery Advocate and the London Conference*, 1855

[Clarkson, Thomas], *An Essay on the Slavery and Commerce of the Human Species, particularly the African*, 1786

[Clarkson, Thomas], *A Summary View of the Slave Trade and of the probable consequences of its Abolition*, 1787

Clarkson, Thomas, *The True State of the case respecting the Insurrection at St. Domingo*, Ipswich, 1792

Clarkson, Thomas, *The Argument that the colonial slaves are better off than the British Peasantry, answered from the Royal Jamaica Gazette of June 21, 1823*, Whitby, 1824

Clarkson, Thomas, *Strictures on a Life of William Wilberforce by the Rev. W. [should be R.I.] Wilberforce and the Rev. S. Wilberforce*, 1838

Committee of Leicester Auxiliary Anti-Slavery Society, *An Address to the Public on the State of Slavery in the West India Islands*, 1824

Conder, Josiah, *Wages or the Whip. An essay on the comparative cost and productiveness of free and slave labour*, 1833

Cooper, Thomas, *Letters on the Slave Trade*, Manchester, 1787

Cooper, Thomas, *Tracts Ethical, Theological and Political, vol.1*, Warrington, 1789

[Cooper, Thomas], *Considerations on the Slave Trade; and the consumption of West Indian Produce*, 1791

Cooper, Thomas, *A Reply to Mr. Burke's Invective against Mr. Cooper and Mr. Watt in the House of Commons on the 30th April 1792*, London and Manchester, 1792

Cropper, James, *Letters addressed to William Wilberforce M.P. recommending the encouragement of the cultivation of sugar in our dominions in the East Indies as the natural and certain means of effecting the total and general abolition of the slave trade*, Liverpool, 1822

Cropper, James, *A letter addressed to the Liverpool Society for promoting the Abolition of Slavery on the injurious effects of high prices of produce and the beneficial effect of low prices on the conditions of slaves*, Liverpool, 1823

Cropper, James, *Relief for West Indian Distress*, 1823

Dannett, Henry, *A Particular Examination of Mr. Harris's Scriptural Researches on the Licitness of the Slave Trade*, 1788

Dore, James, *A Sermon on the African Slave Trade*, 1788

Flower, Benjamin, *National Sins considered in two letters to the Rev. Thomas Robinson*, Cambridge, 1796

Frend, William, *Peace and Union recommended to the associated bodies of Republicans and Anti-Republicans*, St. Ives, 1793

Frend, William, *Patriotism; or the love of our country*, 1804

A Friend of Commerce and Humanity, *Thoughts on Civilisation and the gradual Abolition of Slavery in Africa and the West Indies*, 1789

G.C.P., *Reflections on the Slave Trade with remarks on the Policy of its Abolition. In a letter to a clergyman in the county of Suffolk*, Bury St. Edmunds, 1791

Granger, T.C., *Speech at a meeting of the inhabitants of the City of Durham on 26th of October 1830*, Durham, [1830]

Gurney, J.J., *Substance of a Speech*, 1824

Halley, Robert, *The Sinfulness of Colonial Slavery*, 1833

Harris, Rev. R., *Scriptural Researches on the Licitness of the Slave Trade*, Liverpool, 1788

Heyrick, Elizabeth, *Immediate not gradual abolition*, 1824

Hodgson, Adam, *A letter to M. Jean-Baptiste Say on the comparative expense of free and slave labour*, Liverpool, 1823

Hughes, Rev. W., *An Answer to the Rev. Mr. Harris's 'Scriptural Researches on the Licitness of the Slave Trade'*, 1788

Ivimey, Joseph, *The Utter Extinction of Slavery an Object of Scripture Prophecy*, 1832

Kennedy LLB, James, *An Address to the Inhabitants of Hull and its Neighbourhood on the formation of the Hull and East Riding Association for the Mitigation and Gradual Abolition of Slavery*, Hull, 1823

[Kerr, M.], *Reflections on the Present State of the Slaves in the British Plantations and the Slave Trade from Africa*, York, 1789

Ladies' Anti-Slavery Associations, n.p., [1828]

Letters on the necessity for the prompt extinction of British Colonial Slavery, London and Leicester, 1826

Lowe, John, *Liberty or Death*, Manchester, 1789

More, Hannah, *The Ploughman's Ditty: being an answer to that foolish question, What have the poor to lose ?*, 1803

Pease, Joseph, *On Slavery and its Remedy*, 1841

Peckard, Peter, *Justice and Mercy recommended, particularly with reference to the Slave Trade*, Cambridge, 1788

[Peckard, Peter], *Am I not a Man? And a Brother?*, Cambridge, 1788

Priestley, Joseph, *A Sermon on the Subject of the Slave Trade*, Birmingham, 1788

Pringle, Thomas (ed.), *The History of Mary Prince, a West Indian Slave, related by herself*, 1831

[Raikes, Richard], *Considerations on the alliance between Christianity & Commerce applied to the present state of this country*, 1806

[Ramsay, James], *An Inquiry into the Effects of Putting a Stop to the African Slave Trade and of granting Liberty to the Slaves in the British Sugar Colonies*, 1784

Ramsay, Rev. James, *Examination of the Rev. Mr. Harris's Scriptural Researches on the Licitness of the Slave Trade*, 1788

Roberts, Samuel, *A Cry from the Chimneys; or an integral part of the total abolition of slavery throughout the world*, 1837

270

Roberts, Samuel, *The Rev. Dr. Pye Smith and the New Poor Law*, 1839
Roberts, Samuel, *Autobiography and Select Remains*, 1849
Robinson, Henry Crabb, *Exposure of Misrepresentations continued in the preface to the Correspondence of William Wilberforce*, 1840
Robinson, Robert, *Slavery inconsistent with the Spirit of Christianity*, Cambridge, 1788
Roscoe, William, *A Scriptural Refutation of a Pamphlet lately published by the Rev. Raymund Harris*, 1788
Scoble, John, *British Guiana*, 1838
Scoble, John, *Texas: its claims to be recognised as an independent power by Great Britain: examined in a series of letters*, 1839
Sharp, Granville, *A Representation of the Injustice and Dangerous Tendency of Tolerating Slavery*, 1769
Sharp, Granville, *The Just Limitation of Slavery in the Laws of God*, 1776
Sharp, Granville, *The Law of Liberty*, 1776
Steele, Joshua, *The Mitigation of Slavery*, 1814
[Stephen, James], *The Crisis of the Sugar Colonies*, 1802
The Suffrage. An appeal to the middle classes by one of themselves, 1843
Supplement of Mr.Cooper's Letters on the Slave Trade, Warrington, 1788
The Question, What good will the Charter do? Answered by the Birmingham Christian Chartist Church, Birmingham [1842]
Thomson, Andrew, *Slavery not Sanctioned but Condemned by Christianity*, 1832
[Truth], *A very new Pamphlet indeed!*, 1792
Vindex [Paine, Thomas], *Old Truths and Established Facts, being an answer to a very new pamphlet indeed*, 1792
Wardlaw, Ralph, *The Jubilee*, Glasgow, 1834
Wesley, John, *Thoughts upon Slavery*, 1774
West, Francis A., *The Duty of British Christians in reference to Colonial Slavery*, Newcastle-upon-Tyne, 1830
Wilberforce, William, *Advice suggested by the State of the Times*, 1803
Wilberforce, William, *A Letter on the Abolition of the Slave Trade; addressed to the freeholders and other inhabitants of Yorkshire*, 1807
Williams, Helen Maria, *A poem on the Bill lately passed for regulating the Slave Trade*, 1788
Winn, T.S., *Emancipation; or practical advice to British slaveholders with suggestions for the general improvement of West Indian Affairs*, 1824
Winn, T.S., *A Speedy End to Slavery in our West India Colonies*, 1827

Contemporary works

Allen, William, *The Life of William Allen, with selections from his correspondence*, 3 vols, 1847
Bell, John Hyslop, *British Folk & British India Fifty years Ago: Joseph Pease and his contemporaries*, 1891
Biographical memoirs of the late Thomas Butterworth Bayley, Esq., F.R.S. of Hope Hall near Manchester, Manchester, 1802
Buxton, Charles (ed.), *Memoirs of Sir Thomas Fowell Buxton, Bart.*, 1849.
Complete List of the Members & Officers of the Manchester Literary and

Philosophical Society from its institution on February 28th 1781, to April 28th, 1896, Manchester, 1896

Crummell, Alexander, *The Man, the Hero, the Christian! A eulogy on the life and character of Thomas Clarkson*, New York, 1847

Foster, Joseph, *Pease of Darlington*, n.p., printed for private circulation, 1891

[Haydon, B.R.], *Description of Haydon's Picture of the Great Meeting of Delegates held at the Freemasons' Tavern, June 1840*, n.p. [1841]

Hoare, Prince, *Memoirs of Granville Sharp, Esq., composed from his own manuscripts*, 2 vols, 2nd edn, 1828

Holland, John and Everett, James, *Memoirs of the Life and Writings of James Montgomery*, 6 vols, vols 3–5, 1855, 1856

James, J.A., *The Sunday School Teacher's Guide*, Birmingham, 1816

Magee, W. (ed.), *Biographical Memoirs of the late Thomas Percival M.D., F.R.S. & c.*, Manchester, 1804

Percival, Thomas, *The Works, Literary, Moral and Philosophical*, 2 vols, 1807

Priestley, Joseph, *Lectures on History and General Policy*, Birmingham, 1788

Rawson, M.A. (ed.), *The Bow in the Cloud*, 1834

Rawson, M.A. (ed.), *Hymns for Anti-Slavery Prayer Meetings*, 1838

Richard, Henry, *Memoirs of Joseph Sturge*, 1864

Shaen, M.J. (ed.), *William Shaen. A brief sketch*, 1912

The Sheffield Directory and Guide, Sheffield, 1828

Stephen, Sir George, *Antislavery Recollections: in a series of letters addressed to Mrs Beecher Stowe*, 1854

Stephen, James, *Essays in Ecclesiastical Biography*, 2 vols, 1849

Tuke, Samuel, *Description of the Retreat* (1813), introduction by Richard Hunter and Ida Macalpine, 1964

Wilberforce, R.I. and S., *The Life of William Wilberforce*, 5 vols, 1838

Conference proceedings, reports of meetings, society reports, memoirs

African Institution, *Annual Reports*, 1807–27

Agency Committee, *Report*, 1832

Beverley Anti-Slavery Association, *Speeches delivered in the Town Hall of Beverley*, Beverley, 1824

BFASS, *First and Second Annual Reports*, 1840, 1841

BFASS, *Proceedings of the General Anti-Slavery Convention . . . held in London from June 12th to June 23rd 1840*, 1841

BFASS, *Proceedings of the Convention . . . held from June 13th to June 20th 1843*, 1843

BFASS, *The Slave Trade and its Remedy*, 1848

BFASS, *Address to Christians of all Denominations in the United Kingdom, and especially to Christian Ministers*, 1853

Dinner to Mr. F.W. Chesson at the National Liberal Club on Friday, July 16th, 1886, 1886

Emancipation Society, *List of Officers etc.*, 1862

Glasgow Emancipation Society (GES), *Annual Reports*, Glasgow, 1835–51

GES, *Resolutions and Memorials relative to the Sugar Duties*, Glasgow, 1844

BIBLIOGRAPHY

London Anti-Slavery Conference, *Papers read and Statements made on the principal Subjects*, n.d. [1854]

Manchester Society for the furtherance of the Gradual Abolition of Slavery, *Report*, Manchester, 1827

Minutes of the Proceedings of the Conference of Representatives of the middle and working classes of Great Britain, Birmingham, 1842

Newcastle-upon-Tyne Society for promoting the Gradual Abolition of Slavery, *Report*, Newcastle, 1825

Proceedings at a Public Meeting held at the Town Hall, Chester, Chester, [1823]

Proceedings of a Public Meeting, held in London, August 1, 1859 to commemorate the twenty-fifth anniversary of the abolition of British colonial slavery, 1859

Report of the Proceedings at the Conference of Delegates of the middle and working classes, held at Birmingham, April 5, 1842 and three following days, 1842

A Report of the Speeches at a County Meeting held at the Castle of Leicester on Friday January 20th 1826 on the subject of Colonial Slavery, Leicester, 1826

Sheffield Female Anti-Slavery Society, *The Negro's Friend or, the Sheffield Anti-Slavery Album*, Sheffield, 1826

Society established at Edinburgh for effecting the abolition of the African Slave Trade, *Two of the Petitions from Scotland*, Edinburgh, 1790

Society for the Extinction of the Slave Trade and for the Civilisation of Africa, *Proceedings of the first public meeting*, 1840

Society for the Mitigation and gradual Abolition of Slavery, *Report and Proceedings*, 1824

Society for the purpose of effecting the abolition of the Slave Trade, Manchester, 1788

Suffolk Auxiliary Society, *First Report*, Ipswich, 1825

Swansea and Neath Auxiliary Anti-Slavery Society, *First Annual Report*, Swansea, 1826

SELECTED SECONDARY WORKS

Books and articles

Annan, Noel, 'The Intellectual Aristocracy', in J.H. Plumb (ed.), *Studies in Social History. A tribute to G.M. Trevelyan*, 1955, pp.241–87

Anstey, Roger, 'A Re-interpretation of the Abolition of the British Slave Trade, 1806–1807', *English Historical Review, (EHR)*, lxxxvii, 343, 1972, pp.304-32

Anstey, Roger, *The Atlantic Slave Trade and British Abolition, 1760–1810*, 1975

Anstey, Roger, and Hair, P.E.H. (eds), *Liverpool, the African Slave Trade and Abolition: essays to illustrate current knowledge and research*, Historic Society of Lancs. and Cheshire (HSLC), Occasional Ser., 2, n.p., 1976

Ashworth, John, 'The Relationship between Capitalism and Humanitarianism', *American Historical Review (AHR)*, 92, 4, 1987, pp.813-28

Behagg, Clive, 'An Alliance with the Middle Class: the Birmingham Political Union and Early Chartism', in James Epstein and Dorothy Thompson (eds), *The Chartist Experience: Studies in Working-Class Radicalism and Culture 1830-1860*, 1982

Billington, Louis, 'British Humanitarians and American Cotton, 1840-1860', *Journal of American Studies (JAS)*, 11, 3, 1977, pp.313-34

Binfield, Clyde, *So Down to Prayers: studies in English nonconformity 1780-1920*, 1977

Blackburn, Robin, *The Overthrow of Colonial Slavery 1776-1848*, 1988

Bohstedt, John, *Riots and Community Politics in England and Wales 1790-1810*, Cambridge, Mass., 1983

Bolt, Christine and Drescher, Seymour (eds), *Anti-Slavery, Religion and Reform. Essays in memory of Roger Anstey*, Folkestone, 1980

Brent, Richard, *Liberal Anglican Politics. Whiggery, Religion and Reform, 1830-1841*, Oxford, 1987

Brewer, John, *Party Ideology and Popular Politics at the accession of George III*, Cambridge, 1976

Brown, Ford K., *Fathers of the Victorians. The Age of Wilberforce*, Cambridge, 1961

Burman, Sandra (ed.), *Fit Work for Women*, 1979

Burn, W.L., *Emancipation and Apprenticeship in the British West Indies*, 1937

Butler, Marilyn (ed.), *Burke, Paine, Godwin and the Revolution Controversy*, Cambridge, 1984

Butler, Marilyn, 'Romanticism in England', in Roy Porter and Mikuláš Teich (eds), *Romanticism in National Context*, Cambridge, 1988, pp.37-67

Butterfield, Herbert, *George III, Lord North and the People*, 1949

Cain, Peter, 'Capitalism, War and Internationalism in the thought of Richard Cobden', *British Journal of International Studies*, 5, 1979, pp.229-47

Cain, Peter, and Hopkins, A.G., 'The Political Economy of British Expansion Overseas, 1750-1914', *Ec. Hist. Rev.*, 2nd ser., xxxiii, 4, 1980, pp.463-90

Cain, P.J. and Hopkins, A.G., 'Gentlemanly Capitalism and British Expansion Overseas I The Old Colonial System, 1688-1850', *Ec. Hist. Rev.*, 2nd ser., xxxix, 4, 1986, pp.501-25

Claeys, Gregory, *Thomas Paine. Social and political thought*, 1989

Clark, J.C.D., *English Society 1688-1832. Ideology, social structure and political practice during the ancien régime*, Cambridge, 1985

Cole, G.D.H., *Chartist Portraits*, 1941

Colley, Linda, 'The Apotheosis of George III: Loyalty, royalty and the British nation 1760-1820', *Past and Present*, 102, 1984, pp.94-129

Colley, Linda, 'Whose Nation? Class and national consciousness in Britain, 1750-1830', *Past and Present*, 113, 1986, pp.97-117

Cookson, J.E., *The Friends of Peace. Anti-war Liberalism in England 1793-1815*, Cambridge, 1982

Coupland, Sir Reginald, *Wilberforce: A narrative*, Oxford, 1923

Coupland, Sir Reginald, *The British Anti-Slavery Movement*, 1933

Cowherd, Raymond G., *The Politics of English Dissent. The religious aspects of liberal and humanitarian reform movements from 1815 to 1848*, 1959

Crafts, N.F.R., 'British Economic Growth, 1700–1831: A review of the evidence', *Ec. Hist. Rev.*, 2nd ser., xxxvi, 2, 1983, pp.177–99

Cunningham, A.B., 'Peel, Aberdeen and the Entente Cordiale', *Bulletin of Institute of Historical Research*, xxx, 1957, pp.189–206

Davidoff, Leonore and Hall, Catherine, *Family Fortunes. Men and women of the English middle class, 1780–1850*, 1987

Davis, David Brion, 'The Emergence of Immediatism in British and American Antislavery Thought', *Mississippi Valley Historical Review (MVHR)*, xlix, 2, 1962, pp.209–30

Davis, David Brion, *The Problem of Slavery in Western Culture*, Ithaca, NY, 1966

Davis, David Brion, *The Problem of Slavery in the Age of Revolution, 1770–1823*, Ithaca, NY and London, 1975

Davis, David Brion, *Slavery and Human Progress*, New York, 1984

Davis, David Brion, *From Homicide to Slavery: studies in American culture*, New York, 1986

Davis, David Brion, 'Reflections on Abolitionism and Ideological Hegemony', *AHR*, 92, 4, 1987, pp.797–812

Davis, Ralph, *The Industrial Revolution and British Overseas Trade*, Leicester, 1979

Davis, Richard W., *Dissent in Politics 1780–1830. The political life of William Smith M.P.*, 1971

Dickinson, H.T., *Liberty and Property. Political Ideology in Eighteenth-Century Britain*, 1977

Dickinson, H.T., *British Radicalism and the French Revolution, 1789–1815*, Oxford, 1985

Digby, Anne, *Madness, Morality and Medicine. A study of the York Retreat, 1796–1914*, Cambridge, 1985

Drescher, Seymour, *Econocide. British slavery in the era of abolition*, Pittsburgh, 1977

Drescher, Seymour, 'Cart Whip and Billy Roller: Antislavery and reform symbolism in industrialising Britain', *Journal of Social History*, 15, 1981, pp.3–24

Drescher, Seymour, *Capitalism and Antislavery. British mobilization in comparative perspective*, 1986

Eley, Geoff, 'Rethinking the Political: Social history and political culture in 18th and 19th century Britain', *Archiv für Sozialgeschichte*, xxi, 1981, pp.427–57

Elliott, C.M., 'The Political Economy of English Dissent 1780–1840', in R.M. Hartwell (ed.), *The Industrial Revolution*, 1970

Eltis, David, *Economic Growth and the Ending of the Transatlantic Slave Trade*, New York and Oxford, 1987

Eltis, David and Walvin, James (eds), *The Abolition of the Atlantic Slave Trade. Origins and effects in Europe, Africa and the Americas*, Madison, Wis., 1981

Emsley, Clive, *British Society and the French Wars, 1793–1815*, 1979

Feather, John, *A History of British Publishing*, 1988

Fladeland, Betty, 'Abolitionist Pressure on the Concert of Europe, 1814-1822', *Journal of Modern History (JMH)*, 38, 4, 1966, pp.355-73

Fladeland, Betty, *Abolitionists and Working-Class Problems in the Age of Industrialization*, London and Basingstoke, 1984

Flick, Carlos, *The Birmingham Political Union and the Movements for Reform in Britain 1830-1839*, Hamden, Conn. and Folkestone, 1978

Fraser, Peter, 'Public Petitioning and Parliament before 1832', *History*, xvlvi, 1961, pp.195-211

Fulford, Roger, *Samuel Whitbread*, 1967

Furneaux, Robin, *William Wilberforce*, 1974

Gascoigne, John, 'Anglican Latitudinarianism and Political Radicalism in the Late Eighteenth Century', *History*, 71, 231, 1986, pp.22-38

Gatrell, V.A.C., 'Incorporation and the pursuit of Liberal hegemony in Manchester 1790-1839', in Derek Fraser (ed.), *Municipal Reform and the Industrial City*, Leicester, 1982

Gilbert, Alan D., *Religion and Society in Industrial England. Church, chapel and social change, 1740-1914*, 1976

Goodwin, Albert, *The Friends of Liberty. The English democratic movement in the age of the French Revolution*, 1979

Gray, Robert, 'The Languages of Factory Reform in Britain, c.1830-1860', in Patrick Joyce (ed.), *The Historical Meanings of Work*, Cambridge, 1987, pp.143-79

Griffin, Clifford S., 'Religious Benevolence as Social Control 1815-1860', *MVHR*, xliv, 3, 1957, pp.423-44

Griggs, Earl Leslie, *Thomas Clarkson, the Friend of the Slaves*, 1936

Hall, Basil, 'Allessandro Gavazzi: a Barnabite friar and the Risorgimento', in Derek Baker (ed.), *Church, Society and Politics*, Oxford, 1975, pp.303-56

Hall, Douglas, *A Brief History of the West India Committee*, Barbados, 1971

Hall, Thomas W., *The Fairbanks of Sheffield 1688 to 1848*, Sheffield, 1932

Harrison, Brian, *Peaceable Kingdom. Stability and change in modern Britain*, Oxford, 1982

Harrison, Royden, *Before the Socialists: studies in labour and politics 1861-1881*, 1965

Harvey, A.D., *Britain in the Early Nineteenth Century*, 1978

Haskell, Thomas L., 'Capitalism and the Humanitarian Sensibility, Part I', *AHR*, 90, 1985, pp.339-61; Part II, *AHR*, 90, 1985, pp.457-66

Haskell, Thomas L., 'Convention and Hegemonic Interest in the Debate over Antislavery: A reply to Davis and Ashworth', *AHR*, 92, 1987, pp.829-78

Hersh, Blanche Glassman, *The Slavery of Sex. Feminist Abolitionists in America*, Urbana, Illinois, 1978

Hind, Robert J., 'William Wilberforce and the Perceptions of the British People', *Historical Research*, lx, 143, 1987, pp.321-35

Hollis, Patricia (ed.), *Pressure from Without in Early Victorian England*, 1974

Holmes, Colin, 'Samuel Roberts and the Gypsies', in Sidney Pollard and Colin Holmes (eds), *Essays in the Economic and Social History of South Yorkshire*, Barnsley, 1976, pp.233-46

Holt, R.V., *The Unitarian Contribution to Social Progress in England*, 2nd edn, 1952

Hunt, E.M., 'The Anti-Slave Trade Agitation in Manchester', *Trans. of Lancs. and Cheshire Antiquarian Society*, 1977, pp.46–72

Ignatieff, Michael, *A Just Measure of Pain. The penitentiary in the Industrial Revolution*, 1978

Ingham, Geoffrey, *Capitalism Divided ? The City and industry in British social development*, 1984

Isichei, Elizabeth, *Victorian Quakers*, Oxford, 1970

Jephson, Henry, *The Platform. Its rise and progress*, 2 vols, vol. 1, 1892

Jewson, C.B., *The Jacobin City. A portrait of Norwich in its reaction to the French Revolution 1788-1802*, Glasgow and London, 1975

Jones, Gareth Stedman, *Languages of Class. Studies in English working class history 1832-1982*, Cambridge, 1983

Keith-Lucas, Brian, 'County Meetings', *Law Quarterly Review*, 70, 1954, pp.109–14

Kent, John, *Elizabeth Fry*, 1962

Kirk, Neville, 'In Defence of Class. A critique of recent revisionist writing upon the nineteenth-century English working class', *International Review of Social History*, xxxii, 1, 1987, pp.2–47

Klingberg, Frank J., *The Anti-Slavery Movement in England. A Study in English humanitarianism*, New Haven, Conn., 1926

Knight, Frida, *The Strange Case of Thomas Walker. Ten years in the life of a Manchester radical*, 1957

Knight, Frida, *University Rebel. The life of William Frend (1759-1841)*, 1971

Kraus, Michael, *The Atlantic Civilization. Eighteenth-century origins*, Ithaca, NY, 1949

Laqueur, Thomas W., *Religion and Respectability. Sunday schools and working class culture 1780-1850*, New Haven, Conn., 1976

Laqueur, Thomas W., 'Bodies, Details and the Humanitarian Narrative', in Lynn Hunt (ed.), *The New Cultural History*, Berkeley, Los Angeles and London, 1989, pp.176–204

Leys, Colin, 'Petitioning in the Nineteenth and Twentieth Centuries', *Political Studies*, III, 1, 1955, pp.45–63

Maclear, J.F., 'The Idea of "American Protestantism" and British Nonconformity, 1829–40', *Journal of British Studies*, xxi, 1, 1981, pp.68–89

Maynard, Douglas H., 'The World's Anti-Slavery Convention of 1840', *MVHR*, xlvii, 3, 1960, pp.452–71

McKenzie, Isabel, *Social Activities of the English Friends in the first half of the nineteenth century*, privately printed, New York, 1935

Mendus, Susan and Rendall, Jane (eds), *Sexuality and Subordination, Interdisciplinary studies of gender in the nineteenth century*, 1989

Mitchell, C.J., 'Provincial Printing in Eighteenth-Century Britain', *Publishing History*, xxi, 1987, pp.5–24

Money, John, *Experience and Identity. Birmingham and the West Midlands 1760-1800*, Manchester, 1977

Morris, R.J., 'Voluntary Societies and British Urban Elites, 1780–1850: an analysis', *Historical Journal* (HJ), 26, 1, 1983, pp.95–118

Mottram, R.H., *Buxton the Liberator*, n.d. [1946]

Newman, Gerald, 'Anti-French Propaganda and British Liberal Nationalism in the early Nineteenth Century: Suggestions toward a general interpretation', *Victorian Studies*, xviii, 4, 1975, pp.385–418

Newsome, David, *The Parting of Friends*, 1966

Nicholls, David, 'Fractions of Capital: the aristocracy, the City and industry in the development of modern British capitalism', *Social History (SH)*, 13, 1, 1988, pp.71–83

Owen, David, *English Philanthropy 1760-1960*, Cambridge, Mass., 1964

Perkin, Harold, *The Origins of Modern English Society 1780-1880*, 1969

Perry, Lewis and Fellman, Michael (eds), *Antislavery Reconsidered: new perspectives on the abolitionists*, Baton Rouge, La. and London, 1979

Pickstone, J.V. and Butler, S.V.F., 'The Politics of Medicine in Manchester, 1788-1792: Hospital reform and the public health services in the early industrial city', *Medical History*, 28, 1984, pp.227–49

Porter, Andrew, ' "Commerce and Christianity": the rise and fall of a Nineteenth-Century Missionary Slogan', *HJ*, 28, 3, 1985, pp.597–621

Porter, Bernard, *The Refugee Question in Mid-Victorian Politics*, Cambridge, 1979

Porter, Roy, 'The Enlightenment in England', in Roy Porter and Mikulás Teich (eds), *The Enlightenment in National Context*, Cambridge, 1981, pp.1–18

Prochaska, F.K., *Women and Philanthropy in Nineteenth-Century England*, Oxford, 1980

Rendall, Jane (ed.), *Equal or Different. Women's Politics 1800-1914*, Oxford, 1987

Rice, C. Duncan, *The Scots Abolitionists 1833-1861*, Baton Rouge, La. and London, 1981

Roach, John, *Social Reform in England 1780-1880*, 1978

Robbins, Caroline, *The Eighteenth-Century Commonwealthman*, New York, 1968

Roberts, M.J.D., 'The Society for the Suppression of Vice and its early Critics, 1802-1812', *HJ*, 26, 1, 1983, pp.159–176

Robinson, E., 'An English Jacobin: James Watt, Jr, 1769-1848', *Cambridge Historical Journal*, xi, 3, 1955, pp.349–55

Rudé, George, *Wilkes and Liberty*, Oxford, 1962

Russell, Elbert, *The History of Quakerism*, New York, 1942

Samuel, Raphael (ed.), *Patriotism: the Making and Unmaking of British National Identity. Vol.1 History and Politics*, 1989

Sanderson, F.E., 'Bibliographical Essay: Liverpool and the slave trade: a guide to sources', *THSLC*, 124, 1973, pp.154–76

Scull, Andrew T., *Museums of Madness. The social organization of insanity in nineteenth-century England*, Harmondsworth, 1982

Seed, John, 'Unitarianism, Political Economy and the Antinomies of Liberal Culture in Manchester, 1830-1850', *SH*, 7, 1, 1982, pp.1–25

Seed, John, 'Gentlemen Dissenters: the social and political meanings of Rational Dissent in the 1770's and 1780's', *HJ*, 28, 2, 1985, pp.299–325

Seed, John, 'Theologies of power: Unitarianism and the social relations of religious discourse, 1800-50', in R.J. Morris (ed.), *Class, Power and Social Structure in British Nineteenth-Century Towns*, Leicester, 1986, pp.108–55

Sellers, Ian, 'Unitarians and Social Change. Part I: varieties of radicalism, 1795–1815', *Hibbert Journal*, 61, 1962–3, pp.16–22

Semmel, Bernard, *The Rise of Free Trade Imperialism: classical political economy, the empire of free trade and imperialism 1750–1850*, Cambridge, 1971

Shyllon, F.O., *Black Slaves in Britain*, 1974

Shyllon, F.O., *Black People in Britain, 1555–1833*, 1977

Shyllon, Folarion, *James Ramsay. The unknown abolitionist*, Edinburgh, 1977

Smail, John, 'New Languages for Labour and Capital: the transformation of discourse in the early years of the Industrial Revolution', *SH*, 12, 1, 1987, pp.49–71

Smith, Barbara (ed.), *Truth, Liberty, Religion. Essays celebrating two hundred years of Manchester College*, Oxford, 1986

Solow, Barbara L., and Engerman, Stanley L. (eds.), *British Capitalism and Caribbean Slavery. The legacy of Eric Williams*, Cambridge, 1987

Stafford, William, *Socialism, Radicalism and Nostalgia. Social criticism in Britain, 1775–1830*, Cambridge, 1987

Stange, Douglas Charles, *British Unitarians against American Slavery 1833–65*, Rutherford, NJ and London, 1984

Stanley, Brian, ' "Commerce and Christianity": Providence theory, the missionary movement and the imperialism of free trade, 1842–1860', *HJ*, 26, 1, 1983, pp.71–94

Stoddart, Anna M., *Elizabeth Pease Nichol*, 1899

Swift, David E., *Joseph John Gurney: banker, reformer, and Quaker*, Middletown, Conn., 1962

Temperley, Howard, *British Antislavery 1833–1870*, 1972

Temperley, Howard, 'Capitalism, Slavery and Ideology', *Past and Present*, 75, 1977, pp.94–118

Thompson, Dorothy, *The Chartists. Popular politics in the Industrial Revolution*, Aldershot, 1986

Thompson, E.P., *The Poverty of Theory and Other Essays*, 1978

Thompson, F.M.L., 'Social Control in Victorian Britain', *Ec. Hist. Rev.*, 2nd ser., xxxiv, 2, 1981, pp.189–208

Turley, David M., 'Moral Suasion, Community Action and the Problem of Power: reflections on American abolitionists and government, 1830–1861', in R. Jeffreys-Jones and Bruce Collins (eds), *The Growth of Federal Power in American History*, Edinburgh, 1983, pp.25–35

Tyrrell, Alexander, 'Making the Millennium: the mid-nineteenth century peace movement', *HJ*, 20, 1, 1978, pp.75–95

Tyrrell, Alex, ' "Women's Mission" and Pressure Group Politics in Britain (1825–60)', *Bulletin of the John Rylands University Library of Manchester*, 63, 1, 1980, pp.194–230

Tyrrell, Alex, *Joseph Sturge and the Moral Radical Party in early Victorian Britain*, 1987

Valenze, Deborah M., *Prophetic Sons and Daughters: female preaching and popular religion in industrial England*, Princeton, NJ, 1985

Walsh, John, 'The Origins of the Evangelical Revival' in G.V. Bennett and J.D. Walsh (eds), *Essays in Modern English Church History*, 1966, pp.132–62

Walsh, John, 'Methodism and the Mob in the Eighteenth Century', in G.J. Cuming and Derek Baker (eds), *Popular Belief and Practice*, Cambridge, 1972, pp.213-27

Walvin, James (ed.), *Slavery and British Society 1776-1846*, 1982

Ward, W.R., *Religion and Society in England, 1790-1850*, 1972

Ward, W.R., 'The Religion of the People and the Problem of Control, 1790-1830', in G.J.Cuming and Derek Baker (eds), *Popular Belief and Practice*, 1972, pp.237-57

Watts, Michael, *The Dissenters. From the Reformation to the French Revolution*, Oxford, 1978

Webb, R.K., *Harriet Martineau, a radical Victorian*, 1960

Williams, Eric, *Capitalism and Slavery*, 2nd edn, 1964

Wright, Leslie C., *Scottish Chartism*, Edinburgh, 1953

Theses, dissertations

Dixon, Peter Francis, 'The Politics of Emancipation. The movement for the abolition of slavery in the British West Indies 1807-1833', Ph.D thesis, University of Oxford, 1971

Hunt, E.M., 'North of England Agitation for the Abolition of the Slave Trade 1780-1800', MA thesis, University of Manchester, 1959

Jennings, Judith Gaile, 'Campaign for the Abolition of the British Slave Trade: the Quaker contribution 1757-1807', Ph.D thesis, University of Kentucky, 1975. Copy in Friends' House Library, London

Midgley, Clare, 'Women Anti-Slavery Campaigners in Britain 1787-1868', Ph.D thesis, University of Kent, 1989

Murphy, M.J., 'Newspapers and Opinion in Cambridge 1790-1850', MA thesis, University of Kent, 1971

Owen, Gwynne E., 'Welsh Anti-Slavery Sentiments 1790-1865: a survey of public opinion', MA thesis, University College of Wales, Aberystwyth, 1964

Pilgrim, Elsie I., 'Anti-Slavery Sentiment in Great Britain 1841-1854; its nature and its decline with special reference to its influence upon British policy towards the former slave colonies', Ph.D thesis, University of Cambridge, 1952

Ryan, John, 'Religion and Radical Politics in Birmingham, 1830-1850', MLitt. thesis, University of Birmingham, 1979

Turley, David M., 'Relations between British and American Abolitionists from British Emancipation to the American Civil War', Ph.D thesis, University of Cambridge, 1969

Willmer, Haddon, 'Evangelicalism 1785 to 1835', Hulsean Prize Essay, University of Cambridge, 1962

INDEX

281